"The heart of Tina Martin's memoir is her very readable insider account of the experiences of a 'PCV' (a Peace Corps Volunteer) in Tonga in the early '70s. But the narrative is both an exploration of a very foreign world and, simultaneously, an account of self-discovery. Martin's notion, early on, that 'life has no meaning' sparks an impulse to self-determination and a desire to live life all the more adventurously and deeply—practically challenging life to inhibit her. Indeed, the lifetime experiences recounted here might fill two or three lives. Martin's prose is fluent and charming, marked by a lively sense of humor usually genial, sometimes biting (though never drawing blood). The many lessons imparted here go down easily."

David Hathwell, author of
Muses, Between Dog and Wolf, and The Power of the Telling.

"Tina Martin has written an incisive, funny memoir, an outline for an elaborate musical comedy, and an astute though somewhat oblique commentary on the odd world of the 1960's and 1970s."

Manfred Wolf, author of
Almost a Foreign Country and Survival in Paradise

"Tina Martin's memoir reads like a musical. It is filled with the many melodies of her life and her imagination. We learn about Tonga along with this former Peace Corps volunteer. We also learn about scores of popular musicals through the author's imaginings of incorporating them into her life. The author is a talented wordsmith whose lyrical writing style made this reader laugh, think, and sing."

Evelyn LaTorre, EdD, author of
Between Inca Walls and Love in Any Language.

TINA MARTIN

EVERYTHING I SHOULD HAVE LEARNED I COULD HAVE LEARNED IN TONGA

outskirts press

TABLE OF CONTENTS

Under the Tongan Sun

From one of my twenty-eight Tongan diaries, the excerpt I read for the Journals of Peace at the Capitol Rotunda in Washington, D. C., on November 21, 1988, for the vigil commemorating the twenty-fifth anniversary since the assassination of President John f. Kennedy

I LIVE IN a tiny hut made of bamboo and coconut leaves and lined with dozens of mats, pieces of tapa cloth, and wall-to-wall children.

When I sit on the floor with my back against the back door, my feet almost touch the front door. There's no electricity or running water, so I use a kerosene lamp and draw water from the well. There are breadfruit trees and avocado trees around my hut, and if I want a coconut, the children climb a tree to bring me one.

The kids I teach are always with me, and I love them even more than I once loved my privacy. I've always wanted to have children, but I never thought I'd have so many and so soon. These are the children I would like to see back home — children who have never even seen a television set and don't depend upon "things" for their entertainment because they don't have any things. For fun, they teach each other dances and songs, and they juggle oranges.

They wake me up in the morning, calling through my bamboo poles. They take my five sentini and get me freshly baked bread from the shop across the lawn, and they help me eat it. Some of them watch the ritual of my morning bath—water I draw from the well, heat on my kerosene stove, and pour into a tin, then over a pre-soaped me.

They sometimes braid my hair and help me get dressed for school. Then they walk me there, where I use the oral English method we learned in training — acting out the language so there's no need for translation.

"I'm running! I'm running!" I say as I run in front of the class. "I'm running. I'm running!"

I take a child by the hand.

"Run!" I say, and eventually he does. The goal is to have a running paradigm, which usually ends. "I running, you running, he/she/it running." We do this for all verbs.

English is the link between Tonga and other land masses. And English is the exercise that keeps me skinny, the worst physical defect a body can have in the Tongan culture, where fat is beautiful. I try to compensate for my lack of bulk by being very *anga lelei* (good-natured), which is their most cherished personality trait.

After school the children come home with me and stay, singing Tongan songs and the ones I've taught them—songs nuns and governesses teach children: "Doe, a deer" and "Getting to Know You." But their favorite is the Mickey Mouse Club Song. "M-I-C—See ya real soon. K-E-Y—Why? Because we like you. M-O-U-S-E."

We don't have mice here. Just rats the size of rabbits.

After we sing, I try to help them prepare for the sivi hu, the test they take in the sixth grade, which will determine their scholastic future, and they help me prepare whichever vegetable is to be my dinner.

The children never leave until I am safely tucked into bed under my canopy of mosquito net on top of tapa cloth. Then I blow out my lamp, lie down, and listen to songs from a kava ceremony nearby. Sometimes there is light from what a Tongan teacher told me is now the "American moon," since we put a man there last summer.

On moonless nights, I fall asleep in complete darkness. But I fall asleep knowing that I will always wake up under the Tongan sun.

This memoir is dedicated to Andrea Pannal Goodman Ptolemy, 1946-2010, My Best Friend in Peace Corps Tonga, who was a much better Peace Corps Volunteer than I was and whose spirit lives on in her daughter Jennifer (Jenny) Elaine Goodman, another Super Vol.

Preface to this Memoir

From San Francisco, California, April 2021 and still masked—but vaccinated and permitted inside.

{60 Minutes has just aired the inspiring story about the Tongan school boys who, more than 50 years ago, were stranded on the volcanic island Ata for fifteen months and proved that with ingenuity and cooperation the outcome can be much better than that in *The Lord of the Flies*. Rutger Bregman uses this story in his book *Humankind: A Hopeful History*, as does Peter Warner in his memoir *Ocean of Light*. But I first heard about this from one of the schoolboys, Mano Sione Totau, in Peace Corps Training in 1969.}

A major fear I have is that I'll die before I've finished thanking the people--like these Tongans-- who've made me grateful to be alive. This was a fear I had even before the pandemic, and it's given me a sense of urgency.

I turned 75 during the pandemic and decided that, instead of having a super-spreader gathering, I'd write 75 thank you letters to people who've had a positive impact on my life. Of course, a lot of those people were family and close friends, starting with my son Jonathan and going all the way back to My Best Friend in Fifth Grade, Sara. But a few of them were people I know through the organizations I belong to: Older Women's League, California Alliance for Retired Americans (connecting with AFT 2121 Retirees), Mothers Out Front, and The Affirmative Action Task Force at CCSF. The organizations themselves have kept me busy between the long walks I've taken during the pandemic, often feeling I'm from another planet and just landed on Earth, where everything I see fills me with wonder. Corny but true.

My brother David's caregivers at Garfield Neurobehavioral Center were also among those who made me grateful when I turned 75 years old, and even though I couldn't write to each of them, I wrote to David's social worker as representative of them all. Soon after his death, I'd made, instead of the traditional obituary, a low-tech slide show in memory of David and in honor of them. That was pre-pandemic, when they hadn't yet been declared the heroes they have always been.

I've done other writing too, first about my brother David, who I still feel deserves better than I've been able to relate. After a lot of tries, I finally resorted to writing about him in a letter to the psychologist who gave us Peace Corps recruits, in late October 1969, the sanity test I describe in an early chapter of *Everything I Should Have Learned I Could Have Learned in Tonga*. I needed to know to whom I was addressing the story of my brother's life, during which he was sheltered in place for most of his seventy years.

I also wrote hundreds of letters to Georgia with Working America.

My intention was to write a sequel to my flawed book and call it *Letters of Apology for My First Memoir*, which I will probably still need to do, but I decided I would first go back to editing that first memoir—so much easier to do when it's in book form and with a bar code.

I'm going to keep this re-introduction short, but in *Letters of Apology for My First Memoir* I'll share with you (with their permission) the responses I got from three of the men who star in my coming-of-age memoir of Tonga.

In the meantime, let's consider that however we're living through the pandemic is "a valid expression of human existence" as long as it's anga 'ofa—kind.

Preface to the Earlier Volume

From San Francisco, California, August 2019

In early August 1969, almost immediately after getting word that my application to the Peace Corps had been accepted, my sister Suzy and I took a trip Southeast—to see relatives and friends from our childhood in Atlanta and South Carolina and to visit our father and our sister Missy, who were living in Harrisburg, Pennsylvania.

People were talking about Chappaquiddick and the moon landing, which had occurred within two days of each other just a month earlier—on July 18 and July 20, respectively. I don't think I heard about Stonewall, but this was the year that the news of the My Lai massacre came out; the atrocities had been committed a year earlier, and it was the month of the Charles Manson murders.

This was also the year that I went to staging in San Jose and then to Peace Corps training on the island of Molokai in Hawaii to prepare me to be of some use in Tonga, though not much use. The first lessons I learned were "It's important to get off to a slow start" and "It's better to be people-centered than project-centered."

To celebrate this fiftieth anniversary of my life in Tonga and what I learned as well as what I should have learned and could have learned but didn't, I've gone through old diaries and letters and put some of my reflections into writing for this volume. I hope you will agree with the most significant lesson we learned in Peace Corps training: "It's a valid expression of human existence." That means you and us. In whatever way we're living our lives, it's a valid expression of human existence. Isn't that reassuring?

Because it's been fifty years and because I describe most people so lovingly, I feel free to use the first names of people. But here's my disclaimer: The stories in this book reflect the author's recollection of events. Some names, locations, and identifying characteristics have been changed to protect the privacy of those depicted. Dialogue has been re-created from memory and as recorded in my 28 diaries. If you see the name Jim, for instance, it's not really Jim. It *was* Jim. As I perceived him. Fifty years ago.

I had intended a 2019 revisit (in my imagination) to the psychologist who gave me my 15-minute sanity test in October 1969, but I will end, instead, with life as it was in 2008, when I returned to Tonga, and with "Learning to Read in Tonga" from the perspective of 2019. I ran out of time.

But I do reflect throughout on what I learned or could have and should have. Here's a start: When we don't get what we wish for, we sometimes get something better. I didn't ask to be assigned to Tonga. I didn't even know it existed when I filled out my Peace Corps application form. But I'm very grateful that I was invited there and that I accepted the invitation. Fifty years later my overwhelming feeling in life is gratitude. I'm grateful that I've been able to live my life the way I've wanted to. Things haven't always worked out as I had wanted, but in some cases, that has been a blessing. I wake up every morning excited by the day that lies ahead.

"What's so special about Tonga?" someone asked. "Besides that shirtless flagbearer," she added in reference to Pita Taufatofua of Olympic Games fame, 2016. Everything. My first foreign country was Mexico, where I did volunteer work the summer of 1967, I fell in love with Madrid in 1972, when I lived there, and I found Algeria fascinating the two years I lived there in the mid-1970's;. But Tonga was the culture the most distinct from my own, where my learning curve could have been the greatest had I been a better student. But I did learn.

This morning when I was reading Alex Capus *Life Is Good*, I realized that I might never have discovered this Swiss writer—better known in Europe than in the USA—if I hadn't lived in Tonga, where I met Tavi, a subject in another book by Alex Capus.

If I hadn't met Tavi, I might not understand that segmented sleep can be a good thing and, like a lot of other people, I might be worrying about not sleeping through the night instead of enjoying and using the energy I feel at odd hours.

Living in Tonga also taught me about zero waste, and even though I don't practice it, I think I do better than I would if I hadn't lived in a culture where people were more likely to make what they used and grow what they ate than to buy it.

In 2019, when so many men have been found guilty of past crimes against women, I'm grateful that I've known the good men described in this memoir—kind, smart, funny, innocent of major crimes. I also feel a great deal of affection for other people I describe in this memoir.

In the newspaper this morning, I read that there has been a 940.3% increase in compensation of corporate CEO's since 1978, the year of my first marriage. There's been only an 11.9% increase in wages over the same period. In Tonga our Peace Corps allowance was Thirty-two dollars a month. I know that has increased, but that's the sum I'm donating to Friends of Tonga each month to provide scholarships for Tongan students and in honor of two Tongans, 'Ana Taufe'ulungaki and Kili Silini, and in memory of another Peace Corps Volunteer, Andrea Pannal Goodman Ptolemy, to whom I'm dedicating this memoir.

This year took me to Rome with my Camino walking partner Bill Shoaf, and I also had the great pleasure of staying with Susan and Steve Peeples when I attended the 55th reunion of our class of '64 at Columbia High School, where one of my longest pieces "God, President Kennedy, and Me" takes place. Also in that piece is my sister Dana, who had become partially paralyzed after surgery in February and was back to a very impressive normal in May, when I also went to NYC to see my son Jonathan, whom you'll meet in "Learning to Read in Tonga." This was also the year that my brother David died, and one reason I'm getting this off to the publisher's now is that I want to write about him. But he does appear in this volume in some very significant ways.

Please use any available space to write what you think are the significant events of 2019—personally, nationally, and internationally. But remember: However you are living life, it's a valid expression of human existence.

MARRYING THREE MEN, ALL FOREIGN

MUSICALS AND FOREIGNERS were my two great loves, not counting my boyfriend Steve, who was everything a girl could wish for except foreign. He was a Southern Gentleman, and to most of the world, that was foreign.

For years I longed to be a foreigner because foreigners were the people I admired most—something I may have picked up from my mother, who was a Francophile. Most of the foreigners we met in the South Carolina were from France.

I was awed by how foreigners lived in two worlds, and I loved that magic trick of theirs, speaking a language that wasn't English. I knew the song "Far Away Places," and they were calling me. So many lessons came to me through song. I learned to sing before I learned to speak. My mother would play "Dites-Moi" on the piano, and I would sing along—two words in French!

Mother and I were kindred spirits when it came to foreigners and musicals. She founded the World Friendship Club at Hamilton High School in Los Angeles when she was sixteen, and when I was sixteen, I was the president of the International Relations Club at Columbia High School in South Carolina.

The way that most people worship money or pop singers or movie stars or athletes or sometimes even Jesus—that's how we felt about people from other countries who spoke another language. Actually, we worshipped Jesus, too. He was from another country, and he spoke another language, and if he'd been an exchange student at our high school, we'd have followed him anywhere. When it came to people from other countries, we were stalkers. We wanted to be with them. We wanted to BE them—but not in Columbia, South Carolina. We wanted to be them in *their* country. And usually, their country was France.

I knew that there were other countries out there, beyond the borders of Columbia, South Carolina and beyond the borders of the United States of America. So at about the age of twelve (1957) I started fantasizing about having three husbands in three different countries— France, Mexico, and China. I would have a baby by each husband, and every year the children and I would live four months in France, four months in Mexico, and four months in China seeped in the culture, language, and songs—*living* in each country because I really didn't want to travel to or travel through. I wanted to *live in*.

Of course, I knew this was just a fantasy. I knew it wasn't legal. Then in 1961, President Kennedy signed the Executive Order forming the Peace Corps, "to promote world friendship." College graduates would be trained in the culture and language and get to go to another country and LIVE there for two years. It was legal, and they paid your way. I would go to college and become a college graduate just so I could be eligible for the Peace Corps.

That was my sophomore year of high school and about the time that I fell in love with Steve, an American (although to his credit his father was a professor of Spanish and German, and he spent a summer in Mexico). I told Steve we'd just have to wait to get married until I finished Peace Corps service, and this was after we'd already named our future children. "Maria" (*West Side Story*), "Mariah," (what they call the wind in *Paint Your Wagon*), and Gigi (*Gigi*). He understood. I loved him in spite of his monolingualism. How could I not? He was handsome, smart, and sweet, and he understood my love of musicals and would drive all the way to Charlotte, North Carolina to take me to see summer stock: *The Sound of Music, My Fair Lady, The Unsinkable Molly Brown, She Loves Me,* and *Kismet!*

Steve would be The Boy I Left Behind, or so I thought when I was sixteen.

"Ask not what your country can do for you," President Kennedy said. "Ask what YOU can do for your country."

I knew what I could do for my country. I could leave it. But it was President Kennedy who left the country first.

GOD, PRESIDENT KENNEDY, AND ME

A VERSION OF this appears in the anthology *Even the Smallest Crab Has Teeth, 2011.*

I remember what I was doing on November 22, 1963 even before I heard that President Kennedy had been assassinated. Praying. Not just because I was chairman of Religious Emphasis Week at Columbia High School but because there was a beauty contest that night and, if it were God's will, I was willing to win it. So I kept checking in with God, letting Him know that He was on my mind, and I sure hoped I was on His. I didn't want Him to fix the contest. That wouldn't be fair. I just wanted Him to help me do justice to whatever God-given beauty I might have so that I could honor the Future Teachers of America Club I was representing and serve as a good example for whoever needed one.

"Dear God," I whispered, "tonight's the night. If it be Thy will for me to wear the crown of Miss Columbian, Thy will be done, and"—I added with special emphasis—"I'll give my first summer paycheck to CARE and the NAACP." (In summer I worked in Central Supplies at the South Carolina State Hospital, where my father was Chief Psychologist, but I was too young to work on the wards, so I cleaned needles and syringes instead. I also baby-sat for fifty cents an hour, double what I'd gotten in previous years.)

Living in The South in 1963, I was (1) in the habit of praying in and out of school and (2) in—and out of— beauty contests. We had them for everything, even Fire Prevention Week, and at the urging of my prettier and older sister, Dana, who won the Miss Columbian Contest when she was only a sophomore, I'd decided to work on being prettier than me, if not prettier than her, and carrying on the family tradition of winning even though it couldn't be in my sophomore year. I'd won the Miss Freshman contest my first year of high school, been eliminated in no time at all in my sophomore year, been eliminated eventually in my junior year (bad perm) and now I was already a senior. Last chance.

It was when Dana clearly wanted me to win that I first knew she could be nice, this sister of mine, who'd previously just cursed my birth, beaten me up, taken my lunch money, and made fun of everything about me that was ridiculous, and there was plenty. But now she actually wanted to help me win. To this very day I don't know why.

People sometimes told me that I looked like Natalie Wood and occasionally like Mary Tyler Moore in The Dick Van Dyke Show, but Dana looked like Elizabeth Taylor back in the days when that was a good thing. She had the same oval face, perfect nose and teeth, same-shaped eyebrows. The only thing that wasn't quite the same was the black hair. Dana's hair was really medium brown, but she was not about to be medium anything, so she'd started dying it jet black after she'd first seen Elizabeth Taylor in *Raintree County* in 1957, the year people started noticing the similarity. That was probably the year she took over the upstairs bathroom, too, to do her chemistry lab work for beauty. Six of us used the bathroom downstairs, and she used the one upstairs, where the sink was always stopped up with mysterious make-up-hair stuff. But however horrendous the bathroom was, she was beautiful. She'd also been dressing pretty much like Elizabeth Taylor in *Raintree County,* which made people think she was a strange beauty because *Raintree County* was a period piece. Not that she wore bonnets or anything. But when other girls were wearing matching cashmere sweaters and straight skirts, she was wearing full skirts and lots of crinolines more reminiscent of the War Between the States, as Southerners called the Civil War back then. The War Between the

States: The South's Fight for Independence.

In our family, we called the War between the States the Civil War because, as my friend Sara cautioned people when she introduced me, "Tina's not from here." That's why I was bribing God with my summer wages, promising to give my first paycheck to CARE and NAACP, which my Southern friends dismissed as Communist and against State's Rights. I thought my parents knew better than my peers because they were much older, closer to God's age.

To help along bribe-induced divine intervention, Dana was going to come back to Columbia from Winthrop College in Greenville to help me win the contest. She'd picked out the pattern for the dress I was going to wear and helped Mother find the material at the remnant store because one of Daddy's strongest convictions was that we shouldn't spend money. He would give Mother a budget, for which she'd create envelopes, and she'd put five or ten dollars in each envelope, but sometimes she'd have to borrow from the clothing envelope for the food envelope and vice versa. Daddy was Chief Psychologist at the South Carolina State Hospital, President of Southern Psychologists and had a class of graduate students at the University of South Carolina, but the friend I felt I had the most in common with was Glennis, whose father was a shoe repairman, because Glennis and I both lived poor.

Dana said that with beauty, we could rise above poverty, and beauty was her greatest talent. She knew just how to get my hair to look like Jackie Kennedy's, and I knew I was lucky that she was doing this for me, but I wasn't counting on luck or Dana. I was counting on God, which was why I was praying more than usual that day.

"Please, dear God, if it be Thy will."

The minimum wage had gone up to $1.15 an hour, and I would give all my first pay check to these good causes if God would support *my* cause and let me win the crown. It hurt me, I told God, that not everyone believed in His existence the way I did. And it hurt me, too, that not everyone believed in the existence of my God-given beauty the way I prayed the judges would. Being beautiful—at least for one night—would be an answered prayer.

"A thing of beauty," I said, paraphrasing one of the poems I'd memorized to make up for being bad at math, "would be a joy forever." I wanted to bring joy to the world and prayed that I could do it this special way.

Of course, other girls prayed. This was The South, after all. But their prayers were shallow. Mine had depth because *I* had a social consciousness, which I figured God had too. That was one of my advantages in the beauty contest. I had a better idea of what God wanted, though it never occurred to me that He would want Negroes in our beauty contest. Of course, there weren't any Negroes at our school.

"It's been a decade since the Brown vs. Kansas," my mother would say, "and there's not a face that isn't white at that school."

"Or at any other," I'd say. I knew that Columbia High School was no more prejudiced than any of the others. Most Southerners thought the Supreme Court had been infiltrated by Communists, and the government was going to take over and destroy our way of life. People in South Carolina were saying that President Kennedy and his brother had already gone to Mississippi and Alabama totally disregarding State's Rights, and they'd probably be coming here, but until they did, it was going to be Separate But Equal. Separate water fountains. Separate parts of the bus. Separate schools, and of course, separate beauty contests for the whites and the coloreds, if they had beauty contests.

I knew even back then that "whites and coloreds" sounded like socks, but black was a term reserved for Stephen Foster songs like "Old Black Joe." Black was not yet beautiful. But that night I would try to be. Though I occasionally tried to rise above such petty aspirations, that night, with God's help, I would indulge in and achieve them. Once I'd gotten being beautiful out of my system, I assured God and myself, I could spend my time praying for the outcast. But tonight I would reserve my prayers for me—that I not be cast out—at least not until after I'd made the finalists. I knew beauty was but skin deep, but tonight skin deep got crowned. Skin deep got a dozen long-stemmed rose. And most importantly, skin deep got two full pages in our high school yearbook.

I didn't really have to win that contest to take up more than my share of space in the high school yearbook. I'd been a dismal failure in junior high school, where I'd gotten a bad reputation for wearing red lipstick the first semester of seventh grade when all the good girls waited till the second semester and started with pink, not red. Everyone in the car pool on Stratford and Sheffield Roads and at Miss Sloane's Dance Class had agreed on the second semester. But Dana had told me that I needed color, so my bad reputation was her fault, and maybe also the fault of Nancy Todd, whose brother I'd let kiss me when I was working on a science project at her house, and she'd told people that *I'd kissed back*! Then he'd started riding to my house on his motorcycle, and since I looked a little bit like Natalie Wood, it was *Rebel without a Cause*. People thought I was fast and cheap, and I lived in a neighborhood for nice girls who went to a Hand Junior High, where girls like me were ostracized and left to the boys they let kiss them. But I never "went all the way" or even half of the way with Greg. We never even went steady. Greg was a local boy, and until I met Steve, I was holding out for a foreigner, like Jean-Paul, the French exchange student at Columbia High School.

Fearing that my *kissing back* had gotten me a bad reputation in junior high school, I'd over-compensated in high school—even switching from Dreher and A.C. Flora, our neighborhood schools, to Columbia High School. I'd learned that success consisted of being like everybody else, only *better*, and God willing, *prettier*. I'd almost learned how not to be weird, not to look too eager. I'd learned how not to dress. (Not in my wilted, smelly gym blouse just because I could never get my locker open. Not with my bobby socks crawling down into my loafers.) I'd even learned how to open my locker. I'd learned when to help others and when to help myself. I'd read Dale Carnegie's *How to Win Friends and Influence People* at Myrtle Beach the summer before I began high school, and I'd begun my negotiations with God.

Gradually I'd become socially acceptable—even decent. I was the DAR Girl and Chairman of Religious Emphasis Week. I'd won second-place in the city-wide Youth Leadership Contest sponsored by the "benevolent and protective order of Elks." I'd accumulated awards and been elected to school offices. Now I was a member of Executive Council and the Editor of the literary yearbook, *The Rebel.* This was a big turn-about for a girl who'd been nominated for an office only once in junior high school and had broken out in a cold sweat because she feared the only vote she'd get was that of the kid nominating her. She was right. The teacher forgot to erase the board, and I saw it with my own eyes.

Homeroom Coupon Chairman

Frances: 10
Pat: 16
Tina: 1

Did I mention that my name is Tina?

But now in my senior year of high school, I was president of three clubs, the International Relations Club, the Anchor Club, a girls' service organization, and Future Teachers of America, which was sponsoring me in the beauty contest that night. If I won, in a way it would be a boon to American education. But I have to admit, it wasn't just for that that I wanted to win. I wanted to win so that I'd have a permanent record of how I was before I started to grow old. Dana always said that from the age of sixteen, we start to die a little bit every year. "Nothing can bring back the hour of splendor in the grass, glory in the flower," Dana said, "So gather we rosebuds while we may." I wanted a two-page spread of how I was before I started to wither and wilt.

Dana had told me to cut classes that day so she'd have longer to work on me—after all, she was cutting a day of her classes at Winthrop College to come home to help me— but the principal had a new policy.

He saw how girls were absent from their classes to have their hair done on the day of the beauty contest, so this year he'd announced that roll would be taken, and any girl absent from any of her classes would be ineligible to compete in the Miss Columbian Beauty Contest. So Dana agreed to start in on my Jackie Kennedy "do" right after school got out. That would not only save one dollar and fifty cents (the price of a wash and set), but that would mean my beautician would be a beauty queen personally dedicated to my being one too.

Before I left for school that morning, I caught my mom reading when she was supposed to be working on my dress.

"What's the *Feminine Mystic* about?" I asked her.

"It's *Feminine Mystique*," she corrected me. "Mystique comes from French." She pronounced the word French with a reverence she'd taught me to feel. "It's all about the sacred feminine ideal."

I'd nodded. I had a sacred feminine ideal: God willing, I'd be the prettiest girl of all—please, dear God, just for one night. If mother ever finished the dress!

When Dana woke up, she could keep Mother on task while I was in school. Dana had driven up the night before in the little Fiat Daddy bought her because he wouldn't support the re-industrialization of Germany by buying a VW, and she and I had had a little bit of time to confer on how I should walk, how I should smile, and things like that. She'd been nice until she just had to ask that question she'd been taunting me with all semester.

"How's your campaign going?"

"What campaign?"

"You know. The one for the highest possible moral standards award?"

"I don't know what you're talking about."

"Yes, you do!"

"No, I don't!" I said. I looked at her as if she were crazy and as if I had a low tolerance for the insane.

But I knew. She was talking about the Bill Goldelock Scholarship, which was awarded to a high school senior every year. Bill had once been the president of the student body at Columbia High School, and then he'd been killed in action in Korea. In his memory they gave an award to the senior who most exemplified the characteristics he embodied: Service, leadership, and the highest possible moral standards.

They didn't have the term "short list" back then, but if they had, I'd have been on it. Unless they found out about how fast and cheap I'd been in junior high, kissing *back*!

Mother put down her book and told me to try on what she'd sewn together so far.

My gown was long and straight—something like the one Jackie had worn when she'd gone to France with President Kennedy and he'd introduced himself as "the man who accompanied Jacqueline Kennedy to Paris." Jackie had spoken French with President De Gaulle. Someday I'd know French too. I'd join the Peace Corps right after I finished college and I'd go to some French-speaking country and learn French while I did good deeds. Soon I'd be doing good deeds *in* French!

"Are you sure this is going to be ready by tonight?" I asked my mother.

"Don't worry. It'll be ready," Mother said through the pins between her front teeth. I remembered how I'd had to wear pins in my clothes on the occasions when my formal *wasn't* ready—like for the junior-senior dance the year before.

"Please God, please," I prayed silently. "Let it be ready by tonight. Help Mother *focus*."

There were few occasions when I didn't turn to God, and I prayed silently all the way to school. After our classroom prayer during homeroom period, I added my own silent P.S. "If it be Thy will…"

People came by me at my hall monitor post, and a lot of them said, "Good luck tonight." I looked back at them quizzically, as if the beauty contest were the furthest thing from my mind.

"Why don't you get your hair fixed like Laura Petrie on *The Dick Van Dyke Show*?" someone asked. "You already look a little bit like her."

"But it wouldn't be right to *copy* her," I said, adding with a resigned shrug, "I just have to be myself."

And my *self* was going to be Jackie Kennedy. Dick Van Dyke was cute, but I wasn't settling for *him*. I was going to be the President's Wife, the one he took to Paris.

I walked by the auditorium where we'd be having the contest in just a few more hours. The faculty sponsor of the yearbook, Miss Carter, had vetoed the students' vote for "The Days of Wine and Roses" as the theme because she said it wouldn't be seemly to have wine bottles decorating a high school stage. So tonight we'd hold crescent-shaped cards bearing our numbers, and "Moon River" would play as we walked across the stage—the same stage where Strom Thurmond had stood while getting a standing ovation earlier in my high school career, when the Key Club boys had invited him to speak. I had stood and applauded, too, because even though I disagreed with everything Strom Thurmond stood for, I didn't want to stand out by not standing. I knew I would probably not have made President Kennedy's *Profiles in Courage*, but how many of the men in that book had been rejected for Homeroom Coupon Chairman? How many of those men had *kissed back* in junior high school and gotten a bad reputation? I had a past to rise above, and I didn't want to alienate my Southern friends. I knew their fears.

In spite of Strom Thurmond's stand against civil rights, the Civil Rights Bill might become law, and if it did, those Kennedy Brothers would enforce it, forever changing the Southern Way of Life. We didn't know yet that Sidney Poitier would win the Oscar for "Lilies of the Field" during our senior year of high school, being the first "colored person" ever to win an Oscar. He'd be up there on stage with Patricia Neal, a white lady, and they'd be hugging each other, which was worse than what I'd done with Greg Todd. Greg was white. Hadn't Perry Cuomo kissed Earth Kitt right on the mouth? The world was on its way to miscegenation!

Just three months before our beauty contest, there'd been that big civil rights march in Washington with more than 200,000 people showing up and hearing Martin Luther King talking about making all people equal no matter what color their skin. If God had wanted all people to be equal, my friends reasoned, wouldn't He have made them equally white? And then President Kennedy had sent troops to Alabama to force an all-white school to accept two colored girls, and they'd enrolled in spite of Governor Wallace's rallying cry to protect States' Rights with "Segregation now, segregation tomorrow, segregation forever." If President Kennedy hadn't given that speech saying Civil Rights was a moral issue, that White Council guy might not have had to assassinate the head of the NAACP.

The federal government was becoming Communist and taking over the country, stirring discontent into the heads of colored people who had been perfectly happy before.

It was at the beginning of the school year that those four little girls had been killed by a bomb planted in their church, and that's when I heard my parents talk about the NAACP, but I certainly didn't let my classmates in on my promise to God that I'd give my first pay check to the NAACP if I were chosen our school beauty queen. I didn't think God was a Southerner—though I never told my Southern friend I didn't. The leader of the NAACP had been assassinated in June, and four Negro children had been killed in a church bombing in Birmingham. I had a hunch that God didn't buy that thing about the NAACP being Communist. I was counting on His being pleased with (and maybe persuaded by) my donation!

I don't remember any of my morning classes; I assume I prayed my way through them. But I do remember Miss Pearlstine's Problems of American Democracy class after lunch that day because that was when the news came.

Miss Pearlstine was my favorite teacher. She was a Democrat, too, at a school where the principal himself—Mr. Kirk, an otherwise nice guy who'd coached football before coming to our school—had started The Young Republicans Club, which he himself was sponsoring. The

South had finally caught on that the Republican Party was no longer the party of Lincoln, who had done such terrible things to the South. The parties had switched, and the South was turning away from the Democratic Party. In fact, there was no Young Democrats Club at Columbia High, and Miss Pearlstine had protested.

"If you think the school should have a Young Democrats club," Mr. Kirk had told her, "you're free to start one."

But she wasn't free. She was already the sponsor of the International Relations Club, of which I was president. She was one of the few people who was enthusiastic about my plans to join the Peace Corps as soon as I finished college, culminating a five-year plan that only *began* with tonight's beauty contest.

Miss Pearlstine was the only Jew at our school. As chairman of Religious Emphasis Week, I thought of her and suggested that we drop the "in Jesus Christ we pray" part of our prayers so she wouldn't feel left out. But Miss Webb, the sponsor of Religious Emphasis Week, said, "I'm sure she doesn't mind if we pray our way when there are so many of us and so few of her."

Close to the beginning of our 1:15 class, Mrs. Lindler, a math teacher who had an Algebra by TV class, came to the door.

"You know what?" she said. "They interrupted our Algebra lesson for a news bulletin. There's been some shooting around President Kennedy's motorcade in Dallas."

"Oh, how awful!" Miss Pearlstine said. "I hope nobody's been hurt."

I dropped God a quick line.

"Dear God, let everyone be all right."

But I felt sure that no one had been hurt—not seriously, if at all. I was so certain that President Kennedy was all right that I felt foolish wasting my prayers—prayers that should be directed towards the less certain outcome of the night's beauty pageant.

We went back to our lesson about voting precincts. And then the principal came over the PA system.

"President Kennedy has been shot," he said. "We have not yet received word on whether or not the shot was fatal."

Fatal? Of course the shot hadn't been fatal. Why was Mr. Kirk being so melodramatic? Presidents didn't get assassinated nowadays. Not in our country. Maybe he'd been shot *at*. I could picture him in a Dallas clinic now, charming the staff as the nurses bandaged a slightly nicked shoulder.

"I had hoped for a 20-gun salute," he might say, "but not directed *at* me."

That night I was going to look like his wife. The time he took her to Paris.

A few minutes later Mr. Kirk came over the PA system again.

"May I have your attention please?"

He had our attention.

"President Kennedy is dead."

There were cries and gasps of disbelief. Jeanne Thigpen began to cry. I turned to her.

"It's not true," I told her. "I know it's not true."

A couple of students cheered.

"He asked for it," a guy named Sam said. "He was practically becoming a dictator."

"I think he was a good president," Miss Pearlstine and I said in unison. *Was?*

"This proves that God didn't want a Catholic president," Sam continued.

"Oh, shut up!" I said. And then I remembered my responsibility as a possible future Miss Columbian, and I added, "Please."

I still couldn't believe that President Kennedy was dead. Reporters made mistakes. They were almost always wrong about the weather.

"Dear God," I prayed silently. "Let President Kennedy really be alive. Make this news a false report, and I will give up being Miss Columbian."

I paused for a moment. I knew I had to go further still.

"I'll even give up being among the finalists." I added silently.

In sync with my prayers, Mr. Kirk continued.

"There have been some questions about tonight's beauty contest. If this was a frivolous affair, we would cancel it. But it's been planned for a long time, and the publication of the yearbook depends on the money we raise tonight. So the contest will go on as planned."

I convinced myself—sort of—that since I was representing the Future Teachers of America Club, it was my duty to participate in the contest. I decided I would go on, but I wouldn't smile—not unless the news was false and Kennedy was really still alive. Then I would go on and I would smile but, in keeping with my vow to God, I wouldn't win. I wouldn't even be among the finalists.

It was while Dana was teasing my hair to make it look like Jackie's that we received a phone call from the school secretary.

"Some of the judges don't feel like coming," the secretary said. "So the beauty contest will have to be postponed."

Mother stopped working on my dress, and Dana stopped working on my hair, and we all sat down in front of the TV and watched a disheveled Jacqueline Kennedy stand beside Lyndon Johnson as he was sworn in as our next president. She had a dark smear on her dress, and even though we didn't have a colored television, we knew it was blood. She'd taken his head in her lap and then she'd crawled over the open limousine to get help.

"Now you look more like her than she does," Dana told me.

We all spent the weekend right there in the den, watching all the Kennedys. Caroline, who'd once come to her father's press conference in her mother's high heel shoes, was now crying as she held her mother's hand. John John, sometimes photographed romping around in his father's office, was now saluting our dead president's flag-draped coffin. But the biggest change was in what they were saying about Jacqueline Kennedy. No one was talking about her sable underwear or who had designed the dress she was wearing or how much it had cost. All anyone noticed about her dress was that it wasn't the pink suit with the blood stains on it. It was all black. A black mantilla replaced the pill-box hat. They were using words like courage and dignity. Everything had changed, and I decided I had too.

As Dana was getting ready to drive back to Winthrop, she said, "I came home for nothing."

"Well, you were here to watch President Kennedy's funeral with us," I said.

"But that's not something only I could do," she replied, as if she were a fairy godmother robbed of her mission. "Well, when they re-schedule the beauty contest, let me know the new date, and I'll see if I can come down."

"Thank you, Dana," I said, "But I'm not sure I have my heart in things like beauty contests anymore."

"Oh, that's right. Now all you care about is the Highest Possible Moral Standards Award."

On Monday morning, Mr. Kirk came over the PA system once again. He gave us the new date for the beauty contest.

"And now, let's have a moment of silent prayer," he said, "for our country and in memory of President Kennedy."

That's when I realized that in spite of what had happened, I still cared about the contest, and even though my silent prayer was all about Kennedy and his family and the nation (I was, after all, DAR Girl), I had to add a little PS about the contest. I was too ashamed to ask God to help me win it, with President Kennedy up there within earshot. Still, I had to ask God for something. I knew He was waiting.

"Dear God," I told Him silently, "I guess, the way we left it, I could ask You to help me win this contest because I only offered not to win if Kennedy didn't die, and he died. (I refrained from saying, "You let him...") But, even though we're back where we began, I'd like to move forward and do something to honor Kennedy." I didn't mention anything about meeting foreign men and seeing foreign lands and learning foreign languages like French. I didn't want God to think I had ulterior motives.

"When the time comes and I've finished Winthrop College and have my BA in English, could you and President Kennedy help me get into the Peace Corps?"

It made me a little bit nervous when, on the postponed date of the contest, I won. Did that mean that God was behind in answering my prayers or that He'd chosen having me crowned over getting me into the Peace Corps? I'd have to wait a few years to find out.

Crossing That First Border

WHEN MY FATHER became a director of the Job Corps in 1966, we moved to California, and I wound up at San Francisco State College, where there was an abundance of foreigners. I met a lot of them at the language lab when I began to study Spanish, a language more prominent than French on the West Coast .

I dated a disproportionate number of foreign men, increasing my chances of marrying at least one man from another country. I still wanted my children to have what I was deprived of: Parents from different parts of the world who spoke different languages. I mourned my lot as monolingual. Why couldn't my parents have been newly arrived immigrants? But having suffered this deprivation, I figured that the only way I could salvage the situation was by going abroad myself, which meant going to any country where a foreign language—preferably French or Spanish—was spoken, and I didn't want to wait until I was eligible for the Peace Corps.

I didn't really think I could make it to a foreign country. It just seemed too extraordinary, something to happen to The Chosen Few but not to girls like me from Columbia, South Carolina (not to mention Blackfoot, Idaho; Knoxville Iowa; Hays, Kansas; and Pleasant Hill, California). But I had to give it a try, and if it wasn't to be, as I suspected it wasn't, Destiny would find some way to stop me.

In 1967 I found out about a group called Amigos Anonymous, originally made up of Roman Catholic university students but which accepted non-Catholics, even fallen Episcopalians, we thought. We raised money, learned about Mexico, and prepared to serve in Morelia, Mexico.

I became the most fanatic member of their group. I read everything I could get in Spanish including "La Pequeña Lulu" (Little Lulu) and I memorized all the songs from *Mi Bella Dama*, the Spanish version of *My Fair Lady*, so I'd always have something to say if I ever got to Mexico.

I took down the hems of all my skirts as they asked us to do to fit in with conservative village life in Mexico, and I sold raffle tickets to help fund our trip. I even went to mass with the students at the University of San Francisco.

I had lost my religious faith when I was a sophomore in college. Till then I'd reasoned that there had to be a God because if there weren't one, we'd just live and die, and life would have no meaning. Then, as a sophomore, it dawned on me that life had no meaning.

But now I wanted to go to Mexico, and I wanted to go so badly that I didn't think there was anything unethical about bribing the God I wasn't sure I believed in. I made the proposition that if I got to go to Mexico in spite of all the odds against me (namely that I'd never been abroad before and neither had my mother, who longed to, so it probably wasn't meant to be for mere mortals like us), I'd go right back to the blind faith I'd had until my epiphany in my sophomore year.

After I trained with the San Francisco group, the Bishop of Morelia said he didn't want any non-Catholics, and I thought, "So there is no God." But our group leaders were compassionate and arranged for the other non-Catholic and me to work with a group of Catholic volunteers from Albuquerque, who were going to be in Zamora, Michoacán, whose bishop didn't discriminate.

As the day drew near and nothing happened to make our trip impossible or even unlikely, I kept wondering what was going to happen...just before we got over the border. Probably there would be an accident. We wouldn't necessarily all be killed, but the bus we'd chartered would go no farther, and we'd have to turn back. But why should the whole group have to suffer just because I wasn't destined to go abroad? Maybe I would become deathly ill. But I never got sick, so it would have to be an accident. Maybe we wouldn't be too badly hurt.

When we pulled out of San Diego, I kept looking out for Destiny, coming to get me, to keep me from crossing that border. But then we crossed the frontier into Mexico and got to Tijuana.

"Now I know there's a God," I exclaimed to the Catholic girl sitting next to me on the bus. This comment, no doubt, made her think that I found something inspirational in the tacky border town— a quality that eluded most people. I was, of course, merely acknowledging God's accepting my bribe and letting me cross a border into a foreign country.

I'd just become one of those People Who Travel into Lands with Other Tongues. Now anything was possible.

In Zamora, Michoacán, I lived with a wonderful Mexican family who spoke only Spanish, so the only time I had to speak English was at the high school, where I was an assistant in the English classes. Then, when pre-mature newborns came to Mama Rosa's Orphanage, I started taking care of them, and soon afterwards a full-term baby was born to a maid who had been raped by the son of the family she worked for, so I had three infants to take care of. I bought Dr. Spock—in Spanish!

Many years later, I'd hear about the Summer of Love in San Francisco and wonder what people were talking about. I had had a very different summer of love in Mexico. No regrets—except about the maid who was raped and the mentality that made that possible all over the world!

South Pacific as a Peace Corps Musical Overture

By the time I applied for the Peace Corps in 1969 I knew some Spanish and could sing useful phrases like "Radio, Radio, Alegría" and "Bésame, Bésame Mucho" as well as other songs my Mexican sister Lucha had taught me. She and I were corresponding in Spanish, and some seminarians were also writing to me in Spanish.

I also knew some French from *Les Parapluies de Cherbourg*. I could say, «Un parapluie, un parapluie noir. Geneviève, montre les parapluies à monsieur» and of course «Dites-moi.»

So when I filled out my application for the Peace Corps, I requested, "Any Spanish or French speaking country."

Unfortunately, I didn't know any songs in Chinese, and back in 1969, I'm not sure there was any Peace Corps in Taiwan, and we hadn't yet recognized Mainland China, as my father pointed out in an unsolicited speech he gave at the United Nations in 1969.

In late summer of 1969 I finally got a response from the Peace Corps, inviting me to train for Tonga, and I wondered, "Where in Africa is that?" But it turned out not to be in Africa at all. In fact, it was very far from Africa and every other continent. It was a tiny group of islands

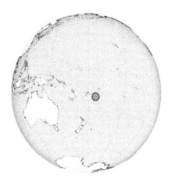

forming an isolated dot in the Pacific Ocean

I knew how Napoleon (a French man!) had been exiled on Elba, and I thought, "I've been rejected! I've been rejected by the Peace Corps."

I knew the Alan Sherman song, "Good advice costs nothing, and it's worth the price." As a volunteer I cost nothing, and I wasn't worth the price? I wasn't worth *nothing*? Maybe I'd have to marry those three men after all.

But then I looked up Tonga in the Columbia Viking Encyclopedia and saw that Tonga wasn't just anywhere in the ocean. It was in the South Pacific, a musical I knew by heart. In fact, it was the only place the Peace Corps went that was a musical show. Tonga was like Bali Hai "lost in the middle of a foggy sea." So, yes, I would go, I would go to Peace Corps Tonga, discarding once again those three foreign husbands and fathers of my children

(to the tune of "This Nearly Was Mine")
Three men of my dreams. Three men to be living with.
Three men to have three kids with
These nearly were mine.

I would be Nellie Forbush, but instead of being a nurse in World War II, I'd be a Peace Corps Volunteer during the War against Vietnam, and instead of my colleagues being in the military, my fellow Peace Corps Volunteers could be Conscientious Objectors.

And instead of living in the barracks, I'd live in the village with the Tongans because I'd never been "taught to be afraid of people whose eyes are oddly made or people whose skin is a different shade." I'd never been carefully taught.

The Peace Corps let us recruits know about the March 1968 issue of *National Geographic,* which featured both Tonga and Iran because there had just been a coronation in each of those countries. I'd already known about Iran because I'd dated Iranians at San Francisco State and people were always hearing about that country (though my dates complained that people thought they still rode on camels). The spread on Tonga was probably the first substantial news ever printed about Tonga in the United States, and it had come out in 1968, in time for us volunteers to benefit.

The Peace Corps also sent us suggestions on the clothes we should pack, and I realized I'd have to extend my wardrobe before I went into training. This was particularly ironic because there was a Ban Deodorant commercial that showed nearly-naked people peeping from around a tree and saying something like "We no wear Ban deodorant in Tonga. But then in Tonga we no wear many clothes!"

Apparently, they wore more than I had, so I'd have to go shopping at Kress or Woolworth's. The Second Hand shops where I usually found clothes didn't have the right stuff for Tonga.

After that and before they sent us to training in Hawaii (on Molokai, the leper colony), we had to go to staging in San Jose. My mother, maybe wishing that she could go along and see the world, drove me there. Of course, we sang along with Dionne Warwick, "Do you know the way to San Jose?" even though that wasn't from a Broadway musical. The song had come out just one year earlier. When my mother dropped me off, I knew I wouldn't be seeing her or the rest of my family for more than two years, but I didn't know that they would feature big in the preliminary interview with a psychologist.

The 50-Minute Sanity Test

Staging for Peace Corps Recruits, San Jose, October 1969

"It's not every day that I'm asked to see a man alone in his motel room," I said cheerily, as I walked in confidently and handed the psychologist the list.

I expected him to laugh and say something like, "Yeah, it is kind of an unusual setting for a screening."

But he stared at me, and after a moment of silence, he said, "I don't know what to say to that."

"You don't?" I asked.

"Well, you come in here and immediately try to seduce me."

"I do?" I asked. I was afraid to protest too much because I knew that line from Shakespeare ("Me thinks the lady doth protest too much."). I also knew that nobody liked having their insights dismissed, and insights were his livelihood.

This was Peace Corps staging in San Jose, October 1969, and a lot hinged on this interview. Would I get to go to Hawaii for training to be a Peace Corps Volunteer in Tonga?

The FBI had already visited the people we used as references, but now we Peace Corps recruits were being screened for basic skills like sanity because they didn't want to send us all the way to Hawaii for training if we were clearly not going to be a good use of tax dollars.

So in October 1969 I'd traveled from Pleasant Hill, a suburb of San

Francisco, to San Jose, where we were asked to fill out a sheet listing everyone in our family—their names, ages, and addresses. Then we were summoned one by one into a motel room for an interview with a psychologist who took the list of family members and began the interview.

I heard the other Peace Corps recruits say they didn't like being psyched out, but I knew that psychologists are just like any other working people, simply trying to do their jobs. They shouldn't be condemned for being licensed. My own father was a psychologist, and I grew up around him and his psychologist friends.

So I had felt confident when I entered that room, but when the psychologist responded so solemnly, speaking of seduction, it threw me off balance.

He asked me to sit down, and when I did, he said, "Well, look at you! The way you sit. Like a queen on a throne."

I guess he meant the way I was holding on to both sides of the armchair because I was starting to fear a rocky ride, and there was no seatbelt.

He explained that our time was limited, and fifty minutes wasn't really long enough to learn all there was to know about a person.

I held back my urge to feign a "Really?" look.

He moved his eyes from me on the throne—or was it an electric chair?—to the list of family.

"Well, I guess we'd better get started," he said. "Describe your father."

"Well, he's very intelligent. And politically active. He organizes his life around causes."

"So he must be pleased that you're joining the Peace Corps."

"Yes," I said, grateful that I wasn't wired for a polygraph. My father was disappointed that I wasn't going to South America to support a meaningful revolution instead of going to a remote South Seas island.

"So, are you close to your father?"

"Well, it's a little bit hard to be close to him because he's very busy and very tense. He's not happy with the way the world is going, and he has a very hot temper."

"So what does he do?" the psychologist asked.

"He yells," I said.

"No," he said, and this time he laughed. "I mean, what does he do for a living?"

"Oh," I said, wondering whether this would help me. "He's a psychologist."

The doctor laughed again. "Well, what does he yell about?"

"He yells about American intervention in Vietnam. China not being admitted to the UN. He yells if we put something away and he can't find it or if we say something stupid."

"You have a different address for your mother."

"My parents are separated," I said

"How long?" he asked.

"Almost a year," I said.

"So what's your mom like?"

"Well, she's idealistic, too, but not as extremely idealistic. She's very smart. She was an only child, so it was her duty to skip a lot of grades. She was at UCLA when she was sixteen. That's where my parents met. He was getting his doctorate, and she typed his dissertation. And then she dropped out of college so they could elope because after Pearl Harbor he had to join the Navy and go overseas. And then she had five children. And then she went back to school through correspondence classes until her last year, when she attended classes on campus. That was my freshman year. We were on the same campus. She graduated with honors."

"And your sister Dana? What does she do?"

"She does beautiful," I said, although I knew that he meant job-wise. But I couldn't say a housewife. Dana was no housewife although she didn't work outside the home. She didn't work in the home either. She called in committees to do her work for her. She didn't work at all except at being beautiful, which was a cushy job for her.

"I'm not surprised she's beautiful," he said, looking at me.

"She's married to a psychiatrist," I said. "They live in Chicago."

"And your brother David, I see, lives in Napa. What does he do?"

Laundry, I thought. He wants to be a brain surgeon, but they're giving him a job doing laundry on his ward.

"*At* Napa," I said. "At Napa State Hospital. He's a patient there." To my horror, I began to sob—quietly but convulsively.

The next thing I heard him say was, "There isn't any Kleenex." Then he added, "You must love your brother very much."

I nodded. My brother and I had always been close, but I'd been able to talk about his psychological and neurological problems since I was seven and he was four and first began having "bad dreams" and "screamers" that morphed into seizures that were sometimes continuous—status epilepticus—and I always talked about him and them with total self-control. I cried only when alone, so I knew I wasn't crying only for my brother. I was crying because I was going to be de-selected on the grounds of "family." The psychologist hadn't even gotten to my sister Missy yet.

Parents recently separated. Brother newly self-admitted to a mental hospital. A younger sister unmarried and pregnant and living three-thousand miles away from the father of her unborn child. We wouldn't get to my twelve-year-old sister, the only one who seemed to be a good model of mental health and stability among us.

I was so good at not crying except when I was alone. It was a talent. And now, of all times, I'd broken down in front of the Peace Corps psychologist screening out the ones who were likely to break down. I hadn't even gotten out of Peace Corps staging! I hadn't even left the mainland.

He was looking around and opened a drawer.

"Could I offer you a Gideon Bible?" he asked, rummaging through the drawer.

"I'm really sorry. I wish there were something I could do to comfort you," he said, reaching into his pocket. "Would you like a piece of gum?"

He unwrapped me a piece, which I took. I knew it was the best that he could do.

I had dreamed of joining the Peace Corps since Kennedy first spoke of it in a 1960 campaign speech, and now it was not to be. They would not send me to Tonga to work, not even to Hawaii to train. I was going to be sent back, damaged goods, to Pleasant Hill. Not even to San Francisco. I'd given up my apartment there. I'd be sent back to my mother's home in Pleasant Hill. I had been tried and convicted, and I couldn't use the insanity defense to get off, to get off to Peace Corps Tonga.

I stifled or strangled a sob and got hold of myself.

"I'm afraid," the psychologist said, sounding genuinely sorry, "that our time is up."

I stood up, no longer crying, and waited to be dismissed, dishonorably discharged before I ever took the oath of service, before I even got into training.

He walked me to the door.

"Here," he said, handing me his card. "I hope you'll look me up in two years, when you get out of the Peace Corps. I feel sure you'll make a good volunteer."

Lessons Learned and Not Learned

WHILE IT'S TRUE that everything I should have learned I could have learned in Tonga, there were lessons available even in Peace Corps staging.

That some psychologists have no sense of humor—or pretend not to in order to see how a "client" reacts.

That self-confidence can dissipate really quickly when a humorous remark is seen as serious.

That some psychologists relate to us better, if awkwardly, when we lose self-control. Now why would that be?

That some psychologists think that the best way to assess mental health in a limited amount of time (50 minutes although I remember it as 15) is to ask those being assessed to describe their family.

Why didn't the psychologists ask us to describe ourselves? Why was our description of people in our nuclear family considered more illuminating than our descriptions of friends or the guys we were leaving behind? What did my way of describing my family reveal about me? Why didn't they ask us how and when we decided to apply for two years in the Peace Corps?

One thing I learned from other Peace Corps recruits that day in staging is that almost all Peace Corps recruits interviewed described their father in terms of his profession. (In most cases, their mothers were housewives. This was in 1969.) It hadn't occurred to me to do that even though my father was a psychologist and saying so might have helped me bond with the psychologist interviewing me. I thought of my father in terms of how he behaved and affected me, not in terms of his profession.

I learned that recent good memories can be repressed if they don't fit a familiar pattern because I described my father as he had been in the past but not as he was two months earlier, when I had visited him in Pennsylvania and he'd taken my sisters Suzy, traveling with me, and Missy, pregnant and living with him, to New York City and two long-playing musicals in New York—*Man of La Mancha* and *Cabaret*—and he hadn't yelled when he found out that I'd left our tickets on the floor of the car. He hadn't yelled even once. He's been both generous and even-tempered, not the way I described him to the psychologist.

Letter from Hawaii, 1969

For General Audiences

Malo ʻetau lava ki he anani! (which means in Tongan "Hello" or—literally—"Congratulations on our surviving to this day.")

Right now I'm on the island of Lanai, which has not only the world's largest pineapple plantation, but also a ditto machine right across the street from where I'm living. I couldn't resist!

Eleven of the Tonga trainees are on Lanai now, and we're student teaching here in preparation for our work in Tonga. I have the sixth grade for language arts, and I'm surprised (and relieved) by how much I enjoy it. The children are predominantly Filipino-American and Japanese-American, and they're really lovely: responsive, thoughtful, affectionate, interested and interesting, beautiful, and all the adjectives that insecure Peace Corps trainees hope they can apply to their students. There are a few white children, also lovely, at the school, and they are treated kindly and without discrimination.

The school on Lanai is very good. Children play the flute, do Filipino dances, read the Honolulu Star-Bulletin, watch (sort of) educational television, draw and make collages, work on plays, and ask personal questions. Most of the children's fathers work for Dole—picking pineapples, irrigating, running tractors, etc. But others work in the school or in the stores, where we Peace Corps Trainees—after having taken our vows of poverty—have to buy milk at 50 cents a <u>quart</u>. Food is really expensive in Hawaii; everything's just about twice as much—except avocados, which sell for 5c each.

My favorite breakfast on Lanai is broiled octopus, orange juice with lilikois (passion fruit) and guavas, and Quaker Oats. When we're invited out, we have fish cakes, veal, venison, and breadfruit for hors d'oeuvres. Lanai is noted for its pineapples, but it also has deer and antelope (but buffalo are extinct), pheasant, goats, mouflon sheep, partridges, doves, wild turkey, lovely beaches, and a glass bottom boat, which we plan to take to sail to the island of Maui, known for its shopping and its volcano.

The life of a Peace Corps trainee is not unbearable, and "it's a valid expression of human existence." That's what they've taught us in cross-cultural training. However people choose to spend their time or money—it's a valid expression of human existence. We're not supposed to be judgmental of other cultures, but I judge our Peace Corps culture in Hawaii very, very valid!

There are 56 people in the Tonga V Training program—eleven married couples, ten single girls, and twenty-five single fellows (which says something about the old draft system). The volunteers are from all over the USA—Hawaii, New York, California, Massachusetts, Texas—and from many types of schools—Marywood College, University of the South, De Paul U., Stanford, Syracuse, Connecticut College, Northwestern, Case Institute of Technology, Yale, UCLA, etc. There are many types of people, which pleases me. Some pride themselves on their ability to be spectacularly bored, but for the most part the Peace Corps Trainees have a positive attitude and a good sense of humor.

The Tongan people are also great. And <u>don't</u> believe those Ban commercials saying the Tongans no wear much clothes. They wear plenty clothes. (deliberate error like the ad) They even <u>swim</u> fully clothed. The women wear tupenus (black skirts) under their dresses, and these go all the way to the ankle. The overall effect is almost puritanical, but it's also very pretty. On Sunday the women dress all in white, and it's like something from another century.

Among our Tongan instructors are Falaetau, who once danced on the Ed Sullivan Show (not as a regular), and Eleni, who once dated the Crown Prince of Tonga. Everyone on the Tongan staff is extremely nice...and patient. The first month we had HILT (high intensity language training) from 6:30 in the morning to 7:30 at night. I know that sounds heroic, but we did have breaks. We fed our chickens and watered our gardens and took three showers a day.

During our usual weeks, we're on the island of Molokai, which has 6000 people—4000 more than Lanai. We get up at 5:45 for language classes. I never thought I'd see a sunrise! And I can't get over the wonder of a garden that <u>grows</u>! Carrots, Chinese lettuce, taro, sweet potato, and radishes all come up in my garden...admittedly, I had a little bit of help. But I've become so earthy. I've even de-beaked a chicken. (They have to have their beaks cut off or they'll cannibalize one another.) We also have pigs, but I don't associate with them much; it's so obvious why they're called pigs.

So many people, before I left, told me that they had been disappointed by Hawaii—that it was spoiled and like Miami Beach. But this really isn't true of Molokai. It's quiet and "uncivilized." We have post-card sunsets—pink and lavender and blue and yellow and sometimes even green. We stay at "summer camp" most of the time, but when we want "culture" we go into town. On my birthday I was treated to a Japanese movie called <u>Destroy All Monsters</u>. But afterwards, for compensation, the PC staff treated me to my first Mai Tai, which is the most delicious drink I've ever had—made from Hawaiian fruits and rum. I had four!

And only on Molokai could you have a picnic in a junk yard, overlooking cliffs and the water of the Pacific AND a Hawaiian sunset.

You know, psychologists are very important people on the PC staff, and we've been interviewed by them many times. But <u>I'm</u> the one who had the distinction of having one for a roommate our first week on Lanai. I think it was just happenstance, but...anyway, they're all "good" people, and I especially like Jean, my former roommate. On December 5th, she told us it was Thanksgiving, and so we had a feast. No one would think of questioning Jean, with her PhD in reality.

It's just a little over a month before we leave for the Tonga Isles. (Two months after we get there, Queen Elizabeth and Prince Philip will arrive for a couple of days in Nuku'alofa, Tonga's capital.) I will then be moving in to my fale, FAH-lay, which means hut. Would you like to improve your Tongan vocabulary? Start with Fale—FAH-lay, and follow this amazing paradigm:

Fale-means hut. Ako means study. So a fale ako is a study hut or school.

Koloa means **goods. So fale ka**loa is a goods hut or store.

Kai means eat, so fale kai is an eating hut or a cafeteria, restaurant.

Faiva means show, so a fale faiva is a show house or theater

Mahaki means sick, so fale mahaki is a sick house or hospital.

Malolo means rest, so a fale malolo is a rest hut or rest room.
Mohe means sleep, so a fale mohe is a sleep hut or dormitory

Maili means mail, so a fale maili is a mail hut or post office. (You can tell which words the English introduced—things they didn't have before!)

Polisi means polilce, so a fale polisis is a police hut or police station.

Got it?

But even before I move into my fale (FAH-lay), we'll have our Christmas-in-July. Some of the trainees have never known Christmas without snow, but I have a feeling that it's going to be a very special Christmas just the same. And for all of you, too, I hope. Merry Christmas "across the miles" and across an ocean!

THE TRUTH ABOUT THAT TIME IN PEACE CORPS TRAINING

I DIDN'T TELL any lies, but I certainly (and prudently) left a lot out of that letter for General Audiences!

The night before I left Molokai for Lanai, I'd willingly gone into a deserted room—the room with the vending machines— with another Peace Corps trainee I felt an attraction towards. We were kissing for the first time when he pushed me down on some kind of cot, which hadn't been part of my romantic fantasy. I pushed him off of me, and he later apologized, but rumor spread that I (not he, but I) had been caught in a "compromising position," as I learned from Broc, another Peace Corps Volunteer I liked a lot. Apparently someone had entered the room before I'd pushed him off of me—unless of course he himself was the one who spread the rumor. He grabbed me on New Year's Eve, too, and when I look back, I think there might be a contingent of women who could come forth 50 years later with their #Me Too stories of him—a great way to celebrate the 50th anniversary of our group's training on Molokai!

I didn't mention how I'd unintentionally insulted P., one of our Tongan training instructors, when on my birthday, after those four Mai Tais, he'd asked me to dance, and I had declined, not wanting to collapse in his arms. He later took me aside and said, "I was for you going to Tonga one hundred percent, but now—-" The cross-culture director told me that same night, the night of my twenty-fourth birthday, that

I had to be very careful not to cause Tongans to lose face. It was culturally insensitive of me, apparently, to say no.

Even then I was aware of not having the "right" responses to whatever was going on. But I genuinely liked the people—Tongan teachers, other Peace Corps trainees, staff.

I didn't mention that Jean, the psychologist I roomed with, couldn't sleep unless we left the lights on all night. That didn't bother me because I've always been able to sleep under any conditions, but it would have been an interesting tale to tell on a psychologist. She was there to give us feedback from our peer evaluations.

I kept my rough draft, but only for the last few pages.

Self-Evaluation

On our mimeographed form, we had 53 people to evaluate, but I had only numbers 33-53, a rough draft of what I turned in.
Beside each name we could express a preference and an opinion. Preference meant that we hoped to be placed near them in Tonga. Opinion meant we thought they'd be good PCVs.

A zero meant we were neutral.

A plus was positive, and a minus was negative. We were asked to make both positive and negative comments about each Peace Corps trainee.

Although no one asked us to evaluate ourselves, I had a lot to say:

MARTIN,	Pref.	Opinion	Comments
Tina	+	+	

I put a plus by my preference (I'd like to live near me) and by opinion (I thought I'd be a good PCV.) I had a lengthy comment. (I hadn't yet understood that the word was Super-Vol as in Super Volunteer. I guess I felt that we, like balls, were just being tossed around from player to player, and there was nothing super about my part in the game.)

Positive: She's not a super-ball, but I've gotten to know her pretty well, and one thing I know is that she's <u>not frail</u>. Contrary to unpopular opinion, she did not grow up in a rose garden. But she sees weeds and pulls them when she can. She's not Wonder Woman, but I truly believe that she's emotionally mature, according to her definition of maturity: willingness and ability to assume responsibility, self-control, patience, capacity to face disappointment without becoming bitter or cynical. (This does not apply to de-selection on the basis of emotional immaturity.) She really likes teaching, and I know she'd work hard and enthusiastically. She has no illusions about Tonga's being a paradise; she knows it's gonna be really hard. But she's stronger than she looks, believe me. She's also very healthy—has never missed a day of work because of health (or any other reason), never missed a day of school because of health, after the seventh grade, and is not a hypochondriac. She realizes that the pressures and stresses in Tonga will be more emotional than physical, and she thinks she can make it, tho' she knows it won't be easy—for anyone, even Steve Cheney. {*Steve Cheney was a SuperVol. He was either de-selected or chose not to go.*} She's not the most striking or outstanding trainee, but I have confidence in her endurance and "good will." I think she should be sent to Tonga. She doesn't like to beg, but: your vote and support would be greatly appreciated.

For Andrea I wrote only positive things: "Enthusiastic, likely to be quite popular with the Tongans, good teacher."

The only thing I'd change in retrospect is that she was an outstanding teacher. I didn't know that in Peace Corps training, but I certainly knew it in Tonga and for the years after, when I had the chance to see her in action at the United Nations and other places. She was gifted.

For Ron Rosenberg I put + and + and commented, "He seems much more a part of things now than he did last month. He's independent and sensitive to other people—he does communicate, and I think he'd be a quiet, hard worker in Tonga. He's 'different' from many of the trainees, but I honestly don't think it's in a rebellious way or a way that could hurt Tonga or the P.C. I think he'd be an asset."

He certainly was an asset in my life!

For Broc Stenman I gave a neutral symbol because I didn't think he liked me anymore, but I still had to rate him high, so for opinion I put a + and commented, "So highly motivated, really does things well. Good language."

For Mike Wimberly I wrote + and + and commented "Warm, thoughtful, conscientious, hard-working, good teacher."

As I said, we were asked to put a plus+ beside the name of anyone we particularly wanted to live near during our two years in Tonga. Jean told me that all the single guys had put a plus+ by my name. (That was before I was caught in that "compromising position.") She also told me that one of the comments was "I like her dream world," and another was "Very feminine. Can she take it?"

"That 'Can she take it' sounds like KD," I said, referring to a married volunteer who was very matronly and inclined to pass judgment and give advice like any good mother.

"Well, I probably shouldn't tell you this, " Jean told me, "but she *is* the one who wrote it. So what does that mean? There's one kind of feminine that means a person is frail and unable to cope, and there's another kind of feminine meaning a person who's sure of herself as a woman."

"That's the one," I said. "The second one" even though I was sure KD meant it as a put down. I really did not want to be de-selected.

I didn't mention any of the guys I'd fallen in love with either.

A Fine Romance?

The same weekend I managed to pass the 50-minute "Shall We Invest Our Tax Dollars on You?" Sanity Test, they put us in encounter groups and gave us games to play while they observed us. There were a couple of guys I was immediately attracted to. I saw one "across a crowded room," and we walked towards each other just like Tony and Maria in *West Side Story* at the dance at the gym although we did not kiss, and my brother didn't threaten him. Another guy I was attracted to was Broc, who was a marine biologist who knew enough to put Tonga down as his first request.

But the first time I met Jim, from Chicago, was after Peace Corps staging, just a day after I was "cleared" by the psychologist in the motel room.

The Peace Corps staff members who had come to San Jose just for the staging saw us off when we were getting on the airport bus from the Auditorium Travel Inn.

"Have a good time," they said. "Good luck."

And we shook hands or hugged.

Jim was the third person to say goodbye to us, so I was surprised when, once seated on the bus, I saw him sit down on the aisle across from me.

"Didn't you just see us off?" I asked.

"Yes," he said. "I like seeing people off."

He was a Peace Corps trainee, too, just like us. Well, maybe not just like us. He was unique—whimsical and smart. He was fairly tall with maybe hazel eyes and curly reddish-brown hair that caught the sunlight in a way that highlighted him. Heeeere's Jim! When I got to know him better, I thought that of all the men I met, he was the one who my brother David would have been most like if he hadn't developed neuro-behavioral "complications" along the way. I later told this to Jim, who was one of the few people I told about David's being a patient at Napa State Hospital.

Jim said, "You're saying that of all the guys you know, I'm the most like your brother who's in a mental institution?"

He knew about David's uncontrollable seizures, and another time he told me, "You know, you're just like your brother only your seizures come out in song." He was referring to my tendency to sing snatches of Broadway show tunes to hold my end of the conversation. Musicals! That's where I got my first notion of what romance was all about.

While our parents were busy fighting, I'd go up to the attic where my parents stored their old records, and I'd listen to their old 78 rps, the records they used to have before 45s and 33rpms. I'd listen to them, imagining that I was in a beautiful restaurant with red velvet wall paper and some wonderful man was singing to me:

"I Hear A Rhapsody" ~ Jimmy Dorsey & His Orchestra w/ Bob Eberly ~ 1940 ~ Decca Records

When you're near the murmuring of the breeze
Becomes a symphony.
A rhapsody.
And when I hear you call
So softly to me,
I don't hear a call
At all.
I hear a rhapsody. (OOOoooOOOoooOOOooo from the chorus)

Another song I liked went like this: (credit goes to Rodgers and Hart)

With a song in my heart,
I behold your adorable face.
Just a song from the start.
But it soon was a hymn to your praise.
When the music swells,
I'm touching your hand,
It tells me your stand-
ing near and
At the sound of your voice,
Heaven knows its importance to me,
Can I help but rejoice
That a song such as ours came to be...

It turns out that "Heaven knows its importance to me" was really "Heaven opens its portals to me." But either was fine with me as long as the man kept on singing.

I knew what love was, and I wasn't settling for anything less than a pair of eyes with "dawn's promising skies, petals on the pool drifting" and an eager mouth with "strange spice from the South, honey through the comb drifting." I required a sky "full of light, with suns and moons all over the place, going mad, shooting sparks into space," etc.

This early education on what love was all about continued with Johnny Mathis, who was "Wonderful, Wonderful," but I found romance mostly in Broadway tunes. In the attic I found the records of SOUTH PACIFIC, and OKLAHOMA, and my mother played those as well as CAROUSEL, SHOWBOAT, and PAL JOEY on the piano. I listened to the records over and over till I knew them by heart. Then, no matter what was going on around me, something beautiful was playing in my head. That's how I got through all the fights at home, as well as Algebra and geometry classes.

When we were really little, my sister Dana and I used to spend every Saturday and every summer day in the movie theater, where we'd see MGM musicals with Ann Blyth, Jane Powell, Debbie Reynolds,

Gene Kelly, Cyd Charise, Marge and Gower Champion. I really became convinced that when you were in love, not only was it The Loveliest Night of the Year, but you always sang to each other about it. It was just second-nature. Then one day I was at a friend's house, and she had a record with a real ugly red, black and white photo on the cover. It showed a girl and a boy running in front of a garbage can, and I wanted to listen to the soundtrack from BEN HUR instead. But Linda, who(m) I liked because she was a misfit like me, said, "No, listen to this," and she made me listen to a song called "Tonight," a song from the ugly album, and that's when I entered a new world, the world of WEST SIDE STORY, the album with the garbage can on the cover. I borrowed it and memorized every song, and I starved for a week so I could buy my own copy with my lunch money—and that was a real sacrifice because the school lunches were so much better than what we got at home. But that's when I learned that there was a whole section of the record shops called "Soundtracks and Original Broadway Show Recordings," and I never ate a school lunch again. Wherever I went, there was always a love scene playing in my head, and the lovers were singing to each other on fire escapes or in the highlands of Scotland or wherever they might be.

Jim didn't sing to me, but he sometimes sang with me. Our relationship was romantic, but it wasn't because Jim was romantic. It was because I insisted upon romance, which wasn't prevalent in Peace Corps training, where our life was largely communal.

Once we took a walk together on Molokai and got caught in a rainstorm, which could have been the height of romance. In high school I'd seen a movie in which Nancy Kwan and Pat Boone get caught in an avalanche and wind up in a little cottage with a fireplace and a featherbed and a long flannel nightgown for her to wear. I thought the rainstorm was romantic because we'd find shelter in each other's arms. It would be like the song "Soon It's Gonna Rain" from The Fantastics. I even sang that to Jim out there in the wet cold.

Soon it's gonna rain. I can feel it.
Soon it's gonna rain. I can tell.
Soon it's gonna rain. What are we gonna do?

Of course, it was already raining. But I went on.
We'll find four limbs of a tree.
We'll build four walls and a floor.
We'll bind it over with leaves
Then duck inside and play.
Then we'll let it rain. We'll not feel it.
Then we'll let it rain. Rain pell mell.
And we'll not complain if it never stops at all.
We'll live and love within our castle walls.

But Jim acted as if he wished it weren't raining. Instead of comforting me, he kept complaining that he was cold. He had a sweatshirt, which he didn't immediately take off and offer to me. But he did put his arms around me, and that felt good.

We found a deserted house, which turned out not to be deserted, and the owner of the house gave us steaming coffee and towels to mop ourselves up with. He also gave me his Molokai sweatshirt.

"I hope this doesn't shame you or make you feel guilty," I told Jim, to bring it to his attention that he should feel ashamed and guilty.

"What do you mean?"

"I mean, I hope you don't feel bad that this nice man gave me his sweatshirt before you had a chance to give me yours."

"No," Jim assured me, "I don't feel bad about that."

"I was hoping you wouldn't," I said.

We stayed with the nice man for about an hour, and then the rain stopped and we made a dash for it. A dash wasn't fast enough to beat the second cloud burst. We ran from tree to tree, shed to shed, and we finally wound up in a barn with horses and hay without the hayride. I always thought hay rides were so romantic—getting in the back with a boy and a bundle of straw and being driven through the night—the next best thing to "a surrey with the fringe on top." But this was a barn, and the horse had his behind to us, and pretty soon the horse had to relieve himself of every meal he'd had for the past three or four months, but there was no bathroom, so he went right there in front of us—generously but unceremoniously.

"I never imagined," Jim said, "that we'd wind up in a stable."

That of course prompted me to say, "For there was no room for us in the inn."

If this was not like an MGM musical, I thought, at least it could be of Biblical proportions.

The rain never stopped—and the horse never seemed to either—so we decided that we'd just run back to camp in the rain. Along the way, we stopped for shelter in someone's carport, and as we were holding each other to keep warm, a man with an umbrella approached us.

"We saw you from our window," the kind Filipino-American man said. "We'd like to invite you into our house."

"We'd like to accept!" Jim said, as I thanked the man profusely.

His wife gave us dry clothes to wear while she was spinning our drenched ones in the dryer. We spent the evening talking with them and playing with their children. I saw that Jim was really good with children. I rarely looked at a guy without wondering what kind of husband and father he would make, and I saw that Jim would make a good father.

They invited us to stay for dinner and then invited us back another time together. "Now we're a couple!" I thought.

"Happy ending!" I said when they dropped us off back at camp.

"Tina," Jim said, "why don't we get married and settle down right here on Molokai and have some beautiful Filipino children like theirs?"

"Okay," I said.

But instead of getting married, settling down, and having some beautiful Filipino children, we went right on—single—with the training program until there was a threat of my being de-selected and sent back home.

FINAL ASSESSMENT ON MOLOKAI

SOUTH PACIFIC WASN'T the only musical that came to mind in Peace Corps training for Tonga. "The Best of All Possible Worlds" is a song from another musical, *Candide*, based on Voltaire but *much* better, with music by Leonard Bernstein and lyrics by Richard Wilbur and Dorothy Parker, and in training on Molokai, I wrote "It's the best of all possible dream worlds" on a banner across my room because I'd been told by the Peace Corps staff there that I lived in a dream world, so they weren't sure I could "take" Tonga. Hadn't I told Jean that I was the "feminine" that was sure of herself and strong? Were we going in circles?

I was really worried, and then Ron and Andrea came by to talk to me about their feedback. Because he'd cut cross-cultural activities, Ron's mental health was in question.

"What do they mean?" Ron said. "The ones who are crazy are the ones who *go* to cross-cultural activities. I'd rather spend time with the Tongans than the staff's misdiagnosis of them."

He'd just made friends with Andrea, who had gotten high ratings on language and teaching skills but had been labeled "lewd and suggestive" because she'd once chased P. with a frog, and Tongans are afraid of frogs, so P. had run into the bush to escape it.

"Aren't you just culturally insensitive?" Ron asked. "How is chasing a Tongan with a frog lewd and suggestive?"

"You're not lewd and suggestive!" I told Andrea.

"They called me anti-social," Ron said. "I'm going back and ask them if I can be lewd and suggestive instead."

"Do you know what they told me?" I asked, ready to hear some reassurance. "They said I lived in a dream world."

"Well, of course, you do!" Ron said, and Andrea nodded approvingly.

"Nobody could know the words to every Broadway show if they didn't live in a dream world. Nobody does routines from musicals while they clean the chicken coop at six o'clock in the morning if they don't live in a dream world. You *are* crazy, and that's your greatest asset."

That was the nicest thing anyone in training had told me, and it brought to mind the musical *Skyscraper* with songs by Sammy Cohn because one of the songs is about daydreaming and how it's an internal coffee break. ("What makes it such a crime if I'm a person who runs away from troubles and hassles, preferring to spend the day in Spanish castles?")

If my best of all possible dreamworlds didn't do me in, what about P.? While Andrea had been labeled lewd and suggestive for chasing him into the bush, I had alienated him by saying no, after four Mai Tais, when he asked me to dance with him on my birthday. He was no longer behind me one hundred percent.

But in January, as a few others were sent back home, Ron, Andrea, and I (with or without P.'s vote) were finally "cleared" by the final Peace Corps Are-They-Sane? De-selection Committee so we could go to Tonga.

We took our oath of service, basically the same as the oath taken by the President of the United States, accentuating certain words:

"I do solemnly swear that I will support and defend the *constitution* of the United States against all enemies, foreign and *domestic*, and that I will bear *true* faith and allegiance to the same, that I take this obligation freely, without any mental reservation or purpose of evasion, and that I will well and faithfully discharge my duties in the Peace Corps. So help me God."

Then we went to Honolulu for our last night on American soil before heading for the South Seas.

A Date I Know by Heart

SINCE OUR LIFE on Molokai had not been romantic, even by Jim's standards, he said he was going to make up for it by taking me out for Mai Tais and dinner in Honolulu, where our Peace Corps training group was going before leaving the United States for Tonga. To make it more romantic, he said we wouldn't go Dutch but he'd pay with his Peace Corps living allowance.

First we took a walk in a beautiful park, where he read to me from a book he loved, *A Separate Peace*. As he read, he'd kiss me between paragraphs or sentences or words, and then we'd really kiss, even though in a public park we knew it was bad manners.

From time to time, as we were kissing, someone would walk by and give us a disapproving look. Once Jim looked back at a disapproving looker and said, "Because we don't have another place to do it." Then he lowered his voice and explained, "That's in answer to their question 'Why can't you kids do that somewhere else?'"

Then we had dinner, and after we had eaten and while I was drinking my third Mai Tai and Jim's second one, he told me The Story of His Life, and I fell asleep in his arms right there in a cozy corner of the restaurant. (Unlike the song from *Funny Girl*, there was no "height of nonchalance, furnishing a bed in restaurants." I stayed seated in our booth.) I had never before had a chance to fall asleep in Jim's arms and now, in my intoxicated state, I thought it was romantic. However, Jim thought my falling asleep was a reflection on the quality of his life story. "Just wait, Tina," he said. "My life story will be a lot more interesting after a few weeks in Tonga." During our three days in Honolulu, we saw *Cactus Flower, Hello, Dolly, Bob and Carol and Ted and Alice*, and we even went to *Closely Watched Trains* at the University of Hawaii because Jim told me it was his favorite recent movie. I liked it better than *A Separate Peace*.

We also slept on the beach—yes, really slept—and when we woke up, we'd made a complete circle in the sand.

But finally our extended weekend was over, and we had to go back to our group. The next morning we got red leis and boarded Pan Am for Fiji, where we had breakfast before boarding Fiji Airlines for Tonga, where we landed just before lunch near a little grass field. When we got off the plane, we were given fresh leis, and our Tongan experience began.

Jim and I held hands as we went by bus through the island's villages to Nuku'alofa, Tonga's capital. Along the way we saw coconut and banana trees, coconut leaf huts, blue sky and smoke rising from underground ovens.

"It looks," I whispered to Jim, "the way you think it's not going to look because things never look the way you expect them to look."

"Yeah," he said.

"You always expect foreign countries to look strange and exotic, but they always wind up looking like Los Angeles or Columbia, South Carolina. But this really looks strange and exotic."

"Yeah," Jim said.

"Jim, we forgot to get married and settle down on Molokai and have beautiful Filipino children," I said.

But Jim was in culture shock and didn't speak again until we were at a communal lunch at the Way In Motel in Nuku'alofa. There he leaned across the papaya to deliver an important message:

"Tina, you're the best date I've ever had," he said. "Dinner in Hawaii, breakfast in Fiji, and lunch in Tonga."

"We should do this more often," I said.

But it was just about time for us to separate. He was going to an outer island, and I was staying on Tongatapu.

"Most people live on a lonely island," I sang to him. I didn't sing the lyrics about the pineapple islands lost in the Doleful Pacific Seas. But I was determined to continue *South Pacific* as a Peace Corps musical.

A few days later I saw Jim off at the wharf, after he'd treated me to several gin and tonics, which I'd drunk alternately with his. We kissed, and he boarded the Just David, the boat that would take him to his island, Nomuka.

I waved goodbye and shouted, "Don't feel bad about deserting me!"

"Okay!" he shouted back.

Moving In

I WAS GOING to a little village called Ha'ateiho. Sione Mafanga, the headmaster at my school, 'Atele Primary (or 'Atele Si'i—Little 'Atele), escorted me there. He was a serious-looking, handsome man, about fifty years old. He reminded me of an Indian chief except that, instead of feathers, he wore the typical Tongan dress: flip-flops, a wrap-around skirt like a sarong called a tupenu, and a ta'ovala, the woven garment worn around the waist.

"You will be on a nobleman's property," he told me. "The noble Havea will look at you."

This disconcerted me a little bit, imagining the inspection like that of Tuptim in *The King and I,* "He is pleased with me, my lord and master?" Then I decided he'd meant to say look *after* me. I went over in my mind the phrase we had learned for greeting nobles. To ordinary mortals, the expression was *Malo e lelei,* literally *thank you for being well.* But to a noble *hello* was different: *Malo e laumalie,* which also meant thank you for being well, but specifying nobly well or a well noble: Thank you, a noble, for being nobly well.

Everything seemed very still and quiet when we reached the lot. There was a tiny hut made of bamboo poles and with a roof made from coconut leaves, and when I entered, ducking to make it into the door, there were lots of women sitting on the floor.

"Malo e laumalie," I said.

They informed me that they were, like me, ordinary mortals.

"Then malo e lelei," I said.

The hut was beautiful. The floor and ceiling were covered with woven mats and the walls were covered with tapa cloth and mats. Because the hut was tiny and the ceiling very low, I had the impression of being in a cushioned cardboard box. As children, we'd played a lot in boxes, since cardboard boxes were an integral part of our furniture, or so I imagined. They were, for examples, tables and drawers. And whenever we wanted to make them less functional and more fun, we'd just clear them off or empty them out, crawl inside them and roll over and over until our cardboard furniture burst. I had the impression of being once again in a cardboard box. The main part of the hut had one little window made of wood and propped open with a long stick. There was a little separation for the part of the hut that had the bed, and there was another window. The windows looked like twelve inch squares (though they were really larger), and a woman, who turned out to be Loiloi, tall and beautiful with a very deep voice and a short natural, was peering in at me through one of the windows, which framed her face. When she smiled, she looked like the Cheshire Cat in *Alice in Wonderland*.

"This isn't really happening," I thought.

In a moment, she ducked into the fale and gave me a *sisi*, a grass skirt to wrap around my waist. The women all presented me with leis and hand-woven gifts and said, "This is your home." I wondered if this was meant literally or more in the sense of *Mi casa es la tuya*. It was literally mine, I soon found out, which made me happy because I'd assumed it was the noble's home; it was certainly worthy of a noble.

As it turned out, the Noble Havea and his family lived in a larger wooden house that was supposed to be appropriate for his chiefly stature but wasn't really as beautiful or as cozy as mine.

There was a feast for me that evening, and everything seemed beautiful and smoky and make-believe. As a special bonus, I was given the Noble's sixteen-year-old daughter Lupe to stay with me and to keep me from being lonely. I smiled brightly but was very disappointed, having looked forward all day to being lonely.

Lupe was a sturdy-looking, good-natured high school girl with a large gap between her front teeth and long kinky hair that, once let loose, went straight up and out for about half a yard. She wanted to help me in return for my teaching her English. She brought a mattress from her house and put it on my floor, thereby occupying half the area of the room. She was going to lie there and get English by osmosis. She sat on her mattress and I sat beside her on the mat-covered floor, while she told me stories about the Peace Corps volunteer who had lived in the fale before me.

"He is a good one. He is very nice, but one thing he do, he bring girls here in his bed and he rape them."

"Rape?" I asked, wondering whether she meant he had "deflowered" them or had consensual sex. "But was it really rape? Didn't they know why he was inviting them here?

"Yes," Lupe said, "but then it is too late. He already rape them."

"How did people know he raped them?"

Lupe pointed to the hole in the closed wooden window. "They looking in the hole." She advised me to keep the hole covered at all times.

"Why?" I asked. "Do people often look in?

"People *always* look in," she said.

And so they did.

I came home one evening and was closing the door and both windows to practice the Polynesian dances my students had taught me that day. I heard laughter right outside my fale. I opened the door to tell them to keep their opinion to themselves, that I was only a beginner. About three Tongan men started running away. The hole was covered. They could see even through matted walls.

But the first night, after Lupe had plopped the mattress down on half my floor and informed me that we were sisters till death, I let her have the petrol lamp, and I lit a candle and took my fire hazard to my bed. I crawled under the mosquito net and on top of sheets that had been placed on tapa on top of springs—no mattress. (Did Lupe have the mattress?) Instead of a nice firm mattress, I had nice firm springs, which I soon got accustomed to sleeping on.

I stayed awake looking at the shadows in my room—and the beautiful tapa and mats, layer upon layer upon layer. Everything seemed make believe.

I knew that for me there was no turning back now. That was what people expected me to do, since I was the frail, delicate ("feminine") one in the group, who had come to PC training equipped only with a private dreamworld—the result of years of living in a rose garden.

They expected me to go crazy, and now I saw that if I did, it would be from too much protection, from lack of loneliness. I was going to go mad, in this beautiful little cushioned hut in this village on this island. Right out here in the middle of the Pacific Ocean. And I wouldn't be able to sail away as the others could because I was the one they were predicting would sail away. I was a High Risk Volunteer. To show them, I'd have to keep my madness a secret so they wouldn't attribute it to my fragility and former life in a rose garden. Because they would hold even my madness against me and say, "Uh huh, we knew it. Her mind—such as it was—has flown away within a week's time."

I fell asleep while planning ways to keep my madness confidential, a village secret.

Once school started my going mad didn't seem quite so certain. After all, we were using the Tate syllabus, which involved our acting out the lessons for the children. I directed a lot of my nervous energy to hopping, running, and jumping, while saying, "I'm hopping. I'm hopping. I'm Hopping. I'm running. I'm running, etc. A woman with so challenging a job does not have time or energy to worry about madness.

Just getting to school was an event. I was generally accompanied by the children, and the same people greeted me as I passed by their huts every morning. Besides "malo e lelei" (thanks for being well), we used the malo e plus whatever verb seemed appropriate. Thank you for washing your clothes/cutting your grass/repairing your roof/—whatever you caught them doing.

I figured this corresponded to our small talk: "Oh, I see you're fixing breakfast/getting ready for bed/reading a book/getting a divorce.".

The dialogue went like this:

Tongan: Tina! Thank you for being well!
Me: Yes, thank you for hanging your clothes on the fence.
Tongan: Where are you going?
Me: To school.
Tonga: Okay! Go on! 'Alu e
Me: Stay. (Nofo a e)

Of course, if I met someone on the road, and that person was also walking but in the opposite direction, my goodbye would be "Go!" instead of "Stay." But generally the people who greeted me greeted me from their yards or huts. They always thanked me for being well, and I always thanked them for whatever it was they were doing.

They always asked me where I was going, and I always told them I was going to school. It wasn't that they couldn't figure out where I was going at eight o'clock in the morning every day, day after day. They knew I was going running, hopping, and jumping, all in English. for their very own children. Their "Where are you going?" was just a smile, a handshake, an acknowledgement.

At eight o'clock every morning the children lined up in front of the school building and walked forward, systematically picking up sticks and "rubbish" as they went. This was the way the school yard was kept clean. On Friday afternoons, they weeded the garden, washed the windows, and mopped the floors. After they finished picking up the rubbish, they lined up for morning prayers, during which time they bowed their heads reverently while their teachers carried on their conversations.

This talking during prayers business was a surprise to me since most of my education had been in the South, where prayers were treated with great care and reverence if only to show those Communist Supreme

Court Judges what they could do with their decisions about separation of church and state. But now, in this very religious Polynesian kingdom where everything stopped on Sunday except church services because doing anything on the Sabbath was taboo, teachers were chattering away as the prayers went on. One of my favorite teachers, Tevita, would always talk to me to put to use his astonishing command of English.

"Tina, you've done something marvelous to yourself. You are sparkling like a glittering star."

"Oh, thank you, Tevita. That's really nice to hear."

Tevita's useful English phrases, of course, motivated me to continue doing marvelous things to myself so that I could go on sparkling like a glittering star and, eventually, be greeted on my way to school with "Tina! Thank you for sparking like a glittering star."

After the prayers had been said, Tevita had practiced his English, the national anthem had been sung, and the headmaster had made his announcements, the children went in lines to their classrooms, where their hands and finger nails were checked, and where their uniforms were inspected. The children were uniformly barefoot. The girls, most of them with their hair in braids, wore white blouses and red skirts. The boys wore a white shirt and khaki shorts.

My job was to teach these children oral English and writing, spelling, and singing on the side. I was also asked to teach afternoon and night classes for the sixth graders, whose government exam would determine whether or not they went on to high school and if so, to which one. Their entrance exam would be in English although none of them really knew English. The prevailing notion was that their success depended on their intelligence test (which is what the entrance exam was supposed to amount to) and perhaps their intelligence itself was dependent upon night study sessions. I was the key.

So I went hopping from class to class, performing my bag of tricks. I think the children thought I was some exotic species, but they did their best to keep straight faces. As teachers, we PCVs tried to make them laugh, to enjoy their lessons. But their teachers regarded English as a serious matter not a source of mirth, so if the kids did laugh, they were reprimanded, and the headmaster switched them.

During the day it was "This is a rat/coconut/boy/girl
There's some cocoa/chalk/milk/water/tea on the table..
Is this/that a bicycle/horse/woman?
Is there any coffee...
And of course I'm/you're/Sione's/ Lupeane's hopping/eating/chewing/skipping/etc.
We used contractions so they'd get accustomed to English as it was really spoken.
Is Sione/Am I/Are they running/standing/paying/working?

All this was brought to them by the Tate Syllabus.

At night all structures and cramming for the high school entrance exam was learned around snatches from Broadway shows.

I had a song for every grammatical point: "I'm singing in the Rain" was good for the present progressive. "Where are you Going"" from *Sweet Charity* was good for the wh-questions. "Climb Every Mountain" from the *Sound of Music* was for commands. "If I Were a Rich Man" from *Fiddler on the Roof* for the subjunctive. I even condescended to teach off-Broadway shows and ballads. "Where Have All the Flowers Gone?" for the present perfect. "I'd Rather Be a Hammer than a Nail" for the conditional.

I returned to Broadway for useful phrases:

"Goodnight, goodnight. Sleep well, and when you dream, dream of me," from *West Side Story*.

"Good-bye, good-bye, goodbye, goodbye, goodbye, good bye" (Don't try to stop me. Please!") from *Hello Dolly*. "Good morning, good day. How are you this glorious day. Have you ever seen a lovelier morning?" from *She Loves Me*.

For pronunciation drills, I had two favorites: "The Rain in Spain stays mainly on the plain" from *My Fair Lady* for stress and "pick a little, talk a little" from *The Music Man* for the voiceless stops.

Pick a little, talk a little, pick a little, talk a little
Pick, pick, pick, talk a lot, pick a little more.

That would have made a wonderful exercise in contrastive pairs had there been any contrast.

The kids and I loved it, and they learned to sing it in rounds, just as Meredith Willson had intended, with "good night, ladies, good night ladies. Good night, ladies. We're going to leave you, pick pick pick pick pick pick pick pick."

Sometimes I'd take a part. "Professor, her kind of woman doesn't belong on *any* committee. She advocates dirty books. Chaucer! Balzac! *Rabelais*!"

Whenever we weren't at school having English lessons, the children were in my hut, and if they heard me singing a song they liked but hadn't come across in the syllabus, they'd ask me to teach it to them.

But of course the biggest success of all the songs I taught them was "The Mickey Mouse Club Song," which I taught them one day when I was in a wicked culturally-imperialistic mood—although rats were big in Tonga, so this wasn't really culturally insensitive. The children and I made a Mickey Mouse club banner to hold high, high, high, and I taught the children to sing in parts.

Mickey Mouse.
    Donald Duck.
Mickey Mouse.
    Donald Duck
Forever let us hold our banner high.
    High, high, high
Now it's time to say good bye to all our company.
Mi-I -C
    See ya real soon!

K-e-y

        Why? Because we like you!

M-o-u-s-e.

I taught the children to sing it with expression and profound respect, and they did. I would just stand by, listen approvingly, and think "And they said I lived in a dreamworld!"

By the time I left Tonga, the song would be known throughout the island of Tongatapu, but I'd never have been able to spread the word if I hadn't managed to convince the shrinks that I was sane.

LICE AND RATS AND LOCAL COLOR

ONE OF THE most "touching" sights at school was that of the little girls at recess, dressed in their red and white uniforms and bare feet, taking turns getting the lice out of each other's hair. There was a method that involved systematically separating the hair with the fingers and running the fingers down until locating lice, which were then ritualistically stabbed with the thumb nails. Lice eggs were gripped with the nails of the thumb and forefinger and slid off each strand of hair. (Sometimes the lice were ritualistically bitten with the teeth, another method.) It all seemed charmingly picturesque to me. So I must admit that I wasn't disappointed or alarmed when I discovered, during my third month in Tonga, that I had lice myself. I was in fact quietly proud, thinking "and they thought I wasn't Peace Corps material!" Welcome to my dream world.

It was inevitable, really, that I should get lice. The children were always with me and very close to me, usually brushing my hair for me, since I couldn't get enough of that. I'd been addicted to having my hair brushed all my life and had always found someone to do it for me—the children I babysat with (if they were old enough to hold a brush) and the boys I dated. Jim had brushed my hair for me in PC training, which may have been one of the reasons for my falling in love with him. Because it was so pleasurable for me, I tried to feign indifference. I started off, with the children, making it seem like a privilege for them to be permitted to do it.

"If you finish your exercises/do my dishes/get water from the well/

sweep the mats/get me a coconut, I'll let you brush my hair." But I was soon reduced to begging: "Don't stop! Don't stop!"

I had very long hair, which I wore piled up on top of my head. At least, that's the way I arranged it in the morning. But I kept imagining that I felt something crawling around up there, and by noon all my hair had tumbled down, due to my giving in to the urge to scratch my imagination. Then one day, right in the middle of our morning prayer, a teacher named Tonga, who'd been watching me with some concentration and interest for a few minutes, came out with it.

"Tina," she said, "you have a kutu on your forehead."

"You aren't just imagining it?" I asked. But I doubted that both of us were. I apologized for having disturbed her morning prayers, and she told me there was no need to apologize, just to wash my hair with kerosene.

This immediately conjured up visions in my mind of my going up in flames. Hinehina would set me on fire. Hinehina was Loiloi's four-year-old daughter, who came around every day, smoking one of her mother's cigarettes and saying, "I AM fine, thank you," which was the only English phrase she knew. She would come around just as I was applying kerosene and, saying, "I AM fine, thank you," flick her cigarette ashes near my hair. No, I wouldn't risk kerosene—not with Hinehina's smoking habits right next door. I opted for getting the lice out some other way. The children could pick them out for me one by one. It would give them a break from the monotony of brushing my hair.

As I have said, I was delighted to have lice. It was a new experience and proof that I was getting right into the culture. Furthermore, it belied my image as the fragile, over-protected Southern girl coming to Tonga straight from her dreamworld—the one that couldn't take the blows of reality. Each time the children got a louse out, I pressed it in a big book the way some people press flowers, then I enclosed a few of them in letters, as positive proof that my boasting lice was true. Lice were a new and wonderful thing...for about a week.

Then the newness began to wear off, and I lost my enthusiasm for them. I was grateful for having had the experience, but enough was enough. No sense over-doing a good thing. Sometimes when I scratched my head, lice would come out in my fingernails. And they kept me awake at night.

It was a little like the rats. At first, when I'd hear them nesting between the mats that made up my ceiling and the coconut leaves that laid the roof, I thought they were great local color. Then one day, while I was undressing for bed, a rat walked right into the room and stood there staring at me. I stared right back unable to think of anything to say but, "My God, I never thought you'd be the size of a rabbit!" I don't think the rat liked my size any more than I liked his, and he ran on his way. But after that, I tucked my feet in more securely under the covers of my bed because I was afraid that the rabbit-sized rat was going to come back and nibble at my toes.

It was about this time—when lice and rats were no longer enough to satisfy me and make my life exciting—that I began having a social life that included more than Jim's letters from Nomuka.

We had been told in Peace Corps training that there would be no social life, especially for a woman. One mighty-looking woman who didn't seem like one easily moved to tears said that she, as a PCV in Tonga, had cried herself to sleep almost every night. A male PCV, newly returned from Tonga, stopped by our training project on Molokai to gather all of us women together and tell us not to go.

"There's just no social life. You can't date. You can't even hold hands. The Peace Corps women I knew there either had nervous breakdowns or became hard and masculine."

So we'd lose either our sanity or our sex-appeal.

I wondered what it would be like to live without a social life. I wasn't really very sociable, anyway, but I had always had one-to-one relationships and had dated a lot since a fairly early age. Men had always been my closest friends and allies. People had said that it was a good thing Jim and I would be on different islands because it just wouldn't work our carrying on the way we did, holding hands, taking walks, brushing my hair. On the other hand, they couldn't imagine me without Jim or someone stronger than myself to lean upon. I'd show them.

And so I'd done all the things that a PCV could do to be strong. I had thrown myself into my work, teaching po'ako, night school, to prepare the children for their high school entrance exams, and giving special lessons to the students and anyone else who wanted to sing. And I'd even gone so far as to get lice. Then suddenly, when I least expected it, I was having a social life.

THE VILLAGE PRINCE

I DON'T KNOW why it was that I fell in love with Line (pronounced lee-nay), unless it was just out of necessity. Loiloi, of course, had encouraged me, pointing out his many assets. He was (1) her husband's best friend, (2) captain of Ha'ateiho's soccer team, (3) manager of the rugby team, (4) small but strong, (5) English-speaking, (6) anga-lelei (good -natured), the most important characteristic according to Tongan values, and (7) the recipient of Pope Paul's kiss upon the foot.

Before saying more about assets one through six, I should explain number seven. Line was studying to become a Catholic priest. While studying in Italy, priests from around the world were selected to represent their people in receiving the Pope's representative kiss upon the foot. There were priests from the African, Oriental (as we said then), Caucasian, and Polynesian nations. Line represented Polynesia. That's how I first saw him—in a photo, sitting there, misty eyed and solemn, offering the sole of his foot to the pope. His mother had one day dressed up in her best black dress, tupenu and ta'ovala and paid the Noble Havea a visit to show him the photograph immortalizing her son's moment of honor as a seminary student. Loiloi had confiscated the photo and brought it to me.

"That Line!" she said. "He a good one, Tina. Maybe you fall in love."

"But, Loiloi, he's a priest!"

"Not yet, Tina," she said.

I kept staring at the picture and liked this priest in training. He had dark skin, short frizzy black hair, dark intense eyes, horn-rimmed glasses and big feet with widely spread toes. I thought he looked funny and nice, and I suppose it caught my fancy that someone in my village had had the Pope kiss his feet. I was looking forward to meeting him and talking to someone serious and nice who really spoke English well. I didn't hold it against him that he was captain of the soccer team or manager of the rugby organization. Athletes had always impressed me as being insensitive and none too bright, though I had been told that there were exceptions, and I associated a certain brainless macho quality with them. I associated machismo with boyishness and lack of maturity. I preferred men. But this priest looked so nice and was probably an athlete only out of a feeling of civic duty, so I was willing to make allowances for him, and I looked forward to meeting him

But I didn't meet him right away. I thought he would stop by to see me at least out of a feeling of civic duty, as with soccer. But he didn't. Still, I knew when he was in the village because people—notably Loiloi—would come by to borrow whatever I had in my cupboard to feed him with. He usually visited them past my bedtime.

"Line here!" Loiloi said the first time, opening my cupboard door.

"Oh, Tina, you don't shopping!"

She looked franticly through my shelves and finally took a couple of eggs, a cup of flour, and a jar of strawberry jam.

"I making pancake," she said. So she borrowed the eggs, flour, and strawberry jam as well as a frying pan to cook them in. Then, after my lamp was out and I was under my canopy of mosquito net with my toes tightly tucked in and out of reach of the rat, Loiloi came knocking at my door again. I got up to see what she wanted this time.

"Please, Tina," she said. "Your stove."

And so she carted out and away my little kerosene stove. And everything in my kitchen had disappeared to feed the priest. I soon learned how much the whole village adored him and how often he came round to be worshipped, responding in his inimitably modest manner.

When he came, people gathered their coins together and ran to the falekaloa (store) for canned salmon or even corn beef. They offered him everything that they had and everything I had as well. He offered them his friendship and the pleasure of his company. He was, after all, *anga lelei.*

I first met him when I was drawing water from the well, and he was standing with a group of men, talking a short distance from the well. As I went by, he spoke to me in Tongan, and I answered.

Then he laughed and did an imitation of my Tongan, which the men found far more clever than it was.

"You put glottal stops where they don't exist and leave them off of words that have them," he told me in flawless English with a British accent acquired in Fiji.

That was not how I had imagined my first exchange with the village prince whose picture I'd memorized and whom I'd indirectly been feeding.

"Did you think I wanted your honest opinion?" I asked sweetly.

"I'm not giving you my opinion," he replied, smiling. "I'm stating the facts."

"Well, the fact is, " I said, "if I want to redistribute glottal stops, putting them in new and better places, you should show some appreciation. That's called progress." (I didn't know the word cultural appropriation then.)

He laughed, but I didn't. I wasn't in love with him anymore, now that I'd met him.

"I didn't mean to make you angry," he said, smiling a brilliantly white smile.

"What did you intend? To flatter me?"

"I was teasing you. Can't you take a joke?"

I shook my head and ducked into my fale, sloshing well water on the floor at the entrance.

Loiloi came running in after me. She was excited by my first encounter with the village prince.

"He a good one, Tina!" she said, almost breathlessly.

"So you say, " I said.

"I think he like you!"

"Yes," I said. "It looks like we've more or less fallen in love."

For the next four Saturdays, Loiloi and I prepared sandwiches for Ha'ateiho's soccer team and distributed them during half-time on the soccer field beside the King's palace. When Line came by, I would hold out his sandwich, and he'd take it without looking at me.

"Thank you very much," he'd say, sort of glancing in my direction.

"At your service, my lord," I'd say, and he'd smile. I watched him play soccer, and it wasn't really such an ordeal. He was, at least, physically attractive. Or maybe it was merely the idea of what he might be. He could be my own private priest, someone wise and understanding in whom I could confide and to whom I could confess feelings and facts and anything else I felt like confessing.

"The only thing I don't like about you," I told him the first time he visited me, "is your personality."

He had come by for lemonade. I was sitting, dressed in a long blue and white kimono I'd bought in Hawaii, on the floor of my fale, surrounded by my students, my constant companions, who were keeping guard over me as usual and taking turns de-licing my hair. It was an early Sunday afternoon, and the door and window were open for light. My back was turned to the door, but I knew someone was there because the fale suddenly became dark.

"Line here!" the children told me. And there he was.

"Why, it's the village prince," I said turning around to face him.

"Have you got lice?" he asked, obviously having seen the de-licing procedure.

"Why? Would you like some?"

"No," he said, smiling. "But I wouldn't mind some lemonade."

I stood up and curtsied. "At your service. Won't you come in? Won't you sit down?"

He did both. He was wearing a short-sleeved shirt and the typical Tongan skirt that all the men wore. And flip-flops.

"Would you like a cushion?" I asked, handing him a matted one.

"Thank you," he said, flashing his brilliant smile.

I got a couple of lemons from the cupboard, cut them in half, squeezed the juice into a small aluminum teapot, and added water. I then bent down on my knees before him and poured it into his cup. He took a sip and told me it was sour.

"Oh, I'm so sorry. I was so dazzled by the presence of the village prince that I forgot everything I ever knew about cooking."

"Why do you call me that?"

"Dazzling?"

"No, the village prince."

"Because that's what you are. Haven't you noticed? Everyone else has. Everyone's always catering to you because you are what you are."

I began spooning sugar into his cup.

"So bright. So talented. So anga lelei. and yet, so humble."

He smiled and looked around at all the children.

"Are you having Sunday school?" he asked.

He tried his lemonade a second time and told me it was too sweet.

"Fie kai" I said, using an expression applied to people whose visit or general behavior was prompted by their appetites.

"Why do you say that?"

"Because that's what you are. Because of you, my cupboards are bare. People borrow from me, the poor PCV, to feed the rich village prince. That's what's called social injustice."

"Well, I didn't know they were borrowing from you. I'll ask them not to."

"Oh, don't do that! They would think I didn't show the proper respect due to royalty."

Line smiled. "You don't like me a whole lot, do you!'

"Well," I said, "I think you're very attractive. I like your looks. I like your English except for the things you say with it. I like your impressive contacts with the Pope. The only thing I don't like about you is your personality."

"I think I'll be going," he said, and he went.

The children stayed, of course, and as they worked on our lice project, I thought about Line. I wondered if I'd been too harsh. After all, he'd taken all the trouble of coming by for lemonade. What kind of hostess had I been? I spent the rest of the afternoon fantasizing conversations with him in which I "reached" him.

Three days later, I did reach him, and he reached me. Loiloi's husband, Fonomanu, came by to take me to see a new house—that of 'Ofa and Fusia. 'Ofa had just returned from Hawaii, where he'd worked and saved all he earned. He had had a "real" house built, and I was invited to inspect it. Line was there, and so was home brew, made from pineapples and yeast. Fusia and Loiloi were serving and sampling, so I felt it was my place to partake and participate too. I was seated next to Line, who looked better and better as the evening progressed.

"Talk!" Loiloi commanded us.

"She wants us to talk to each other," I told Line. "Just as if we were two civilized people."

"Well," Line replied, "What have you got to say today?"

"Nice weather we're having."

"Would you like to get on with your words about my awful personality?" he asked, looking directly at me.

"My God," I said. "You're looking directly at me."

"Pardon me."

"No, it's just that you never look at me. You have the shifty-eyed look. You look over, around, or through me. But you never look *at* me"

"Well, has it ever occurred to you that maybe I'm a little bit shy?"

"No."

"Well, I'm human, aren't I?"

"You are?" He looked at me again. "Oh, Line, I'm sorry! I never suspected. But I think that's wonderful."

"I got off on the wrong feet with you because I criticized your Tongan."

"You criticized my glottal stops."

"I got off on the wrong feet—"

"Foot."

"With you because I criticized your glottal stops."

"You got off on the wrong foot with me because you were selfish, insensitive, and cold."

"Those are harsh words."

"Do they wound you to the very core?"

"Well—"

"See? I told you."

Line smiled, and then he tried to look wounded to the very core.

"You know, Line, now that you're human and I'm drunk, I'd like to say a few words."

"Okay. Go ahead."

"Thank you. Maybe I'm just getting sentimental because of all the yeast and pineapple, but I just want you to know that against my better judgment, I do like you. Maybe it's just because I keep thinking of what a beautiful relationship we could have if you were just totally different. But whatever it is, I like you. I like you so much that I keep fantasizing, imagining how it would be to be close friends with you."

"Well, I appreciate your thoughts," he said modestly.

"Unfortunately, I can't really talk to you."

"I don't see why not," he said with an air of magnanimity. "No one here understands much English."

"It's not through fear of being overheard by them," I said. "It's through fear of being overheard by *you*. I just don't think you'd understand anything."

"I appreciate your confidence."

"Still, I can't resist the urge to try to talk to you. Although I know I'll regret it in the morning. You know, Line, I'm not really all that religious. Not like you."

Here I laughed, and so did he.

"But I have a kind of mystical belief in Mass Destiny. And I think it may be Destiny that we're here together on this island now. Destiny put you here to comfort me and be kind to me. After all, here I am a foreigner, far from home. Far from my old friends and family. And here you are someone who's lived in Fiji and Italy. Someone who speaks English well and knows something of my culture. So Destiny put you here to listen to me and understand me. To be warm to me."

"Woman!" he said, smiling. "I'm not supposed to be too warm, you know. I have certain vows."

"You're not over-hearing me right. I'm not even talking about *that* warm. I'm not attempting seduction. It's just that I sometimes wish I could really talk to someone. More specifically, I wish I could talk to *you*. And that's what I think Destiny put you here for. To listen! And Destiny put me here, I think, because you're going to become a priest, and you just have no idea of the complexity of human beings. Life's been far too simple and easy for you for you to understand people. So Destiny put me here to make you a better person, a better priest."

"You're a conceited one."

"Well, I'm not saying that I'll *succeed* in making you a better person," I said humbly. "I'll just do my best. You see, Line, if you're going to be a priest, you've got to be really concerned about people. You've got to understand them, and you've got to really love them. Take me, for example I don't think you really love me."

Line laughed.

"No," I continued, "I really don't think you do. I wish you were warmer. And older. And more mature. I wish you'd suffered, just a little bit, and had some idea of how wonderfully complex and confusing life is. And I wish I could just put my arms around you without your considering it seduction."

"Woman!"

"I wish we could really get to know each other and be really close emotionally—and even physically, while we're at it."

"Woman!"

"I don't mean *that* close. I just wish I could put my arms around you and just sit beside you for a while without your misinterpreting it all."

"You can put your arms around me if you really want to, but I wouldn't suggest that you doing it here."

"I don't think I'll do it anywhere. The problem, Line, is that you don't need me. Well, I mean aside from the need you have for me to make you a better person. But you don't even know you have that need. The problem is, you're satisfied with yourself and with your life the way it is. And that's just fine for you, but what about all the people whose lives you're going to be ruining, once you're a priest, by not understanding dissatisfaction?"

Fusia refilled our glasses, and we emptied them.

"I've lectured myself almost as seriously and long as I'm lecturing you now, and I've told myself that my interest in you is totally unwarranted and infantile. And yet I still have an interest in you. I care about you for some reason, and I really wish we could be friends."

"Well, then, let's be friends."

"Oh, but it's not that simple. I want to be close friends."

"Well, then, let's be close friends."

"Starting when?"

"Starting now."

"Right now? Okay, then, if we're close friends, can I tell you something confidential, friend to close friend?"

"Yes, of course."

"Okay, I've got a confession for you. Prepare yourself, and try to take it like a good, close friend and a kind, wise old priest. I sometimes want to touch you. I would never do such a thing, of course, but sometimes I want to touch you so badly that I can hardly stand not to. Like right now."

"Tina!" He had called me by name!

"I mean, just touching. Like this." I touched him on the arm, quickly as if I were testing an iron. "Just like that, see? Is that so bad?"

"No," he said, smiling his brilliant white smile.

"Also, I think I'm falling superficially in love with you."

"Tina!"

"Superficially, I said. Anyway. I shall be strong. I wouldn't tell you all this," I added "if I weren't so disgustingly drunk. In fact, I might not want to touch you. I might not even be superficially in love with you if I weren't disgustingly drunk. Drinking always makes me more affectionate than I ought to be. More affectionate than most people deserve."

When Line and I—mostly I, of course—had stopped talking, I realized that there were others there, who had been there the whole time, talking in Tongan and not understanding our eloquent conversation. Hopefully.

It was now time to go back, and Fonomanu and Line were going to accompany me. Loiloi had already returned to their hut.

There was no moon that night. Fonomanu had a flashlight. He walked ahead of Line and me.

"You've drunk a lot," Line said, putting his arms around me. "Are you all right?"

"No," I said.

"I'll have to help you walk," he said.

"Yes, you'll have to."

He put his arms around me more tightly and Fonomanu kept walking, a bit farther ahead of us, not looking back. It felt very good, just having his arms around me, and then he kissed me—astonishingly well considering that (1) he was studying to become a priest and (2) he was walking at the same time. It was inevitable that, in the dark, walking and embracing at the same time, we would fall into a ditch, and the inevitable happened.

Fonomanu seemed uncertain as to whether or not he should rescue us, but in no time at all, Line and I had let go of each other and we were walking side by side. Line kept his arm around my shoulder, and it felt delicious and warm and other things that prompted me to remark, "Maybe you're going to be a better priest than I had imagined."

Fonomanu and Line got me home, where Lupe was waiting for me.

I was tucked into my tapa-over-springs bed, and Line called from the partition, "Sweet dreams."

He left and Loiloi came rushing in.

"Oh, Tina!" she said, clasping her hands. "He a good one!"

Guilt and Ethics

LINE AND I did become close friends, and my goal was for us to have a beautiful, make-believe relationship that I could look back upon when I returned to the real world and that he could look back upon when he was an ordained priest, chaste and celibate. My other goal was not to feel guilty.

All my life I'd felt guilty, and I was tired of being hunted and haunted by my conscience. I wanted to change, to be a Great Woman, and I knew that A Great Woman was one who did what she wanted to do instead of what other people wanted her to do. A Great Woman indulged her senses, satisfied her appetites, abandoned herself to passion, and held her head neither bloody nor bowed. A Great Woman, in the tradition of Carmen, Isadora, Helen of Troy, Scarlet O'Hara, didn't give a damn except about what she wanted. And yet, my tendency was to feel guilty.

Feeling guilty was a family tradition. Everyone in our family felt guilty except my father, who devoted too much time to making us feel guilty to feel very guilty himself. But all the rest of us were haunted, and we each expressed our guilt in astonishingly similar ways, by shouting at ourselves.

I started first, as far as a know. I would think of something horrible I'd done, like saying something incredibly stupid in Shakespeare class, and when it flashed into my mind, this scene of shame, I would shout, "Death!" I don't know why I shouted "Death!" instead of something else. Perhaps I meant "Death to the memory, the rude intruder," or perhaps I just wanted to die myself because of the humiliation I felt at having said something so stupid. Whatever the case, whenever the memory came back to haunt me, to make me feel guilty or ashamed for not being what I should have been, not doing what I should have done, not saying what I should have said, I shouted, before I could stop myself, "Death!" This might happen on city buses, at parties, or in quiet department stores just before closing time—anytime I was lost in thought and an unpleasant memory struck, it was "Death!"

I first noticed this habit of mine when I was in college, saying—evidently—dumb things in Shakespeare class. I didn't know that anyone else in the family was given to the same habit until my older sister Dana and I were re-united after three years. She had been in school in North Carolina while I was in California. The summer she came to visit us, after this three-year separation, I heard her scream from another part of the house.

"No!" she shouted. I, being very attentive since she was a relatively new arrival in the household, went running in to find out what the matter was.

"What's wrong?" I asked.

"Huh?" she said.

"I just heard you scream 'No!'"

"Oh, yeah," she said. "Just thinking."

She told me that she always shouted at herself when she thought of something she wished she hadn't done or said or thought.

"I was very much impressed by the fact that both she and I had developed this habit while separated by three thousand miles.

After our younger sister Suzy went away to college, she started doing the same thing. Her cry was "I hate you!" and, when she was really haunted, a still ruder and less delicate "Fuck you, you creeps!"

One night Suzy, Dana, and I were having dinner with some friends of our father who were, like him, psychologists. We were having a lively but uncontroversial conversation, since Daddy was managing somehow not to discuss our war crimes in Vietnam. Then there was a moment of silence, which Suzy—who'd been lost in thought—suddenly broke by declaring, "I hate you!" (It could have been worse, of course.) Our friends didn't know what to make of this, but I did. Suzy had said her lines without wanting to, but Dana and I willingly joined in.

"No!" she said.

"Death!" I said.

There was a pause while people exchanged glances.

But when I told my mother about it later, she caught on.

"Hmm," she said. "I do that too. Only I do it when I'm alone in my office and think of something I wish I hadn't said. Then I say, 'I didn't say that!' but I don't shout. I just proclaim, loudly and clearly for all those around me, 'I didn't say that!' as if to reassure them that they hadn't overheard my thoughts correctly. But of course," she continued, looking chagrined. "I *did* say that."

I didn't say more about this, but I entertained the thought that David's psycho-motor epilepsy, his "screamers," were also representative of his guilt or shame about something he wished he hadn't done or said or thought. And I even wondered if it were genetic. After all, we didn't know anything about Mother's origin, except that she looked like an Eskimo or an American Indian. She had been adopted.

I tried to remember if there had been anything before we went away to college comparable to our screaming at ourselves, and it occurred to me: Daddy.

When Daddy was around us, there had never been any need to shout ourselves down because he took care of that for us.

His voice boomed on every topic from "What?!" to "You are NOT sorry!" He would say "What?'" in response to something dumb we'd just said or something less dumb that we'd just mumbled or expressed incoherently or in a rambling way. Or to an observation that lacked depth or an opinion that lacked Truth. Or to our failure to understand what he'd really meant when he asked us to roll up the car window.

That was one of my earliest childhood memories. There I was pressed to the car door in the front seat where my father was driving.

He asked me without really booming to roll up the window. I jumped to the task but was somewhat hindered in my performance by the fact that the car window was already rolled up. Just the same, an order was an order, especially from my father, so I tried to roll it up more without breaking the glass.

A few seconds later my father turned towards me and asked, "Well, what are you waiting for?" That one stumped me, but I tried to get it right because I knew that if I guessed wrong, Daddy would boom "What?!" But try as I did, I couldn't figure out what it was I was waiting for.

"Well, are you going to roll down the window as I asked, or are you just going to sit there?"

"Roll it down?" I asked. "But you said to roll it up."

This really made him furious.

"It was already rolled up. It if were already rolled up, why would I want you to roll it up?"

That had been my question, too, but I'd tried to overcome it, to not let it interfere with my blind obedience.

"Can't you use your head?" he asked. "I obviously meant for you to roll it down."

I rolled it down without further delay, mumbling that I was sorry.

"What?!" he boomed.

"I'm sorry," I said again, trying to articulate better.

"You are NOT sorry," he said, as he so often did.

I can remember numerous occasions on which I thought that I was sorry, at least for having gotten screamed at, but Daddy always insisted that I was NOT sorry, and that left me with very little left to be or say.

Perhaps once away at college, with our father no longer there to shout at us for our manifold sins and wickednesses, we had to do it ourselves and that was why we screamed down all the memories of our moments of imperfection.

Whatever the case, I'd always felt guilty, even before I'd started screaming out about it, and sometimes I was guilty. My being close to

Line was, after all, hardly comparable to my failure to roll down a car window or to my saying something stupid in Shakespeare class. It was more like my wicked behavior at age eight, when I stayed with cousins in Georgia all summer.

I developed an interest in my seven-year-old cousin, with whom I slept. We played with each other, but not in the way his mother, my aunt, thought we played with each other. And I knew that it was a sin, and I knew that I was more to blame than Timmy because I was a year older and knew better and should have been stronger and not given in to my base instincts. I was a child molester in both senses of the word. I was molesting a child, and I was a child molesting. It was all doubly wrong because I was a hypocrite. I was the angel in the family, the good one all the relatives trusted. I was sweet and quiet and well-behaved. My aunt praised me for being a good influence on her children, and all the time I was corrupt and corrupting.

I don't know why I was so precocious for my age, so wayward so young, unless it came from my listening too much to soap operas on the radio. I especially like "Young Widow Brown" because there was a wicked artist who was supposed to be painting her portrait but instead—and unknown to her—he was drugging her and then asking her to walk around the room and then to kiss him. I liked the deep and somewhat sinister way he spoke. I listened to all this with my grandmother, who would put raisin cookies and milk before me during our radio time. But in spite of all the wholesomeness in the room with me, I got lost in the program, drugged like Young Widow Brown, and found the program titillating, and I never missed a single fifteen minute segment of it. If we were at a church reception creating a time conflict with "Young Widow Brown," my grandmother would unlock her car and let me listen to it on the car radio.

Sin and worldliness held an attraction to me. When I was at my parents' home, whenever they'd leave and I'd be alone in the house, I'd dance all around and go through all the musical numbers I could remember or imagine, and that was good clean fun.

But sometimes, instead of wholesome fantasy, I'd climb up in the cupboard and get down my father's cherry brandy, and I'd get my mother's cigarettes, and then I'd sit and look at myself in the mirror— smoking, drinking, and pantomiming a song with music by Romberg and lyrics by Oscar Hammerstein.

Softly, as in the morning sunrise,
The light of love keeps stealing into a newborn day.
Burning, with all the glow of sunrise,
The light of love...etc.

I was rehearsing all the time because I wanted to be a movie star. In fifth grade, my best friend Sara and I used to act out scenes from movies, and to my astonishment as I look back, the kids didn't make fun of us. They gathered around and watched. Then in sixth grade I used to do scenes from the *Three Faces of Eve*, the Joanne Woodward movie about a Southern woman with a multiple personality. I'd do Eve White, the painfully timid one, and then I'd do Eve Black, the wicked one, who would come out when she got too bored with her timid self.

"I go out on Saturday night and get gassed up, and then the next morning I let her have the hangover!"

I also did the scene where she surprised her clueless husband. "Honey, there a lot of things you never seen me do. That don't mean I don't do 'em."

My Georgia relatives were good old-time Baptists and Presbyterians, so there was no brandy and there were no cigarettes when I stayed with them. There wasn't even any Romberg. I had to settle for Timmy. So there I was, eight years old, in Georgia corrupting my little cousin Timmy, seven, who took a liking to being corrupted. We got carried away with our explorations of each other's bodies and did a number of highly imaginative things that I'd certainly never read about. I thought I had invented oral sex though I didn't have the name for it then.

Sometimes his parents took us up into the Georgia mountains on a religious retreat, and Timmy and I would sleep together in a room in the cabin next door to my aunt and uncle's room. We would wait until they had heard our bedtime prayers and we were tucked in and kissed good night before we'd start in on our adoration of each other because of course we didn't want to get caught. But one night we were almost caught, and it was almost enough to make me give up premarital sex at the age of eight.

Aunt Katherine had already kissed us good night and gone to her bedroom. We counted to fifty and then we started in. Then right in the middle of our stimulating exploration, Aunt Katherine came back to the door.

"I forgot to hear your prayers," she said.

I was afraid to move my hand from where it was and shouldn't have been for fear that Aunt Katherine would notice from whence it came. So without budging, I began to pray out loud. Aunt Katherine always preferred my prayers to Timmy's because all he ever came up with was the one about thanking for the world so sweet, food to eat, birds that sing, and everything. That was okay for a grace, but my prayers were less sing-songy and more personal and appropriate for bedtime.

Grateful to God for getting me through that moment without detection, I gave up pre-marital sex when I was nine and hoped that over the years Timmy would forget my— or our—transgressions. But he never forgot, and whenever our families got together, he'd say, "Remember when we—" And I'd shout, "No! I don't remember! And neither should you!"

Guilt was not the same as shame, like the shame I felt when I was twelve and was supposed to be working on my science project but instead let Greg Todd kiss me and even kissed back. I hadn't sinned again till I was sixteen and had a real boyfriend. By then I had found out that what really mattered was virginity, not all the other things you did, so I was okay. Steve's parents had a beautiful country home, where they often left us alone, so we had beauty and space in which to do everything we wanted, most of which we would do. I was older now and there was no need to climb up and get into the cupboards for cherry brandy.

Steve's parents had a bar behind the bookshelves, but Steve and I ate instead of drinking, played records, planned our eventual marriage, named all of our future children, and spent the rest of our time doing everything except losing my virginity. Not losing my virginity was being virtuous, but I—being me—had to feel guilty.

I went to a very old-fashioned high school at which the principal, Mr. Kirk, wouldn't let us wear dresses above a specified length because we were supposed to be "ladies," and our Problems of American Democracy teacher Miss Pearlstine didn't want us to read *Time Magazine* when there was an article on contraceptives or the New Morality because she said, "I think it would shock your finer sensibilities," and our Latin teacher Miss Mc Dearmon told us every other day not to let our minds fall into the gutter because we could ruin our lives if we let them fall down there.

So even when Steve and I were just "making out," as the sensitive adolescent phrase put it, or "petting," and not "going all the way," I knew I was going against everything that Mr. Kirk, Miss Pearlstine, and Miss McDearmon had ever taught us. My dress, hiked up, was too short, my sensibilities were shocked, and my mind was lying there in the gutter.

And yet it felt so good.

So all I could do was to do what felt good and then feel guilty. And I did almost enough feeling guilty to make up for all the feeling good.

Now, though, I wasn't going to feel guilty. I was a college graduate. I even had a teaching credential. I should have outgrown guilt by now.

I knew, of course that the New Morality, as in those confiscated issues of *Time Magazine*, was on my side, but I didn't want any part of that. I wanted to be a Great Woman, and a Great Woman never had the masses on her side. Her specialty was rugged, earthy, strong-willed and daring individualism. But I couldn't really damn the masses there in Tonga because I liked them, especially the children. And then there was Tevita, who thought I sparkled like a glittering star. How could I let him down? I couldn't not care what these people thought about me. And the Tongans had been influenced by the missionaries. They wouldn't approve of my carrying on with a seminary student. Whether they approved or not, I wanted this to be a private affair because everything was more beautiful when it was private. I didn't want people to meet me at the well in the morning, as they greeted married PCVs on other islands, with "How many times last night?"

So after our kissing behind Fonomanu's back and our stumbling into the ditch (symbolic of my Latin teacher's gutter) Line and I met only during the daytime and only for conversation for a while. When we talked, we were never alone, but no one, as far as we knew, could keep up with our fluent English—especially with Line's English, so rich in metaphors and wise sayings, which it takes most people a lifetime to acquire.

He knew them all. I encouraged him to talk about his family because knowing about him—and getting him to tell me things—made me feel that I was becoming part of his life although I suspected that the feeling wasn't real and never would be. He told me that he once had a sister.

"Well, what happened to her?" I asked

"She went to the man upstairs."

"She died?"

"Yes, she kicked the bucket about seven years ago."

"Such fluent nonchalance you've got."

"Well," he said, "there's no need crying over spilled milk."

"You've really mastered English," I said, "down to the most insensitive clichés."

"Well," he said philosophically, "the early bird gets the worm."

"Mmm," I said. "I'll have to give that one some thought."

I wanted to write fiction while I was in Tonga, and I created a Mormon missionary modeled after Line. I named him 'Ofa, a Tongan name when capitalized, and the word for love.

'Ofa was also the captain of a village soccer team, and if he felt that his soccer team was talking too big and not getting down to "the nitty gritty," he'd tell me "Talk, talk talk. We've got to stop talking and put our foot where our mouth is."

If something went unexpectedly well, he'd say, "That was the golden goose that laid the egg."

If something went unexpectedly badly, he'd say, "The best laid plans of mouse and man sometimes goes astray."

For no reason at all, that I could see, he came forth with something like "It's the greasy wheel that gets the oils" or "A stick in time saves mine."

At first I jotted down my story in bits and pieces, but I soon had a whole notebook just for a fictionalized version of Line.

The real Line told me he was one of the few men who had been abroad who continued to wear the Tongan skirt (tupenu) upon his return.

"The others are afraid of what the Europeans will think," he said. "They're afraid to be the laughing of the stock."

"But not you," I said, patting him on the knee. "You wear the Tongan skirt because you know you've got cute legs. Just the way women with good teeth laugh at men's jokes."

Then I added quickly, "But I'm not speaking of me. I'd laugh at you even if I didn't have good teeth."

I would and I did, getting a high on laughter.

I think it was partially—perhaps mainly—Line's proverbs that made my love for him go beyond curiosity and gentle, restrained lust. But I soon loved him so much that I couldn't go to sleep at night without first replaying our conversations in my head. Sometimes I laughed out loud, and Lupe would laugh back from the adjoining room. Sometimes I'd even hear someone outside my window laughing back!

After about five months, Lupe moved back to her parents' house, taking her mattress with her and leaving me alone, once the children left me, to fictionalize Line.

Around that time, May of 1970, Jim invited me to visit him on his outer island, Nomuka.

NOMUKA

I HAD TO go by boat to visit Jim, of course, and the boat got near the edge of the island at night when the winds were strong. To prevent a collision, the boat signaled to the shore, and small canoes came to get us. So I arrived to shore in a canoe and in the moonlight. It would have been very romantic with Jim there to meet me if I hadn't had the disturbing feeling that I was being unfaithful to someone or other. Was it to Jim or to Line? I had a feeling that Jim's interest in me was more profound, even if he deserted me to live on Nomuka. He'd written me every week and sent me poems from *The Atlantic Monthly*. But I felt faithful to my nascent love for Line and different towards Jim, and he noticed this almost immediately.

"You seem different," he said, after feeding me.

"I've got lice," I said. He showed an interest in this but said that wasn't it.

"No, there's something different besides the lice," he said. "You know, I've thought of so many things I've wanted to tell you and talk to you about. But now it's not so easy to talk to you."

"I'm sorry, Jim," I said, and I meant it. I was about to have an attack of guilt. "It's just that I've decided to become a Great Woman."

"A great woman?"

"Yes, a Great Woman in caps. Now, don't tell me that I'm a good woman but not a great one."

"I won't." After a pause, he asked, "What's a great woman?"

"You'll just have to watch," I said. "It's hard to explain."

"I'm watching."

"Yes," I said, "but I haven't gotten very good at it yet. I feel too guilty to be a Great Woman. Guilt is what keeps a woman good instead of great."

"You know, Tina, I've been thinking that we've never had any privacy. We never have had a chance to make love. For example."

"It's just as well," I said. "I have much too much respect for you."

"Well, I don't have too much respect for *you*. I mean, I have a lot, but I don't have too much."

"Well, I don't know what to say except that I would never make love to a mortal man. I make it a point, in my efforts to become a Great Woman, never to make love to a man unless he's a nobleman or a priest."

"Well, I was a Brother." It was true. Jim had been a Brother among the Jesuits when he was in his teens.

"Has-beens don't count," I said. And then I felt guilty. I hadn't gone there to be flippant. I'd gone there because I really cared about Jim, and wanted to see him. I wanted to talk to him and take walks with him and maybe get caught in the rain again. And he was being so nice, feeding me and talking to me and everything. So what was wrong with me?

"Death!" I said.

"What?"

"Oh, Jim, I really care about you. I even love you. But I'm so sleepy, and I want to go to bed. Alone. Not here. Far be it from me to ruin a young man's reputation."

"I don't care if you ruin my reputation."

But I wouldn't do it. So Jim walked me to the home of a Peace Corps nurse, who had left me permission to use her house, if it came to that, while she was on another island. Jim and I kissed good night, and when he was down the road a few paces, I called him back.

"Jim, I'm sorry," I said. We met each other half way and kissed again, and then I went to bed to feel guilty all night about our not having made love or anything approaching it.

There was always something to feel guilty about.

The next day we rode horses into the Pacific Ocean, but it wasn't a one-way trip.

I realized that I was a disappointment to Jim and that I'd rather be disappointed than disappointing.

Betty, the Peace Corps nurse, returned from Fiji while I was still there, and she thought it was time that we paid some attention to the sores I'd been ignoring—sores on my legs and feet.

"Oh, yeah," I said. "I don't know how I got these sores. They look sort of like jewels to me. Like gems. They glisten."

"Well, that's one way of looking at them," Betty said. "They could be scabies. That's when itch mites get into your clothes or mats or tapa and then get into the skin and lay eggs, and then the eggs hatch."

"Wow!" I said. "I thought I'd just scratched some mosquito bites."

"They could be mosquito bites. They can turn into a tropical ulcer. That's why you don't want to scratch them."

"But I *do* want to scratch them," I said. "I know I shouldn't. But I just have the urge, and sometimes I give in."

"Uh huh," Betty said, sympathetically. "Well, I can give you some phisohex to wash them with, and then we can apply benzyl benzoate."

She gave me medicine for them and for my head lice.

The restraint I'd shown with Jim, I'd show to other itches. I needed to go back to a better me, from top to bottom.

BACK ON TONGATAPU
ON THE SABBATH

I REMEMBER VERY little more about my stay with Jim on Nomuka except that we had very little contact with the Tongans on his island except for one day when I was asked to give a lesson at his school. To this very day, I have a faded picture of Jim hanging in my bathroom in San Francisco. He looks as if he's in the middle of the ocean. Jim and I stayed inside a lot too in what he called the bomb shelter.

What I remember more clearly is that when the return boat arrived in Nuku'alofa, it was Sunday at 2:00 am, and no one would touch our bags because it was the Sabbath. In my diary I say "we," so I must have met someone I knew on the boat, and I write that we had to wait with our bags near the water until someone who was also smuggling a turtle into the city offered to help us. At the time I was completely unaware of the ramification of tortoise smuggling, and I was happy that someone took us and our bags back to our villages.

When I woke up, there were seven children—one for every day of the week—standing over me like dwarfs.

"Malo e lelei," I said, sitting up, then noticing I didn't have any clothes on and going back under the tapa cloth.

This was of course a show of absurd modesty since the children always watched me bathe, but it was, after all, Sunday, and almost everything was taboo on Sunday.

I asked the children to hand me my kimono. A couple of children were holding siblings not much smaller than themselves, and they handed these tots over to me too while they got my kimono. (In my second year it was stolen along with my other dresses. I'd find it weeks later when I passed by a church and saw it on a woman who'd made it into a maternity dress.)

I asked the children how they got in. Hadn't I latched the door?

Yes, but I hadn't latched the window. That meant, of course, they were expected to come in through it.

The children watched me bathe, helped me dress, then braided my hair for me.

They wanted to show me their drawings, sing me their songs, and catch me up on all that had happened during my absence.

Gossiping was acceptable as a Sunday pastime, but there was some debate as to whether or not it was taboo to sing secular songs or draw pictures on the Sabbath. Those whose theology forbade singing and drawing reprimanded the singers and drawers who, in their turn, defended their activities.

You could sing secular songs on Sunday if no one could hear you and if you didn't think about the words.

You could draw on Sunday if you sat down to do it.

As long as you were sitting it wasn't work and it wasn't play. It was next to nothing, and nothing was the right thing to do on the Sabbath before, after, or instead of going to church.

I listened very carefully in an effort to grasp the finer points of theological interpretation, but I was not given a vote. Anyway, I was home, back in my village.

Jim's Arrival and Departure

Someone's been sitting in my hut, and he's still there

A week later I stayed at school after classes to finish a letter I was writing to Jim, and when I returned to my village, I saw that people were crowded around my fale. There must have been a fire, I thought, because there had been a flare-up in my stove earlier in the week. Then Loiloi motioned to me from her fale, indicating that someone was in mine. I thought, "Line?"

It was Jim, and I was very happy to see him. I thanked him for being well, and then I noticed his bandaged hand. Had he come to visit on the pretext that his wrist was sprained?

He told me that he was returning to the United States by way of Japan.

I introduced him to the children as the Nomuka Pisi Kolopisi on his way to Japan. (Peace Corps: no r, no consonant clusters, no silent s, but Pisi Koa was an alternate to Pisi Kolopisi.) They thought his going to Japan was treason unless he was going there to fight the Japanese.

"Oiauei!" one child said. "They wants to dead to us," which meant that the Japanese wanted to kill us, a notion still prevalent on this island, which was "protected" by the Americans during World War II. The Tongans learned their lesson well. Japan was part of the Communist conspiracy to take over the world and make all Tongan children go to school on Saturday and even (Godless Communists!) on Sunday.

"The Japanese have surrendered," Jim announced in an effort to bring the kids up to date. But the children would not be fooled. They knew that was just a rumor the Communists were spreading to catch the Tongans off-guard. The Japanese were after Tonga's oil.

We could point out that the Tongans didn't have any oil, but that would just strengthen their case. The Japanese and other Communist agents were piping Tonga's oil under the ocean to Holland.

"Can we speak in front of the children?" he asked.

"There's no other way to speak," I said. "Besides, they don't understand. Except when you mention J-a-p-a-n, that land of godless Communism."

I had the same experience in Mexico, when I crossed that first border. A bright young woman I taught with thought the swastika was the symbol of the Communist Party. American propaganda had worked. All evil was Communist-inspired.

Jim told me he was leaving Tonga and suggested that I go with him.

"I propose a Wednesday night dinner in J-a-p-a-n," Jim said "We'll stop by Samoa on our way and have lunch. How's that sound? Breakfast in Tonga, lunch in Samoa, and dinner in Japan. Sake, tea gardens, tea ceremonies, Geisha girls. You could learn the art, Tina. That would broaden your horizons."

"I'll broaden my horizons here for a while," I said.

"Tina, what to keep you here?"

I indicate the children who line the walls around us, and then I sing (from *The King and I*) "The children, the children. I'll not forget the children. No matter where I go, I'll always see those little faces looking up at me."

"Okay, so they're nice kids. But there're nice kids all over the world. There're nice kids in J-a-p-a-n."

"Hah! Godless Communist spying tots!!" I said.

"Tina, really you've seen the Tongan horizon. Now it's time to move on and see something new."

"I'm not a tourist. I'm not sight-seeing. I'll move on it a couple of years."

"Why a couple of years? Because the contract's for a couple of years? Don't let a document determine your life for you. Don't sacrifice your life. Live it."

"I don't consider it a sacrifice to remain here for a couple of years. It's a valid expression of human existence. I know how fashionable it is to break contracts. It shows you're a free spirit and an individual. I know it's tacky to keep commitments. Commitments led to Vietnam. Except that I want to make a commitment. To Tonga. I know that's proof of my reactionary spirit. But I want to carry out my two-year plan. I'd feel that I was deserting the children and the whole village if I left now. I'm not making any accusations of course, or in any way implying that that's what you're doing."

"But Tina, don't you see that it doesn't matter? I know you love these kids, and I'm sure they like you. But a month after you've left, they'll have forgotten you."

"Maybe so.. But they'll remember the songs."

"Whereas I'll remember you," here Jim paused, as if calculating, "at least a half year.. Seriously, Tina, you've got to face reality."

"I do not. And I will not. I did not come all this way to face reality. I came here to get away from mental and physical clutter. I came here to live like Thoreau but in a warmer climate. I came here to produce and direct and star in a musical extravaganza with my cast of thousands. I did not come here to face reality."

'Okay, okay! But just don't delude yourself that you're letting people down if you think about what's good for you."

"But I am thinking about what's good for me. And what's good for me is believing that what I do here matters. Maybe it doesn't matter. Maybe nothing matters. But I want to believe that something does. And this is what I've chosen to believe matters. And if I want to believe it matters, I'm going to believe it matters, and there's no stopping me."

"I'm just worried about you."

"Why? Because I believe that something matters?"

"No. Because I think you're out of touch with reality."

"Watch your tongue with that R word."

"And I'm afraid you'll be even more out of reality in two years."

"I thought my dreamworld was supposed to be my greatest strength. Reality is only straw to be spun into gold. You've got to take what you're given—reality, for example—and make it into something better and more beautiful. Why do we have to resign ourselves to clear Kodak prints?"

"You're right. I'm tired of my Instamatic. The first thing I'm going to get in J-a-p-a-n is a camera. Come with me, Tina, and we'll get you a camera that you can focus as much or as little as you like."

"I don't need a camera like that. I *am* a camera like that."

"I hate to leave you here."

"I hate to see you go."

"Don't look. Will you write?"

"Of course."

"Will I write?" he asked.

"I think you will," I said. "If you don't, I won't answer."

"I'll write."

"I'll answer."

"And I'll answer your answers."

"This could go on for years," I said.

"Oh, Tina, I'm scared."

"Why? I can think of several good reason for your being scared. But what reason for being scared have you chosen?"

"I'm not well."

"Not well?"

"I'm losing weight. I've got stomach trouble. My jaws flare up."

"What are you doing? Practicing your speech for Dr. Wiley? He'll probably just tell you to cut down on your diet of green mangoes."

But the Peace Corps doctor gave Jim a medical discharge, and on Tuesday night Jim, Ron, Larry, and I got together for a farewell dinner. Ron, in soil development, brought the salad, and Larry, in rat control, killed and cooked a couple of chickens and made a chocolate cake in his magic toaster oven. I, as chief mourner, didn't have to do or bring anything. All I had to do was mourn.

We overate and drank to Jim's health and his New Frontier and to tomorrow's hangover. Then, till eleven, we told our favorite Twilight Zone episodes.

At eleven o'clock, they left Jim and me in Larry's house so that we could say goodbye till dawn, there, alone with the supernatural.

I put my arms around Jim and told him I was frightened.

"I'm the one who should be frightened," he said. "I'm the one who's making the move."

"No, I mean I'm frightened by the Twilight Zone episodes. I can sort of feel the supernatural seeping into this hut like black light or air and wrapping itself around us."

"Tina, you're not frightened by the right things."

"What are the right things to be frightened by?"

"By my leaving. By your staying."

"I'm frightened about that too. I'm frightened that you're going to regret leaving."

"But isn't it better to regret what you do than what you don't do?"

"It's best not to regret at all."

"I hope you don't feel I'm deserting you."

"The thought didn't even occur to me," I said. "As obviously it didn't occur to you."

"I've asked Ron and Larry to take care of you."

"To take care of me?"

"Yes, to feed and clothe you and give you shelter from the rain."

"And from Japanese bombs?"

"I also asked them to keep an eye on you. So watch your step."

"I'm watching."

"Would you consider taking a nap with me?""

"Yes, I'd consider it."

"And then would you do it?"

"Take a nap with you?" I asked. "Yes! We can lie down here on the mats in good Tongan style. And we can hold each other and whisper until dawn, at which time I'll say goodbye and walk back to my village to be home when the children get there."

Andrea's Visit and Revelations

LINE WOULDN'T SPEAK to me for weeks because of what I'd done to him. I tried to find out just what I'd done, but this was difficult since he wouldn't speak to me, and no one else seemed to know why he wouldn't. So there I was, with Jim gone and Line silent, in mourning for them both and alone once more with only my hutful of children to keep me company.

Then one day Andrea ('Ana in Tongan) bicycled from her end of the island to mine to bring me word of rumors being spread about me. The children announced her arrival, and we greeted each other effusively.

"I remember you," I said. "You're the lewd and suggestive one."

"And you're the one who lives in her own private dreamworld," Andrea said.

"Right! Come in and see it."

She said she had come because she had things to tell me, so I invited her to sit down, and I sat down on the floor with her to be told things.

The kids kept oohing and ahing about her beauty. "Faka 'ofa 'ofa!"

"I wish they'd stop that," Andrea said.

"But they're saying that you're beautiful," I said.

"Yes, and I know they're sincere. But 'beautiful' is just Polynesian for 'fat.' Anyway, enough of me. I've come here to tell you about yourself. I think you should know you're getting a bad reputation."

"Uh oh," I said, thinking of Jim and thinking of Line.

"Yes, rumor has it that you're happy in Tonga, and everyone knows what that means. You're mentally retarded or, at best, simple-minded. Because people with brains that function know how inappropriate it is to be happy in a place like this. With no intellectual stimulation, with no social life. I mean of course, from the point of view of the other Peace Corps volunteers. They're the ones spreading the rumors."

"Is that all they say? That I'm happy?"

"Isn't that enough? You're happy. Therefore you're brainless and insensitive. You know, easily satisfied."

"I never realized I was coming across like that. But how could I be coming across at all? No one in the Peace Corps ever sees me. So how can they go around saying things like that? That I'm happy?"

"All I can think of is that there's a leak in the village. It may not be intentional badmouthing. Maybe it's a Tongan passing the word just not knowing what a negative connotation being happy has in our culture if we're being happy in another one."

"But, Andrea—and you don't have to answer this question if it's too absurd or indiscreet. Aren't *you* happy?"

"Well, I guess I can tell you. Yes. But at least I have the good judgment not to let it show. If you keep acting happy, you're going to alienate everyone. It's so tacky. So unchic."

"What can I do now?

"Well, as Ann Landers used to say back home, if you get yourself a bad reputation, you just have to bend over backwards to lose it."

I bent over backwards and hit the tapa cloth lining the walls.

"Another thing they're saying about you is that you never want to play."

"Play what?"

"Play with them. You don't come to Peace Corps parties, for example."

"But remember that statistic? That the farther Peace Corps Volunteers are from the capital or from one another, the more satisfied they are? Peace Corps parties depress me."

"But isn't that just what you need? To be depressed? Then maybe people will think you have some depth and character. If you don't come to parties, they know you're cold and unfeeling. A person who doesn't need people."

"People...people who need people," I sang, realizing I hadn't yet taught the songs from *Funny Girl* to the village kids.

Andrea joined in for "Are the luckiest people in the world."

"But the Tongans are people," I said.

"As it is, they can't forgive you for not going to pieces when Jim left."

"How do they know I didn't go to pieces? Maybe I went to pieces in private."

Andrea laughed. "There's no point in going to pieces in private. You're supposed to do it where it can be seen and appreciated. So people can think 'Aha! Unhappy and unable to cope. A real person.'"

"Andrea, I wish you hadn't brought all this to my attention. I was feeling so good until I realized how happy I seem."

"Well, we can't dwell too much on your bad reputation because there are other items of interest. There's someone in Nuku'alofa who wants to meet you."

"Who?"

"Vincent Williams. He's an Englishman and the administrator of the new hospital they're building."

"Why does he want to meet me?"

He just likes you."

"How does he know if he's never met me?"

"He's driven by your village, and he's seen you."

"How romantic. He 'did but see me passing by and yet he'll love me till he die'?" I asked, quoting a verse that made the same impression on me that some woman made on the poet.

Andrea laughed. "I guess that's about it. Anyway, the first time he asked people about you, they told him—"

"That I'm dim-witted and shallow?"

"Yes, no doubt. And easily satisfied. But they also told him that you were more or less engaged to an outer-islander. That was Jim."

"I had no idea Jim and I were engaged. I don't think he did either!"

"Anyway, for that reason he didn't ask about you for a while. And now he's gotten word that your outer islander is altogether out of the islands, and he wants to meet you."

"I think that's nice. But how? Where?"

"Well, you could try coming to a Peace Corps party."

"Isn't there some other way?"

"That's about it. You could come just once."

"I know. It's just that I've really been trying to get into the culture. Nothing takes you out of it faster than a Peace Corps party. All them white folks."

"Yes, but among all those white people is Vincent Williams, the nice man who wants to meet you."

"But if I do meet him, what then?"

"Then you fall in love and live happily ever after."

"Oh, good. That's just what I've always wanted to do." I sang a few lines of "Happily Ever After" from *Once Upon a Mattress*.

"I know. So here's your invitation."

"To living happily ever after?"

"To a dinner party at Dr. Wiley's house. It seems that before Jim left, he asked Dr. Wiley to take care of you for him."

"My God, he's asked everyone to take care of me! I'll be getting more taken care of than I've ever gotten in my life. Especially when Jim was here."

"Dr. Wiley told him that he'd do his best but that he never saw you since you never seemed to get sick or sociable. And Jim said, as Dr. Wiley tells it, 'Just feed and clothe her.' so Dr. Wiley decided he'd begin by feeding you. So he's giving a little Peace Corps dinner and he's inviting Vincent, who—in his turn—may someday clothe you."

"Is that what Jim had in mind?" I asked. "This sounds serious!"

"Yes, everything's been arranged for you. All you have to do to get your life on its way is to show up at the Peace Corps dinner."

"I am kind of hungry," I said. "And Dr. Wiley's such a nice guy."

"That's the spirit."

"But how can I face those people who think I'm happy? And what about you, Andrea?"

"What about me?"

"Well, don't you want to live happily ever after too?"

"Not yet. You can go first. I'll be a beautiful fat lady-in-waiting."

Andrea was not fat. She wasn't really in-waiting either. She was one of those Super-Vols loved by all except by other volunteers.

She had brought a roll to sleep on, but I offered her my bed. When she tried it, she returned to her roll.

"Don't you have a mattress?" she asked. "You're sleeping directly on the bedsprings?"

"Well, there's some tapa cloth over the bedsprings."

"Even the prettiest tapa cloth can't hide a torture rack," she said. "Don't you get bruises when you turn over?"

"I don't turn over—except the things in my mind," I said.

I went back to my torture rack and to turning things over in my mind.

Meeting Vincent

I HAD A dress made in Nuku'alofa by the same woman who made clothes for the wife of the King of Tonga. It cost six dollars, about one-fifth of my monthly living allowance. It was a silky blue print dress with elaborate sleeves, and I wore it over a tupenu and with a ta'ovala.

I knew that I was over-dressed.

I was seated beside Vincent Williams and did my best to look tragic and appealing.

"You must be Tina," Vincent said, reading my place card.

"Yes, "I said, "the dim-witted, soulless, happy one. But tonight I'm in mourning for a loved one."

"Oh, really? I'm sorry to hear that. Someone in your family?"

"No. I was recently jilted."

"Oh," he said, smiling

"You take that lightly?" I asked somberly.

"Not at all," he said, darkening.

The rest of our conversation was polite and friendly. I asked about the new hospital and how his work in Tonga compared to his work in Fiji, Australia, and Britain. We started to compare my work in Tonga with my work in the US, which had consisted mostly of baby-sitting.

"When I was twelve, I took care of three children after their mother attempted suicide," I told him.

"How old were the children?"

"Four months, two years, and four years."

"Weren't you awfully young at twelve?"

"Oh, I was much more mature then than I am now," I said. "But I'm still surrounded by children. It's just that now I have to prepare them for the high school entrance exams that will determine their futures."

After dinner, Dr. Wiley asked Vincent if he could take me home, and Vincent acquiesced.

"I hope you'll forgive me for my bad table manners and all the rest," I told him in the car. "But it's so rare that I leave my village, and I really have no idea how to behave in public. All I know is that I have to bend over backwards. I have a very bad reputation."

"Oh? I hadn't realized."

"But it's not an interesting bad reputation. You're forgiven if you've got one of those because then at least you keep people entertained."

"Well, just what kind of bad reputation is it you've got?"

"The reputation for being innocuous. Insipid. Simple."

"I'm very sorry to hear that."

"I don't suppose we'll be seeing each other again."

"Why is that?"

"Because you must be so bored."

"Could you bore me again next Sunday?" he asked. "I'd like to invite you to dinner."

"Are you sure you're not just being kind?"

"I know a good restaurant. The only restaurant on the island."

"The 'Ofa atu!" I say. "I can tell you're a really nice man. Very understanding and tolerant. Next Sunday?"

But we bypassed the 'Ofa Atu, an Italian restaurant (because it served spaghetti) and the only restaurant independent of the hotel although there was the Beach House for communal dining, where Ron took me after Jim had left Tonga.

Vincent and I ate at the Dateline Hotel, a hotel so named because of Tonga's being on the dateline, where time begins. We tried to choose exotic things, but we were already spoiled. We had tortoise soup, and

I wondered whether it was the turtle rescued with us on the Sunday I came back from Nomuka.

Vincent and I drank coconut milk through a straw inserted in a chilled coconut. We had nondescript beef as a main course, and we drank Mateus, which I'd never had before.

"I only drink the kind of wine that comes in a jug with a screw-off top," I told him. "Or I used to. Now there's a boycott of Gallo because of the grape pickers' strike in California."

I wondered how he would respond. Was he the British equivalent of a Republican, who thought the grape pickers should pull themselves up by their bootstraps?

But he responded in a way sympathetic to the strikers.

Then our conversation turned courtly because we talked about the king.

The king had been advised that the Tongan economy depended upon the tourist trade as much as upon the exportation of copra, dried coconut meat. At an executive meeting, when they were planning to build a hotel, the king suggested this location, along the wharf. The wharf was not awe-inspiring, and someone protested, "But the wharf is so unattractive. The tourists wouldn't like it."

"If the tourists don't like it," the king replied indignantly, "they don't have to come."

Through dinner we talked about Vincent's work and my children, and then he asked, "Would you like to come to my palace to see my Benedictine?"

Vincent smoked his pipe and followed me while I wandered around his house. It was big and roomy, with high ceilings and white walls, and clean, smooth floors, furniture, books, records, and—it wasn't just a line—Benedictine.

"What do you do with all this house?" I asked.

"I hire a housekeeper."

"No, I mean, don't you ever get lost?"

"No. Not lost."

"Well, then, what do you get?"

"Lonely."

"And what do you do when you get lonely?

"I paint. Or I drink too much. Or I overeat. Or I go to bed early. Or I take a trip to Fiji. Or I drive into your village."

"Do you really drive into my village?"

"Yes. Well, not exactly in. By."

"Next time you drive by, I'd like you to step in and tell me about your loneliness."

"All right. And I'd like to hear about yours."

"What makes you think I've got any?"

"Well, you were jilted recently, weren't you?"

"Oh, that's right. I forgot."

"Oh youth, How easily they forget."

"Are you so much older than youth?"

"I'm old enough to talk about youth objectively. And objectionably."

"How old are you?" I asked.

"How old would you like me to be?"

"Old enough to be the older man in my life—like Emile in *South Pacific*."

"I like you at the age you are now," he told me.

"Then I'll try not to get any older," I said.

"And I'll try not to let our incredible age difference interfere with our friendship."

After this we ate together at his house every week, and he was a good cook as far as I could tell. We talked and read to each other from the *Manchester Guardian* he got and *Harper's*, which Jim sent me. He explained the most recent economic crises in the US, like the meat freeze.

He was not very aggressive. He kissed me when we met and before he let me out at my door. I wondered whether he was disappointed in me now that he'd met me. He didn't seem truly attracted to me, and that inhibited any attraction I might have felt towards him.

A couple of times a week Vincent drove into my village and knelt down with the children and me to talk. When he picked me up for dates, the children wanted to go too.

"Someday," Vincent told them one day, at my prodding, "Tina and I will take you to the beach."

The children screamed ecstatically and literally jumped for joy, though a little girl named Kili jumped the highest, and when she landed, she asked, "What's the name of the day?"

I marveled at this pointed phrase and tried to think of the Tongan Kili was translating from. ko e ha e fakahingoa 'aho? Ko e 'aho ha eni?

Asked for the name of the day, Vincent had to make a commitment and did.

I marveled at the wisdom of that phrase, which I shared with Andrea later. We vowed that anytime someone we really wanted to see said "Let's have lunch sometime," we were going to ask, "What's the name of the day?" with or without the preliminary screaming and jumping for joy.

Kili had already impressed me, but she went even further.

During the week before the day that Vincent had to name, she asked, "Other child will going or only we go?"

"Only you," I said, and her eyes lit up. She recognized "Only you" from a song I'd sung around the fale.

She broke out into song.

"Only you, only I. World farewell, world goodbye!"

She remembered the song "Follow Me," from *Camelot*, a song that a spirit sings to lure Merlyn away from Camelot, and she knew how to apply it.

I had accomplished something during my Peace Corps service— and in my first year in spite of doing my best to follow the instructions "Get off to a slow start."

It felt so good to know that I'd be leaving behind something besides "The Mickey Mouse Club Song."

Lesson Learned: ESL stands for English is a Singing Language

Lesson Learned: If you want a commitment from someone who says "Let's have lunch sometime," ask "What's the name of the day?"

"What's the Name of the Day?" Is Here

The children and I were much more enthusiastic about the outing than Vincent was, good man though he was. Maybe there were reasons for his remaining a bachelor, and maybe one reason was children.

The children piled into Vincent's car, which seemed to sink into the lawn. It was the first time a couple of the children had ever ridden in a car, and since Vincent's car was a snazzy sports car, they were appropriately hysterical.

It happened that on our way to the beach, we were spotted by Tevita, the teacher at my school who thought that I was doing marvelous things to myself and sparkling like a glittering star.

I of course loved Tevita for his way of seeing things (me), so I was concerned that he looked so worried. I would talk to him on Monday.

The children found shells and made wreaths from seaweed and played Vincent's ukulele and sang. Afterwards, Vincent took us all to his house so that they would know what a palace looked like, and they danced around the rooms.

On Monday Tevita said he wanted to talk to me.

"Tina," he said. "I worry to you when I see you in the man's car. I think the man is going to do bad things to you."

"No, Tevita. That was my friend Vincent."

"I think very bad things what wants that man."

"But Tevita, with all those children, what could he possibly do to hurt me?"

"I think he will doing his best. The man have a bad look in his eyes. I tell to my wife that I see the Peace Corps in the car, and she tell to me that's okay. But I think it's not okay."

"Well, Tevita, it is okay, after all. Your wife was right."

Later that week I told Vincent about Tevita's concern for me, and Vincent told me about the children's concern for him.

"A couple of them have come by since our day at the beach," he said.

"Oh, I never thought of that," I replied. "Now that they know where you live, you may never be lonely again."

"Well, they've asked me some very specific questions about my salary and my general standing in the community. They wanted to know if I have credit at the village shop. They also asked if I had a wife in my country and if I had any children or wanted to have any. Do you suppose they were taking this inventory for any particular purpose?"

"I think they want us all to live happily, happily, happily ever after. Together. All of us."

Very soon Vincent, not Line, had earned the most points. If he had credit at the fale kaloa (store), that cinched it. He was now the children's favorite among my "suitors."

Even though one villager still insisted, "Line is a good conduct boy, and you are a good conduct girl," Kili and Tonga insisted that "Line not bath" and "Line not enough for you."

Oh, if they only knew.

The Day the Ship Came In

June 1970

It was the year Tonga gained its independence (from being a protectorate), and the British—maybe to show that they were better sports than they'd been when the United States won its independence (or that there was no oil in Tonga, after all), sent a ship with Prince William of Gloucester aboard. As one of four "government girls—single," I had been invited aboard the visiting British warship to meet Prince William of Gloucester and all the crew who had embarked in Nuku'alofa for a week of receptions, parties, dinners, parades, and other celebrations.

"What do you do as a government girl—single—on a visiting British warship?" I asked the Peace Corps director, Layton Zimmer, who had extended the invitation but was, himself, a government man—married. "This wasn't in our Peace Corps job description."

"Just make small talk," he said.

"Fefe hake?" I suggested. "'Alu ki fe?'?" (How are you? Where are you going?)

"Maybe in English," he said.

The captain of the ship, who looked like Oskar Werner, an actor I liked, greeted me and introduced me to "the man who really *isn't* married," a very nice guy named Nigel, who showed me around, danced with me, and got me a gin and tonic, a glass of wine, a rum and coke and a Manhattan because I wanted a combination of tastes.

Nigel was a perfect gentleman if you can overlook his approval of the US's presence in Vietnam and Cambodia, his reading TIME Magazine and his patronizing comments about the Tongans.

"The Tongans have no class," he said within earshot of a Tongan waiter.

"My mother once told me that anyone using the word 'class' doesn't have any," I said. (There are times in life when you have a moral obligation to be rude.)

Nigel recovered, and he and other men plied me with compliments, which was very enjoyable and a nice contrast to village life, where I was palaku (ugly—literally scarfaced—because I was too thin).

I enjoyed the attention. ("When men say I'm cute and funny as around in a dance we whirl, I just lap it up like brandy. I enjoy being a girl." FLOWER DRUM SONG) But equally enjoyable was the incongruity: I was a Peace Corps teacher serving Tonga by spending an evening aboard a British warship and dismissing class. But what I really particularly enjoyed was the singing, which we all wound up doing as a result of conversations that began with poetry.

The captain, after paying me a compliment that I'm too modest to repeat here, told me that he was part of all that he had met, which is a line from Tennyson.

"'Yet all experience is an arch where through gleams the untraveled world whose margin fades forever and forever when I move,'" I replied.

"You know Tennyson!" he said.

"Not as intimately as I'm sure you do," I said, but the captain asked some other men to come over and listen, and we began reciting alternate lines. The men applauded and then, instead of slipping away to have some fun, they asked for more. We recited some Shakespeare, Donne, and Milton.

"An American who knows English literature!" the captain said.

"I know American literature too," I said.

"IS there any?" he asked.

I recited evidence that there was.

Because it was supposed to be small talk, I stuck to easy-to-like poems like Poe's "The Raven" and "Annabel Lee" with an exaggerated southern accent, which they really liked. And Frost's "The Road Not Taken" plus the last stanza of "Wild Grapes." But I also recited "The Love Song of J. Alfred Prufrock." They thought "Oh, Captain, My Captain" had something to do with sailing. (It's really Walt Whitman mourning the death of Lincoln.), so I suggested Gilbert and Sullivan, which really did relate to the Queen's Navy.

I am the Monarch of the sea
The ruler of the Queen's Na-vee.

I figured if they liked that, they *had* to like Rodgers and Hammerstein and Lerner and Lowe, so we moved on to Broadway, and every now and then they'd be able to sing along.

It really surprised me that, instead of people backing off and away, more gathered around as if it were a strip tease they were watching.

We sang all night, and it was "a grand night for singing." (STATE FAIR)

Nigel accompanied me back home in a taxi.

"That was the most fun we've had on the entire trip, he said. "We don't usually sing like that. You've given the fellows something to fantasize about."

"What's that?" I asked.

"Being me," he said.

I wasn't quite sure what he meant by that. Was he expecting something to happen between us? Did the label "government girl" suggest the same thing to him that it did to me? Or did he mean he would be a source of envy just because he had the privilege of escorting me home and reviewing more poetry?

He took me to the door and kissed me in a very socially acceptable way. Drinks always arouse me, but I was reserving my arousal for Line, even though he'd been giving me the silent treatment. I could sing "I loved you once in silence, and misery was all I knew." from *Camelot.*

"When someone with eyes that smolder says he loves every silken curl that falls on my ivory shoulder," I sang as I walked from my door to Loiloi's, where I hoped to find Line and did.

"I enjoy being a girl!" I sang as I entered.

I approached Loiloi and embraced her as a preview of coming attractions for Line. I told them about the evening and sang a medley of the musical numbers, ending with one we hadn't sung, "He touched Me" from DRAT THE CAT. It described the feeling you had when you were really attracted to a guy and the smallest contact, the slightest touch, was thrilling.

If there were only the smallest contact, the slightest touch with Line that evening, I'd find more in my fiction with 'Ofa.

I sang "He Touched Me," changing the tense from past to future: "He'll touch me. He'll put his hand near mine and then he'll touch me. I'll feel a certain tingle when he'll touch me. A sparkle, a glow."

Then I sat down beside Line and whispered in his ear.

"You are a Priest in Training," I said, "and I am a government girl."

"Kreecht," he said, smiling

"Jesus loves you," I sang, "So do I."

Line smiled and said he would see me safely to my door, and sure enough that far he saw me safely. We closed the door.

"Light the lamp. Light the lights. We've got nothing to hit but the heights!" I sang. (GYPSY)

"Shh, " he whispered, and he didn't light the lamp.

"Please touch me," I sang to the tune of "He Touched Me." (DRAT! THE CAT!)

"Shh!" he said.

"If you want me to stop singing, you'll have to seal my lips," I told him, and he complied.

"So what did you do aboard the ship all night?" he asked when he took his first breath.

"I told you. We recited great poetry."

"Yes, I'm sure," he said.

"And we sang."

"I bet YOU did.

"You know what they gave me on board the ship? They gave me magic love potions guaranteed to turn me helplessly amorous towards the first handsome Tongan I gaze upon. I kept my eyes downcast until just now," I said, looking up at where I felt his breath in the pitch black air. "I'm looking in the eyes of love," I said, staring deeper into darkness. I couldn't see Line at all, but there was strong evidence that he was there.

"Oh, I wish I could marry you."

"No, you don't, and neither do I. But I wish we could be very, very close. I deserve a beautiful, funny Catholic priest to love until he jilts me to run off with the Church."

Line began reciting lines from some romance love comic book he must have come across somewhere.

"You're the only woman for me," he said. "The only one I ever love. I wish I could hold you in my arms. all night. I wish I could press my lips against yours and—"

"'Line!" I said. I wanted to believe that he was being to some degree sincere, but I couldn't arrive at a stage of willing suspension of disbelief.

"Line, that's so sweet. But do you know what I really long to hear? I long to hear you tell me about the greasy wheel that gets the oils and the golden goose that laid the egg. And I want you to stop talk, talk talking and put your foot where your mouth is."

Was I confusing Line with 'Ofa?

I began laughing with delight, which impressed Line as unromantic. But his funny proverbs made me feel so close to him.

"I'm only laughing because I love you," I tried to explain, but he said he had to return to Loiloi, who would be speculating on what could be keeping him so long.

Line came by the next day to tell me that, as the manager of the rugby team, he had to go to another island for a few days, leaving this government girl alone with her fiction.

TIKA

TIKA WAS AN Australian archeologist named Nigel who had gotten his new name through phonological change. A Tongan once asked him what his work was, and he replied, "I'm a digger." There is no *d* or *g* in Tongan, (though there is an ng) and the final *r* in Australian English isn't pronounced, so digger became tika, and Nigel, inseparable from his work, became Tika.

Tika was a very handsome man who looked just a bit older than I was—maybe in his late twenties. I'd have loved to know him in his days as an archeologist, but I met him instead when he had given up digging to dedicate his time and skills to religious fanaticism.

Loiloi was the first to spot him when we were riding the bus to Mu'a, another village on Tongatapu, and she told me, "The handsome man staring to you, Tina."

"How do you know he isn't staring at *you*?" I asked.

"No, to you, Tina."

A few days later Tika spotted me at the post office and did, in fact, show a great interest in me. He found out what village I lived in, came to visit me, and bought me fish from Nuku'alofa.

Loiloi was ecstatic. She told me he was her dream man.

I was flattered by his attention until it became clear that he was after only one thing: My soul.

I'd always been interested in religion and the mystical, but I'd ceased believing in literal interpretations like the six days of creation and water into wine, bread into flesh.

When I was younger, I reasoned that there had to be a God. If there were no God, we'd just live and die and life would have no meaning. Then, when I got to college, I thought, "Oh. Life has no meaning."

I'd gone to an Episcopal church when we lived in the South, where everybody except my father went to church, and I went again in college when I lived on California Street in San Francisco just a couple of blocks away from St. James Episcopal Church. But the Episcopal Church isn't evangelical or fundamentalist or Born Again, and I thought people who were well-educated were unlikely to be any of those things.

I was fascinated by Tika. For him to be so well-educated and intelligent and still have his fundamentalist beliefs made me think he must have a great need to believe.

During our time together, I spent as much energy trying to discover what that need was as Tika spent in trying to get me to have the need too.

"Do you believe in God?" he asked me when he first visited.

I didn't know what I was in for. I thought it was going to be just a simple philosophical discussion, and I plunged right in.

"Yes, I do. And even if I didn't, I wouldn't say so. With all God's been through I wouldn't want Him to hear and get His feelings hurt."

"Have you accepted Jesus Christ as your savior?"

Now, that's the kind of question an Episcopalian was too polite to ask.

"Yes, I think I did that once. I was confirmed at St. John's Episcopal Church when I was twelve."

"But do you believe in Christ?"

"I believe he was a very good man.'

"A good man? You don't believe that he was the son of God?"

"No, I don't think God has any children—other than all of us, I mean. It's common in Greek mythology that the gods fathered children. But I don't think the God in monotheistic religions does that sort of thing."

I saw at once that Tika had no appreciation for flippancy. He told me that Jesus Christ was the son of God. There was proof right there in the Bible. He began quoting me verses.

"'Knock and it shall be open onto you." "Believe and ye shall be saved."

I joined in with a recitation of Ruth's "entreat me not to leave thee" speech, which I'd always liked, but Tika said that had nothing to do with being saved through the blood of our Lord Jesus Christ.

"Have you been washed in the blood of the lamb?" I asked, quoting Vachel Lindsay. "Mumbo jumbo and voodoo you!"

"Have you ever thought about what hell would be like?" he asked.

"I think I know. I think about that when I'm at the dentist's. You're forever under a dentist's drill, and there's no laughing gas or piped in music and no one to talk to you to make you feel better."

"Would you like to spend the rest of your life in hell? In pain and separated from God and all that's holy?"

"No!" I said. "Maybe from all that's holy, but not in pain and separated from God."

"Then believe. All you have to do is believe."

"Don't you have to be good too?" I asked.

I thought it would be fun to get into ethics. There once was a little girl whose mother asked her not to eat the cookies in the cookie jar...

Nigel insisted that there were verses—and he knew them all by heart—that made it quite clear that believing was the key.

"But you can't offer the Bible as proof unless you offer proof for the Bible," I said.

"Don't you believe in the Bible?" he asked.

"Yes, I believe in the Bible. But I don't believe it's necessarily true."

This got me started in on Gershwin's "It ain't necessarily so. It ain't necessarily so. The things that you're liable to read in the Bible, it ain't necessarily so."

"That's blasphemous," he said.

"No, it's Porgy and Bess," I said..

Our conversations always began carefully and politely, but we were soon raising our voices— and not always in song. He was calling me unsaved and headed for an eternity at the dentist's, and I was calling him superstitious and sanctimonious.

I apologized.

"Tika. I really like you. You're..." I tried to think of something nice and sincere.

"You're very handsome."

"Why do you say that?"

"Because you are. Loiloi says you're her dream man."

"You only like what titillates," he said.

"Huh? I really like you, Tika, except when we get on the subject of your religious beliefs. Can't we just talk like friends?"

"I want for us to be friends. I love and care about you. You're one of God's children, if you'll just recognize it and accept Jesus Christ as your savior."

I tried to change the subject, but I soon discovered that there was no subject on which his views didn't outrage me.

He loved my country for what it was doing in Vietnam.

He liked Jerry Lewis—even his takeoff on victims of Cerebral Palsy.

I didn't dare ask him what he thought about the grape pickers' strike in California.

I found myself spitting out accusations like "If you really believed in Jesus Christ, you'd understand that he'd have protested against the US intervention in Vietnam and against Jerry Lewis. And he wouldn't buy grapes."

I became a self-appointed authority on what Christ would and would not have approved of. I even found myself making comments like "Every time you espouse a reactionary cause, and you always do, you're crucifying Christ all over again."

I became a match for Tika in self-righteousness, but he kept coming back for more.

"I don't believe that rumor that God is dead," I said, "but don't you ever get the impression that He's getting old? That He's senile? That He's gone mad? Or maybe He's just so depressed that he doesn't think it matters anymore, and so He let a whole nation get wiped out in Vietnam."

"Nothing ever happens without reason," Tika said. "Everything is either reward or punishment."

"You mean all those Vietnamese—like the ones in My Lai— are being wiped out because they aren't good Christians?"

{I first learned about My Lai in Peace Corps training on Lanai, when my host teacher told me in November 1969, after the massacre of March 1968 had just been made public by a independent journalist named Seymour Hersch. When Mrs. Hobdy told me, I thought the incident had just happened.}

"That's right. That's why it's so important to send missionaries."

"And I suppose you think that someone who has epilepsy is really possessed by demons?"

"In many cases, yes."

"My brother has epilepsy."

"I'll pray for him."

"You really believe in witches and demons?"

"Yes. Because they do exist. It's in the Bible. Even my father admits that. He's a skin specialist and not really a confirmed Christian. But he believes that ninety-five percent of his patients' skin problems are due to demon possession."

I was silent for a moment, choking on indignation and incredulity. I didn't ask how his father broke this news to his patients or what kind of prescription he wrote them, but when I got back my voice, I made a plea.

"I don't mind your telling me things like this," I said. "Just spare the Tongans, who don't need any more myths or ghost stories."

But no one was spared. He even said that the Catholics were not Christians, something I shared with Line, who, returning from the rugby tour, had the chance to speak to Tika about this in my presence.

As they sat on the matted floor, I decided to give them the chance to debate on this issue. Tika expressed himself in a more diplomatic way, and afterwards he was disappointed in me.

"I can't believe that you would tell him that I'd said that."

"But you did. Don't you have the strength of your convictions? I wanted him to have the chance to defend the Catholic Church and for you to have the chance to attack it."

I was surprised but also touched that Tika cared about not offending people with his proclamations.

When Tika's sister visited him from Australia, she brought him a plastic blowup chair, which he brought as a gift for me so I'd have some furniture in what he referred to as my cave.

My cave? The most beautiful, plush and lush fale on Tongatapu he sees as a cave?

I speculated before this visit that his need to believe in the unbelievable was due to guilt feelings he had—perhaps about a wild past.

When I commented on his purity, he told me, "I certainly wasn't pure when I was in my teens."

"Oh, I wish I'd know you then," I replied, just to be playful. (I "only like what titillates.")

The day he came by with the plastic chair, I decided his deep-seated fear might be of germs. We took turns blowing up the chair, and when he had to put his mouth over the areas on which I've had mine, he spent about three minutes rubbing it clean. Even the most germ-conscious would be too polite to spend that long. Maybe he thought that only God could make him clean. Out damn spot! Was I the spot?

At Christmastime 1970 he invited me to a choral concert in Nuku'alofa. We went on his motor bike, so I was obligated to put my arms around him. When we got to Nuku'alofa, he told me he had a headache.

"Aha!" I said. "Nothing happens without a reason. You've sinned, and God must punish you."

"I know," he said, with a humility that threw me though I stayed on the motorbike.

"Well, what have you done?"

"I don't want to tell you," he said. "But I think I know."

The music was beautiful. I'd always loved Christmas carols, and I told Tika how much I was enjoying the songs.

"Yes," he said, "and they're singing about a man who really lived."

"Don't spoil it," I said.

"That's what makes it so wonderful," he said, "for me."

At the end of the evening, he took me back on his motorbike and saw me to the door. His headache was worse.

"What terrible sin have you committed?" I asked.

"I don't want to tell you."

"Come on. Confession is good for the soul."

"I've thought of someone and looked upon her with lust," he said.

I looked at him sympathetically.

"Oh, that's so sweet," I said softly.

He got back on his motorbike and rode away.

One day I let it slip that Loiloi had a child with water on the brain. Tika promptly (but only temporarily) left his mission of saving me to save the child. Meliani was two years old and very pale. Her head was swollen, her eyes large and haunted-looking, and all she had done since birth was lie on the bed and move her arms back and forth.

Loiloi lovingly spoon-fed her and changed whatever she used for diapers and took one day at a time.

The Mormons in the village had offered to take Meliani to Honolulu and have her operated on. All Loiloi and Fanomanu had to do was become Mormons, and the church would pay for everything.

Tika's solution was simpler. He explained to Loiloi and Fonomanu that prayer could cure Meliani. All they needed to do was believe and pray and bring Meliani to the faith healing the following Saturday.

Loiloi, excited and hopeful that at last there was a solution, came to me to tell me the good news.

"Oh, Loiloi," I said. "Don't get your hopes up."

I couldn't wait to get my hands on Tika. I'd give him a headache like he'd never had before, and this time it wouldn't be from lust.

"But Tina, I think it going to working. Meliani going to be good. Pray."

I prayed.

I sent a note to Line, asking him to save Loiloi and Fonomanu from the faith healing. Meanwhile I lectured Tika.

"Don't you see how cruel you're being? Not only is she going to be disappointed when Meliani's head doesn't shrink miraculously, but she's going to feel guilty. Because she's going to think it's through her imperfect faith that the faith healing failed."

"If she believes strong enough, the faith healing won't fail."

Loiloi invited me to go, as if it were a baptism or confirmation. I declined. I sat there with the children all evening, but I lived through it all anyway.

And right now they'll be saying the prayer, and Loiloi will be holding the baby...and right now they'll be...

When they returned to the village, Loiloi and Fonomanu went straight to their home with the baby. I got word that they were waiting for sunrise to see if there would be a delayed reaction to the attempted faith healing.

At sunrise I got word that Meliani was lying there as usual, head swollen, eyes large and haunted, arms. moving back and forth. I agonize over the guilt and disappointment that Loiloi must be feeling.

Then I got word that it was clear: The faith healing didn't work because of someone who willed it not to. God forbid that they thought that was me.

Song of Song of Solomon

Line sometimes sulked about my social life, saying that it was not my place as a Peace Corps Volunteer to have one. I explained to him that I was having a social life only because I loved him and didn't want him to be forced into taking me for granted.

"The whole village thinks you're a harlot," he said one day with what I hope was exaggeration.

"Why do you think that they think that?" I asked.

"Because they see you going out with a different Tom, Dick or Harry every night."

"That's ridiculous. I don't go out every night, and when I go out with Vincent, half the time we take the kids along. Tika visits me only in a futile attempt to save my soul. Ron was told to look after me and is only doing his duty."

Ron was the one who was declared psychologically unfit because of his cutting cross-culture activities in Peace Corps training. This judgment of unfit was over-ruled by the same psychiatrist who declared that my dream world might be more of an asset than a liability. Now Ron was on the same island and coming by every week to bring me vegetables or to take me to dinner at his house on the other end of the island. When he invited me to dinner, I always offered to help, but he refused to let me into the kitchen, saying, "Tina, cooking is a man's job." I loved his attitude, and I loved him.

I first saw him as someone affectionate when, on January first 1970, when we were still in training on Molokai, I greeted him, putting my arms around him to wish him a happy new year, and he hugged me as if he meant it. It was then that I suspected that unsociable, psychologically unfit Ron was not unaffectionate, and if he were affectionate, what did it matter whether or not he attended cross-culture activities? He had, I judged on the basis of a hug, a great capacity to love, so he was a good man.

Whenever we got together on Tongatapu we talked a lot, since that was my favorite pastime, and I read aloud to him (Elinor Wiley's poetry, James Dickey's latest macho production, *Deliverance, Time Magazine, Harper's* from our friend Jim) while he cooked. But it had never occurred to me to fall in love with him—perhaps because it was Jim who gave Ron to me or me to Ron, and falling in love with someone's gift would be a betrayal of the gift giver. Or maybe because of my secret meetings with Line, which were all I felt I should permit myself on the earthy (and literary) plain. So Ron and I never did anything risqué like kissing.

"Ron and I never do anything risqué like kissing," I told Line, as further proof that I was a harlot only in my fiction with him.

But a week later, Ron and I kissed. We did it after he'd brought me home from dinner at his hut. I lit the kerosene lamp and he closed the door. Then as we were saying good night, we were overcome with affection and kissed, right there behind the closed door.. It didn't last more than thirty seconds. But that was enough.

The next morning Line, dressed all in white like a milkman, came by on his way to play cricket. He ducked into my hut where, exceptionally, there weren't any children at the moment. We put our arms around each other and kissed quickly. Then he said, "I thought you said that you and that Peace Corps chap never kissed."

"That was true," I say, slurring the past tense.

"Oh yeah? What about last night?"

In Tonga there was never any privacy. But the unfair thing was this: Everyone knew what you did, but no one knew what you didn't do and with whom you didn't do it. That's why everyone, according to Line, who I think exaggerated, thought I was a harlot. They didn't know all the things I didn't do and all the people with whom I didn't do them. But fortunately no one minded my being a harlot. The important thing was to be a good-natured whatever it was you were.

Whenever Line wasn't sulking because of my social life, he came by and brought me little gifts like Cadbury chocolate bars and cans of corn beef imported from New Zealand to offer as proof that he, under my excellent tutelage, was becoming a better, more generous person and less of a free-loader.

"This means a lot to me," I said.

"Oh, what's a bar of chocolate," he said in his modest way.

"No, I mean it means a lot to me that you're becoming a better, more generous person and less of a free-loader."

He sat on the floor among my children and drank lemonade and talked. The children watched him closely and with disapproval because, in spite of our formal behavior in their presence, they considered him a threat to my future happiness with Vincent, whom they of course preferred. What did Line ever do for them? Did Line ever take them to the beach or to his home? So they defended Vincent by attacking Line after each visit.

"He's a bad one. He didn't bath. He's not enough. He didn't worthy of you."

"We must think of the children," I imagined telling Line. "You didn't worthy of me. You're not enough. You didn't bath. You're a bad one."

I imagined other things when Line became 'Ofa. in my factionalized version of my life in Tonga (See "To Whom It May Concern: I Am Your Mother)

Letters and Diary Entries

I have twenty-eight diaries from Tonga, notebooks I carried around in the basket I always had with me, one notebook at a time, so I could write down whatever Tongan words or thoughts in English came into my mind. I often scribbled letters, which I'd later copy over onto aerograms in a more legible hand. For this reason, I have many and maybe most of the letters I wrote the second year—at least in their first-draft form, and sometimes I kept writing a letter I never sent. Sometimes I'm not sure which was a letter to someone else and which was just a diary entry. I wasn't even always sure of which year I was looking back on!

But here's something for you, dear reader. (I think I have at least one.)

Lesson Learned: Put the date and year on every diary entry and also on the front of every notebook you use for a diary.

(I acknowledge that blogs are for some today's equivalent of a handwritten diary and with blogs come dates.)

To make this memoir truly eclectic, I'm using my letters to describe the second year of my Peace Corps service in Tonga through October.

I'll interrupt the letters only when they aren't self-explanatory, but this won't be quite like an epistolary novel.

Late January 1971

Dear Mother, Suzy, and Kathy,

I hope you got my postcard from New Zealand. I'm in love with that country now.

Fiji was nice too, and that's where we spent Christmas Eve and day. Mike/Marshall, one of my favorite Peace Corps volunteers, originally from Alabama and now living on the outer island Ha'apai, went with Andrea and me as far as Fiji. Mike and I sometimes went to church together on Molokai during training because that's what Southerners do, and the other PCVs think of me as Southern. Back in training I sent you a picture of me in my blue dress and white tupenu posing on Molokiai beside the sign saying "The Episcopal Church welcomes you," and we found an Anglican church in Suva. Andrea, who isn't religious because she was brought up in the Baptist Church, liked the beauty of the Anglican Church and expressed dismay that no one had ever told her how pleasant a church service could be.

On Christmas we tried to find a place to eat, but all the restaurants were closed. Finally we spotted one with big windows and a lot of Indians in saris, so we knocked on the door and asked whether they were open, and they let us in. They didn't have a printed menu, but they served us Indian food, like nothing we've ever had before. Please try it if you can find any in the Bay Area. It's delicious—very spicy with bread a little bit like tortillas. We drank a lot of water. After we paid—about a dollar each—we left a fifty-cent piece on the table for a tip, and they thought we'd forgotten it and tried to give it back!

Later I got to thinking about this: What if that really weren't a restaurant? What if that was really a private home, and they'd just let us in because we knocked and said we were hungry and couldn't find any place to eat? I'm just so glad they did open because that was about the best food I've ever had in my life.

Then after only three days in Fiji, Andrea and I flew to New Zealand without Mike. We stayed at Youth Hostels and at YMCAs, and we hitch-hiked from place to place and never had to wait more than a few minutes for a ride. New Zealanders are excellent drivers even after they've had a whole pitcher of beer and have to drive on really steep and curvy mountain roads. The people who picked us up almost always took us pub crawling, which is what they do instead of bar hopping, but they managed to land safely!

The New Zealanders were so friendly that even the official who took our passport numbers spoke to us between the digits he had to write down. When we went into a book store, the manager invited us to her home, and when we went to a fish and chip place, the Rumanian family who ran it invited us to their home for dinner—and it was a very beautiful, bountiful Romanian dinner, not fish and chips, they served us. We absolutely loved the people.

We visited the family of Mike Monti, the volunteer from New Zealand who worked at the broadcasting station and refereed games. Mike and I haven't had a of contact, but I do like him and liked his family—mother, father, sister Gabriel, who sings really well, his brother Pete, who's really sweet. I think I fell asleep in Pete's arms after one of the pub crawls (in the car and with a lot of people in attendance).

New Zealand is also a beautiful country, and we managed to see it while also seeing 33 movies the month we were there! Better not tell Daddy! He'd be horrified that we went into dark theaters when we could have spent ALL of our time out in nature, but we needed to see those movies, and think of it: There are 24 hours in a day. The movies took only 2 to 4 of those hours, leaving us 20 to see beautiful sights and people.

The only negative thing about the trip was me. Andrea is much better organized and ambitious than I am, so that put a strain on things sometimes. Also, whenever they'd pick us up, I'd sit in the back seat and go to sleep, and she had to entertain the drivers, so she asked me to start sitting in the front seat, and I did, but I still fell asleep, so she still had to entertain the drivers.

But we are still friends, so that says something about overcoming obstacles like my basic personality. Andrea is funny, as well as efficient, and she's a great storyteller. She can tell a story all the way through instead of speaking it in rough drafts the way we do.

Oh, one story she tells is about the night John from a chicken fast food place came by. We'd met him at the fast-food place earlier in the day, and he knew we were staying at the Y on the ground floor. At midnight, he came to our bedroom window with a roast chicken. While I slept on, Andrea woke up and took it, thanking him. Then she woke me up and said, "Tina! John just passed us a roast chicken through the window." She says my waking words were, "Oh, I was hoping he would."

Well, I'm now back in my village, where they gave me a very warm welcome back.

Love,
Tina

Jim,

Here I sit, waiting for a new white tupenu to be sewn, while Fehi lies on a bench and chews on a ribbon from a package I just got, and Hina paces. Just 24 hours ago I landed on my flight from New Zealand, and now I'm starting over again with Tongan life. It was beautiful, NZ, but as I tell every Tongan I meet along the street, "Oku ou lata o foki ki Tongani," which I hope means I am happy to be back in Tonga. My language hasn't made the strides you suggested in your letter. I'm sincere when I say my Tongan was better on Molokai. As for me, I don't know. Maybe I me myself was better there too. Remember Jerry Lesser, who said we'd lose either our sanity or our sex-appeal? Which do you think I've lost? Which would you rather?

to be continued...

I can't remember what I brought back for Ron. Lesson learned: Note things like that within your diary or at least within your letter to the recipient so he'll remember! But let's place our bets: A Cassette of Kiss Me Kate? *The classic comic book of* The Taming of the Shrew?

To Ron,

who writes well, I present William Shakespeare, who also writes well. *The Taming of the Shrew* as a Broadway Musical is *Kiss Me, Kate*. The film version without music stars Richard Burton and Elizabeth Taylor and is a Paramount Production.

So this is a souvenir from New Zealand though I realize that you, though a science scholar, are well-acquainted with the BARD.

With much love and literary taste, Tina

January 29, 1971, Ha'ateiho, Tongatapu, Kingdom of Tonga, Having just returned from a successful tour of New Zealand.

Dear Mother,

To continue the letter I sent you, Kathy, and Suzy just a day or so ago—or to replace it if it doesn't make it to you:

My job's going to be different this year. I'll be trying to give demonstration lessons to teachers on teaching oral English to classes 1 & 2—real little kids. These classes are very hard for me, but maybe I'll improve. For some reason the director of Education has me at Fasi Primary

School's Teachers' Retraining Center in the afternoon although in the morning I teach at 'Atele (right by my village), five miles away from Fasi, and they have the 'Atele Teachers' Retraining Center right there! So I'll spend my lunch hour commuting.

Oh, I was really surprised to get more packages yesterday—the Moroccan dress from Dana & the books from David. David has very good taste! *{I don't remember what books were sent in David's name.—See Lesson learned above—but I don't think he chose them himself. He did sign the card, though.}* I'm spending this weekend talking to my Tongan family so I can spend some of next week not talking to them. But I'm liking them these days, and Likua, the woman whose falekaloa (shop) provides me with kerosene and bread, the two staples in life, wants to take me to the bush on Sunday so I can get some rest. The father of her son has a big piece of land in Vaikeli, something his father, who married another woman, gave him after his wife had only daughters. I like Likua a lot, and it's so quiet and peaceful there. I'm not really suffering!

I'm not sure whether I get this across or not, talking as I do about my emaciated body and the water shortage. I just complain for effect, for the sake of the picturesque. I'm really not unhappy here.

Did you get your tenure? What kind of work are you doing now? Where's David? Missy?

Love,
Tina

At that time, my mother was a counselor with Kathy at Juvenile Hall. I don't know what I meant by tenure. I'm not sure whether David was still at Napa or Missy was still with our father.

After dropping out of the Peace Corps in May 1970, Jim got into a musical in Chicago, a play I make reference to several times without giving it

a name. Guess, and I'll tell you later! In the following letter I also make reference to Larry, who was in Rat Control, and to Jim's days in a Jesuit school when he was a Brother before joining the Peace Corps. According to what I later found online, the play opened in Chicago in February 1971.

Ha'ateiho,   January 29,
1971

Dear Jim,

Here I sit, on top of my mosquito coil, cross-legged on the floor with my right knee against my little floor table, which has letters and flowers on it and the white thread little Hina is going to use to string the flowers for me to put over Kalea's head when she dances tonight at an outdoor party to meet the VSAs (Volunteer Services Abroad—New Zealand and Australia) and PCVS who've just come. After that Ron will pick me up and take me to dinner with Larry and Mike, who's going back to Ha'apai tomorrow after writing a song for family planning. We'll make a toast to you and to your stage career because I see that this is opening night and I'm excited for you, as Larry, Ron, and Mike will be when I tell them and show them the clipping from the Sun, Jan. 10 *Showcase/Chicago Sun Times.*

Thank you so much for the Oh, happy Christmas telegram. I got two from you—and your postcard. Thank you for getting your friends from Jesuit school to write to me!

All this as you delve into show business! Special thanks for the long letter, which I read over and over and will try to comment upon in depths to your satisfaction. But be patient, please, because I have no typewriter.

'Ofa atu and "Break a leg" as they say in the theatre, don't they?

Love,
Tina

Ha'ateiho, Tonga

January 29, 1971

Jim opens tonight in your city!

Dear Dana,

The Moroccan dress is beautiful and unusual, and I love having it. See how I'll break the stereotype of the plain, simple, self-sacrificing PCV with my bikini panties & Moroccan dress and Nabokov's *Ada* under my arm? (I read that the title of his book is pronounced something like ardor!)

But why don't you write? I wait, I look, I wonder.
I write!

Nuku'alofa, Tonga
Same day but later
around 1:00 PM

I went with a Tongan friend to a social tonight and little had I realized we'd be socializing with my own people whom I love but avoid because I bore me when I'm with them. So I spent the evening with an older but wiser (but not older than me) ex-PCV, who let me tell him my dreams.

I'm very sleepy and there's a feast waiting for me back in the village.

Good night,   from Tina with love.

February 1, 1971

Dear Suzy,

It's good to know how you're progressing through your adolescence. I've just about progressed through mine too. For the past few days I've told people that I'm really 28 years old, that I lied on my passport, which has my birth year as 1945. I am, in fact, 28, a mature woman, pushing 30 and unashamed. I know at least 4 people who believe me.

Are you singing? What? What new records do you have? How do you like the midi?

At the moment I'm sitting with Mele on a mat on the ground of 'Atele GPS, where I taught last year. Mele's a Tongan teacher who studied in Australia, speaks English fluently, and is going to be a head teacher at 'Atele's Teachers Retraining Center— for re-training teachers in Oral English. I, who live around the corner, have been assigned as assistant tutor to a center in Nuku'alofa, 5 1/2 miles away. Maybe I won't be teaching kids at all this year.

Think of it: I've been in the PC (counting training) 15 months. Another year to go. Do you think I'll extend?

You said that Dana didn't understand the mutual friendships you have. What mutual friendships are those? I mean, with whom? Are Mary Beth and Jennifer and Patty still your best friends?

You're quite right about furniture. "Who needs it?" When I go back to America, I'm going to spread out a mat and my tea tray and that'll be it. Then I'll buy a midi cape to wear out into the world.

What have you been reading lately?

When are you going to get a job? Are you learning to drive? Are you taking singing lessons?

The children are out cleaning the yard now with their long brooms and bush knives. Tonga's really beautiful, when you look <u>at</u> it instead of <u>through</u> it.

Suzy, please tell Mother that I just got her pictures. They're really pretty. My Tongan family and Kaleni (Tongan equivalent of Karen) said Mother's "faka'ofa'ofa," which means beautiful. About Kaleni: She's not the child I was going to adopt, although I like her. Kaleni lives on the grounds of 'Atele Si'i, where her father and I teach. I think sending her postcards each time she writes is a good idea because postcards are pretty and you don't have to write a lot.

Please send me some more pictures of all of you. Please! Soon. Please.

Love,
Tina

{I loved the Tongan children and really did fantasize adopting one—officially or unofficially. I think Kaleni may have already been borrowed from her birth parents by a couple who couldn't have their own children.}

Elmer Skold was our country director the second year I was in Tonga. He and his wife Patty replaced Layton Zimmer and his wife. Apparently there was someone named Mr. Graham I was supposed to meet at a party in Nuku'alofa.

Dear Elmer and Patty,

The party sounds good, but I'm afraid I've already committed myself for Friday night. Mr. Graham is welcome to come to Ha'ateiho if he likes. I'm sorry to miss the rest of the new PCVs, but the ones I've met seem very nice, enthusiastic, relaxed but not too relaxed, and I hope to see all of you again someday too!

'Ofa atu,
Tina

Dear Line,

Are you still sick? If you are, I'm sorry, but here are a few magazines, some throat lozenges, and a word of sympathy. Either it's tuberculosis (too many cigarettes. Have you seen the doctor?) or else it's all psychological: You've had to wait too long to begin a new life. But soon your papers will come & you will leave us all forever.

to be continued...or discontinued...

February 4, 1971

Dear Jim,

Yesterday Ron brought me the books you sent me, and they are beautiful: Everything I ever wanted to know about sex (but was afraid to ask) and 2 other less technical books. (Hahahah, as Dostoevsky says.) There's nothing technical about Reuben, who's just as cute as can be. But I like his book, and the others. I've been wanting to read *Zelda*. The *Papillion* I hadn't heard of but obviously should have. I'll come back educated, Jim. You'll be so proud of me. Maybe I can pass as a college graduate.

Oh, Jim, my legs are erupting again, oh most beauteous sight. And I've tried Merthiolate in vain. When I come back, I will be a marked woman—scorned and covered with scars, to be sung to the tune of "The Impossible Dream" from Man of La Mancha. I am 28. That's what I tell people now. They express surprise, but not appropriate disbelief.

P. is the Head Tutor at Fasi's Teachers Retraining Center, where I'm assistant tutor. I have made name tags for Monday and stuck pins in them and thought about my demonstration lesson. I want to remember to get off to a slow start, the way they advised us in training.

But Jim, you must tell me all about your play!

Tonight I go to a PC party with Naomi, a teacher I've taught with at 'Atele Si'i, and will leave shortly because I like parties most when I go for 45 minutes, eat, drink, look, talk, and go. I like Elmer and Al (assistant director) and the others—don't misunderstand me—but my place is in my fale.

Did I tell you that Andrea and I saw 33 movies in New Zealand?

I almost forgot. I dreamt of you: I was combing my hair in front of a mirror in the Ladies Lounge when your face appeared in the mirror above my right shoulder. I was so surprised! I covered my face, said, "Jim!" and took you out of the Ladies Lounge. I was very happy to see you. But while I was gone, someone stole money from my basket that I'd left in the Ladies Lounge. Still, it was worth it. You said, "See? I've appeared in your mirror—just as I promised." But I had thought your promise was to appear in my fale, and it was less of a promise than a wish. I'll re-read your letters.

But please tell me about your play! Were you discovered?

'Ofa atu,
Tina

{to Mike Monti, a New Zealand volunteer, who worked in broadcasting and knew Line}

Dear Mike,

Could you give Line the addresses of your family in Dunedin and of Peter? I want to send them a card to thank them, but only Andrea has their address, and I can't get in touch with her without going to her village on the other side of the island. I've just realized I don't have their addresses.

{Mary and Leif, a Peace Corps couple, were my nice neighbors, living and teaching at 'Atele College, across from 'Atele Primary, where I taught. People who went to prestigious colleges as they did—Northwestern and Stanford—were assigned to educational posts in institutions of higher learning while those of us who went to state colleges were assigned to the lower grades.}

February 7, 1971

Dear Jim,

I hope you've gotten my telegram. I didn't get yours till a few hours ago, when Mary brought it and a small stack of letters over and apologized for not bringing them sooner. She and Leif had picked them up at the PC office for me a couple of days ago. I don't think the people around here honor a telegram appropriately.

I'd gotten 2 identical (oh, happy Christmas) telegrams from you, and when I saw this one, I thought the Tongan Government was doing everything in duplicate. I was really shocked when I read it. I said, "Oh, my God, Jim's father died!" and Mary said, emotionally, "Oh, shit!" which you know in "their" language represents all sort of sentiment and sympathy. But I just thought of how no one knows what to say about death.

I think about death and shout it, but I really feel sad about your father's death, and I don't know how to express it. Winchester's book tells about Mrs. Johnson trying to console Jacqueline Kennedy after the assassination. "What I regret most," she said, "Is that it happened in our state of Texas." What I regret most is your father's dying, but I also regret my inability to express how I feel.

He must have died just about the time your play was opening—when Larry, Ron, and I were toasting you. And he must have died unexpectedly. Some people say that's good because it means there hasn't been a lot of pain and senility and feeling of worthlessness. But it's sad in the sense that you can't prepare and do and say the last things you want to have done for him and said to him. I have a picture of your father with your mother, Jean, and Mary at a wedding. He doesn't look at all close to death. It's good that Kathleen came home for Christmas!

I'm sending along a silly letter I wrote before I got your telegram. As I said in my telegram, I really wish I could be with you—especially now.

What about the "new splash musical." Is it going well?

Love,
Tina

PS It's raining now, and I have nothing to eat but peanuts. I'm sad, but not because of the food. I'm sad because this is such a stupid letter, and I really love you.

{It's clear from my second-year diary that I much preferred teaching the Tongan children to "re-training" Tongan teachers. The Tongan teachers were good teachers, but even though I believed in the "Tate Method," it really didn't work very well with the children, and we used children in our demonstrations. It didn't help that I was working as the assistant of a Tongan who didn't want to work with me, a feeling he was articulating to other people like Sione Kite, who was the Secretary of the Tongan government at the time and whom I was going out with my second year.}

<u>March 1971</u>

Dear Mother,

Thank you for sending *Living Poor*! I'm reading it now! I'm doing it too!

I wanna go home! I love Vincent and Ron and the children but no one and nothing else here. Except Likua and her family. I do like them. Well, I like a lot of people here. What I don't like is working with P. at the Teachers Retraining Center because he doesn't want me as his assistant, and I've risen to the level of my incompetence. {Daddy and I heard Dr. Peters talk on his Peter Principle, which Daddy said made a good article but didn't need to be turned into a book.} I was competent teaching kids, so I got promoted to a job requiring totally different skills. Now I am incompetent in my job. I almost feel as if I'm serving a sentence and am on probation. I'll be "out" in nine months.

I met Andrea, My Best Friend in Peace Corps Tonga (if we don't count the men) on my way to the Peace Corps Office today, and she said she'd heard rumors about me —that P. wasn't happy with me, that I didn't prepare my lessons, and he'd once told Mele Taufe'ulungaki (one of the sisters whose brothers all died and who now lead the island in education) to tell me not to bother showing up if I weren't going to prepare my lessons, but Mele was too kind to tell me.

Apparently P. decided the first couple of days that I was timid and not commanding the respect of the other teachers. He told Mele and Sione that he wanted me to work in Mele's Center—at 'Atele, which would be much more convenient for me since that's where I am in the morning—and have Linda Bassett, another hard-working PCV, work in his center. He told Mele my lessons only lasted 3 minutes and he imitated the way I stood by taking the posture of a person shrinking inwardly. He told Linda Bassett too.

All this without a word of criticism to me! I see so well how my cautious tact backfired. I was too careful about getting off to a slow start and not offending people while they were— or at least he was— judging this as a sign of meekness and incompetence. When he makes mistakes (and he makes a lot because he's never taught kids before), I'm so kind about it. I mean I'm gentle when I point out the most gross mistakes. And I never talk to other people about his weaknesses. I'm surprised and infuriated by his lack of integrity—especially about his lying and telling Mele I didn't prepare my lessons. I've lost a lot of respect for him.

I approached P. and asked him about this "rumor" I heard about his dissatisfaction with me, and he said that the first day he thought I lacked confidence because I didn't deliver my speech well. (I didn't deliver a speech at all! I thought he was trying to keep me in the background!) Anyway, he says since then his opinion has changed and he thinks I'm doing "a fine job." Maybe better than he is, distractedly looking out the window and missing the point when Sandy, resident Super Vol(unteer) criticizes him in her inimitable way.

I remember when we were on Molokai the night he asked me to dance, but I'd had five Mai Tais and said no—just so I wouldn't collapse in his arms. Could he still hold a grudge? (The Cross Culture director did caution me after that incident, saying that face was very important to Tongans. Did I cause him to lose face?) Or have I truly just risen to my level of incompetence?

Thank goodness I have my Sunday in the enchanted woods with Likua, Hea, and Sipaisi on land that his father Masao Soakai gave Hea after the woman Masao Soakai married (not Likua) didn't bear a son.

Am now at Vaikeli/Tokomolo.. Sepaisi has prepared a mat on banana leaves on a stone table here, and I have a pillow. It's beautiful and cool up here on the table.

I brought them a big can of pulu (beef) which the people of Tokomololo brought me. Now they're preparing the feast. I like their food—curry and sheep and bananas and coconut milk—beautiful and hot.

Hea's weaving baskets from coconut tree leaves to put hundreds of green bananas in. Likua's on the floor on top of coconut leaves with her head on a red and white cloth bag. She's such a good woman. She's very small and her feet are also small and hardened. She's wearing shoes with missing shoelaces on one foot and nothing on the other and a stained skirt, a multicolored (yellow, blue, purple in swirls) blouse. Her hair's gray and frizzy and braided at the nape of her neck. Sipaisi, Hea's wife (Liku'a's daughter-in-law) is very sweet-voiced and pretty, and now she's stirring something for us to drink.

Do you remember the Swiss banker I met at the airport when I was seeing Nils off to Sweden in 1968? He invited me to share his taxi back into SF that day, and then he took me to dinner. We've corresponded for a couple of years—lots of postcards from him!— as he's travelled all over the world. He's getting married, so I'm sending tapa cloth to him and his wife-to-be for their wedding present. I got a special price on the tapa because the woman selling recognized me as a Pisi Koa (Peace Corps Volunteer), so now I just have to come up with the $15 to mail it to Hong Kong, where he is now.

Last night on my way home from a party, I felt the urge to run away.

What I want to do is avoid The Group (dissatisfied PCVs) and maintain what I can of my private little world, my island on this island.

"How I love the simple, reserved countrymen, my neighbors, who mind their own business and let me alone...I avoid myself." Thoreau

I wish I could avoid my incompetence.

Love,
Tina

～～～

Dear Dana,

There's a couple up the hill from me who come by occasionally. They tell me a lot about their sex life and she commented recently that I was very good at bringing people out, but that I never disclosed anything personal about myself. I confided in her that I saw her point.

My heroes all are freaks, but handsome ones. I like private people. I don't like this "Hurry up, hurry up and know me" encounter-group stuff, this "Here I am, the real me" business. Mystery and privacy and quiet loves are much more beautiful. Maybe that's why you feel the need to keep so much from Herman, though I guess in my world the Man in My Life would be the beautiful private love rather than the one I was keeping my beautiful private love a secret from. (Remember how Daddy used to say "Never use a preposition to end a sentence with"?)

This year I was applying the "Get off to a slow start" dictum to my job at the Teachers Retraining Center in Nuku'alofa, where I was slowly "assisting" the head tutor P., who felt insulted when I didn't dance with him on my birthday on Molokai. Did I tell you about that? For my birthday the staff treated me to five Mai Tais at a small club in Kaunakakai. I remember your telling me "There's no limit to what you could be drunk," and I think they wanted to see how I would behave. I was doing my best to remain in control of my wits when P. asked me to dance, and I declined. He was furious. He told me he'd spoken in favor of my being sent to Tonga. "I said 'Tina one hundred percent.' But now...." and then he walked away. I was sitting with the Director of Cross Culture Training, and he said, "Be careful. You don't want to cause any Tongan to lose face."

So now I'm working as his humble assistant, but he's criticized my humility and even my slow start! But there's a new Super Vol (that's a Volunteer who's super or outstanding) who must not have heard from the Cross Culture Director. Her name is Sandy, and she must pride herself on her frankness (total lack of tact). Today she told P. that he looked out the window too much and that it was very distracting. When P. left her criticism on the floor and talked about something not related, Sandy said, "No, I think you missed the point." I don't think he missed the point.

The Fasi Teachers Retraining Center is right across the street from Vincent's house, which I can see from where I sit not paying attention to a discussion about the anomalous *have*. I'm between Vincent's house and ZCO, the radio station where Mike Monti , an Italian-Kiwi volunteer from New Zealand, works. Isn't it strange that I like Vincent so much, but we've never kissed, whereas Mike's almost a stranger to me and we have kissed. It's much easier for me to be affectionate when there's no chance of its leading to something terrifying like marriage-too-young.

But I like Mike too. I went to the Yacht Club with him and then to the Government Bachelor Quarters, where he's stayed these two years. He lay on the bed, and I sat on it, and we sang together songs from *Show Boat, Oklahoma, My Fair Lady, West Side Story*...

We hugged each other quite a lot and held hands, but I told him I was too shy to kiss him. I guess I overcame my "shyness," which I think is really just loyalty to the other men I love.

We ate Tongan food palangi style at the home of his Tongan family, whom we told we were getting married. They gave us advice and two pairs of slippers. I really needed some new ones because the ones Line (the priest-to-be) gave me are in terrible condition

Mike begged me to go to a party with him afterwards, but I told him I couldn't possibly and I didn't give in. However, I did kiss him a few more times.

The only one here I have to really fantasize about is the priest in training, the one my Tongan family wanted me to marry. When I protested that he was a priest, Loiloi, the beautiful Sophia Loren Tongan woman who is sort of my big sister, said, "Not yet!" So during this "Not yet" period, we are rising to the occasion...occasionally.

I'm now spending Sundays in the enchanted woods, called the bush, with Likua and her illegitimate son Mongahea, who thinks I love Line. He says it came to him in a dream. "Laupisi," I said. That means nonsense, which my love for the priest-to-be is only at times.

I find a certain serenity in making visual aids. Hemingway fished.

Thoreau gardened. I draw, color, cut out visual aids.

I just dread going to class now that I know P. and I don't get along.

I went to the beach with Kalea (the Tonga equivalent of Clair) and smelled like the sea at the party for Mike Monti, the only one I talked to at the party, when Kalea and her boyfriend stayed outside. Mike was, after all, the host and guest of honor. He refilled my mandarin and Bacardi glass twice and was beautifully attentive.

I drank some magic brew and fantasized going to my Tongan priest and whispering in his ear, "I love you and am always faithful to you."

"And I'm always true to you, darling, in my fashion! Yes, I'm always true to you, darling, in my way!" *Kiss Me Kate*

I'm going to another party tonight—this one for the Minister of Education, Langi, and I'll be going with Mike, who has spoken more than once about the copulating tiger the former "tenant" of my fale had. That was Mosesi, the Peace Corps Volunteer who lived in my fale before I did and the one Lupe, my Tongan sister, says brought women here to rape them. I hope "rape" just means "have sex with."

Mike's home is in Dunedin, where my Tongan priest is.

Be faithful to me and WRITE.

Love,
Tina

Dear Vincent,

I'm in a letter-writing mood, and I've been reading letters Tongan children wrote to the kids I set them up with on Lanai, so let me write to you faka-Tonga:.

How are you? I am fine, thank you. The name of my mother is Nadine, and the name of my father is Elmore. The name of my sisters is Dana, Melissa and Suzy, and the name of my brother is David. The name of my uncles is Tom and Jack. The name of my aunts is Katherine and Mary. The name of my cousins is Tommy, Timmy, Ted, Nancy, Miki, Patsy, John, and Sarah Beth. What is the name of your family?

Last year the Queen came to visit.

I live in a Tongan fale.

'Ofa atu,
Tina

PS You've got to think of new, cute, and imaginative things to do to keep our relationship from growing stagnant and new ways to please me and make yourself desirable. I'm tired of doing all the work, and I've risen to the level of my incompetence. (Remind me to tell you about this.)

<u>April 1971</u>

April 14, 1971

Dear Jim,

Your packet was so wonderful—full of your 8 x 11 and Japanese Warriors, *Love Story* and the NBA. I wish I could have been there to hear your fine falsetto. But I think I c'n remember it. (I'm writing can as "c'n" as part of teacher-training to remind them not to pronounce the vowel because when they do, it sounds like can't. C'n is never stressed.)

Please don't feel defensive about your bitterness. I didn't mean it as a criticism although I'd rather you not be bitter for your own sake. I'm only thinking of you. I'm only thinking of you. (From *Man of La Mancha*)

I take it you liked *Love Story*. Why? Couldn't we do much better than that as both writers and star-crossed lovers?

I'm thinking of getting my ears pierced. That always seemed like a barbaric rite to me, but now it seems like something that would make wearing earrings much less painful, and they have such pretty tortoiseshell earrings here. They have shark teeth, too. *{Author's note: I was unaware...But going back in 2008, there was increased awareness of saving turtles—and not for jewelry! Shark teeth have also, perhaps, gone out of favor.}*

Before I go back to America, I want these things:

A dress made of real tapa
turtle earrings
A tapa bag
tapa cloth for myself
woven mats
Tongan oil
Then of course gifts to give

Now I really must write a set of exercises for the kids in Class VI. Tonight I'll teach *po ako* and maybe take a picture. *po ako (night school from the words po night and ako study)*

Around April 16, 1971

{Andrea, My Best Friend in Peace Corps Tonga, had asked why an attractive man we knew had married a woman who was very plain.}

Dear Andrea,

About why he married a woman so plain. Maybe because she was sweet, kind, and home-centered and would be a faithful wife and a loving mother. Also never underestimate who's "good in bed." You never can tell. Maybe she turns into someone wild and exotic under cover. Here I'll quote: "There are two types of women: Those who want power in the world and those who want power in bed." Jacqueline Kennedy as quoted by Gloria Steinem.

Hope you like the CARE package. Still haven't recorded anything but I plan to next week—will pass it on.

How long do cassette batteries last? I mean how many songs before they die?

This CARE package contains:

1. 3 cassettes—Sgt Peppers, *Hair*, Judy Collins
2. 4 books: *Zelda, Love among the Cannibals, The Golden Notebook, The Peter Principle*
3. 1 Mickey Mouse balloon
4. 2 exotic tea bags Shui Xian
5. 1 copy of *Harper's* featuring Norman Mailer

I have $5.17 to last these two weeks before we get our living allowance. Are you better with money than I am?

{Susan was—and is— a very bright friend from high school days}

Dear Susan,

I really love you, meaning that I respect you, think you're a smart and sensitive person, and feel we have some things in common in spite of all the differences. But you don't pay any attention to my good advice. ("Good advice costs nothing and it's worth the price.")

What I'm really afraid of (please don't resent my saying this) is that you've become comfortable in your unhappiness and don't want to live without it. Just be miserable half the time. Devote at least a few hours a day to joy. So much depends upon self-hypnosis. Either you've got to do what makes you happy or be happy doing what you're doing. You sound martyred to me. If you want to get married, you'd make a very good wife. Didn't you win the Betty Crocker Good Housekeeping Award over all the Home Ec girls? And you're good with kids, etc., etc.

I remember our sexy, romantic ideas in high school, and a girl must never lose her sexy, romantic ideas. Just be careful that you're not acting like a spinster at your age. I don't think anyone wants to marry a spinster or have one to play bridge with.

Now that the Feminist movement is going on, it's been brought to our attention that women shouldn't depend entirely on men for their sense of worth or sense of identity. "Getting married" isn't woman's greatest achievement. Look at the unattractive, dull-witted women who've done it. Studies have also shown that next to the unmarried man, the most dissatisfied person is the married women. Marriage isn't magic. So instead of trying to please a man or find a husband, maybe a woman (You, me, etc) should concentrate on being the person she enjoys being around, respects, and loves.

You always seem to have yourself around (generic you).

My favorite quote (maybe I've already quoted it?) is from a disillusioned socialite and globe-trotter who said, "No matter where I go, I'm always there and spoil everything."

Dear World, who never wrote to me:

Emily Dickinson had funerals in her brain. I have wars there. And the air's polluted by the gunpowder. (No matter how your analogies limp, you can always drag them a little bit farther.)

I am what I can't believe in. I have risen to my level of incompetence.

April 22, 1971

Dear Jim,

I'm at school now—at the TRTC, where the children are saying "skee skay skoo" during a demonstration lesson I'm not teaching . The children are really beautiful. Dark children are so much more appealing than pale ones (with the exception of Irish-American kids many Christmases ago, who weren't too pale after all but quite appealing). Sitting on the floor in their school uniforms they look like ribbons—their skin, white blouses, khaki shorts or red skirts.

April 30

Dear Jim,

Think of this: The more you do without the more you can do without. If you don't have bread, you don't need jam. If you don't have a cassette player, you don't need a cassette recording. Someone sent me a cassette player, Jim. But I'm doing without bread and jam.

May 1971

May 1, 1971

Dear Line,

"Tra la! It's May! The lusty month of May!" (That's from *Camelot*.) I miss you and the way our skins together (as we sit upright together on the tapa cloth) make Neapolitan ice cream. I'm happy, but I'd be happier if we could be together committing secret offenses against no one.

I wish we could snuggle up together on the matted floor and talk about God. I've just finished *Leviticus*. (You can imagine the self-discipline it took to leave *Song of Solomon*.) Your father tells me you're playing lots of soccer. Didn't you say you were tired of it? Is it just that they need you so badly? What sacrifice! But we can't serve you sandwiches during intermission.

You know who likes you? Ed Shore. I had dinner with him and his wife Joan and kids the last night they were here, and he said he didn't think he'd get down to the South Island of New Zealand, but he'd like to see you. He said he knew you very well. He doesn't, does he? Anyway, you made a favorable impression on him.

You made a favorable impression on me too. But isn't there something you want to send me? Something beautiful and holy that I can wear around my neck and pressed between my sweet little breasts?

May 1, 1971

Dear Jim,

Kalala is living with me now. She's a very bright six-year-old who speaks English fluently and listens well to stories I tell her of Sleeping Beauty and other famous American historical figures and who wakes up crying when she has wet the bed and asks to go to the falemalolo. (bathroom if you've forgotten your Tongan). Her grandfather is headmaster at a Catholic primary school for which I write tests, and her uncle is a priest-in-training (as you, sort of, once were) and the captain of the soccer team, which opponents say isn't fair because his team has God on its side.

It's now May 2nd

Kalala was stung by a bumble bee while she was in the bush picking guava for me, and she's now crying with great indignation. How dare it sting her when she was picking guava for *me*? I need to tell her your stories—about Abiyoyo and about my king who is bigger than your king.

Do you know any poems by Elinor Wylie? Ron says you owe HIM a letter. (Ron is doing wonderful things for Tongan soil.)

It's the prince's birthday. Ron came by this morning with cantaloupes marked for his evaluation (3, 4). I get to make this report. Broc is deeply in love with Phyllis, who he says is beautiful in mind, body, and spirit. He spoke of "moon." How's your sister Mary? Your friend and her love Neil? Your mother? American popular music? Would you care to discuss China? What about your teaching? How are YOU, Jim? I am fine, thank you,

Love,
Tina

May 6, 1971

Dear Dana,

Oh, why don't you write? Why? I've written Mother about you, and she's said nothing. Neither has Daddy. All I could get out of Suzy was that she and her friends have a mutual respect and you couldn't see it. I've asked Jim to call you, but I think he's afraid after the way you responded to his first call. ("I don't know you!") Sometimes I think you're dead and they're sparing me. And you? Are you sparing me too? Why don't you write? I have so much to tell you. And you have so much to tell me. I dreamt that you'd dyed your hair a fluorescent yellow. I thought, "Now I'll have to take over." I am getting uglier but less neurotic.

Please write. I'll tell you about everyone I love and where and how.

Don't worry. I am still neurotic. Just less or in a different way.

WRITE

Ah, my fellow teacher Naomi was so sweet and just came by to talk—about whether she could have my iron and my stove when I leave Tonga in seven months. I said no because someone else asked first.

Love,
Tina

Dear Jim,

I just got back from the Way In Motel where Ron took me to talk to Mike (Wimberly) about the surprise birthday party we're having for Ron on Friday. It's a picnic at some beach and Elmer Skold and other DC VIPS are going to come in with the tides and shout "Surprise!" Anyway, I discussed the plans with Mike with only occasional and monosyllabic interruptions from Ron. Then, while Ron stood, Mike and I sat at the piano and sang our favorite Schmaltz and then Mike played his birth control song (to be broadcast over ZCO eventually to promote Family Planning) as well as Debussy, Chopin, Beethoven, and Bach. Ron brought me home on his motorbike, and I was handed your letter. I am responding promptly.

There is no storm except in my forever-disturbed mind. I feel as if I'm undergoing psychotherapy though and that I am getting better. "Good, petter, pest," write my sixth graders.

Why didn't you visit my family when you were in CA? And did you call Dana?

Yes, someday I'd like to go to the Grand Canyon and all over America with you, showing you places my family camped out when we were vagabonds—gypsies with our 10c pots and pans, sharpening scissors while Daddy restored minds. Yes! Yes! Where we picked spuds when we were poor Mexican white trash. Yes! Yes! I'm listening to Brahms and I'm on Deuteronomy now.

Yes, I often say "Death!" when I think of Shakespeare class or a play I was in or anything else really humiliating. Yes, mosquitoes sometimes but not always. Did people use to follow me?

Carla Child came home from the PC office with me. She's an anthropology major from Radcliff and she speaks an obscure Indian dialect she learned in Mexico. Yes, I am sometimes nervous or scared. My dreams are too numerous and too long to tell. If they were made into a movie, it would be longer than the Russian version of *War and Peace* (Last week I dreamt of the Russian actress who played Natasha) and would have to be dubbed when distributed.

Many strong desires, but we mustn't talk about it.

Love,
Tina

~~~

May 14, 1971

Dear Jim,

Last night we had a picnic for Ron at Larry Pierce's house (changed plans) and after no more than 6 inches of cheap wine, I was thoroughly and blissfully drunk. Jim, I find that I love a lot of people—not promiscuously but affectionately. I find I want to hug a lot of people. Last night I wanted to hug Ron, I wanted to hug Mike, and I wanted to hold Larry's hand. I hugged Ron, I hugged Mike, and I held Larry's hand. (My mother has met Mrs. Pierce, who lends her Mormon documents and *The National Geographic Magazine*. My mother refers to Mrs. Pierce as "Rat Control's mother.") And as I sat there with them, I really loved them and I loved you and wished you were there too because I wanted to hug you and do other things. I wonder what it is that makes me want to go around hugging people. I wasn't unhappy or frightened, and I'm not now. I thought of a letter your Mary once wrote about how she loved Neil and Gary, etc. I feel like Mary. Please tell me more about her so I can understand myself better.

Oh, I wish you were here. But I'll see you in a few months.

Please call Dana!

Love,
Tina

Sione Kite, the Secretary to the Prime Minister, asked me out to the picture show next Tuesday.

Also Elmer Skold, our PC director, has "nominated" me to be in a fashion show at the Dateline Hotel. At first I wanted OUT, but now I think it might be a good thing—just to give my life some variety.

Love,
Tina

~~~

May 17, 1971

Dear Jim,

There are some things we must discuss. Have you read Lawrence Durrell's *Justine*? If you haven't, let's read it together. I love it!!!

But this is what we have to discuss: Ireland. When I get back to America, I'll stay with my California family for a couple of months, probably, and then I'll come to Chicago to see you and Dana. Then I'll go to Europe. I'm going to London where I plan (the best-laid plans of mice and men) to stay at a flat that belongs to an Englishman I've met here in Tonga. I may stay in London a month. Then, when June comes and you're out of school, would you like to meet me in Ireland? We could visit your friend and travel together as we'd once planned. (The best-laid plans...)

to be continued...

Even today I love Vincent. (I love the others too.) But our relationship was fraught with problems, and now I realize that he was almost certainly gay, but I didn't understand that. I just felt insulted that the desire he professed to have for me wasn't real, so I felt insulted. I behaved badly—pushing him away for not really wanted to be close and then wanting to be close to him again. I was very tedious. Sorry, Vincent.

Dear Dana,

It's Sunday morning May 16, and I'm thinking about last night when I "let" Vincent kiss me for the first time. We all have our methods and responses, I guess, but I didn't like his. Lately, when he's touched me, I've felt a delicious sensation, but last night when he kissed me, I felt like a well-brought-up Victorian waiting to get it over.

It happened, as I felt it would, when he was brushing my hair and leaned over and kissed me on my neck through my hair. When I didn't yell "Rape!" at that, he waited a few seconds and came back to stay longer. I sat there very still and then he moved my face to kiss it, and I put my sweet big hand over his arms, which were around me, and then he began gnawing at me, the way some people do. I wouldn't have thought of Vincent as a gnawer. There was something wrong with it all—as if Vincent's movements were greater than his desire, but he hated to lose this opportunity. I really didn't like it. When he whispered, his voice became higher (and more cockney if only in my imagination) and sounded almost like a woman's although it's usually not. I think higher is less affected than the seductive lowering an octave, but I didn't like it. This is what his new voice said, "I've wanted to do this for so long." Mind you, we were just necking. We were still fully clothed.

I don't remember anything else. I kept my eyes closed as if I were asleep until the water boiled and I gave him a little cupful of coffee.

He thinks he understands me because I told him lots of interesting things about Daddy. I was so silly last night with Reichlech (spelling?)

wine and Vermouth, soda water and bitters. I got cold and he wrapped me up in a beautiful blanket one of his sisters sent him from America, where I guess she moved from England.

He had given me some poems to read—the usual rather good, very autobiographical (and perhaps highly romanticized) poems. One had "J" in it, but I don't think Vincent knows about the *Sensuous Woman*. I asked him about her and "Who did you love most? Who gives you the most pain looking back upon?' Things like that—silly, nosy.

He talked while I listened and slept and didn't interrupt as much as I usually do. Then he said he'd talked a lot about himself, wouldn't I tell him a little bit about me? And I thought for a minute, I really did, and then I said, "No."

That was wise, I think.

It's funny, but I can take a line from Vincent's "new" (recently given me) poems to describe him:

...kisses digging deep

In the semblance of satisfaction.

It's now May 21, 1971! I've got to mail this letter!

A note to Vincent May, 1971

How dare you be angry with me?! It was you who made the drinks. I'm angry with you if you're angry with me, and I have reason to be because you're angry with me for no good reason, whereas I'm angry with you for being angry with me for no good reason, and that's a reasonable reason to be angry.

Question   1. Are you angry with me?
               2. Why?

You may answer these questions on paper or, preferably, in person, when you come for coffee someday (soon, hopefully, tho' of course I realize you can't "commit" yourself, to use your own word and the one we Americans use to enter mental institutions and to stay in Southeast Asia.)

In spite of your unprovoked bad temper and cool manifestations of unelicited hostility, I miss you when I don't see you often.

May 22, 1971

Dear Vincent,

Would you like to come for coffee on Saturday morning after—or be-fore—you do what you must do at the hospital?

I could try to make you French toast and I promise not to make you read scriptures unless you really have your heart set on it, in which case I wouldn't be making you, would I? I'd be letting you!

Love,
Tina

Dear Ron,

The butter is beautiful and it's a wonderful world with favorite people riding up on motorbikes to deliver such things. Thank you!

Andrea told me Friday night that she'd gotten your letter, and it was really funny. "I don't want to paraphrase it for you," she said, "because something of the prose quality would be lost." But she appreciated it very much, and so did I because I can imagine.

Ron, would you like to have dinner at my house on Saturday before we go to the movies? It would be something simple with an incompetent cook standing over a one-burner kerosene stove, but I'd do my best.

Maybe we could have a sunset-indoor-picnic. If you'd like, so would I, 'cause I've never had you to dinner.

Love,
Tina

One of the people I corresponded with in Tonga was a Swiss banker I'd met at the airport when seeing off my boyfriend, who was going home to Sweden for the summer. I had sent him and his new bride Susan tapa cloth as a wedding present, but I hadn't heard from him.

May 23, 1971

Dear Joe,

I'm worried 'cause I don't think you've gotten my package. I sent it to Susan's address that you gave me, and I sent it by air on April 20. (I think it was put on the plane April 22.) Obviously, she should have gotten it by now

It was kind of a big box, covered with lots of stamps for your collection. Inside was some tapa cloth—the specialty of the South Pacific and very detailed work. It depresses me to think you haven't gotten it But I'll try to send you some more at a later date. This I'll probably have to send by boat, and I'll send it to one of the appropriate addresses you gave me in your recent letter.

Please let me know 'cause I don't want to weigh you down with tapa. I know people make an effort to travel light.

Love,
Tina

Sometimes I wrote notes that I didn't plan to send.

Dear Vincent,

I love you and want to be lovely for you.

Dear Ron,

I love you. How could I not?

Dear Jim.

I love you although I could not.

Dear Sione Kite,

You interest me because you're a friendly, enthusiastic snob.

Dear Mike Wimberly,

I like you very much in spite of what a disappointment I am to you.

Dear Line,

You are my most sensuous synthetic friend.

Dear Joe,

You represent the world I want—beautiful traveling but secure and conservative and kind. Lots of lovely things that money buys but none of the despair we poor people try to see the rich as having.

Dear Scotts Fitzgerald,

I've been reading *Zelda*. Yours is not the world I want.

Dear Vincent,

This is just a little insignificant note to say hello.

Hello.

I'd like to add that I can hardly bear the exhaustion I feel when I think of the exhaustion you feel working too hard. I feel guilty about having diluted your scotch simply to empty the bottle of soda water. You deserve so much better than that. But—Hello again,

Love,
Tina

May 25, 1971 from my village

Dear Me,

Here I am again, all bathed and in my Jane Austen dress and sitting against the back door beside my cup of hot lemonade. My front door is open and blowing in a cool light wind. I've got to get over this spoiled mood I'm in that makes me bored with boring things like lesson preparation and makes me want to sit (or lie) by myself and read. I felt so much more interest in my work before I found out that it wasn't going well. Now it's as if I have a self-fulfilled prophesy on my hands.

from the Fasi Teachers Re-training Center

I'm at school now and trying to get rid of the apprehension of mine. Why can't I relax? I think maybe I can. I must put "attitude" before "results." What happens is less important than how.

But the classes I teach are too large. It's dishonest of me to keep this to myself. I should ask the teachers to help me so the kid'll learn something. As it is, I get it over with.

Today I went to the Dateline Hotel with Elmer Skold to meet Mrs. Bateman, the wife of the cook and the one who's planning the fashion show. She said it was "Super" that I was interested, but her facial expression was more like "Oh, dear." I looked awful. I was dressed in a dowdy brown outfit that makes me look like the well-protected female duck and my hair was blah and my face was pale. But I think a bad first impression is very important to a relationship that will continue for two weeks. Her husband the cook, whom I've met under better circumstances (when I was on a date and looking pretty) said, "This is good luck. This is the girl you've spoken about before and said you thought she'd make a good model."

"Really?" said Mrs. Bateman with a tact that would continue.

I could tell almost immediately that she planned to intimidate me—to make me feel guilty or foolish if I refused to wear what she wanted me to wear (a bathing suit, a bikini, a negligee, and hot pants) and whenever I agreed to something, she reacted with an attitude that said, "Now, that's a good girl."

{My father, taking my sister Suzy on a trip to the USSR, had offered my mother, his ex, a trip to Israel, which she had turned down. I also mention Gloria Tate, the author of The Tate Syllabus, a method of teaching Oral English used in the South Pacific for about twenty years, between 1968 and the mid-1980's when it fell out of favor, as far as I can tell. If anyone knows anything about Gloria Tate, I think she deserves recognition for what she accomplished even if it did fall out of favor. At the time I wrote this letter, I thought we'd have a late-December departure from Tonga .}

Dear Mother,

Thank you very much for the summary-in-verse of all literature. *Shrinklit*'s good to catch up on the great pieces without having to lose time turning pages—just the essence of the books in verse I can commit to memory.

May I have your trip to Israel?

Your letter was great—"informative" and interesting. Yours is a valid expression of human existence.

I'll be home by Christmas at the earliest. I'm really looking forward to it, but I'm using a lot of restraint and not talking about it ahead of time. I still have several months to concentrate on. I'll say this, tho'. I'm going to talk to you for a couple of months, then go to Europe because I've become, by nature, a vagabond and will have to spend my life wandering.

Gloria Tate, who wrote the Tate Oral English Series used for the elementary grades throughout the South Pacific, is here now, and I met her. She's nice! She smokes, looks a little bit world-weary, and has a good sense of humor—self-deprecating.

At noon I went to the post office with Andrea and got a package by surprise—the type-writer from Jim! I'll write him a type-written thank you note!

I borrowed a *Ladies Home Journal* from Andrea, and it has Sophia Loren on the cover and inside. It turns out that she uses surgeon's tape to lift the skin above her eyes and to her ears. I'm really sorry to hear that. Bones, she says, are the things, and that's what I have an awful lot of. They rattle when I walk. But she meant the bone structure in the face—enhanced by surgeon tape.

What I want is only two of everything. It's absurd to have twelve bras. Wear one, wash one and don't leave stuff hanging in the mildew. I hate clutter, and I believe it's more than the fascist pig in me.

Vincent left me a nice note today—full of hearts and arrows and talk of pâté, golden, hot appetizing toast and biscuits and tea. It was beautiful and circular with a little jar of something to spin it around under.

We discussed pornography.

I told him what Dana said: That she was trying to convince Herman that Andy Warhol 's films were innovative and artistic. When I said,

"Yes, they really are, they say," Dana said "Well, they really aren't. They're dirty, is what they are." I told Vincent what you said, that you wouldn't mind seeing dirty films if there were no one there to see you seeing them. He seemed to think that was funny.

Love,
Tina

May 28, 1971

Dear Jim,

It's beautiful, this orange machine that's in my hands at last. I'll type you a letter just as soon as I get a ribbon.

I remember when you used to sit in the fale kai (dining room if you've forgotten your Tongan) and type long letters leaving me out and journal entries putting me in —but not importantly. I admired you and I admired your typewriter. Thank you, Jim. I'll bring it to you in early '72 when I stop in Chicago on my way to Spain. You must meet me in Ireland.

I continue to read the Bible, but some of the verses you gave me (ex: Solomon) aren't in my Bible. I'm on Ezekiel, prophet in exile, and I have my very own Billy Graham Bible dictionary designed for people who want a better understanding of the Word of God.

Remember Trickster theology? There's an infinite number of possibilities. Have you read *God Is an Englishman*? Is it any Good?

Gloria Tate is here now—a friendly, pleasant woman with a face full of wrinkles that smooth out when she laughs, which she often does.

I find I'm trying to get my kids to make mistakes because they make such cute anecdotes.

Dana doesn't write, but she sent me *Harper*'s "An American Innocent in the Middle East." Please try to call her again. Her husband's name is Herman Langner.

Much love to all of you.

To Mike Monti, May 28, 1971

Dear Mike,

I'm at Po ako now and have given the kids a nasty test so I can write to you. How's the lovely land of sheep and motion picture theatres? I'd love to have your job in the music library and to be in the chorus of *Brigadoon* —that sounds awfully good too. What d'ya mean, it doesn't have much of a plot? It's practically existential. What choice would you have made, had you been the hiker? Better to stay in Brigadoon and disappear for a hundred years than live without all that heather on the hill. I think that I believe in Brigadoon.

Do you have access to a cassette recorder? If you do, I'll send you a few blank cassettes and you can let them pick up whatever you like in the music library. And also I'd like to have "Old Man River" with the bath-tub drain effects. If you have a cassette player, I'll talk to you and bring you the sound of Tonga. If you don't have a cassette player, I'll have my children draw you pictures.

Last night I dreamt that I took a secret trip to Argentina, which was just over the border from Tonga. Even my subconscious knows better geography than that, and I mentioned Chile and Peru. But everyone assured me that I didn't know what I was talking about—that it was right over the Dateline from Tonga. It was snowing, Mike, and I put on a brown- knitted cap. I was making my getaway first in a canoe and then in a truck parked in the depths of the forest. What I dream affects my mood the next day, and this is the next day.

Tell me what you miss most about Tonga so I can pay close attention to it while I'm here. Are you doing any refereeing? I've heard that Father (to-be) Line is playing soccer once again, though he swore he was tired of it

Thanks for the pictures. You look good, I think, but I look hard-working and underfed. Now you have 3 bad pictures of me.

That was a nice letter to the *Chronicle* about you. Who do you think wrote it?

I'm sorry you still haven't gotten your farewell gift from Langi. He's been working hard—both with education and rugby—and he's now down with the flu.

Well, see lots of good films and plays and tell me about them so I can live vicariously. Say hello to Pete and the others for me.

'Ofa atu,
Tina

~~

Can you guess who Dulcissime is?

May 28, 1971

Dulcissime,

I must really need you in my life—not necessarily here tho' that would be nice) but somewhere and in touch. Because I've been happy enough and enthusiastic here with people I love who are kind to me, etc. But I've felt sort of depressed lately for no reason I could understand, and then your letter came.

You write beautiful letters. Funny beautiful letters. When I see your family, I look for you in their faces, but you're not completely there. Your mother's beautiful. (I didn't notice that at first) and there's a definite resemblance. F.'s attractive, and the soccer-playing one looks somewhat like you, but something of you isn't in their faces. You with your sad, dark eyes—cozy, warm you with your arrogant, hurt voice and your easy smile at just about everything. What a funny man you are. Magic, I think as if you were some perfect, plastic giant balloon to blow up into a perfect, life-like man. What are balloons made of? I like it, whatever it is. Oh, I love you, it's true, but I don't intend to suffer for it.

How well I remember the joy I felt at being drunk near you. All the drinks I'd had aboard the ship gave me an excuse for doing all the lovely foolish things I'd always wanted to do with you. You know for so long after that every time I had a drink, I'd feel such desire for you—as if my inebriated state belonged only to you. I haven't had any wine tonight, but I feel the longing returning.

to be continued...

{I liked Jim to talk about his family—his sisters Jean, Mary, and Kathleen— and his friend Neil. At this point he was sending me their pictures.}

Dear Jim,

I loved your letter, wonderful as it was, and full of pictures. I too love pictures. Mary and Neil look so different. And you!!! ... That's how I like you best—with your curly hair uncombed and a poetic mustache. There's a greatness, a soul, in your profile, I think. Kathleen looks pretty too.

A mixture of mad artist as epileptic linguistic professor—more psychotic than neurotic and only slightly stupid around the mouth. Remember when I washed your hair for you? Better still, remember when I dried your feet with my hair near some waterfall in Hawaii? We have a history, you and I together.

Are you going to meet me in Ireland?

to be continued...

May 31, 1971 for June 6, 1971

Dear Daddy, Happy birthday June 6th! I really don't know which year you were born, so I don't know how old you are, but as the Little Prince would say it's not the numbers that matter.

{Drawing of an elephant within a boa constrictor, a sheep within a box}

I remember way back in Blackfoot when you used to read us that. Most of the people I know who love the book didn't discover it till they were in college. I read another book by Saint-Exupéry, *Night Flight*, but it's just not the same!

It looks as if I haven't risen to my maximum level of incompetence after all—tho there's still time. I'm kind of enjoying working with the teachers and I've resigned myself to being responsible although it'd been my wish to walk around blissfully lobotomized. I still have time to myself, and I date a lot—another PCV, a hospital administrator from Great Britain (Are they the bad guys?) and, occasionally the Prime Minister's First Secretary.

You've asked about money, but I really don't need any now. What I would like, tho', is your specialty. I'd like a whole lot of pamphlets from SANE—things that document because people are suspicious of propaganda. If there are a few you could send me airmail, I'd appreciate that and memorize them all. Then, if you could send a box by surface mail, I could (in 3 months) distribute its material to the Peace Corps office so people could get hold of it.

Also, anything you think it worth my while to read. Right now I'm reading the Bible (as a lit major rather than as a religious fanatic). I've read all the New testament and Genesis through Isaiah. I'm now on Jeremiah. I'm also reading a series of articles on the Middle East in *Harper's*.

Did I tell you Mike Michaelski, from Columbia, South Carolina, sent me a cassette player/recorder? So now I can listen to Broadway's Best, Brahms, Mozart, Joan Baez, Simon and Garfunkel, etc. etc. right here in my fale. (two syllables—FAH-lay—hut). I don't have electricity of course, but it runs on batteries.

How's your August trip coming along? Still coming? It sounds great, and I think Suzy's really lucky. If Mother doesn't want the trip you've offered to Israel, I'll take it. I'll go to a kibbutz in Israel and pick grapes just like Justine (in a book by Lawrence Durrell).

Yesterday was such a lovely day, and so was I—happy, alert, interested, and patient with all the kids who came to visit. I told stories in English and in Tongan, sang with them, and answered their questions—the perfect mother.

June 1971

{Line and I had a running joke about cappuccino, and I think it was because when he first said he liked cappuccino, I asked, "Who's Cappucchino?"}

June 1, 1971

Dear Me,

The day's just begun (I've been in it or it in me for two hours), but I like it so far—even though I always wake up with a little bit of fear.

I'll go to Fasi early and plan things with Vaoke, another teacher-trainer. {I don't say or remember what happened to P.} When things are well-organized, I feel tranquilized. I'm too much bothered by my sloppiness to benefit from a laissez-faire approach.

{At this time, Kalala, Line's adorable 6-year-old niece, would sometimes stay with me in my hut.}

Dear Line,

How can I send you a picture—you who have no appreciation of my exceptional beauty? My pictures are worse than reality.

But someday I'll send a picture of cappuccino.

I'm worried about Kalala. I think I hurt her feelings, and she moved out! One day when she came with her school uniform and books, I told her I had to go somewhere that evening, and she said, "Oh, dear," and that was the last I saw of her.

Right now I'm wondering what contribution I'm making to your becoming a great priest instead of a greater degenerate. But I'll bear your cross—all of them.

How can I see you again, Line? When you're a newly-returned priest, secret rendezvous will be impossible.

Even now, when I'm deliriously happy and everything in my life seems to be going well, I think of you with such affection—so I know you're not just escape for me—escape from reality and practicality. Everything about our relationship is unrealistic and impractical and doomed. But the funny love I feel for you is real, and I sort of enjoy the meaninglessness of it all. Besides, anything that's beautiful and fun and a culture-exchange has its own meaning and is a valid expression of human existence. Yes, Tina, there is a Line. You are my favorite priest-to-be.

June 4, 1971

Dear Suzy,

This is Tonga's Independence Day, when Vincent's hospital opens.

Last night I finished Jeremiah and I've decided that before I go on to Lamentation, I'll learn what I've already read because I haven't been reading for history—just for nouns and images, and I can't tell Hezekiah from Zechariah. (Hezekiah was good and wise; Zechariah was bad and foolish—but I had to look again!)

Last night Ron came by with everything I need: a beautiful new flashlight, a pound of butter, and a fork. Ron's really thoughtful and remembers things like my eating with a teaspoon and having no butter for the buns he brought.

Right now I'm waiting for the bus to go to town to re-mail Daddy's birthday letter—this time with a stamp—and to see my hot pants and skirt for the fashion show a week from today. I suspect that the buses will be packed for a while 'cause people are going to watch the opening of the new hospital. Maybe Mrs. Bateman, the wife of the Australian cook at the Dateline and the woman who's producing the fashion show, forgot about that when she asked me to come in today. If so, I'll return home quickly, shave my legs, and read until Vincent comes at about 2:00. Then we'll go to his house, where we'll read, I hope, and eat leftovers from today's celebration. Chocolate éclairs are what I'm hoping for.

The most beautiful thing in Tonga is late afternoon just before sunset when there's mist of smoke blurring everything just a little bit and all the colors are shades of browns and greens except for little dabs of red, orange, blue, white from the clothesline. As I guess you know, I have a thing for clotheslines, if not for doing wash.

Here's my plan: I'll finish here in December—maybe in time to be home for Christmas. I'll talk with you all for a couple of months until everything I say becomes a re-run. Then I'll buy a one-way ticket to Europe. I'll spend most of my time in England. Vincent says I'm welcome to stay with him for as long as I like. Jutta, my German pen-pal from 1963, is teaching German in Paris, so I could maybe find a place to stay through her. I can visit Laurence Durrell's Alexandria and Marshall Friday's Southern Baptist Biblical Israel.

I'm reading the Old Testament now and have gotten to Ezekiel, the one right after Jeremiah. Anytime I have gentlemen callers, I read it out loud, and I have learned quite a lot about God as He was back then.

I'm also about through with a series of articles in *Harper's* called "An American Innocent in the Middle East." Very good!

When Dana calls next, please ask her how come she never writes to me. Tell her if she doesn't write, she should call me once a month and talk and talk and talk. (The thing is there's no telephone.)

I'm really excited about seeing you all again although I've had dreams in which I've met you at Safeway, and you go on with your shopping as if my reappearance on the scene were no great thing. God, just about 6 more months. Oh, it's gonna be great to get home although I'm happy enough here. Two years is enough happiness. I'll treat you all to some Winchell's donuts. One thing though— I think I want always to travel. I only regret that there's so much ocean between countries. I can't see myself getting married for quite a while, and I've almost dismissed Dana's and my Latin teacher Miss McDearmon's and Robert Herrick's "Gather ye rosebuds while ye may." I think I'd like to get married someday, but not when my bargaining power's the greatest.

Jim sent me an orange typewriter, which I'll start using as soon as I get a ribbon. That'll be a strange feeling. Mike Monti sent me *South Pacific* for my cassette player, which another Mike—one from Columbia, S.C.—sent me.

Someone I like a lot but as a brother has said several things about marriage—reminding me of my advancing age, telling me of the benefits he'd get from his military insurance if he were married. etc.

Sometimes I think it's not just the prospect of marriage that frightens me but the idea of being married to only one person. I think a certain amount of continuity is desirable, and I want marriage for that. But more than one continuity, more than one man. "There's safety in numbers! That's what I believe." (*The Boy Friend*)

Thanks for answering so many of my questions!

Say hello to Mother, Kathy, and Finney.

Love,
Tina

Saturday, June 12, 1971

Dear Dana,

Before I read *Ezekiel* or *The Grass Harp*, a word about yesterday's fashion show. Before catching the bus to Nuku'alofa, I got a beautiful funny letter from Ron, who had also left me eggs, and I took it along to the "Fashion Show" to try to keep me in a good mood. It was kinda hard because when I got to the Dateline Hotel, the hairdresser was extremely rude, even tho' I was friendly and polite. When I made a suggestion about how my hair could be done, she sighed with disgust and said, "Look, we haven't got all night." My suggestion was extremely simple: I wanted something different because the way I always wore my hair made me look too much like a Peace Corps Volunteer.

"But that's what you are. Are you ashamed?" she asked.

I had spoken with levity, but she would not be levitated.

She was working beyond her usual hours, and it turned out that she and the other staff members at the hotel hadn't been told anything about it till the morning of the fashion show. I sympathized with her and said, "You should have been asked in advance and not made to work from 8:30 till now. That's a very long day."

She readily agreed. It was then that I sensed all her rudeness was resentment at being treated so badly by those in command.

I asked, "Are you being paid overtime?"

"Not on your life!" she said.

"Then you're just helping out to be nice?"

"I'm helping out because I work for the hotel."

I explained to her that I'd been working all day and hadn't waited until six o'clock just to ruin her evening by keeping her here. She seemed to respond well to this "news." Maybe she'd thought that I'd come late just to show my self-importance?

...By the time I left to be in the fashion show, she was being so friendly, telling me how beautiful I looked and stuff and stuff. She helped us dress and loved to give us advice.

I felt strangely relaxed—no more nervous than I feel when entering a room of strangers. I didn't model "properly," and I cut corners when I thought the audience had had enough. My hair did NOT look beautiful, but I felt attractive enough.

Andrea told me that Elmer Skold kept telling them, "I'm so proud of Tina! I'm so proud of Tina."

Yeah, it was a great thing I did for the Peace Corps, for Tonga, and for Los Angeles.

(Mr. Riechelmann introduced me as Tina all the way from Ha'ateiho—originally from Los Angeles, California." I whispered "San Francisco" to him, but no one ever listens to a mannequin.)

I saw Gloria Tate and tried to catch her eye so I could say, "I'm walking! I'm walking." acting out the present progressive tense as she has teachers do in the oral English lessons.

Elmer bought me and all the guys around me a drink of our choice, and I had a delicious Brandy Alexander.

I've been thinking of a new image—one to go with the underground personality I have.

Now for Ezekiel.

Love,
Tina

PS I'm all bathed and dressed and wanting to go out with Ron, but he told me his motor bike had been acting up, and if he didn't come for me, that was why. If he doesn't come, I'll just lie here and read *Balthazar*.

{For my whereabouts on Sunday I sometimes wrote Vaikeli, and sometimes Tokomololo, so I looked up both online and found a court case indicating that Tokomololo was and is a township, and Vaikeli is either a place within that township or a place nearby. The court case concerned the theft of five cartons of canned corned beef among other things.}

Sunday, June 13, 1971 from Vaikeli

Ron and I did go out, and it was very pleasant. We ate at the Beach House, where we met a very young American couple I found lovely because of their gentleness and naturalness. They've been traveling around the world since September and, like us, they've been reading a lot. We listed our books, and tomorrow I'm taking them by some.

When I asked Ron why he didn't take part in the conversation, he said, "I take you to the Beach House so other people can talk to you. If they try to draw me into the conversation, they've defeated the whole purpose."

Tuesday morning, June 15, 1971

I regret my thoughtlessness. Until this morning, I didn't even think of having a tea for Miss Tate or putting fresh flowers on her table or getting her a real ashtray. She's been using a Sun Bell Tuna Flakes can every day, and I 've been emptying it, and that's all. I just picked some weeds for her, and I think they're beautiful—white and lavender, red and yellow—and there's even an orange rose.

Dear Vincent,

Oh, that I had Clea's iron hand to paint and draw and make great art. But I can't draw pictures for you as you do for me. Just the same, I'm feeding your cat and being altogether terribly responsible and careful as if to prove I'm good for something. How pretentious I am.

I had a beautiful afternoon at your house listening to Rimsky-Korsakov-Scheherazade and finishing *Clea* (Once upon a time...) and making an elaborate chart for Sandy {another teacher trainer}and the TRTC (full of dates and numbers, lessons) and eating chilled asparagus spears while the cat ate mutton.

I've just begun a wonderful new (to me) book, *Giles Goat-Boy*. It's really funny at least to my warped sense of humor.

{To Mike Wimberly, a Peace Corps Volunteer on Ha'apai, who had written and recorded a song for Family Planning}

Dear Mike,

We on Tongatapu continue to follow your career and I am secretly waiting for the State Department to make its move.

I've also been waiting to send you these tapes. The Philips store was out of invoice slips, and that delayed it a month. Now I find even with alcohol on applicators, I can't remove the static from my recorder. So I'm sending you Simon and Garfunkel, Barbra Streisand, and *South Pacific* without Chopin and static. I'm sorry.

Maybe in a week or so I'll be able to send you some more music, which you can listen to, erase, and record over. I'd still like so much to have a tape of you and your songs before I have to pay $4.00 for the LP.

Are you sane these days? I've gotten past the point where I can judge myself. I feel mindlessly happy though—making substitution tables with purple textas (felt-tip pens), reading (I just finished the Alexandria Quartet, which I loved—*Justine, Balthazar, Mount Olive, Clea* and I have begun *Giles the Goat Boy).*

I don't even think about how much time we have left. (5 months, 14 days) but when the time comes, I think I'll be happy to return home and reflect upon Tonga. Maybe I'm judging prematurely, but I think all and all it's been a positive experience. What is sanity, when sacrificed for a positive experience prematurely judged?

Is there any chance that you'll be sailing down here in August? I'd really like to see you, and so would my neighbors. One day I was listening to *Funny Girl* and your choir came on where it had been recorded on the same side as *Funny Girl*. Havea (my mysterious noble, who hides away in his house playing cards) was suddenly at my door. He said he'd heard you at the conference and liked your "clever singing." He stayed for it all. I told him I'd play it again, but I'd have to play *Funny Girl* first (because I can't rewind), and he walked away. Pesi and Loiloi, though, stayed and patiently sat through Barbra Streisand so they could hear you. It's clear you're in demand.

Love,
Tina

June 23, 1971

Dear Dana,

I think I mentioned the fashion show to you! They had a spread on it in the Tonga Chronicle on June 17, calling it "Fashion 'First' for Tonga." Vainga, the wonderful young teacher I have a crush on (but do nothing about because he's married), asked me why my picture wasn't among the four they had. I said with mock indignation, "Maybe they didn't like me. You can't imagine what a blow this is to an egomaniac like me, but maybe my picture will make it into the *New York Times* when they report on our fashion show. on the front page of their Week-in review."

Then today Mele, the only other "model" not pictured besides me, hailed me from across the street at Morris Hedstrom's (Nuku'alofa's general store) and said, "Tina! What happened? Why didn't they put our pictures in the paper? That Jack Reichelman put two of Anau because she's his wife's sister, and I know his ways. I didn't feel sorry for myself, but I felt sorry for you because you don't know his ways. Everyone asked me why they didn't put our pictures in the paper. And you didn't even want to join us. We waited for two weeks for you to come. And I told my mother, it's all right. they didn't put my picture in, but they're not going to bury me alive."

"Right!' I said, patting her on the shoulder.

She suggested that I come for coffee at her house someday. She also told me she'd waited to say anything because she thought the Peace Corps would do something about it.

July 1971

July 1, 1971

Dear Line,

I love the cross and the apprentice priest who sent it. (Did you bless it?) Your letters are sometimes mystifying, as was especially your last one.

Right now K's here. I've given him tea and handed him a magazine to read. I once mistook him for you, and he still remembers. Until tonight I thought he was one of your brothers. He looks like a cruder you. He's not as handsome, well-educated, etc. etc, but he has something of your family in him. I used to wonder why everyone else in your family had front teeth except this brother.

How much I love the cross and the picture with you dancing a go-go—and letters—especially the most recent one, which you must have written when drunk. Keep drinking. It's obviously food for your soul. It makes you 75% sensitive.

I thought, "Oh, if drinking makes him gentle and romantic and sensitive, let him drink." But Line, last night Loiloi told me she'd got a letter from you and so had Saia and you'd said in both letters that you suspected you'd failed your exams because of your drinking too much. Why, Line? I'd thought that the drinking was to supplement your priestly life, not replace it. If you have failed, what then? I'm frightened for you because I feel you've planned to become a priest for so long, and I don't know whether you'd be happy in an alternative life. I really love you, and I have this nightmarish picture of you returning bitter and wild and aimless. You hate teaching, and what a waste for you to work on a taro patch. What are you going to do?

Lupe speculates that you've fallen in love with Pua, with whom you've spent a lot of time. I think Pua's pretty and athletic and good at the high jump. But could you and she live happily ever after on the soccer field?

To Ron in Fiji from Tina in Tonga

July 1, 1971

Dear Ron,

The interview with the fashion duck deserves to be made into an LP album with all my beauty (bill, webbed feet) on the cover with a long discussion on back.

I miss you of course, but at least I know you're not here to not come around when I'm at home, so it's less hurtful…although you had been doing better lately.

Tell me about Fiji—the Chinese food, the soil, my sleeping bag, the Indian women as bony as me but wrapped in saris with Indian sandals on their webbed feet. (They've changed a lot since Christopher Columbus discovered them accidentally in his search for a shorter route to the new world—but they weren't in Fiji then.) Do you eat curried chicken and read American magazines and see British films like "Dracula Has Risen from the Grave" and "Cul de Sac," the movies Andrea and I saw in New Zealand back in January?

There are donuts and drug stores and supermarkets in Suva! Enjoy, enjoy.

This week I'm working on being a nice person—being sociable, I mean. I've accepted two invitations for the same night: a campout with the Bazettes, Andrea, Roger, and George and dinner at the Dateline with the Glomsets' parents, the Glomsets, Vici and Fred, Larry and Leslie. I think they were counting on my not accepting because notice how everything is paired—or was until I accepted.

Here's a great idea: Send Pauline a postcard. Oh, please do, Ron. She was begging you to deny your smirk in the 'Ofa atu that day—to tell her that you didn't feel contempt and great antagonism toward her. And you refused to reassure her. You just re-affirmed by smirking. Pauline's a basically good woman who deserves your postcard, Ron. Don't be cruel. Write! Send her a magazine or a cup of soil. Rise to the occasion!!!! Write on!

I would write on, but I need to prepare a test for Fapiano, Solo, and Tevita, who want their sixth graders to get into Tonga High School. Fapiano is the headmaster at Pea School, Solo is a colleague and the father of the remarkable Taufe'ulungaki women, and Tevita is the wonderful teacher who tells me I'm sparkling like a glittering star. So I'm preparing a sample test for the students to take as practice for the one that determines the rest of their lives—and I want to take one to Va'inga, another teacher I love.

{I use more "musts in my writing than I would now.}

July 2, 1971

Dear Jim,

You were born today. Oh, I'd thought of sending you a telegram. It would have read "Dear Jim. STOP."

You once described a writer who was so succinct, concise, and compact in his writing that each word was as carefully chosen as if for a telegram. "STOP Happy Birthday. STOP Love Tina."

But I have no money. You'll receive a gift soon, though—a token of my esteem and of the Peace Corps living allowance.

Dana loved your letter to her so much that she sealed it in an envelope to me with a note asking me to send it back to her unless I really wanted it badly.

I really wanted it badly.

I guess you go over best with Dana when you're not presumptuous.

I also enjoyed your letter in which you said my wish was your command. Oh, Jim, do you really feel that way? I just never realized. And me too! We could have a beautiful cheap time in Europe, you and I.

First I must go to Spain alone to think. I know that's why I joined the Peace Corps—to think. But now I've got to think about the Peace Corps. If I go to Spain in February, by June I'll have thought enough, and then your school will be out, and I can show you around the country. We can visit Aquinas and Angels and go on to your Greek ex-brother-in-law on Crete. Then on to Ireland. We can see the world, you and I, together. But you must give me a head start.

I'm moving out of the TRTC, Jim, because there's a Tonga VI Super-Vol who was after my job. I had risen to my level of incompetence anyway, so I gave it to her the day before yesterday. Now I can devote my time to doing follow-ups on our "graduates" and to making up intelligence tests for our sixth graders.

I sometimes forget how to do the problems after I've created them.

Jim, have you read The Alexandria Quartet? Would you like to go to Egypt? Or we could work on a kibbutz in Israel. I don't think we could do both—at least not at the same time.

Please send me John Boylan's address and I'll write him in Madrid.

{Apparently Larry lent me his bike—unless it was the bike Andrea fell off of, breaking her leg, and he was keeping it for her If you figure it out, please let me know. I'm happy to see that I did something nice for Vincent.}

Dear Mother,

The parents of the PCV couple L. and M. who live up the hill from me are in Tonga now, and they invited some of us to dinner at the

Dateline, Tonga's finest (and only) hotel.

They were very nice. The mother asked if Leslie and I had had trouble adjusting at first, and it immediately came to my mind that she knew L. and M. had, and I didn't want to sound like a goody-goody, but I didn't want to lie 'cause M. and L. knew I'd been happy from the start. So I said something about mindlessly going through the motions, and Leslie elaborated upon that. I wish instead of sacrificing myself, I'd just turned to Leslie and said, "What about you?" instead of answering the question myself, at my expense.

But I'd forgotten that at the very beginning I did have some days of asking you to report a family emergency to call me back. I don't even remember when or why I felt that way. I see myself as culturally shocking rather than shocked.

On Monday, I'll pedal in to Nuku'alofa and put flowers in Vincent's rooms.

I love riding the bike, and today I've come about 30 miles. I just got back in the rain. "My children" were in the center of the village to welcome me back—shouting cheering, and making me glad that Ha'ateiho is my village.

They took the bike to Larry's house for me and drew and carried water from the well. Now I've finished washing my hair. I'm waiting for more hot water to come to a boil for my bath and tea and hair brush.

On my way home I feared that I'd become reckless—doing too much what I feel like and using too little restraint. I decided my life was too much like a rambling novel and too little like a poem. So I'm going to be stricter with myself and less prosaic.

Dear Dana,

Vincent and I just "broke up." After our omelet and Chablis, he said he couldn't bear seeing me so much without touching me, and he sensed that I didn't want a physical relationship with him. I let him talk for about 15 or 20 minutes without interrupting him. Then when he asked me to comment, I didn't tell him that I didn't believe he really wanted to touch me.

Vincent said I could keep the key to his house. but I gave it back to him,

I got a postcard from Line, who's in Auckland, and from Mike Monti, who'd written to Langi asking about me, and from Mother and David. David's letters were beautiful and sad, written in his big handwriting that takes him such a long, long time. I really love David, and I know that he loves me. He told me so. And he asked about my hair—had I cut it? He also asked for a color picture. I'll write him tomorrow now that I have his address. I remember when we were little children and used to play communion with cherry Kool Aide. And when he was just five and had had seizures for about a year, he had a nose bleed, and I asked him to bleed into a Maraschino cherry bottle so we could take it to the laboratory and test it and find out what was wrong with him. Mother and Daddy very gently explained that David had already had a lot of blood tests—and other kinds.

Mother tells me you have the lead in another play.

"Oh to be a movie start! A beautiful, glamorous, radiant, ravishing movie star!" (*The Apple Tree*)

Dear David.

I just now got a letter you wrote last year! I wondered why you never wrote. I really miss you, too, and will see you in December—just five months from now.

Are you still working on the laundry truck? I'm still teaching English to little kids and acting it all out for them—things like "I'm eating" "I'm hopping" "I like yam."

It's not the most interesting job in the world, but I like the people a lot.

I don't have any recent pictures of me in color, but here's an old one.

An American named Skip who was traveling around the world asked some Peace Corps Volunteers he met in New Zealand whether there were any single women he might meet in Tonga, and I was one that he contacted. I thought someone who taught in Harlem would be interesting to meet, but he seemed more like my unfair stereotype of a business executive in the end.

Dear Skip,

Yes, I'd love to meet you. Nothing impresses me more than a man who gives up his executive position in advertising for a teaching job in Harlem unless it's a man who gives up his teaching job in Harlem for an executive position in advertising. What do you teach in Harlem? I'm a teacher, too. I teach oral English, but I've never taught it in Harlem. I've never even been an advertising executive.

Dear Dana,

People do gossip! Andrea told me that Umu told her that Sione Kite's secretary told her that Sione and I were having an affair. What she said was that I was Sione Kite's girlfriend, with all the implications, and that Sione once told her, when they were out my way, that he wanted to stop by to see me but there was another car parked by my house. "Just thought you might be interested to know the rumors," Andrea said. I was interested. But I wish it were a recent rumor.

July 10

Dear David,

As a reward for writing, you get an illustrated letter—full of photos of village life in Tonga.

The rest of the letter is written on the back of the photos.

I miss you, but I'll see you at Christmas time.

Love,
Tina

PS Send me a picture of you if you have one. If you don't have one, write anyway.

July 12, 1971

Dear Vincent,

Just so you won't forget me during this period of self-imposed separation, an almost illustrated letter and thanks for the leftovers. Ah the lifestyle of you palangis!

Yesterday I was stung by a bee (or wasp) and my face has swollen. All the new PCVS think I'm deformed and look away.

"Do let's keep in touch."

Love,
Tina

Dear Jim,

Last night I dreamt I was on a plane to Madrid, but I hadn't made a proper booking so they stopped the plane, and I went down to buy my ticket. While I was being "served," the ticket girl got a phone call straight from *Airport*, and so she screamed. I never did find out how much it would cost.

I have a seminarian friend in Mexico, and he says he can find me a family to live with if I go to Mexico.

I'm so excited. You in New York, my favorite city. How long will you be there? Will you go back to teaching in September? You never mention your teaching job. Why?

{This letter is interrupted by my diary entry.}

July 15, 1971

Last night Vincent came by when Kalala and I were reading "The Animal Book." He'd come by with some anti-histamine for my bee sting 'cause he'd gotten my note today. (I took a special trip to Fasi to put the note under his door.) He stayed, talked, had a cup of coffee with me. L.came by in a blanket and straw hat to return my unsatisfactory tape player/recorder. It's full of static. Vincent invited me to dinner this Saturday.

Kalala may be my "Tongan friend" for the picnic on Saturday. It's BYOF Bring your own friend, and some of the PCVS are irate and threatening to go instead to Suva for free food, free love, and free friends.

Yesterday I got a letter from Susan Martin and from Claude, the vaccinating doctor from Los Angeles. He sent me the picture he took of Ron and me at the Beach House.

{Notice how what I read in the New Yorker appears to have been the

Letter to Jim continued after July 17, 1971

Rod McKuen is better through the air from New York and when he writes for me instead of for the masses—although, of course, you will be immortalized posthumously if not before because I keep your letters for posterity for the masses.

I've been reading *The New Yorker*, Feb. 20, 1971, along with *Time* you sent me, and I want! I want! I want a cape coat from B. Altman & Company, a sterling silver pair of be-dangled earrings by Cini.

Did I tell you I have pierced ears now? Fuiva, the beautiful wife of the Minister of Education did them for me. She jabbed in a blunt needle and said, "This is some needle!" and added that she'd done Tupou Havea White's ears, and Tupou had to have injections for the infection that developed. Fuiva said I should put thread through my ears for a few days, but I couldn't wait for the real thing.

"It's just that some people have a reaction to the metal," she said.

"I have a reaction to the thread," I said.

I now have tiny little 9-kt gold earrings from Fiji. *{I can't remember whether Vincent or Ron got these for me.}*

I want patches for my jeans and a black dress with slits like Catherine Spaak's when she finally got a divorce in Italy, and I want to read *Citizen Kane* by that reviewer who lost it in the movies (Pauline Kael?) "Oh, so many types of innocence are lost there." She reviewed *Love Story* as "maudlin."

Ron took a trip to Fiji the same week Greg Meehan did, and by chance they signed up for the same room in the same apartment. Ron said Greg sat—bearded, sweatshirt inside-out, in blue jeans—by a window for hours at a time—just looking out and munching on an apple. Then every few hours he'd get up and ask Ron, "Could I bother you for the time?" and Ron would tell him. Then Greg would say, "Wow, time really flies!"

I have a little girl now—named Kalala. She just brought her uniform and moved in one day. She's having Elizabeth Skold (5 year old daughter of our new Peace Corps country director) over to spend the night this Friday. I'll get popcorn ("What's popcorn?" Kalala asked) and peanut butter and chocolate cookies and let them eat and tell them stories and let them play cards and sing and stay up past their bedtime.

Kalala says she wants to have Sharon Robinson (our new doctor's daughter) next week.

A week ago I was stung by a wasp and my right cheek moved out. Kalala said she wished she'd gotten stung all over so she could be fat. I told her my newly-gained beauty wasn't worth it to me, but it was clearly worth it to her. Now that I have a little girl, I can tell you all the darling, precious things she says.

Jim, I'm gonna try to get a $99 flight to Spain in February. Then you can come in June and we'll go all over the world together, as if we were married almost. Could you give me the address of your friend in Madrid so I could write him and find some quiet convent to live— away from English-speaking tourists and away from Fascist police who might shoot through my frail body with machine guns? All I want is a convent full of Spanish language, security, and Spanish cooking— paella, olive oil—so I can learn Spanish. I could work in the kitchen or with children or I could do light housekeeping (dusting)—and I'm more than willing to listen to Spanish tales of God, provided that they're told in Spanish. I'd even wear a crucifix. Tell him I am not a hippy but a reasonable, middle-aged young girl, full of restraint and linearly-oriented, whose greatest pleasure in life is doing exercises in her Everyday Spanish Book and reading her Bible and *Citizen Kane*.

Tell him I dress conservatively, my only flair being a cape coat and sterling silver ear bangles, which I'd be willing not to wear if necessary. I could easily be disguised as whatever is approved of.

Tell me more about NY! I love that city and will see movies there too at 3:00 am before I catch the plane to Madrid. Oh, yes! I do like my life!

I want to see you in January when I get back. I want!

Now it's July 20, 1971

I want! Oh, we'll have a good time and we will have midnight dinners and carpet drinks at Dana's house. (She's an actress now—had the lead in a Feiffer play and now is in a Moss Hart revived musical)

Love,
Tina

After this letter to Jim I meet the advertising executive who "chucked it all for Harlem," who goes with Kalala and me to the Beach House.

Dear Line

Are you safely back? And what's the news? Are you or aren't you? Did you get my letterful of wisdom and encouragement? It's been so long. Thank you for the postcard from Auckland. Did you have a chance to see your referee in Wellington?

Yesterday I had an appointment with an American man I didn't particularly like and Kalala's been staying with me, so I took her along, and he refused to pay for her dinner!! He didn't want to cash a twenty-dollar traveler's check. He paid for only him and me, and I paid for Kalala. I don't have any money, but I still value my time more than money, and I was spending my precious time with HIM! I think he was the most selfish man I've met in three years, but I had fun with Kalala anyway. We took her to the Moana Hotel, where we stole green lesi (papaya—but why am I translating for you?!) for her basket. Then we took her to visit Justine Warner, whose brother and mother the American visitor knew. Kalala played with Janet Warner, who's at the Side School with her. Then we ate at the Beach House and walked around in the cool night with Kalala under my great big pancho bought in New Zealand. {*It wasn't until I was on the Camino in Northern Spain in 2016 that I realized I meant poncho.*} Kalala's a darling girl. I think she's closer to Ana than to Luseane. Ana takes such good care. I took Kalala on a PC picnic with me this past Saturday, and Ana boiled and fried some chicken for us and made some ufi (yam) Kalala played with Elizabeth Skold, Cheryl Johnson, and Sharon Robinson, and when Mrs. Skold was driving us home, Elizabeth asked her if Kalala could stay for dinner. I invited Elizabeth to spend the night with Kalala (at my fale) this Friday. Kalala asked if she could have Sharon Robinson next Friday.

'Ofa atu,
Tina

In between these letters, I taught po'ako, night school from the words po meaning night and ako meaning study. I also went to the home of our Peace Corps doctor, Dr. Robinson, and his wife to visit My Best Friend in Tonga Andrea after she broke her leg in a bike accident and was in a cast and crutches, but she'd already left so I talked to Mrs. Robinson and her Indian friends. I also did observation reports at a government primary school in Nuku'alofa and wrote reports to turn in to Mr. McMurdo, the Director of Education.

July 24, 1971

Dear Claude

I'm writing you by flashlight because I'm at night school and they've "killed" the light from town. Thanks a lot for the picture. It captured a certain something although I haven't yet come to terms with what the something is. Do you know "Golden Helmet" from *Man of La Mancha*? My helmet reminds me of that even if it's not golden.

Later

Po ako was over days ago, and I'm now in Vaikeli, where I hide away on Sundays. It's so quiet out here with my favorite Tongan family, who know how to make curried breadfruit, raw fish salad, and other delicacies. It seems strange and often wonderful that I won't be here in five months or ever after that. But I'm happy here. So mindlessly, peacefully happy. Are you happy there?

You know (you don't), I wrote you a letter a couple of months ago.

I'm excited about going back to the US. I have dreams in which I see my family at Safeway, and they go right on with their shopping. But I know they'll be more excited than that. I picture us all talking at once, and their making daiquiris for me and bringing me cushions and playing my favorite records for me and telling me funny stories of what's been happening to them. I'll see about three movies a day to catch up and then I'll go to Chicago to see my sister and brother-in-law and then to Pennsylvania to see my father and another sister and then to Spain to see all the little fascists. I've never been to Europe. In a week my father and my youngest sister are going to Eastern Europe to visit—Moscow and the Balkan countries. Daddy's intent on over-throwing the American government, and he thinks he's going to be "expelled" from the country, so he's looking around for a new place to live. He's very dramatic, but I suspect that he'll remain in America so he can continue not paying his part of the federal taxes used to finance our war crimes in South East Asia. He and other people who feel as he does don't pay on their phone bill and give what they don't pay to a housing development project in Harrisburg. They won't throw them out for that, will they?

How could you suggest that nothing has been happening here in Tonga? Why, just last week I had my ears pierced. You can't imagine the difference it makes. I walk around feeling exotic. Also, I have a little girl now. She just came with her school uniform one day and moved in.

She's really darling and speaks English fluently because she goes to the Side School, where all the English-speaking palangis (foreign) kids go. She asked me if she could come live with me in America, and I told her I was going to Spain. She said that would be all right too.

Linda L.R. is trying to make pretzels, and Sandy O. is collecting jars for pickled onions. So you see, there's lots of activity here.

And I love it.

And I'm so excited about leaving it.

But I'd like to come back here someday and see how everyone turned out and whatever everyone turned into. And you must come back to see if the kids are accomplishing marvelous things because of vaccinations.

I am fictionalizing my life here. Making South Pacific into a Peace Corps Musical, and the cast keeps getting longer. I'm also writing a novel about a Peace Corps Volunteer who falls in love with a Mormon minister.

I need to read for inspiration, but my favorite books are *Hertzog, Alice in Wonderland, Beck a Book, Green Mansions*, and *Pale Fire*. What kind of writing would that mélange inspire?

Mostly, I'm just disappointed in myself because I just don't write enough.

I try to focus on superlatives.

The woman I admire most is Gloria Steinem because she writes, is not a housewife, is beautiful, and Mike Nichols admires her. Mike Nichols is the man I admire most. I don't expect him to get the Democratic nomination, but if he does, I'll vote for him. *{I have no idea where I got the idea that Mike Nichols was running for office.}*

My greatest fear is growing old and being mistreated the way old people are, of being senile or thought to be senile and condescended to and pitied and considered an annoyance.

{Kelea (Claire in English) was a lovely young woman who became a friend, but I think she was from a different village—Vaini?—so I don't remember how we met. She's not to be confused with Kalala.}

Late July, 1971

Dear Kelea,

I have a bad cold and I'll have to stay at home tonight and sip hot tea and lemon.

Guess what! I can go with you to Vava'u in August! I'm really happy. I'll talk to you about it later.

Love,
Tina

{Once again I try to visit Andrea, who isn't at home.}

Am at Andrea's now, but Andrea's not. I've been here for a couple of hours. I'm looking forward to talking to her.

...I bought Andrea 3 apples, some chocolate nut biscuits, and 2 cold Cokes.

{Here I mention a writer who was my first creative writing professor, George Cuomo, who was a much better writer than the mentioned review indicates. Looking him up online, I see that he has been mentioned more than once in lists of unfairly neglected authors, for example by Richard Yates in Ploughshares }

George Cuomo's most recent novel was reviewed in *Saturday Review* in the issue I got today. It was summed up as "less than successful," but they (David McCullough, free-lance critic) mentioned his wry under-stated humor.

July 30

I'm glad I stayed and talked with Andrea. It was fun, and I feel better as a result of it. Our senses of humor don't clash, and it was just very pleasant.

Dear Andrea,

I just thought of something good about that American Harlem executive: The best movie he's seen in years.

"You probably didn't like it," he began, "but the one I liked the best was *Ryan's Daughter*."

July 30, 1971

Dear Dana,

I know what's gonna happen. You're gonna be discovered, and they'll say you have Elizabeth Taylor's beauty and vulgarity and Natalie Wood's beauty and youthfulness. You'll be a bigger success than Ali McGraw and you won't even have to die. ("A person would have to have a heart of stone to read of the death of Jennifer Cavilleri without laughing." *Time*) Suzy and I will play your records, and you can lie on the carpet with your Seagram's 7 and roll over to where Herman lies and say, "I did it for you, Hermie. Just so you'd be proud of me."

I'm proud of you, Dana, and so jealous! I wish you'd write and tell me more about this Moss Hart musical you're in—with the Dixie drawl.

There's a lot to tell you, but I'll do it in person. I'll visit you and Herman in January before I leave for Spain. It'll be so much fun!!!

I am getting old. It had to happen.

Dear Susan

Have you read *The Feminine Mystique?* If you haven't, please do, and we can discuss it. It came out when we were seniors in high school, but I didn't get around to reading it till now. It's good.

The time of my release from my South Seas Paradise is drawing near, and I'd like to know where you'll be in January 1972. I'll go to Chicago and Pennsylvania and NY, but I don't think I'll go south of that. Could you come north? I'll treat you to lunch.

We can talk and talk. You'd be welcome to stay with us in Chicago, but probably NY would be more convenient, right? I'll show you my new tapa cape coat and my turtle buttons. That'll impress you.

I'm leaving for Spain in Feb.

God, when I think of all the movies and shows and conversations I'm gonna have to pack into the time. and January! When shall I meet you?

And how's our gang 2 years later? Are the married people still married? Dal and Linda? Lynn and What's His Name?

Is our friend (probably more yours than mine) Charles married yet? To whom? You must find out. If he's not married, you must marry him, and I'll be his mistress to keep him in the family. I have my heart set on being his mistress. If you see him, remind him. And please see him. I must know how he turned out. Tell him he can have lunch with us too.

I have a feeling I might marry Jim, but I hope not for a few years. I love him, but as you know, I equate marriage with failure.

August 1971

Dear Andrea,

P. told me to write to you about a meeting tomorrow at the Nuku'alofa GPS math center—to discuss supervising the *sivi hu* {*entrance exam for high school*} on Saturday. I told him your condition, and he said it was up to you. If you had your heart set on attending the meeting, you wouldn't be excluded because of your handicap.

Yesterday I discussed God with Dr. Robinson and Mrs. Dixit. Mrs. Dixit is the Indian woman whose goal in life is to write God 1, 400,000 times on dough and then give the dough to the fish. I ate with her—3 platefuls of rice and curry, reminding me of our Christmas Eve dinner in Suva! I got magazines and Dr. Seuss books for Kalala at Liahona. Did you know Liahona is owned and operated by the Church of the Latter Day Saints?

It's about 7:30. A few minutes ago Kalala "broke wind" while she and Fehi were playing. Kalala immediately insinuated it was Fehi and waved her hand in a graceful Polynesian hand movement to push the bad air away. Fehi said, "Ko koe" {*It was you!*} and made the same gesture in the opposite direction. They accused each other for 30 seconds and then Fehi turned to me in hope and earnestness and said, "Ko Kalala!" And Kalala in desperation said, good-naturedly, "Eenie meenie miny, moe." But Fehi wasn't going to go along with that, so Kalala pretended Fehi had hurt her arm and began crying.

Dana told me of a friend of hers, Petie, who farted when she and a boyfriend were dancing. She loved the boy and wanted so much to be beautiful and romantic for him. After she broke wind, she asked, "What was that?" Then they both laughed. Then she burst out crying.

I'd like to have rings for my toes the way Mrs. Dixit does.

Tomorrow Kalala, Mrs. Dixit, her 2 sons, and I will see *Funny Girl*—but I'll go without rings on my toes.

'Ofa atu,
Tina

August 6, 1971

From the Nuku'alofa math center.

I didn't want to get to this meeting early, but I did. It's raining and Lupe will leave this morning for Hawaii. I'll try to leave the meeting at 10:00 to catch a bus to the airport to see her off.

From the blackboard:

In a feast there were three types of meat, fish, chicken, and pork. 16 people ate fish, 18 ate chicken, and 21 ate pork.

If there were 5 who ate fish and chicken, 8 who ate chicken and pork, and 7 who ate fish and pork, how many people in the feast if 3 ate fish, pork, and chicken.

{Letter to Gloria Tate, who wrote The Tate Oral English Series, requiring an acting out of each verb, used throughout the South Pacific Islands at that time. Around August 26, 1971}

Dear Miss Tate,

On my way home in a tugboat yesterday from Vava'u to Tongatapu, I almost threw myself overboard—not because I was depressed but because I was seasick and I didn't want to prolong the agony.

But while I was clearly and unambiguously presenting the new item

("I'm dying. I'm dying") I thought of all the fan letters I hadn't written to the people I admire. I thought of you along with Audrey Hepburn, Mike Nichols, and Gloria Steinem.. My feeling of justice took priority over my flight from floating stomach, oh most gentle of euphemisms.

I'm writing this note to tell you some of all you've heard before.

I've always had the fear that if people aren't told over and over again that they're admired (when they are) that they'll stop being admirable. I know you've heard enough speeches. But even if a person knows his candidate's gonna win, he feels good about casting his ballot, so...

Of course you know everyone appreciates your warmth and enthusiasm, and so do I. But one of the things I appreciated most during the short time you were here was your originality. I admire wit when it's not mean. (Actually, I admire wit when it's mean too; I just don't like it), and your sense of humor (or humour in your country) was never at anyone else's expense. I liked your remark in response to what one speaker (Paul Bloomfield?) said about how good it was to get the word from the horse's mouth.

"Well, I'll tell you, the old grey mare ain't what she used to be."

But I can't believe it's true. People around here who met you are still saying to newcomers (like the latest group of PCV) "You should meet Gloria Tate!" in tones that convey that you're far from a stiff, priggish purist.

It was nice meeting the mystery writer of the books we use every morning and every afternoon.

I plan to plagiarize the Tate Series a little bit. I know it was written especially for the South Pacific, but we plagiarists have to make some compromises besides moral ones.

I hope you'll be able to come to Tonga again so some more people can meet you. But if you're too busy to make the trip, I think Mr. McMurdo should send a group to you—but not in a tugboat.

'Ofa atu,
Tina

<u>September 1971</u>

September 8?

Dear Ron,

Everyone's vain. I just joke about my vanity more than most people, so it's all more obvious. And I parody vanity, singing the Passionella song Jules Feiffer inspired.

And I did feel resentment about being discussed because I've come to feel that whatever I say or do with one person can't be private. I don't feel I can trust anyone—not you or Andrea or anyone else. Because on this tiny island we all gossip so much and no one uses any discretion. Everything's repeated.

But you're right of course. "It's not just that." I like you so much—even love you—but I feel confused. I feel bored with myself and tired of being childish and cute. I have the chilling idea that I'd rather talk or read or learn something than kiss. Is it because kissing is so exciting? Or is this Gloria Steinem's influence? I don't know. But I really do have this idea. I really feel this way. I become frightened at the prospect of someone's doing more than kissing me now. I'd rather be held, just held—or maybe hold, to do my part.

On an island we have to set limits—or be very good swimmers.

Love,
Tina

{My diary has reference to Germaine Greer—The Female Eunuch and Kathleen Tynan. I also have notes from chapter 4 of "the Museum of the Revolution" from Behind the Lines—Hanoi by Harrison E. Salisbury.}

Dear Vincent

It makes me so sad that such a lovely evening—and your anniversary too—should have ended so (check one) unpleasantly/hostilely/rotten even if it was your fault. You may not acknowledge this, but it was. It was you who rejected me, not I who rejected you. My not following you into the bedroom should not have been construed as a sign of rejection or (even) iciness. I felt quite warm towards you—even when you were sitting there pouting on the couch and saying unfriendly things.

After September 8, 1971

Dear Ron,

I'm eating a carrot right now. Thank you for all the eggs and the vegetable garden. You're wonderful, Ron, and I would be better company if I were less manicky and more sane, less confused and better adjusted in this and all hostile environments.

Really, I am confused these days and would like to keep my confusion to myself.

But I'll be thinking of you and warmly.

Love,
Tina

September 1971

Dear Claude,

Have you been sailing lately? Just think—your ownership of the boat is a third of our readjustment allowance. If there's one thing I resent, it's affluence—someone else's I mean. But happy sailing anyway.

During the holidays I went aboard a boat. I think it was a tugboat, but people tell me there's no such thing in Tonga. I had taken one of those magic Dramamine tablets and for three hours I sat by the rim of the boat and sang B'way hits to myself and the sea—all I could remember, A to Z. (*Annie Get Your Gun—Zorba*) But now I know Dramamine lasts exactly three hours. I crawled downstairs and collapsed in somebody else's cabin.

This was the first time in my two years in Tonga that I was sick—except with a cold. But it made up for a lot of healthy days.

My project for the next 2 1/2 months is a crash teach-yourself-course in economics so I can better understand the US on my way back through. I want to grasp such concepts as floating yen and dollars cut from (away from) gold, and the way trade works with Germany, Japan, and Canada, who are giving us more than we're giving them, and this is bad?

I got hold of some *Cosmopolitan, Vogue, Glamour, Mademoiselle*, magazines and am taking notes on skirts and hairstyles and deciding what I'll conform to and what I'll to do without. As a feminist who aspires to be among the Radical chic movement, I spend a lot of energy trying to resent these magazines that perpetuate an oppressive, even rather de-humanizing image of women...

All I really want in life is a cape coat and great big earrings as I march around with my autographed copy of the *Pentagon Papers* and my vocabulary of Germaine Greer, Gloria Steinem, and Kay Millet. And my indignity and abuse. (I'm not denying that women really are indignant and abused) I read in the June issue of *Vogue* that it's no longer considered vulgar to wear diamonds before breakfast. But that doesn't really affect me because I rarely have breakfast.

Do you remember Ani Losoff from Antioch and Vaini? She and I are working together at 'Atele Teachers Re-training Center this term, and today we got to singing Tom Lehr Songs, though not with our teachers! Before they came in.

Tom Lehr, Alan Sherman, and Stan Freberg are the three satirists I miss the most—and all from our parents' generation. I wonder if I'm hopelessly behind the times. People I ask say "Yes."

Dear Ron,

Thanks for the chewing gum and popcorn and official judge badge and agriculture booklet and letter reuniting us with Broc.

{As was so often the case, Ron came through in such a wonderful way, and thanks to his supplying me with popcorn kernels, I was able to perform my magic trick of putting corn kernels at the bottom of a pot on my kerosene stove, covering the pot with a lid, letting the children listen to the magic going on inside, and then showing them how I'd transformed those simple kernels into the incredible white fluffy stuff, filling the pot. Oyaiye! Word traveled fast, and soon my head master was asking for a few of those kernels so he could plant them in his garden and grow the fluffy stuff. I felt a little bit like the hero in "Jack and the Beanstock"!}

Dear Mother,

Carrots do have feelings, but fewer, I think, than pigs and cattle although maybe it's a mistake to judge sensitivity by protest at slaughter. Anyway, we've got to eat something that's not one another. I used to under-esteem animals and have for them the same kind of indifference I felt towards sunsets and the great outdoors. How boring! But I've read about ESP in dogs in *Harper's* and about the courage of turtles, and I have more respect for them. I rarely have kiki (meat) here anyway. And

I really love the sunrise, which I can watch from my front door as the morning rises over Likua's shop of kerosene and freshly baked bread.

After I get back from Spain and Europe, I'm thinking of re-enlisting in the Peace Corps but only on the condition that I go to a country like Turkey or Thailand or India because I probably won't get to them on my own.

Oh, I'm excited about traveling.

I like your idea about making foster parenthood my career. I mean it.

Congratulations on your weight loss, but I wish I could have some of what you lost. I weigh what I weighed in high school but without the glow of youth.

Have you finished *Female Eunuch*? I'd really like to borrow it. Also *Pentagon Papers, Khrushchev Remembers*, and anything at all by John Kenneth Galbraith. Then when I return in December we can have a seminar!

Here are my plans as they stand now:

Late December—arrive home for Christmas—talk, talk, talk

January: Talk and see movies

Middle January visit Dana and Jim in Chicago

Late January —Visit Daddy and Missy in PA

Early Feb Leave for Spain

August Visit Western and Northern Europe

Have you seen any movies like *Love Story* or *Man of La Mancha*? I guess you don't really need to read John Barth. Once I was past the intro, *Giles the Goat Boy* got silly, and *Sot Weed Factor* no longer seems original after page 3.

I too got a postcard from Suzy in Leningrad. Is she back home now? How long was their trip? She sounded happy when she wrote. What an opportunity and at her age, while the rest of us, her elders, go about our business on our respective islands. But soon it'll be my turn. And your turn's way overdue. Wouldn't you like to work on a kibbutz in Israel? Maybe you can visit in Spain when I'm established.

Sorry about your job change. Has it turned you against welfare?

Do you understand things like floating yen and balance of trade?

I'll write to David this evening. Hello to Kathy and Suzy if she's back.

Love,
Tina

Late September 1971

Dear Dana,

I wish I could have seen your play. Will you be in anything when I come in January? You said Herman would be "no problem." when you got back from Mexico. Are you getting a quick divorce, or was the order of events only coincidental?

You know, back in my days at CHS, we didn't have an orchestra. Sometimes we didn't even have a piano. So coming in at the right time was no problem. Being in the right key often was.

Right now I'm not particularly happy in Tonga although I'm not miserable either. I'm definitely glad I joined the PC. I don't know whether it's changed me or not, but I know it's changed my attitude and plans. For example, I'm less anxious to marry than ever before. My being two years older makes marriage look less attractive, and I'd thought I'd become desperate with age. Maybe I'll marry eventually, but I'll put it off.

Right now I'm working at a job I do not like—as a teacher trainer. I like the teachers, but in spite of my astonishing knowledge and grasp of the techniques in teaching oral English, I don't do a good job. It's more my personality than anything else. I come across "teacherish," at least that's the way I feel. (Only in a teaching situation, though. I'll say that for myself.)

Dear Vincent,

You loved me in terms of two months, and I loved you in terms of always. That's why you wanted an exclusive relationship, and I didn't.

<u>October 1971</u>

{I loved my grandparents, but I was very bad about writing to them. I felt especially bad when my maternal grandparents died because my mother was an only child and not a frequent letter writer, and I remember how anxiously they waited for a letter to drop into their mail slot when I visited them in Los Angeles. I was already clear on how rotten older people were treated, so I vowed I'd do better with older people. One older person was Miss Pearlstine, who was just about retirement age when we were in her class on November 23, 1963, when the principal of Columbia High School came over the PA system to let us know that President Kennedy had been shot and killed. After my graduation from high school, we started corresponding.}

Letter typed on Jim's orange typewriter to Miss Pearlstine

October 1971

Dear Miss Pearlstine,

I'm writing you from the 'Atele Teachers Retraining Center, where I'm head tutor now. We re-train teachers to teach oral English through the Tate South Pacific method. It's not the most fascinating job in the world, but I like the teachers. This term they're the older teachers, head masters and such, whose education must have been in Biblical English. One teacher is always beholding things.

One of our Tongan teachers is leaving in a few minutes to fly to New Zealand to get rich, so I'll leave for the airport to see him off in an hour or so. It's about 7:30 am and I've been up since 3:30. Last night I went to bed at sunset because I was out of kerosene. Someone brought me kerosene sometime last night and I graciously accepted it through the window without waking up. I remember the days when I slept till noon, but then I didn't go to bed at 6:30.

I'm happy here. The girl I work with said something I completely agree with: "Tonga is a dollhouse, and life is make-believe." {Really?}

It's beautiful here in a sort of a wholesome way—open air, trees, sun, water—and I really prefer the more exotic, secretive unwholesome such as—oh, maybe Turkey. But there is a happy superficial friendliness here that provides a pleasant background for whatever I want to do.

I think I'd always like to live simply—with physical simplicity, that is, so I can keep my mind as cluttered and chaotic as I like. Living without too much, without more than I need, like electricity: who needs it? makes me feel virtuous and almost (not quite) serene. I'm attached to my ugly black kettle in which I boil water for my bath and water for my tea and coffee.

This morning I had sweet sherry in my coffee—provided by Ron Rosenberg, a Peace Corps Volunteer from Texas, who possesses one of the characteristics I admire most in a man: generosity! I think he must spend most of his living allowance on me. He left for a faraway island (Niua Fo'ou—Tin Can Island) to do some soil surveys, and he left me with his sherry and *Time Magazines*. (I don't know why not *Newsweek*—I remember your pointing out to us when we were in Problem of American Democracy class how smart-alecky *Time* was and is.) Since he left, every week someone brings me a basketful of vegetables—papaya, eggplant, carrots, onions—and eggs, arranged by Ron. Besides being thoughtful, Ron's very smart and very nice.

It doesn't fit the image I had of the Peace Corps, but I do date a lot. I don't date a lot of people, but I date often—Ron and Vincent Williams, mainly. Vincent is a hospital administrator, gift of the British government, from a suburb near London. He lives in what looks to me like a palace—tall white rooms, a stereo, lots of records and tall and beautiful bottles of vermouth, gin, scotch, port, and cherry brandy. He's very, very smart and explains things like the American economy to me. We read to each other and have periodic fights—all very civilized, in the British tradition, I supposed. He's almost 40. Ron's 24. Ron and I almost never have a disagreement.

I haven't dated any Tongans—none have asked me, except that I went to an Anglican Church with one a couple of times before he got married. Now I spend my Sundays with him and his wife and mother out in the bush where it's quiet and calm. They're my favorite family here. The one exception to my not dating Tongans is Sione Kite, who's Secretary of the Government. He's young—about 30—and lived in Australia for 18 years while he went to school and taught history. I've only dated him a few times. He's now in the US doing something or other with Peace Corps selection. I used to think he was very pompous and very formal until one evening he was driving along and announced that he'd sing me some Negro spirituals when the radio signed off at 11:00. And when the radio signed off at 11:00 he sang me Negro spirituals. I thought that was a particularly charming thing to do, with no prompting at all from me and a particular pride in his rather good voice. After that I liked him much, much more. I really like to be entertained.

I think sometimes of what I want to do with my life, and right now I think this is what I want. I'd like to live like this all over the world. I'd like to be a professional volunteer and never work—just always be given an allowance and work at different things. I'm glad (not proud but glad), that I'm an American because in spite of all the sins of Amelika, it's a fascinating country, the United States, and I'd like to have it as a base. But every time I see a map, I really feel excited and I know I want to spend a lot of my life traveling.

I used to want life to be meaningful, profound. Now I think life is too mysterious to understand its meaning, and while I want to make certain assumptions—that people matter, that what I do makes a difference, at least to me, I'm not always trying to create a theology about it. I want life to be beautiful, that's very important to me. I don't want to become so self-indulgent that I'm insensitive…I don't want things to happen terribly fast. I don't particularly identify with my generation or any other. I'm bored and bothered by the smugness and cynicism of my generation, living it seems only for the next angry confrontation. But the mindlessness of our parents (not mine; mine are exceptional) the stupid blind acceptance of such outrageous things as our government's foreign policy in (yes, you've heard it before) South East Asia, is incredible and of course immoral too. I can't accept the values of any generation—only my own private set. I don't want to be smug either, though.

Women's Lib fascinates me. I can't accept men as my enemy. And I'm so suspicious of generalities—even my own. But women should be brought up to want more than they're brought up to want. They shouldn't think it's feminine and sweet to limit their lives and to direct their every attention to pleasing a man. I don't believe women are slaves, but I do see an awful lot of women who are serfs. It's most evident in marriage but there are symptoms even before they take the vow. Isn't it nice that I feel I can sit back and talk about slaves as *they*?

I agree so much with what Betty Friedan says in *The Feminine Mystique*, and to think that it came out the same year you were suggesting to us that women were too emotional to be national leaders, that men somehow had an inherent better understanding of news. You were a great teacher and my favorite both at the time and in retrospect. But you should be ashamed of yourself for that. Life is much more interesting and full of joy when a person of either sex is learning new things and using all his or her intelligence and originality. Women are told they are not designed for understanding things outside the home, and they believe it. And so they get married and cook sweet little meals and have a couple of children and find new ways to make Jell-O interesting and concentrate on furniture and live sad and limited lives.

Don't you think it's interesting that every woman dreams of getting married and living happily ever after, and every survey shows that married women are less happy than unmarried ones? I'd like to get married someday because I'd like to have children from all over the world, and it would hard for me to have them either naturally or through adoption without a husband. But I want to put off marriage for as long as I can.

I no longer believe "Gather ye rosebuds while ye may." Dana suggests that I get married while I'm at the stage "most attractive to men"—and she means looks. I used to get a little bit nervous when she told me that. Now I can't imagine myself getting married out of desperation, before I'm ready for it and while I like my life the way it is. If I lose my "golden opportunities," that's just too bad. It's worth it to me to run that risk. and I'd certainly rather not marry a man who wants a doll-like wife whose greatest joy is in washing his socks and who avoids reading anything for fear that she would disagree with her husband if she were informed. I dislike wives who belittle or nag their husbands. But I dislike men who belittle or nag their wife. I like gentleness and kindness in both sexes. I don't think sensitivity is a female characteristic; it's a human characteristic. I like human beings, and I want to be one.

When I think of what makes me happy, it's things like teaching the Tongan children Broadway songs and supervising the kids while they clean my rooms and taking walks. It's being with Ron or Vincent and reading the *New York Times* Week in Review. Every inch of it—and trying to keep up with what'll happen next with the Supreme Court, with McGovern, with the proposed amendment to the Constitution. I don't want to be protected from knowing about Attica and Belfast while I rave about a detergent that works wonders.

Life is over so quickly, and a woman's life is often over at twenty-two. I think that women should be drafted into some kind of national service—with the military if they choose; I wouldn't.) or with Acción. Another year I'd like to join a United Nations project. If not that, then maybe VISTA. And you could join too if you really wanted to. And you could still take the advice given to Taurus: to have a good time and enjoy yourself. I'm a Scorpio, and I'm taking that advice.

Joining the Peace Corps wasn't motivated by saintliness, only by interest. and it has been interesting. I want the rest of my life to be. But you shouldn't complain because even without the PC your life has been interesting.

I am looking forward to returning to the US—to seeing my family in Pleasant Hill, in Chicago, and in Harrisburg. And I'm looking forward to movies and shows and glazed donuts and San Francisco.

I'm going to buy one of those beautiful magical cape coats. I'm going to go to the FS {?} Bookshop and buy a carton of books to where I'm going next. Oh, I'm so excited, when I think of it. Of course, I'm a manic-depressive, but right now I adore life.

If you'll be anywhere near Harrisburg in January, let me know, and you can treat me to lunch. I envy you your seeing Kennedy Center. I could only read about it. Write again sometime!

'Ofa atu,
Tina

Above: Sisters Suzy and Missy—The photo Suzy is describing in her poem
Below: Missy as she was in first grade,
when she visited our 6th grade classroom

59, Columbia, S. C.

'MISS COLUMBIAN'

Miss Dana Martin, daughter of Dr. and Mrs. E. A. Martin, has been chosen "Miss Columbian" of Columbia High School, where she is a sophomore. She was chosen in a beauty contest at the school Thursday night. Individual class beauties selected are Miss Senior, Bobbie Lu Satterfield; Miss Junior, Marianne Engram; Miss Sophomore, Nina Nelson; and Miss Freshman, Jane Duncan. (Record photo by Tutte)

Dana won the Miss Columbian Contest in 1959 without bribing God.

In 1963, after the assassination of President Kennedy, I stopped bribing God for that crown in favor of His help getting me into the Peace Corps, so when I won the contest the following year, it occurred to me that God had de-selected me from serving my country by leaving it.

Columbia High School Beauties Chosen

Collage of Tonga 1970-71

Collage of Tonga 1970-71

Andrea with Linda and Sid, Tonga 1971

With 'Ana and Kalala in 2008

*Obama on window of post office in Nuku'alofa, August 2008, and an ad
for the commemorative stamps of the coronation of Kingi Siaosi Tupou V*

Reunions with Tongans in 2008

Looking forward to the king's coronation

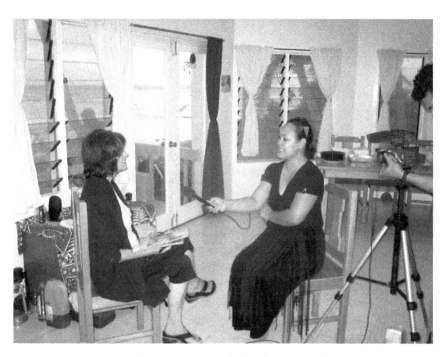

Being interviewed for Tongan TV

Collage of Tongan Families, revisited, 2008

Kili, Sipaula and me 1971; Kili and me 2008

Leaving Tonga:
My Diary Goes Missing

When did I start leaving Tonga? Isn't there something about how you can walk into a forest only halfway because after that you're walking *out* of the forest? That's assuming you don't get lost in the forest and walk around in circles, which might be a better metaphor for what I had been doing. I probably began leaving Tonga at the beginning of my second year. But of course I kept the summary of everybody and everything for the diary that would go missing in late November before my departure on December third.

I had put the basket down at the Fua'amotu Airport when I was seeing off a Tongan teacher leaving to become rich in New Zealand, and when I reached down to get my diary out—almost a reflex— my basket wasn't there.

Whenever anything traumatic or dramatic happened, I'd whip out my diary if it wasn't already in my hand, and I'd take note. That steadied me, made me feel less vulnerable. Maybe I couldn't cope, but I could take copious notes on my inability to cope, and I felt that somehow if I took notes on a catastrophe, I could learn from it. I loved that saying "A writer is a person upon whom nothing is lost." Lost!

Losing my diary was a catastrophe, traumatic and dramatic, but now I had nowhere to write down the traumatic and dramatic catastrophe.

It probably wasn't theft. The only thing that had ever been stolen from me were my hen's eggs (before I gave up on keeping a hen) and my clothes—a kimono I'd bought in Hawaii and the muumuus I wore over my *tupenu*, the long straight skirt women wore. (Men wore them too, but theirs were shorter, showing off their legs.) Tongans didn't usually need to steal because there was such a convenient *kole* or borrowing tradition.

I figured someone had taken my basket thinking it was theirs since we all carried the handwoven Tongan baskets everywhere we went. When I looked around but didn't spot anyone carrying it or bringing it back to me, I went to an official at the airport to see whether someone had turned it in. No one had.

In Tonga everybody knew everybody else, so they knew me, Tina Pisi Koa, and they knew where to return my basket. But when the airport official offered to help me get an ad on the radio to offer a reward for the return of my basket, I accepted his offer.

Whoever took my basket would definitely see the diary because I kept it right on top for easy access—mine, not theirs, whoever they were who had easy access to my diary now.

What if it had fallen into the hands of someone who knew English well enough to decipher my handwriting and was interested enough to read it?

I walked outside just in time to get a bus back to Ha'ateiho. I told the bus driver I had lost my basket with my pa'anga/seniti (money/cents) in it, and he knew I was Pisi Koa, so I didn't have to pay anyway.

Maybe when I got back to my fale, the basket would be there. Then I remembered. So would Andrea! We were getting together to finish our Description of Service reports for the Peace Corps and our report on the respective Teachers Retraining Centers where we'd been head tutor. We were also celebrating the end of the term and planning our trip back to the USA mainland by way of Samoa and Honolulu.

We'd timed it so I'd be back from the airport when she arrived, but I hadn't allowed for my unsuccessful lost-not-found misadventure. She would be able to get inside my fale because I rarely closed the padlock

Ron had gotten for me after someone stole my clothes. Until then all I'd had on my door was a bent nail I'd push back to keep my door shut, no less effective than an open padlock. If anyone wanted the two dresses I still had, they could take them. The only thing I kept locked up were my diaries—in a Samsonite suitcase, of all things—under my bed. All but the current one, the one gone missing.

I thought of that Oscar Wilde quip that comes out of the mouth of Cecily. "It is simply a very young girl's record of her own thoughts and impressions, and consequently meant for publication."

I didn't mind the world's seeing my diary, but I certainly didn't want anyone I knew to see it.

Just what thoughts and impressions had I scribbled in this missing diary? My love for and fidelity to Jim, Line, and Ron? My avoid-approach relationship with Vincent? My recent dates with Sione K.? The discussions with Tavi? My feelings about Tika? My disappointment in my job and myself as the head tutor at the Teachers Retraining Center? My regrets about the evening with my Peace Corps neighbors, whom I'd insulted. in a way—and yet they invited me to their farewell party and, when his parents were visiting, even to the Dateline with other Peace Corps Volunteer they didn't like. What Kili had told me about the gossip at the kava ceremony? What Andrea had told me when I stayed with her in Fahefa?

When I arrived at my fale, neither Andrea nor the basket was there.

I ducked inside and went straight to my UNICEF calendar, and then sat down on the matted floor and, leaning against the plastic chair Tika had brought me, I tried to remember what all I'd "covered" that might now be uncovered.

I remembered writing on the first page of this final notebook: **Since I'll soon be leaving Tonga, this will probably be my last Tongan journal, so sometime within the next month I'll "summarize" how I feel about people and things.**

What would be the most damning thing they could find? Or did that depend upon who "they" were?

In this diary I'd written about my recent dates with Sione K, which were usually dinner, a movie, and a ride home, bypassing my village so we could keep singing. He told me I was "the prettiest of the lot," but I suspected he was really after my repertoire of songs. He never said he liked my voice, but he liked the songs I sang, and he'd drive us down the Taufa'ahau Road past my *fale* so we could keep on singing. He liked "Summertime" because he said it sounded "Negro," and he identified with Blacks. He wanted me to write down the words to "Some Enchanted Evening" because it was good for his voice range. But the week before he'd been my date for the Thanksgiving gathering the Peace Corps country director Elmer Skold and his wife had for Peace Corps Volunteers.

True, recently, there had been more flirtation, and I'd written it all down. He'd taken me to the 1963 movie *Cleopatra*, Tonga's premiere in 1971, and then invited me to his home for dinner, which his sister prepared and served. He played me a cassette of a calypso song about the Queen of Tonga when she went to Queen Elizabeth's coronation and "stole the show" by leaving her carriage top down in the rain. Sione spoke of writing a book about the independence of Tonga since he'd seen it behind the scenes. Then he'd gotten out an old volume of *The Works of Shakespeare* and proceeded to read the parts of Antony and Brutus in *Julius Cesar* before handing me the hefty volume and inviting me to read Portia. I declined, feeling that Portia deserved better and I should really be getting home. When he was opening the car door for me to take me home, he moved closer to me, and I didn't move away. I wrote about that.

I wrote about his saying that he'd read *The Sensuous Woman* and thought it was supposed to be satirical, but he had been assured that it was meant to be taken seriously.

I wrote about his saying, "Oh, honey, honey, honey, honey, honey" and his asking me to write from San Francisco "now and again" and promising to send me all the gossip "because I know that's what women are interested in."

I wrote about my gentle but scornful laugh.

Did I write about his description of me as "tiny," and my telling him I'd become fifteen pounds tinier in Tonga? About his trying to fatten me up a little at the Dateline, where he'd taken me for my birthday two weeks earlier and spoken as if he were courting me rather than saying farewell?

It was when I was ruminating on this that Andrea arrived, escorted by some admiring Ha'ateiho children, uttering what they always uttered when they saw her, "Faka 'ofa 'ofa" Beautiful. I, on the other hand, was "Faka 'ofa," pitiful, because of my being so tiny (and now because of my lost basket. Did they know?) What a difference one single 'ofa made.

It was starting to get dark, so I lit the kerosene lamp, a prelude to shutting the door, and after I reminded the children that they were spending the night with me tomorrow, my last night, they clapped their hands, jumped in the air, and scattered. Before their voices faded away, I could hear them singing, "Good night, good night. Sleep well and when you dream, dream of me" from *West Side Story*.

"I just heard your farewell message on the radio," Andrea said, putting down her basket and her sleeping bag.

"My farewell?" I asked.

"Well, it was in Tongan, so I couldn't understand every word, but it sounded like you were thanking the Tongans for their gifts and saying goodbye."

Andrea's Tongan was better than mine. But this made me aware of how much guessing goes into listening to a foreign language. I explained what had happened and what the ad really said.

"And now, while I wait for my basket to be returned, I'm trying to remember what all I put in my diary," I said, lighting the kerosene stove for the tea kettle and, indicating the plastic chair Tika had brought me, asking, "Would you like to take the throne?"

"Is this a variation of the bean bag that's become such a craze?" she asked, sinking into it. "Or a swimming pool float?" She got back up and out and sat against the side wall. "I don't think the plastic throne is conducive to finishing our reports on the TRTCs."

"Oh, no," I said, remembering. "I wrote the rough draft of my report in that notebook—the missing one, the one I use as a diary."

"That's too bad. But at least it's not too personal."

"Maybe that's the *most* personal," I said. "Remember when you said you'd heard it was a zoo at our teachers retraining center? For some reason some teachers took it as a joke. A really nice nun named Sister Loreto was taking our course, and she didn't think 'Ani should sit on the table Indian style. I thought the teachers saw us as too unstructured and informal. But the feedback showed me how bad I am at judging a situation. Their main criticism was that we demanded too much."

"They actually gave you criticism?"

"Oh," I said, getting out the tin cups from my cupboard and putting them on the floor table. "You got only praise?"

"Well, they know I'm leaving, and they want me to come back," Andrea said, quickly adding, "I'm sure they want you to come back too."

"Oh, Andrea, you've really done a good job," I said.

"I'm sure you have too," she said. "And you've taught the kids all those songs. I can just imagine some traveler thinking they've come to a desert island, uncharted territory, never before inhabited—and then suddenly they hear a chorus of children singing 'Hello, Dolly.'"

"My headmaster talked to me for about twenty minutes yesterday," I said. "He's such a good man. He took our retraining course this term, and now he doesn't switch the kids when they laugh anymore. I should put that in the progress report. He told me he was ashamed because he really didn't know what he was doing when he gave the pronunciation lesson, which was what he gave. It didn't have anything to do with the Tate Syllabus. And he felt like a failure because none of the kids at 'Atele got into Tonga High School."

"None of ours at Fahefa did either."

"But last year three of our students did, and what I didn't understand at the time is that I was given the credit because I'd been teaching po ako. They thought it was me. This year I hardly ever taught afterschool classes."

"Oh," Andrea said with a nod, "so now they think it was you that caused them to fail?"

"I'm afraid so. Because I didn't teach night school three times a week."

I got out the instant chocolate mix and put some in each of our cups and began imitating a Tate Oral English lesson.

"This is a cup. These are cups. I'm putting some chocolate mix into these cups."

"You're putting some chocolate mix into those cups," Andrea said in response.

"Now I'm pouring hot water into the cups."

"You're pouring hot water into the cups."

"Now I'm stirring the hot water in the cups."

Andrea had already dropped out of class, so I continued on my own.

"Now I'm pouring milk into the cups," I said as I got the thick evaporated milk to come out. "And I'm stirring the milk in the cups."

"You know," I told Andrea as we sipped our hot chocolate. When I first came here, I didn't want to disturb the balance of nature, so I tried to live in harmony with the cockroaches that were crawling up and down that cupboard." I indicated the three leveled cabinet with the screens on the front next to the kerosene stove. "Then one day I was stirring my hot chocolate, and you know the way the evaporated milk goes to the bottom and you have to keep stirring as you drink. I'd stir and sip, stir and sip. And then, when I got closer to the bottom, the milk was still thick at the bottom—even lumpy."

"Oh, and was the lump a cockroach?"

"You guessed it. That was the day I decided not to live in harmony with nature. I got a spray and sprayed all over, and I never saw another cockroach."

"I'm stirring my cocoa," Andrea said, bringing her spoon up to be sure the thickness was only the sweet evaporated milk.

It was time to get back to agonizing about my lost diary.

"I wrote about what the head master said, and part of it worried me. He was apologetic about the teachers who didn't take the classes seriously, and that made me feel good. But he also made a judgment about a younger teacher who really has a better grasp of how to teach oral English than another. He said he was going to give the younger teacher the sixth-grade classes another teacher had been teaching for years."

"Not the prestigious sixth-grade classes!" Andrea said.

"Yes, and I think that will be really humiliating to the teacher who's been teaching that level. I like him so much. He's the one who used to say that I was shining like a glittering star back in the days when I was doing that. So that was confidential. I'd hate for someone to read it."

"Oh, I thought you were worried about what you wrote about your social life."

"Well, that too," I said. "Remember when they told us we wouldn't have any social life?"

"And I really haven't except for Roger, and we've been very discreet about that. You, on the other hand…"

"I'm still trying to remember what I wrote about that social life in my diary."

"Anything scandalous?"

"I haven't done anything scandalous. But I have described 'what lips my lips have kissed and where and why,' and I haven't forgotten because I wrote it all down in my diary. I've done what gave me such a bad reputation in junior high school. I've kissed back! And more than one man."

Here I sang the beginning of a song from Barbra Streisand's Third Album, changing only the number, "'One kiss, five men to save it for.'"

Andrea laughed. She loved musicals as much as I did, so I sang a line from *Finian's Rainbow*. "When I'm not near to the man that I love,

I love the man who's near."

"Isn't it *girl?*" Andrea asked.

"In the song, but not in my life."

"That's from *Finian's Rainbow*, isn't it? I saw that in Nuku'alofa."

"So did I! Ron took me. Or maybe it was Vincent. Or Sione." I sighed and sang again. "When I can't fondle the hand that I'm fond of, I fondle the hand at hand."

"I'm glad we both love musicals," Andrea said.

"Yes, that brings us closer," I said. "You know, you're the only girl in the Peace Corps that I feel close to. I feel close to a lot of men. You can be affectionate with men in a way you can't be with women. And I've avoided Peace Corps couples although Tavi brought us all together a couple of weeks ago, and I managed to alienate them further."

"By doing what?"

"Being me. You know a lot of the PCVs flock around Tavi. He's the closest they can get to a mountain top in India. They think of him as their guru, so he leads a lot of discussions, and he invited me to join in one up at L &M's place. He brought up the subject of Women's Lib and read something from a book he had about how well housewives are treated in Denmark. That's where he comes from. No one responded very enthusiastically when Tavi brought up the subject, but we talked about it long enough for me to call Judy an Uncle Tom—and I really like her—and Bill a male chauvinist—those stupid labels—though I did preface them with 'You *might* be called…' They said they were happily married, but I wanted to make analogies—The happy Negro before the Black Movement, the Happy Housewife before Women's Lib. I can be so obnoxious. Last year I attacked *Love Story*, and this year I attacked marriage. I'm surprised Tavi wants to include me in these gatherings. Is he trying to save me the way Tika was trying until he gave up—not for Our Lord and Savior Jesus Christ but for something New Age?"

"I wonder why he dresses the way he does," Andrea said. "He looks like someone who's been shipwrecked. And left on a desert island too long."

"Is that my cue to sing 'Hello, Dolly'?" I asked. "He's a nice person. He asked me to take some pictures of him at Leafa's. She's the widow of the Havea that was brought up to be the chief of the village. Tavi told me the younger brother was kept uneducated so there wouldn't be any competition between them. But then the big brother died. Anyway, he wanted some pictures to send to his mother in Denmark, and after I took them, he asked me to see him tomorrow at five. That'll be between the time I have lunch with Kalala's family and dinner with Sione at Langi and Fuiva's. Then the kids are coming over to spend the night."

"You do keep a packed schedule," Andrea said.

"That's my social life," I said. "I hope they bring the diary back before then. I'm not leaving that behind."

"So if you don't get it back, we won't be boarding Fiji Airways together?" Andrea asked.

"That's another thing I have to look into tomorrow. I made a reservation with Fiji Airways three weeks ago, but they don't have any record of it. But even if they find my ticket, I'm not leaving until I get my diary back."

"And if you never get it back?"

"'Alu e i," I said, using the word for saying goodbye when you're staying and the other person is leaving.

Andrea and I spent the rest of the evening on our Description of Service Reports for the Peace Corps and the report on the Teachers Retraining Centers for Mr. McMurdo, who was the foreign Director of Education. In the morning we went into Nuku'alofa together to turn in our reports and to check with Fiji Airways about the reservation just in case my diary was returned in time for me to be on the plane the next day. But the first stop I made was one to get a new notebook.

I filled in the blanks on the cover:

My Government of Tonga Exercise book
Name: Tina Martin
Standard: Lower than I'd like
Subject: Leaving Tonga—or Staying If My Other Diary Isn't Returned.

Thursday, December 2nd, 1971 Last Full Day in Tonga

I had wanted to pay close attention to every detail of Nuku'alofa because I knew that I might never see it again. But all I remember is that my diary was still missing even though several Tongans stopped me to tell me that they'd heard the announcement on the radio and wanted me to take a brand new basket they had made. I thanked them but explained that I needed what was inside the old one—"A teacher's report." I remember a lot of dust and a bus ride back to Pea, the village stop right before Ha'ateiho, where Kalala's grandparents 'Ana and Pepe, had prepared a private feast for me.

They apologized that there was only chicken instead of the more ceremonial pig.

"They was going to kill my little piggy!" Kalala said with a sob.

"I'm glad they didn't," I told her. But in my heart of hearts I was also sort of sorry about the chicken. One of the many things I'd loved about Tonga was that animals were permitted to move around in families before they were slaughtered. Quite often in front of my *fale* I'd see a mother hen with six chickens crossing the lawn. I'm not quite sure where they were going, but they had freedom of movement—at least for a while.

But my freedom of movement was restricted by my determination to get my diary back—or stay.

During our private feast we focused on Kalala and how bright she was. I asked about Line only to the degree that would be polite, certainly not to the extent that I'd written about him in my missing diary.

After lunch Kalala and I went on to my fale in Ha'ateiho to check for my missing basket—not there—and then she walked me to Leafa's home to meet Tavi, so I wouldn't get lost. She then ran back to her village and her little piggy.

Tavi was wearing a tupenu, a sheer open shirt, and a big straw hat. He led me to a lagoon, where he helped me into a boat, saying, "Give me your hand."

That may not have been the first time we ever touched, but I couldn't remember another time.

He took me out on the boat, which reminded me of my reunion with my high school crush just weeks before I went into Peace Corps training. Because my sister was being such a conscientious chaperone, the only chance we had to be alone was out on the boat. But I drained that lake from my "inward eye" and looked at Tavi. He was probably only in his forties, but his beard made him look older—like Jesus, who lived to be only thirty-two but looked older. He had the same coloring as Jesus in the Mormon churches that seemed to delineate each village. Light brown beard and hair, blue eyes, slim build.

"A Peace Corps Volunteer spoke very wisely to me," he said as he rowed. "She said that I shouldn't let my feelings go unexpressed. She said, 'Tell Tina.'"

Oh, my God, I thought. He has read my diary, and he wants to give me advice like "Don't. Don't do what you do. Don't be who you are. And if you do, don't keep a diary. Don't."

But it turned out that the operative word was *do*. I can't remember his exact words, but he told me he had tender feelings for me, that he loved me, and he wondered if I would consider becoming his wife.

"You're asking me to marry you?" I asked in astonishment. (He had said, "Give me your hand.")

"Yes, if you would consider it. You don't have to give me your decision today."

"Oh, Tavi," I said. "I feel very honored that you'd ask me such a thing, but we really don't know each other."

"I feel that I know you," he said.

Oh, my God, he's read my diary!

"You remind me of myself when I first came to Tonga," he went on.

"Oh, Tavi," I said. "I really appreciate the thought, but…"

I thought of what a responsibility we have to those who love us or think they do. I felt both touched by his having such an idea and also protective of him. How could I be both clear and kind?

"You don't have to give me your answer today. And as my mother says, a wife needs a nest. We could live where you chose."

"Thank you so much, Tavi," I said. "But I'm afraid you're too much like Jesus Christ, and I'm too little like Mary Magdalene."

I can't remember coming ashore, but we must have. It was time for me to return to my village and check on that basket before getting ready for my date with Sione, who was taking me to dinner at Langi and Fuiva's home.

"So, this is your last night in Tonga," Sione said, as he drove us there. "Have you gotten back your basket? I heard about your loss on the radio."

"I didn't really lose it. I just put it down and someone must have taken it by mistake."

"How long does it for them to figure out they have the wrong basket?" he asked.

"Longer than I'd hoped," I said.

Fuiva was very warm and welcoming. She'd prepared a card for me that said on the envelope, "To Our Darling Tina."

"We heard about your lost basket on the radio," she said.

"I haven't gotten it back yet," I said.

"And you leave tomorrow afternoon?"

"Not without my basket," I said.

"I'm going to get her ticket straightened out with Fiji Airways tomorrow," Sione said.

"What are you going to do when you get back to America?" Fuiva asked.

"I'm going to take my Peace Corps readjustment allowance and leave," I said. "But I'm not going back without my basket."

"A pretty girl like you. Don't you want to get married?" Fuiva asked me.

"If I could marry more than one man. I believe in fidelity, but I'd like to be faithful to more than one man. If polygamy were legal, I'd choose to be a polygamist."

"You mean polyandrist," said Harvard-educated Langi, who had been very quiet throughout dinner.

And that's all I remember about the evening. I don't even remember which songs Sione and I sang as he was driving me back home to Ha'ateiho. But I do remember his telling me that he'd pick me up the next morning and help me straighten out the ticket problem with Fiji Airways.

When we drove up to my fale, the children—Kili, 'Aivi, Kalala, and Fehi— were waiting outside. At first Sione tried to shoo them away, but I reminded him that I'd invited them to spend the night, and he drove off.

Once inside I performed my magic trick of putting little corn kernels into a pot, covering it with a lid, and placing it over the kerosene stove until mysterious popping sounds could be heard. Then, just seconds later, I took the lid off, and in the place of the little corn kernels were puffy white pieces called popcorn. Shouting with joy and disbelief, the children were as elated as if I'd pulled a rabbit—or maybe a rat—out of a hat.

We practiced the Tongan dance to "Hopo'e la'a" and sang some English songs I'd taught them.

I was very tired and when I excused myself to go to my "bedroom," the part of my fale partially separated from the other by mats and tapa cloth, there on my bed was my basket. I looked inside, and there was my diary, right on top, where I'd left it. Where they'd left it, whoever they were.

"Someone returned my basket!" I announced.

The children cheered! They'd heard the announcement on the radio but didn't know who had returned it.

"Whoever had it didn't get a reward," I told them. "How did they get into my *fale*?" I asked. No one knew.

I was too tired to read it to figure out what someone else might have read, but I kept my diary in bed with me and fell asleep while the children were still chattering. I woke up in the middle of the night and looked in on the four little girls sleeping, spread out on their own mats, semi-covered with their own small blankets or sweaters.

The kerosene lamp was still lit, and I moved it to the table behind my bed and started looking through my newly-found diary, which this time opened automatically to the page of who got what after I left Tonga.

My green plastic garbage can for storing water. Pot and lid. Tea kettle. Bath tin. Dish tin. Tin cups. Food in cabinet. Towels. Frying pan. Kerosene stove. Thermos. Blue wine glass. Children books. Card games. Jigsaw puzzle of the world. Magic slate. Blackboard with abacus.

It must have been a village effort, getting back that basket. If I stayed, they wouldn't get all these valuable possessions. But the stove had already been promised to Malia, who after doing some wash for me, had asked for it several weeks earlier. Should I have bequeathed it instead to Likua, who took me to Vaikeli and fed me all those Sundays? Or even Loiloi for all the help she gave me the first months I was there? Too late.

I had already given the blackboard with abacus to 'Aivi, whose family lived on the grounds at 'Atele Si'i. The last day of school, she'd come around to help me pack the gifts the villagers brought me, and I asked her what, of all the things from the closet, she would like to have. She gave it her complete attention, touching one item at a time, and then she chose the blackboard with the abacus. Tongan children didn't have any toys. They created their own play, juggling oranges, singing, dancing. Now she had an educational toy. I hoped it would only enhance what she already had, not dimmish it.

I sat on my bed and wrote a farewell letter to Tonga.

"This is my letter to the world that never wrote to me." Emily Dickinson, who had funerals in her brain. I have wars in mine or at least battles.

This was the year three new things entered my house: Jim's orange typewriter, Tika's plastic chair, and Mike's cassette player/recorder—Fie palangi (For posterity *fie palangi* means "want to be white man" and is not *faka-Tonga*, the Tongan way.)

Did those fie-palangi possessions take over my soul? I was more "into" Tonga the first year. I started leaving at the beginning of the second. That's something I've learned. I'm better at the beginning than at the end. There's something about anticipation that takes me out of the present, and I start closing down, the way I did when I took voice lessons. I'd run out of breath at the end of a line, and my voice teacher would have me sing that line twice to prove that I had plenty of breath until I came to the end the second time and let down.

I wondered how many people I had let down.

Since my dad is a psychologist, I've taken the Minnesota Multiphasic Personality Test just for fun and, to the question, "I know who's to blame for all my problems," I've always checked True, even though I now realize that's supposed to be a sign of paranoia—a belief that the whole world is against me. I've always known I was to blame for my problems. I still know that. So I can't really blame my *fie palangi* furnishing. But this second year has left me feeling not so much disappointed as disappointing, what I hate most to be.

I don't think the world is against me, but I think I sometimes sabotage some really good situations and hurt some really good people, and I feel dangerous. On the battlefield of my brain, I try to shoot me down, but I miss and someone else gets the bullet.

I want to sum up what I think of people now, as I prepare to leave this island.

Of course I still love Jim, Ron, Vincent, and Line, which makes me love myself a little bit less for acting up the way I sometimes do with them, as if I were warding off love—or warring off love? Or is it just marriage I battle against? I think of that song from *Flower Drum Song*, "Don't Marry Me!" I want to warn these wonderful men I love how punishing marriage to me would be, as if they were down on their knees begging. How presumptuous of me—although I'd never have presumed that of Tavi.

There are men I like, like Tika and Tavi. Funny how they sound almost like twin brothers. But Tika is really Nigel, and Tavi is really Preben Kauffmann.

Tika wanted to save my soul, and Tavi, to my great surprise, wanted to marry me.

I feel an affection for both Tika and Tavi. They were good to me, and they're living according to their convictions. That's something to admire, even if I don't share their convictions.

But neither Tika nor Tavi got what they wanted from me. Did any of the men I love?

I've always loved the children, even when they came by and, peering in my *fale* window, blocked the sun, which was the only source of light during the day. The whole *fale* would go dark until they either came inside away from the window or went on their way. There were days when I showed impatience. "I can't see! You're blocking the light."

But I know that they *are* the light. They are definitely what I've loved most about my Peace Corps experience. (I don't count, Jim, Ron, Vincent, and Line as my Peace Corps experience since I have in no way been of help to them.)

Kili, of course, stands out. She told me earlier this month that she was glad I live alone. "The man angry to the wife, then I afraid," she said. I think of how I felt during my parents' frequent fights and wonder how much that has to do with my wanting to put off marriage and back away from men I love. I'm conscious of wanting to put off marriage until I can hold my own in a way my mother never could, but maybe I'm not conscious of everything that goes on in my warring brain.

Kalala is up there with Kili. I love her not just because she's Line's niece. I love her spirit! "They was going to kill my little piggy!" Of course, Kalala has had advantages other children haven't had. Mele Taufe'ulungaki, of the distinguished Taufe'ulungaki family of women, got her accepted at the Side School, where the children of expatriates and of Peace Corps country directors and of visiting dignitaries go.

Fatafehi, who used to join me for breakfast after I gave her 10 *seniti* to cross the lawn to Likua's *falekaloa* and get a loaf of bread and bottle of kerosene. Fatafehi's little sister Hinahina, who used to come to my door with one of Loiloi's cigarettes in her mouth, and she would take a puff and say, "I AM fine thank you."

I look over my diaries and realize that I've written a lot more about the children and the men than I have about the teaching, which was my assignment and my justification for being here.

For days villagers have sent farewell presents my way, as I suspect they have been instructed to do, and I feel ashamed because I haven't "earned" these gifts and don't deserve them.

Pesi, the wife of the village noble Havea and the mother of Lupe, is such a sweet woman. She sent Fehi over with some pretty tapa cloth and two mats for my family. "You mommy," said Pesi.

What was I leaving behind at the Teachers Retraining Center? When the young teacher was acting goofy, maybe rebelling against our "demanding too much," we got a note from another teacher: "Dearest Tina and Ani, I'm terribly sorry that we teachers shouldn't act like children. So please do forgive us."

I'm so ready to forgive other people—when I think about how grateful I'd be if they forgave me. But I am superlative: Most defective.

Was I indirectly responsible for the demotion of Tevita, devoted sixth-grade teacher, who used to tell me "Tina, behold, you are glittering like a shining star"?

My star is tarnished, and I no longer glitter, but what about him? I'll bet whoever had my diary—if they read it—won't obsess about my "social life" and my wickedness in "kissing back." But how did I make them feel? How did I make Tevita feel? And what about the others?

I feel as if I have two black eyes and a bloody mouth—all self-inflicted.

It's time to leave.

This would have been my grim and final melodramatic self-assessment if it hadn't been for Kili and the other children. Sione was picking me up, but in the meantime I was waiting with the children who were waiting for the bus, because there were too many to fit into Sione's car. I suggested that we review "The Twelve Days of Christmas" with the Tongan images I'd substituted. The kids remembered it better than I did, and I told them how impressed I was by their memories after almost a year.

"It's because," Kili said, "We sing in school. The teacher ask to us what we know, and we tell to her 'Chim Chiminee' and one boy stand up and sing 'Mickey Mouse, Donald Duck, Mickey Mouse' and everybody laugh to him. And we sing 'The First Day of Christmas,' and our teacher tell to us where we learn the song and we tell to her from the Peace Corps name Tina, and she say that you a good Peace Corps."

By the time Kili finished her explanation I felt an elation mixed with sweet hysteria. My mission had been a success. After 2 years of sacrifice and grueling labor, (theirs, not mine) the children were carrying on my songs. I sang, I danced, I cried aloud.

"Oku fiefie e Tina!" {Tina's happy} one kid said, and I agreed.

I thought about what Sali, one of the teachers at 'Atele Si'i, had once said. "Usually when a person go down the street singing and dancing, people say that a foolish, but when you do it, people think it okay. They don't say foolish. They just say 'Tina.'"

I don't remember breakfast and I have only the vaguest recollection of my farewell to the teachers at 'Atele Si'i, who liked me better the first year. At the airport we were given kahuas (leis), and Ron, who was staying in Tonga longer, stayed with me until the end. So did my headmaster Sione Mafanga. Sione K. straightened out my ticket for Fiji Airways so I could fly. But when I got on Fiji Airways, and we were taking off, I felt hope that my redemption was in the children and the songs.

{When I got back home, I finished typing up my fictional accounts of Tonga. One began "It's not true that I went mad and burned down the village." Another began, "It was a valid expression of human existence." But this one, I'll give you in its entirety. To Whom It May Concern: I Am Your Mother.}

TO WHOM IT MAY CONCERN: I AM YOUR MOTHER
A work of fiction by Tina Martin

The Fiji Isles, February 1971

To Whom It May Concern:

I am your mother. Or I was your mother. I am, as I write this. I was, as you read this, if you read this, years from now. It occurs to me that if I pack you enough luggage before I leave you on the doorstep, even though I'll no longer have you, you'll still have some of me and you'll have all of you, not just the part that's left after adoption. I'm packing with you everything I think you would want to know and I hope not too much of what you wouldn't. I would like you to remember me, even though you've never met me, and I'd like to help you like yourself, which I think is a mother's main job. Maybe it's already done, by the time you get this. Some people like themselves almost instinctively.

I'm sending you word-photographs of me and other members of the family you'll never have met. I've heard they won't let you see real photographs of your first mother and father. All you can get are words giving their vital statistics and medical histories, which may tell you about your chances of getting diabetes or breast cancer (and I don't even know whether you've got breasts since I don't even know whether you're male or female or what age you are when—and if—you read this). But statistics and medical histories won't tell you what you really want to know about blood relatives or about yourself. So I'm thinking of including my diaries—all the journals I kept when I was a Peace Corps Volunteer in Tonga. I always kept a notebook in my basket so that wherever I went, I could write things down any chance I got. I'd tell the Tongans I was writing down new Tongan words or letters home, and it would be true. 'Oku ou fai Tohi. (Tohi is the Tongan word for both letter and book.) I wrote to everyone in my notebooks—not just to myself. I've always felt that, no matter where I was or how frightened I was, I wasn't alone as long as I had a pen and paper. So my Peace Corps diaries have all kinds of notes—my thoughts and feelings, observations on what was going on around me, and descriptions of the men I loved—your father among them.

I'd really like to keep the diaries, but I don't want anyone who knows me ever to read them, so I'm afraid to take them home. Nothing's safe there. Somehow it doesn't bother me that YOU should read them someday. I've always found it easy to reveal things to strangers, and I can't imagine that I'll have enough time to tell you all you'd want to know before I have to leave Fiji to give birth to you, and then put you in a basket and sail you down the Nile to the pharaoh's daughter. (Moses was also adopted and managed to do quite well—eventually— even without his biological mother's diaries.)

Of course, I'm not really leaving you on a doorstep or sailing you down the Nile in a basket. I'm arranging your adoption through an agency in New Zealand because I love that country and no one knows me there. That's where Victor's from originally, and he's gotten me a job there. I'll leave Christchurch right after I give you birth and sign the papers. Right now I'm in Fiji, in an office that's really for the use of Victor, one of the men who may be your father. I thought of letting a

Tongan family adopt you. That's common. They'll borrow your kerosene. They'll borrow your kerosene lamp. They'll borrow your children. It's not at all uncommon there for a mother to give her child to someone else in the village to bring up, and children don't address their mothers as "mother." Just by the first name. Mine is Sarah. In Tonga they pronounce it Sela. But I don't think adoption officials will let you know my name. They'll probably cross out things like that. Biological mothers have to remain anonymous, like poems.

No one knows the real reason that I left or where I am now. Everyone thinks I'm back in South Carolina for a funeral, but I'd never go back there to have you because you might be half-Tongan, and in South Carolina, that would be like being half-black. Black is beautiful, but not in South Carolina. There you'd be an example of miscegenation, something gone wrong with genetics. But it isn't true. Half caste children are the prettiest, I've noticed. I grew up believing they'd have polka dots.

I'm so sorry to say that you MIGHT be half Tongan or that Victor MIGHT be your father. You probably wonder what kind of ex-mother doesn't know for sure. But I promise that my not knowing doesn't reveal what you might think it does about me. I'll explain all this later.

I'm going to make sure that you're adopted by a good family who can give you a good start in life and prove what a good mother I was for the short time that I was one. There's so much I want to tell you while I still have time. It's strange, but I sometimes feel not as if I'm about to give birth, but that I'm about to die, and I want to be sure my child will be provided for. But a dying mother has seen her child before leaving it. And the child has seen her. I'm just a ghost to you, though you're much more than that to me. You have a very definite physical form. And I'm not dying, but my days are numbered, that's for sure! I'm in my eighth month. I'm not terminally ill, but terminally pregnant.

And so now's the time to arrange to be the anonymous donor who gave you not just a kidney, but every organ you've got and gave your adoptive parents you. So what do you want to know? And what do I want you to know? How much will they let you know about me beyond my medical history? There's usually just a form to fill out, I hear. I want to leave you volumes. Everything you need to know before we never meet again.

Well, let's see how much I can sum up for you now that I have Victor's electric typewriter. (It's taken me more than an hour to learn to use it. The good thing about a typewriter over pen is that you can go faster and keep up with your thoughts. But this electric typewriter gets ahead of my thoughts and spurts out letters and skips lines. And it does seem strange to use an electric typewriter—such a modern contraption—to write about my life in a place that didn't have electricity.)

I have to tell you, too, that this isn't the first letter I wrote you. I wrote you last night, but when I read it over, it was so rambling that I thought you would stop reading. This time, I'm going to try to write it all down very systematically—as if it were a book with chapters. And I guess the first chapter should be Family Background.

Your Family Background

The last time I described everyone in our family, I broke down sobbing—not just out of sympathy for them but because I was afraid the Peace Corps would de-select me on the grounds that with a family like ours I couldn't be normal, and that's what they were testing for—normalcy. Before sending Peace Corps trainees from the mainland to Hawaii for training, they had a staging in San Jose to de-select anyone whose airfare they thought was a bad investment.

They put us in encounter groups and gave us games to play while they observed us. But the big moment was the psychological screening in the motel rooms in San Jose.

There were about eight psychologists—one in each motel room—and we were to march in, one by one, so they could sum up our mental state in the fifteen minutes allotted. If we didn't pass, we'd be sent back home to straighten ourselves out and apply again or decide that the Peace Corps wasn't our bag. If we did pass, we'd be sent on to Peace

Corps training in Hawaii to be screened some more.

Before I learned better, I was sometimes spontaneous, so when I walked in the motel room, I said, "Well, it isn't every day I'm asked to meet a man alone in his hotel room."

I thought he would laugh and say something like, "Yeah, it is kind of an unusual setting, isn't it." But instead, he was completely silent for a moment and just stared at me.

"I don't know what to say to that," he said when he finally spoke.

"You don't?" I asked, wondering what he meant.

"Well, you come in here and immediately try to seduce me."

"I do?" I asked. I was afraid to disagree, for fear he'd think like Hamlet's mother, "The lady doth protest too much." That's a good thing to remember when you go through life. Don't deny too much or they'll think you're guilty. Besides, I thought it would hurt his feelings to know that I wasn't trying to seduce him—not because he would feel undesirable, but because he'd feel like a bad psychologist who hadn't figured me out right. So I just left it at that.

"I do?"

He asked me to sit down, and when I did, he said, "Well, look at you!" And so I did. I looked at as much of me as I could see, being me. And he went on.

"The way you sit. Like a queen on a throne." And I guess he meant the way I was holding on to both arms of the armchair because, frankly, I was afraid of a crash landing, and there was no seatbelt!

Having established rapport or broken the ice or whatever, he then explained that our time was limited, that fifteen minutes wasn't really long enough to learn all there was to know about a person, so they'd devised a clever scheme to maximize our short time together. Ahead of time, they'd asked us to fill out a list of people in our family—their names, ages, and addresses—and now I was supposed to describe them as he called their names.

"Describe your father," he began.

At this point, I was too nervous not to be candid. I just let it all spill out. (Well, maybe not all of it.)

"Well," I said, "he's very intelligent. And politically active. He organizes his life around causes."

"So he must be pleased that you're joining the Peace Corps."

"Uh huh," I said, grateful that I wasn't wired for a polygraph. Your grandfather thought I should go to a South American country and help start a meaningful revolution instead of being a pawn for the Peace Corps, which he thinks is a branch of American imperialism.

"He's the kind of person who gives us birthday and Christmas presents in the form of contributions in our names. To SANE, CORE, the NAACP."

"So your father is a generous man."

I looked at him quizzically. "Well, to causes. He's also very frugal. He doesn't believe in spending money on things like clothes and furniture or appliances. Everything at home comes from Good Will. He says he's never wanted us to be more privileged than the rest of the world's children. He's been successful."

"So, are you close to your father?"

"Well, it's a little bit hard to be close to him because he's very busy and very tense. He's not happy with the way the world is going, and he has a very hot temper."

"What does he do?" the psychologist asked.

"He screams," I said.

"No," he said, and he laughed. "I mean, what does he do for a living? What's his job?"

"Oh," I said. "He's a photographer. Maybe you've heard of him? Paul Nye?"

"No. Should I have?"

"Well, he's well-known for some photographs he took during the Civil Rights Movement. Of sit-ins. He had an anthology a few years ago, too, that gave him almost celebrity status. It was just after the March on Washington, and it was kind of a photo history of what led up to that."

"Well, well," the psychologist said. Then, almost as an after-thought, he asked, "What does he yell about?"

"He yells if we put something away and he can't find it or if we say something stupid. He yells about China not being admitted to the U.N."

"Uh huh," he said, looking down at the form. "Now, your parents must be separated. Your father lives in South Carolina and your mother lives in California."

"Yes," I said. Los Angeles."

"So, what's she like?"

"Well, she doesn't worry a lot about China not being admitted to the U.N. My mother's more into...herself. She's into acting."

"Oh, would I know her?"

"No. She's never actually made it a career." I refrained from saying, "She's just made it a way of life." I refrained from telling him that she acted all the time because I didn't want him to think that was what I was doing.

I decided it was all right to mention the fact that she was beautiful.

"I'm not surprised," the psychologist said.

"Thank you," I said, and then I wonder if maybe I shouldn't have acted like I knew what he meant. Your grandmother and I are really quite different in our appearances. I have red hair, from your pater-nal grandfather's side of the family, and I'm tall. Your grandmother's "petite" and dark. I decided not to describe her beyond that, but you should know that she's funny. She never stops talking. Absolutely nev-er. If there's a silence, she panics and tries to fill it as quickly as she can. Your grandfather calls it her staccato repartee. Whatever it is, it's inces-sant. She interrupts everyone. She even interrupts herself. Right in the middle of a sentence. And she lies. She lies for no apparent reason ex-cept for the thrill of deceiving. And she's always getting dressed. It takes her three hours to get dressed just to go to the grocery store because she wants to be sure everything's just right, and it's a dress rehearsal for other places.

"So you grew up with just your mother?" the psychologist asked.

"No, Daddy got custody," I said, knowing he'd expect an explanation. I couldn't just say, as Peter did, "Mother ran away." I was trying to pass a normalcy test. And oh, if he knew about life with Daddy!

"My father got custody of us because he married again soon after my mother left, so he had someone to take care of us." I didn't mention that the person who took care of us was me. Our stepmother Helen, while brilliant, was addicted to talking on the phone, and whenever she got off, she just wanted to die. She attempted suicide more than once. I took care of HER from the time I was in first grade.

"To take care of you and your brother Peter," the psychologist said, glancing at the Family Inventory Form. "And Delana and Mel."

"At the time, there was just Peter and me. Delana and Mel are half-brother and sister."

"Describe your brother Peter."

"Oh, Peter's brilliant. He has a really good imagination. And he's really good with words." I stopped, thinking of the irony of this.

"And he still lives at home?"

"Yes," I said, beginning in a very matter-of-fact way. In fact, he'd recently been admitted as a patient at the South Carolina State Hospital. "He has some neurological problems," I said.

"What kind"

"He has a nervous tic, and he screams out things."

"Like what?"

I began to cry. I couldn't just say (close your eyes if you're too young for obscenity) "Screw you, you goddamned fucking bitch."

"Obscenities," I said, and it came out in a sob.

"It sounds like he might have Tourette Syndrome," the doctor said.

"What?" I asked, amazed that he knew a name for what my brother did.

"Tourette syndrome," he repeated. "Not a lot's known about it, but—I'm sorry there's no Kleenex." He looked around and opened a drawer. "Could I offer you a Gideon Bible? I'm really sorry. You must really love our brother very much."

And then I really sobbed. I sobbed because I really love my brother very much but I'd always loved my brother and yet I usually had the ability to talk about his problems with almost clinical detachment.

You uncle was a child prodigy. He was just exceptionally bright, and he caught everyone's attention because of that. He was tested at the age of 4 and found to be a genius. He could manipulate numbers in an astonishing way. He could get nuances of words, too. He was just exceptionally bright. And then when he was about eight years old, he developed a nervous tic. We thought it was an unfortunate mannerism. It came soon after our mother left, so doctors thought it might be a response to being abandoned. And then he started having spasms. He'd start kicking or flailing his arms. And then, he started shouting out profanities. This was in the Bible belt, where the strongest language I heard, outside m father's, was "Good Lord!"

That's not what your uncle was saying. He'd say words I'd rather not repeat and he didn't want to repeat them, either, but he couldn't help himself. He'd shout until he was hoarse. And he started hurting himself in other ways.

That's how I always summed up my brother when people would ask. I'd speak with detachment. It was like reading the headlines in the morning. If you let yourself feel them, you wouldn't be able to get on with the day. So you try to read them without feeling them and then you can eat your breakfast and otherwise function. So, I'll tell you what I didn't tell the psychologist. I was crying because I knew now that they'd de-select me from the Peace Corps. They were going to reject me because I didn't come from a normal home, and if I were rejected, I'd have to go back to that not normal home because they needed me there.

The psychologist really looked sympathetic.

"I wish there were something I could do to comfort you," he said, reaching in his pocket. "I don't have any Kleenex. Would you like a piece of gum?"

He unwrapped me a piece, which I took because I didn't want to hurt his feelings, even though I don't like to chew gum because it bothers me that no matter how long you chew, it's still there, exactly the same.

"I wish I could comfort you," he said. "I wish I could put my arms around you and comfort you, but I guess that wouldn't be very professional."

"I know," I nodded. I looked at him, looking anguished. "Maybe if I put my arms around you?"

And I walked over to where he was sitting on the bed—not to seduce him, please understand, but just to make it possible for him to comfort me without being unprofessional. I figured that I really needed comforting because my dream of joining the Peace Corps and going to Tonga had just been shattered, and it was all his fault.

I slipped into his arms, and he stroked my hair in a very nice way.

"I'm afraid," he said, after I'd had his arms around me for a couple of minutes, "that our time is up."

I stood up and waited to be dismissed from the session—discharged from the Peace Corps.

He walked me to the door.

"Here," he said, handing me his card, and I thought, "God, so this is how he builds up his therapy business."

"I hope you'll look me up in two years when you get out of the Peace Corps," he said. "I'm sure you'll make a great volunteer."

And so I was "cleared" and sent to Hawaii, where, in training, I met one of the men who might be your father.

DANNY

Of the three men who might be your father, Danny was the first I met. He was another PCV, an American from New York City, who I first met in Peace Corps staging just a day after I was "cleared" by the psychologist in the motel room. The people who had come to San Jose just for the staging saw us off when we were getting on the airport bus.

"Have a good time," they said. "Good luck."

And we shook hands or hugged. Danny was the third person to say goodbye to us, so I was surprised when, once seated on the bus, I saw him sit down on the aisle across from me.

"Didn't you just see us off?" I asked.

"Yes," he said. "I like seeing people off."

He was a Peace Corps trainee, too, just like us. Well, maybe not just like us. You'll read about him in my diaries. But for now, I just want to say that he was very funny and very smart and I sometimes thought that of all the men I met, he was the one who my brother Peter would have been most like if he hadn't developed "complications" along the way. I later told this to Danny, who was one of the few people I told about Peter, and Danny said, "You're saying that of all the guys you know, I'm the most like your brother who's in a mental institution?"

I also told Danny that Peter was at State Hospital, something I hadn't put down on the list of addresses.

Another time he told me, "You know, you're just like your brother only your tics come out in song." He was referring to my tendency to sing snatches of Broadway show tunes to hold my end in the conversation. Musicals! That's where I got my first notion of what romance was all about.

While our parents were busy fighting, I'd take Peter up to the attic where they stored their old records, and we'd listen to their old 78 rps. (That's what they used to have before 45s and 33rpms.) Or I'd listen to them alone, over and over again, imagining that I was in a beautiful restaurant with red velvet wall paper and some wonderful man was singing to me:

When you're near the murmuring of the breeze
Becomes a symphony.
A rhapsody.
And when I hear you call
So softly to me,

I don't hear a call

At all.

I hear a rhapsody. (OOOoooOOOoooOOOooo from the chorus)

Another song I liked went like this:

With a song in my heart,

I behold your adorable face.

Just a song from the start.

But it soon was a hymn to your praise.

When the music swells,

I'm touching your hand,

It tells me your stand-

ing near and

At the sound of your voice,

Heaven knows its importance to me,

Does my heart still rejoice

That a song such as ours came to be...

This early education on what love was all about continued with Johnny Mathis, who was "Wonderful, Wonderful," but I found romance mostly in Broadway tunes. In the attic I found SOUTH PACIFIC, OKLAHOMA, CAROUSEL, SHOWBOAT, and PAL JOEY, which I listened to over and over till I knew them by heart. Then, no matter what was going on around me, something beautiful was playing in my head. That's how I got through all the fights at home, as well as Algebra and geometry classes.

When we were really little—before Peter developed the tic and when Mother was still with us—we used to spend every Saturday and every summer day in the movie theater, where we'd see MGM musicals with Ann Blyth, Jane Powell, Debbie Reynolds, Gene Kelly, Cyd Charise, Marge and Gower Champion. I really became convinced that when you were in love, not only was it The Loveliest Night of the Year but you always sang to each other about it. It was just second-nature. Then one day I was at a friend's house, and she had a record with a real ugly red, black and white photo on the cover. It showed a girl and a boy running in front of a garbage can, and I wanted to listen to the soundtrack from BEN HUR instead. But Linda, who I liked because she was a misfit like me, said, "No, listen to this," and she made me listen to a song called "Tonight," a song from the ugly album, and that's when I entered a new world I wish I could share with you. Have you ever heard of WEST SIDE STORY? That was the album with the garbage can on the cover. I borrowed it and memorized every song, and I starved for a week so I could buy my own copy with my lunch money—and that was a real sacrifice because the school lunches were so much better than what we got at home. But that's when I learned that there was a whole section of the record shops called "Soundtracks and Original Broadway Show Recordings," and I never ate a school lunch again. Wherever I went, there was always a love scene playing in my head, and the lovers were singing to each other on fire escapes or wherever they might be.

Well, the man who may be your father didn't sing to me, although he sometimes sang with me. Our relationship was romantic, but it wasn't because Danny was romantic. It was because I insisted upon romance, which wasn't prevalent in Peace Corps training, where our life was largely communal. Once we took a walk together on Molokai and got caught in a rainstorm, which could have been the height of romance. In high school I'd seen a movie in which Nancy Kwan and Pat Boone get caught in an avalanche and wind up in a little cottage with a fireplace and a featherbed and a long flannel nightgown for her to wear. I thought the rainstorm was romantic because we'd find shelter in each other's arms, but Danny acted as if he wished it weren't raining. Instead of comforting me, he kept complaining that he was cold. He had a sweatshirt, which he didn't immediately take off and offer to me. But he did put his arms around me, and that felt good. We found a deserted house, which turned out not to be deserted, and the owner of the house gave us steaming coffee and towels to mop ourselves up with. He also gave me his Molokai sweatshirt.

"I hope this doesn't shame you or make you feel guilty," I told Danny, to bring it to his attention that he should feel ashamed and guilty.

"What do you mean?"

"I mean, I hope you don't feel bad that this nice man gave me his sweatshirt before you had a chance to give me yours."

"No," Danny assured me, "I don't feel bad about that."

"I was hoping you wouldn't," I said.

We stayed with the nice man for about an hour, and then the rain stopped and we made a dash for it. A dash wasn't fast enough to beat the second outburst. We ran from tree to tree, shed to shed, and we finally wound up in a bar with horses and hay without the hayride. I always thought hay rides were so romantic—getting in the back with a boy and a bundle or straw and being driven through the night. But his was a barn, and the horse had his behind to us, and pretty soon the horse had to go to the bathroom, but there was no bathroom, so he went right there in front of us the way our half-brother Mel did because for some reason Helen potty trained him on newspapers.

"I never imagined," Danny said, "that we'd wind up in a stable."

That of course prompted me to say, "For there was no room for us in the inn."

If this was not like an MGM musical, I thought, at least it could be of Biblical proportions.

The rain never stopped—and the horse never seemed to either—so we decided that we'd just run back to camp in the rain. Along the way, we stopped for shelter in someone's carport, and as we were holding each other to keep warm, a man with an umbrella approached us.

"We saw you from our window," the kind Filipino-American man said. "We'd like to invite you into our house."

"We'd like to accept!" Danny said, as I thanked the man profusely.

His wife gave us dry clothes to wear while she was spinning our soaked ones in the dryer. We spent the evening talking with them and playing with their children. I saw that Danny was really good with children. I have to say that I rarely look at a guy without wondering what kind of husband and father he would make, and I saw that Danny would make a good father.

Well, maybe he did, but not quite in the way I had in mind.

Anyway, we all had dinner together and they invited us back together. Now, I thought, we were a couple!

"Happy ending!" I said when they dropped us off back at camp.

"Sara," Danny said, "why don't we get married and settle down right here on Molokai and have some beautiful Filipino children like theirs?"

"Okay," I said.

But instead of getting married, settling down, and having some beautiful Filipino children, we went right on—single—with the training program, took our oath of service, and went to Honolulu for our last night on American soil before heading for the South Seas.

Since our life on Molokai had not, even by Danny's standards, been romantic, he said he was going to make up for it by taking me out for Mai Tais and dinner in Honolulu, where our Peace Corps training group was going before leaving the United States for Tonga. To make it more romantic, he said we wouldn't go Dutch but he'd pay with his Peace Corps living allowance.

First we took a walk in a beautiful park, where he wanted to read me a book he loved, A SEPARATE PEACE. I was anxious to love it, too, because I loved Danny, but I just couldn't love the book, no matter how hard I tried, because I thought it was melodramatic. But I managed to keep my opinion to myself and from time to time he'd kiss me and then we'd really kiss, even though in a public park it was bad manners. From time to time, as we were kissing, someone would walk by and give us a disapproving look. Once Danny looked back at a disapproving looker and said, "Because we don't have another place to do it." Then he lowered his voice and explained, "That's in answer to their question 'Why can't you kids do that somewhere else?'"

Then we had dinner, and after we had eaten, and while I was drinking my third Mai Tai and Danny's second one, he told me The Story of His Life, and I fell asleep in his arms. I fell asleep because I had never before had a chance to fall asleep in his arms and now, in my drunken stupor, I had an excuse. I thought it was romantic. However, Danny thought my falling asleep was a reflection on the quality of his life story.

"Just wait, Sara," he said. "My life story will be a lot more interesting after a few weeks in Tonga." So would mine. And yours, of course, would begin.

During our three days in Honolulu, we saw CACTUS FLOWER, HELLO, DOLLY, BOB & TED & CAROL & ALICE, and we even saw CLOSELY WATCHED TRAINS at the University of Hawaii because Danny told me it was his favorite recent movie. I liked it better than A SEPARATE PEACE.

But finally our extended weekend was over, and we had to go back to our group. The next morning we got red leis and boarded Pan Am for Fiji, where we had breakfast before boarding Fiji Airlines for Tonga, where we landed just before lunch in a little grass field. When we got off the plane, we were given fresh leis, and our Tongan experience began.

Danny and I held hands as we went by bus through the island's villages to Nuku'alofa, Tonga's capital. Along the way we saw coconut and banana trees, coconut leaf huts, blue sky and smoke rising from underground ovens.

"It looks," I whispered to Danny, "the way you think it's not going to look because things never look the way you expect them to look."

"Yeah," he said.

"You always expect foreign countries to look strange and exotic, but they always wind up looking like Los Angeles or Greenville, South Carolina. But this really looks strange and exotic."

"Yeah," Danny said.

"Danny, we forgot to get married and settle down on Molokai and have beautiful Filipino children," I said.

But the man who might be your father was in culture shock and didn't speak again until we were at a communal lunch at the Way-In Motel in Nuku'alofa. There he leaned across the papaya to deliver an important message:

"Sara, you're the best date I've ever had," he said. "Dinner in Hawaii, breakfast in Fiji, and lunch in Tonga."

"We should do this more often," I said.

But it was just about time for us to separate. He was going to an outer island, and I was staying on Tongatapu.

"Most people live on a lonely island," I sang to him. And I decided to write whole new lyrics to SOUTH PACIFIC, a musical you should get, if your adoptive parents don't have it, with *your* lunch money.

At 10:30 that morning, I saw Danny off at the wharf, after he'd treated me to several gin and tonics, which I'd drunk alternately with his. He kissed me and boarded the Just David, the boat that would take him to his island.

I waved goodbye and shouted, "Don't feel bad about deserting me!"

"Okay!" he shouted back.

But he returned to my shore the weekend the ship came in, and he became one of the three men who might be your father.

The Best of All Possible Dreamworlds

Whatever mystery there is about who fathered you, we do know where: Tonga, a tiny Polynesian kingdom made up of lots of tiny islands, in the South Pacific. SOUTH PACIFIC is the name of a musical, and "The Best of All Possible Worlds" is a song from another musical, CANDIDE, which is another really good way to spend your lunch money. (It's based on Voltaire but MUCH better, with music by Leonard Bernstein and lyrics by Richard Wilbur and Dorothy Parker. If you're a girl, you've got to get the Portable Dorothy Parker for the verse. I wish I could get it for you. I wonder if they'd let me leave this extended "background information" AND a few Broadway albums and Dorothy Parker. A Life Kit.)

I once wrote "It's the Best of all possible dream worlds" on a banner across my room on Molokai because I'd been told by the Peace Corps staff there that I lived in a dream world, so they weren't sure I could "take" Tonga. I was really worried, and then Danny and a female PC volunteer named Pesi (Betsy) came by to talk to me about their feedback. Because he'd cut cross-cultural activities, Danny's mental health was in question.

"What do they mean?" Danny said. "The ones who are crazy are the ones who GO to cross-cultural activities. I'd rather spend time with the Tongans than the staff's misdiagnosis of them."

He'd just made friends with Pesi, who had gotten high ratings on language and teaching skills but had been labeled "lewd and suggestive" because she'd once chased a Tongan with a frog, and Tongans are afraid of frogs, so the Tongan man ran into the bush to escape it.

"Aren't you just culturally insensitive?" Danny asked. "How is chasing a Tongan with a frog lewd and suggestive?"

"You're not lewd and suggestive!" I told Pesi.

"They called me anti-social," Danny said. "I'm going back and ask them if I can be lewd and suggestive instead."

"Do you know what they told me?" I asked, ready to hear some reassurance. "They said I lived in a dream world."

"Well, of course, you do!" Danny said, and Pesi nodded approvingly. "Nobody could know the words to every Broadway show if they didn't live in a dream world. Nobody does routines from musicals while they clean the chicken coop at six o'clock in the morning if they don't live in a dream world. You ARE crazy, and that's your greatest asset."

That was the second nicest thing the man who might be your father ever told me, and maybe the staff came to the same conclusion because I, along with Danny and Pesi, was finally "cleared" by the final Peace Corps Are-They-Sane? De-selection Committee so we could go to Tonga and he could tell me that I was the best date he'd ever had (the first nicest thing he ever said).

But when he made that comment about how a dream world could

be an asset, I remembered a musical called SKYSCRAPER with songs by Sammy Cohn, and one of the songs is about daydreaming and how it's an internal coffee break. ("What makes it such a crime if I'm a person who runs away from troubles and hassles, preferring to spend the day in Spanish castles?")

That's a concept that I want to pass on to you just in case heredity makes you more like us than maybe you'd choose to be. Just try to make the most of heredity. A dream world could be part of your heritage because you were conceived in one. Pesi was the one who said that Tonga was "fakamuno," which means make-believe. (I should explain that "faka" means "pertaining to" and is nothing obscene.) There's a phrase by a poet, Marianne Moore, about "imaginary gardens with real toads in them." Whatever "imaginary" things happened here, you and I have both been left with something very real—and no toad! You. And I'd tell you at bedtime if I were still your mother:

Once upon a time in a faraway kingdom that was a valid expression of human existence, your once upon a time mother lived on a little island in a little village in a little hut made of bamboo reeds and coconut leaves, with walls lined in tapa cloth and floor covered with mats. The hut was so small that when she sat on the matted floor with her back touching the back door, her toes could almost touch the front door. It was a little bit like sitting in a straw basket or falling deeply into a wicker chair. There was no electricity or running water, so she used a kerosene lamp and drew water from the well. There was a wee little garden where six chickens, two pigs, one goat, one horse, and a family of ducks came to dine until there was no wee little garden anymore. But there were breadfruit trees and avocado trees and coconut trees to climb anytime she wanted a snack. At night, she would go to sleep on a pile of mats under a net and listen to the rain coming down all around her until her wee little hut became a boat and gently rocked in the lake once her lawn. Then pigs would fly over her roof like reindeer. In the morning after a rain her hut would be an island completely surrounded by water, and the children she taught would wade, water to their waists, to get her, and together they would float to school.

Whether they were floating or walking to school, the same exchange would be made every day:

"Malo e lelei!" (Hello or, literally, thank you for being well.) "'Alu ki fe?" (Where are you going?) And she would always be 'aluing ki fale ako (going to school) to teach English that wasn't Shakespeare's or Milton's or Melville's or Mark Twain's or Vladimir Nabokov's. It wasn't even Mailer's. But she taught English that, once learned, would enable the students to set sail for the English-speaking kingdom more comfortable than their legitimate expression of one. And she taught this English by acting out verbs and demonstrating count and non-count nouns.

Has this fairy tale, AKA your mother's Peace Corps experience, minus the week that the ship came in, put you to sleep?

I worked all day and spent all afternoon, into the evening, talking and singing with the children, who loved Broadway show tunes. People remember words better when they're set to music. The only Spanish I remember, for example, is "Bésame, bésame mucho, como si esta noche fuera la ultima vez." (No doubt you think I was singing that the week of your conception.) And of course the French phrases from LES PARAPLUIES DE CHERBOURG. So I taught the children useful phrases from songs like "Good morning, good day. How are you this glorious day?" from SHE LOVES ME, "Good night, good night. Sleep well, and when you dream, dream of me" from WEST SIDE STORY, "Goodbye, goodbye, goodbye, goodbye, goodbye, goodbye. Don't try to stop me, Harris" from HELLO, DOLLY, and I even delved a little into AMAHL AND THE NIGHT VISITORS for "Thank you, thank you, thank you kindly...you are welcome too." This may not be exactly what linguists mean by choral drills, but...

Of course, the song that became the island hit was "The Mickey Mouse Club Song." I like to think that when tourists arrive on that island paradise they'll be greeted by "Hello, Dolly," but I know for sure that they'll hear "M-I-C, See you real soon. K-E-Y. Why? Because we like you. M-O-U-S-E."

Anyway, this was the setting for my meeting 'Ofa, another man who might be your father, a Tongan Mormon Elder with whom I fell in love. I used to think, partly out of need (I could never seem to go more than 6 months without being in love with someone present and Danny was on another island) and partly out of compliance: Taita, the very nice woman-of-the village who belonged to me, suggested that we fall in love.

'OFA

When I'd moved into my hut, Taita had been presented to me by the village committee, who said that she had worked for a French family in Tahiti and for an English family in Fiji and that she was "a good one."

"She smart to speak English," one of them told me. "She's yours."

So she was mine, and I valued her and liked her and sang French songs with her and appreciated her living next door instead of with me, and then, one day, I went to church with her, and that was where she suggested that I fall in love with 'Ofa, whose very name meant Love. No, she suggested that I marry him. But maybe that included love.

Most of the churches in the village were made either of coconut leaves or of third-hand lumber. Worshippers brought their own mats and sat on the floor. But Taita, this woman who belonged to me, worked hard all week and wanted to go somewhere nice on Sunday morning. So three years before, she'd become a Mormon, giving up the rich Wesleyan heritage that had been in her family since Christianity had been discovered on the island in the nineteenth century. All Mormon churches on the island (and on all islands) were large, cement, and painted white with blue trim. Inside were smooth wooden benches to sit on. Everything shone. I had heard that the Mormon missionaries believed that the Polynesian people were one of the lost tribes of

Israel, but the pictures I saw illustrating the Seven Steps to God at the entrance were of blue-eyed blonds.

"Funny, you don't look Jewish," I said, and then we were seated and I was introduced and thanked for all my loving kindness to the people of the island and asked to name the town in America I came from. (Later I could see that some people confused South Carolina with South America, and since I'd said Columbia, it was a cinch.) Then hymns were sung, prayers were said, verses were read, and there was a sermon.

The minister wore a suit and tie. Most of the people did dress up on Sunday, and most men wore coats and ties they bought at the Mormon second-hand store at Liahona. But most wore the skirt-like tupenu instead of trousers. Few wore shoes, and those who did wore them without socks. But the minister was wearing shoes and socks and trousers and coat that fit. He was dark and healthy looking. Attractive but not spectacularly. Mostly he looked clean and young—maybe about thirty-two. I sat and listened to his sermon and understood a preposition or a conjunction here and there. Later Taita gave me the English translation.

"Oh, he make a good one about a wife and husband he visit to. The woman come to the door and she have scar in her face and she didn't could shake hand because she not have it. But her a childs love to her and they kiss to her and her husband come home and he love to her too, and everyone love to her. And the priest ask what happen to her hand and her face. And they tell to him that her and her husband go to play a card and put the childs to bed. And they tell there a big fire and the mother run into the house and save the childs. And she burn herself. And her hand burn off her. And now they remembers what she do. And they see her scars and she have no hand and they love to her."

"Oh, that is a good one," I said. "What do you think it means? I mean, about the Seven Steps to God?"

"That she the same like Christ. Because Christ die to the cross for us and we remembers. And the wife burn herself and they remembers."

While I sat quietly trying to take the analogy further, Taita added, "Maybe you marry with 'Ofa."

"Who's 'Ofa?" I asked.

"The minister," she said.

'Ofa turned out to be a frequent visitor at the home of Taita because Taita's son and 'Ofa were good friends and on the same soccer team. It was from my cupboard that Taita began to get 'Ofa's nightly snacks.

The first time he paid an unexpected visit during my stay in Tonga, Taita came running into my hut to take quick inventory:

"Oh, Sela! You don't shopping!" But she borrowed what there was: eggs, flour, strawberry jam, a frying pan. Then after my lamp was out and I was under my mosquito net with my toes tightly tucked in and out of reach of the rat I shared my hut with, Taita came knocking at my door again, and I moved the bent nail that served as a latch to see what she wanted.

"Please, Sela," she said. "Your stove."

And so she carted off my little kerosene stove. Everything in my kitchen had disappeared to feed the Latter Day Saint.

Then one weekend Taita told me we were going to her son Viliami's estate. I knew something about the original stipulation that every son be given an acre of land, but the land was running out, and the men were looking for square feet of home in other countries. What was this about an estate? What I found out later was that Taita's son (and isn't THIS a meaningful coincidence?) had been fathered 20 years earlier by a high Tongan official who later married a better educated woman and had four daughters. Even though all but one daughter (one was wild and rebellious) were brilliant and excelled at everything they did, he wanted a son to inherit his land, so he finally acknowledged his illegitimate son and gave him a huge hunk of his estate.

So that's why Taita's son had told me, almost the first time that we met, that he was a bastard. And I had protested that no, he was 'anga lelei—very nice!

There in the bush it was quiet and children didn't come to joyously visit and stand in the door and at the window, blocking the sun that I was learning to like. I loved the children, but they were with me in my hut before school, all day at school, after school at special po'ako (night school) sessions, and back in my hut all evening until I crept under my mosquito net to go to bed. As much as I loved them, I also loved getting away from them on Sundays.

So after church, Taita and I walked to the bush and shaved vegetables and prepared an underground oven while we ate ripe bananas and sang French songs. Singing was taboo on Sunday because singing was considered recreation and recreation was taboo. But either the Mormon Church or Taita took exception to this because we sang secular songs on Sunday if we wanted to.

We sat on the floor, and everything looked ready to eat, but Taita said we should wait. Then 'Ofa rode up on a brown horse. He still had on trousers, but he wasn't wearing a coat. He had on a white shirt and I could see a white undershirt under it. Underclothes were usually hand-made. That meant that women made their own underpants and men rarely wore undershirts. That was the first thing I thought about that afternoon—that his undershirt was not hand-made. He excused himself and came back wearing a tupenu.

Taita told me that 'Ofa was a real man, not a "fie palangi," a Tongan who rejected his own culture in favor of the White Man's. (Fie means want. Palangi means white person.)

'Ofa said he'd already been to the church's feast, but he'd come here to rest. Taita took him to a shelter made of coconut leaves and spread out a clean mat and a tupenu (a cloth usually used as a wrap around or under skirt) and gave him a pillow for his head. The rest of us ate. Then we made a kettle of coffee over a open fire and Taita asked me to take a cup to 'Ofa. I stopped at the door and asked him in Tongan if he were asleep, and he said that no, he wasn't. I walked in and went down on my knees to give him the cup of coffee.

He moved his arms from beneath his head and sat up.

"Such servitude, you getting on your hands and knees for me," he said in English. "Thank you."

"I didn't know you could speak English," I said.

"A little bit," he said.

"Yes, I can see how little. Where did you learn it?"

"In school."

"Really? Here?"

"No, in the land of the free and the home of the brave."

"In the United States?"

"Yes, in Hawaii. I believe that's part of America."

"You seem pretty clear on your geography, " I said. "I'm from South Carolina, and some Tongans confuse South Carolina with South America. When they hear that the South seceded from the Union, they think that means South America."

"I know the difference."

"Well, I don't always know what's going on in the world because I don't have a radio, and people are always coming to me with reports like 'There's a terrible earthquake in your country,' and when I ask them in what state, they say, "Peru.'"

"Well, how could I learn English in South America? They speak Spanish there except for Brazil, where they speak Portuguese."

A scholar, I thought. "Yes, I know," I said.

"You should get a radio," he added, "so you know what's going on in the world and won't have to depend upon local gossip."

"I know I should."

"Then why don' t you?'

"Because I like not knowing what's going on in the world."

"No news is good new? Do you have relatives in Vietnam?"

"No. No friends, either."

"The reports make it sound like everybody and its brother is there."

"Not mine."

"So your family lives in South Carolina?

"Yes, Except for my mother. She lives in Los Angeles."

"Oh, near Hippy City."

"Hippy City?"

"San Francisco," he said. He moved his cup in my direction. "Aren't you having any coffee?" he asked.

"No, thank you. Coffee makes me over-emotional. But why are you having coffee? You're a Mormon."

"Well, Sunday's a feast day. Besides, I'm not setting a bad example. No one's here to see me."

"Ah!" I said. "This is what's known as the New Morality."

"I wouldn't go that far."

"How far would you go?" I asked.

"Well," he said, "I really don't agree with today's mode of perversion. Are your parents still alive?"

"Yes."

"Good for you."

"What do you mean?"

"Well, some people don't have all the luck."

"You mean you? Your parents aren't alive?"

"That's right. I'm sorry to say that they kicked the bucket some year ago."

"I'm sorry."

"Well, that's the way it goes."

"Such fluent nonchalance you've got."

"Well, it's not in our hand."

"Whose hand is it in?" I asked.

"I like to think these decisions are make by the man upstairs."

I laughed.

"You think that's funny?"

I changed the subject.

"Did you study religion in Hawaii?

"At Church College everyone studies religion," he said.

"I know. But did you study it more than most people?"

"Well, I'm an elder, so I had to."

"I'm not asking that you apologize."

"I also studied art."

"Art? The history or the actual thing?"

"Well, I wanted to dabble in the actual thing. So I took drawing and painting and woodcraft. I still like to indulge now and then."

"Uh huh," I said.

"I think you have a very fine heritage in your country of painter."

"Really? Like who?"

"You should know your own culture."

"I know I should. But I only know Andy Warhol and Campbell Soup cans. I'm part of the culturally-deprived majority."

"What about Keane?"

"Keane?"

"I think he has some of the best exhibit I ever saw. I'd give my right hand to paint like that."

"Is painting your main interest?"

"Yes, but I'm not vaunting my authority. My talent's nothing to write home about."

"Okay," I said. "I'll think of something else to tell them."

"I painted that," he said, pointing to a goat tacked to the matted wall. It had protruding eyes.

"I can see Keane's influence," I said.

"Krittch," he said from his throat, dismissing the possibility of truth in so extravagant a compliment.

Taita came into the room with something steaming in two halved coconut shells. She bent down and put it on the mat next to 'Ofa.

"It for both of you," she said.

We thanked her, and she smiled and left, winking at me.

It was desiccated coconut mixed with ripe bananas and maioke and baked in an underground over. It was good.

"It's not sweet enough," 'Ofa said. He put it down.

"Would you like some sugar?" I asked.

"That would be nice." He smiled.

"Would you like me to go get it for you?

"I wouldn't complain if you do."

I did.

He added three teaspoons of sugar, stirred it and ate the whole thing. I got half way through mine.

"Eat till you burst," he said. "That's one of our proverbs."

He lay back. "If you'll excuse me, I'll take a snooze."

I looked at him lying there, more or less asleep. His eyes slanted more noticeably when they were shut. His skin looked bronze and smooth and strangely soft, and his hair looked like steel wool. Then I stared at his goat for a while, and then I lay down across the room from him and went to sleep.

Being with 'Ofa was the next best thing to being alone. He didn't get on my nerves. I liked him. I began planning our future together. We would talk together—he and I—about his country, about my country, and even about God, eventually. We'd share the lofty things we couldn't share with anyone else. He'd come to hold me in higher esteem than even the woman who dived into the fire in his sermon. He'd find me exquisitely beautiful the way men do in gothic tales, and I'd come to depend upon him in a truly touching way. It would be his compassion, interest, and appreciation that would keep me from having a nervous breakdown or becoming hard and masculine the way they said PCVs with no social life became. He would give me the impetus to become a super-vol.

On the other hand, he was a Mormon, not a Jesuit Priest or a Unitarian. How long could he sustain me? Then I would sustain him?

When I woke up, he was gone. It was just about dusk, and Taita and I walked back to the village.

I saw 'Ofa, this Mormon elder, several consecutive Sundays after that, and our conversations remained stilted and stupid and full of insensitive figures of speech, and the only thing that made him the least bit attractive to me—it made him very attractive—was that he seemed just a little bit self-conscious about his being so charming. As if his being so charming were immodest somehow. He had a way of smiling when he thought he'd said something clever, a mixture of apologetic pride and humility that didn't convince him. Once he told me I had some brain in my head, and he seemed very embarrassed afterwards, as if he shouldn't be such a flatterer, that no one could fall for a line like that. It's kind of hard to explain, but it's sort of like the kind of confused emotion a person feels when slipping change into the muscular dystrophy box on the counter. You don't know whether it's going to do any good, and you don't want anyone to see you, though you know there's nothing wrong with it, and you wind up feeling very awkward.

When 'Ofa wasn't complimenting me on my brain, he often spoke with a scratchy sound in his throat—like the ch in Hebrew, I suppose, though the only Hebrew I know is from FIDDLER ON THE ROOF. ("To life, to life, L'Chaim")

"Krittch," he'd say, and he gave me advice on how I should dress for example.

"Not with your clothes just hanging around you," he said.

I told him it was a butterfly dress, and he asked whether I thought I was an insect, and he seemed so amused and proud and embarrassed by his wit. I wondered if it weren't something maternal I felt for him, so vulnerably corny. Maternal. Ah, the irony of feeling maternal about the man who might be the father of the child I can't keep.

After several Sundays of eating and taking naps and talking silly we were invited by Taita and Viliami to partake of home brew. It was a joke, of course, because it was illegal any day but especially on the Sabbath, and Mormons couldn't have alcohol. They were teasing 'Ofa, who didn't drink even coffee officially, and he smiled. He was no prude. I, though, thought of it as a new and broadening cultural exploration and coaxed them into giving me a cup.

It was made of bananas and pineapples and yeast—the last item gotten from the baker who was Taita's cousin. It had fermented a week. I didn't make a face, and I asked for more. Then more. I thought what an excuse for letting myself go. I was right, of course. I said hilarious things since the Polynesian humor was not subtle, and I hugged Taita, patted Viliami, and said, "I love you" to each in turn, ending with 'Ofa, who made a scratching sound in this throat and said he'd better help the drunk to bed.

I leaned on him. He let me down on the mat in the coconut shed, and I could feel myself looking beautiful, my auburn hair spread out upon the pillow, my head back, my neck long—beautiful, vulnerable, helpless without inhibition and at his mercy.

I knew I was irresistible.

"You look disgusting when you're drunk," 'Ofa said, standing over me. He started to walk out, but I grabbed his foot.

"Would you kindly let go of my foot?" he asked.

I spoke apologetically, contrite: "No."

"What is it you want, woman?" he laughed a little laugh, self-conscious now.

"Conversation," I said.

"You're in no condition for conversation."

"You're right." I let his ankle go. I was no beggar.

"Everybody and its brother can see us now with the lamp on and the walls with holes."

I turned over and away from him.

"Good night. Sleep tight. Don't let the bedbug bites," he said.

He spoke staccato when he was self-conscious.

He left, leaving me lying there betrayed. My mood immediately changed to dignity. But then I realized I had to go to the bathroom. The bathroom was an outhouse, and it was dark and difficult to find my way, but I did, and when I finished, I felt sober and cool and walked out into the night air. That was when someone grabbed me.

Rape! I thought. Oh, rape, and everyone would think I'd asked for it with my unseemly drinking, alcoholic fruit upon my breath.

But it wasn't rape after all. It was 'Ofa, the elder, with his arms around me.

I thought you were a rapist!" I said.

"Shh!" he said.

I put my arms around him, happy to have him to tremble into, rewarding him for rescuing me from the rapist I had mistaken him for. And he kissed me in the most progressive European style. (Fie palangi!) He walked me behind the outhouse. He was very well-coordinated, I remember thinking, being able to kiss so well and walk straight simultaneously.

As we kissed, I said, "Oh!" and he said, "Shh!" and I said, "Oh," and he said, "I wish this could go on forever," and I laughed, and he said "Shh!" and took me back to the coconut shed, where he said, "Good night, sleep tight, and don't let the bedbug bites." He kissed me once again and whispered, "Sweet dreams," which were what I had. ("Out of my dreams and into your arms I long to fly" OKLAHOMA "Dream of now. Dream of then. Dream of a love song that might have been." THE MUSIC MAN. "I have dreamed that your arms are lovely." THE KING AND I.)

That was the beginning of rendezvous on Viliami's "plantation" in the bush where we could "kiss in the shadow...hide from the moon. Our meetings were few and over too soon." (THE KING AND I) We would meet publicly only at soccer games for which I helped make the sandwiches.

It was always with great excitement that I anticipated our meetings. ("How can I wait...till that golden moment when I'll be seeing him again?" PAINT YOUR WAGON)

But it made me somewhat uneasy. It was so soon, and I'd be there for two years. They say you shouldn't have a romance with someone in your office because professional obligations and personal lives don't mix well. He was a Latter Day Saint and I was a Pisi Kopsi in our professional lives on a small island. What kind of mix would that be? Maybe the kind of mix that created you that fateful weekend when all my loves converged.

VICTOR

The third person I was with that fateful weekend was Victor, with whom I was really having a "social life" more than a love life. They had told us in training that we wouldn't have any kind of "social life" at all. (Did they mean love life?) One returned volunteer came to our Bitch-In and said that all the women he knew either had nervous breakdowns or became hard and masculine because there was no social life. So, I concluded, we'd lose either our sanity or our sex appeal.

Maybe my daring to have both a social life and a love life indicated that I had lost my sanity. 'Ofa was my love life, but not really my social life. Our rendezvous were secret and took place only after the lamp was blown out because even though his name was Love, pre-marital love was against his religion.

Victor was my social life. Sweet, romantic, generous, talented Victor. Dr. Victor Williamson. He's the one whose typewriter and office I'm using now. He's the only one who knows about you, though he knows even less than I do because he doesn't know about Danny and 'Ofa.

There's a song from SOUTH PACIFIC called "Some Enchanted Evening" about two strangers who see each other across a crowded room, the way Tony and Maria do in WEST SIDE STORY. Victor, who knew the song, says he first saw me across a crowded lawn. It was a dry period when my lawn was not a lake, and on it were a family of chickens, some pigs, a goat—and me, crossing with a group of children towards the road. And he had the feeling I'd wanted 'Ofa to have. The feeling that I was beautiful and we belonged together. That's one thing you'll learn as you go through life: Sometimes to find all the qualities you love in a person you have to find more than one person. Sometimes even to be all that you want to be you have to find more than one person.

I have a belief that I call my Musical Instrument Theory: Every instrument has a basic quality, depending upon who crafted it and what it's made of. But how each musical instrument sounds depends also upon who's playing it. The most finely-crafted instrument won't sound very good if the musician playing it is inept. And the greatest musician probably can't get an unworthy instrument to great musical heights. Each of us have certain qualities, and it's up to us to find a talented musician to play us.

I'd found Victor or, rather, he'd found me.

Victor, being a doctor, was invited to the Peace Corps doctor's house along with a pre-med student, Jacqueline, and other volunteers in family planning and rat control because they all had certain things in common. But later the wife of the Peace Corps doctor made a special trip out to my village. She said, "Sela, there's someone who wants to meet you. We clearly aren't very good at match-making because we had a party to introduce him to Jacqueline, since she's in the field of medicine, and she says he kept bringing up the topic of you."

"Me?" It actually occurred to me that she was talking about 'Ofa because I didn't know any other non-Peace Corps man. Also, I guess, I liked the idea of his spending a whole evening talking about me.

"Victor Williamson. He's a doctor from New Zealand, and he said that one day he saw a beautiful redheaded girl walking across the lawn and he wanted to stop his car, but he had no excuse for stopping. He said he kept wishing that a pig would charge so he could come to your rescue."

You can imagine what a good impression he made, thinking I was beautiful and wanting to come to my rescue. What could be more gallant? I was glad that I was the only one with red hair, or I'd have had to wonder if they'd correctly identified the object of his interest.

"Anyway, we're having a party next month, and we'd like you to come."

I came, and Victor drove me back to my village afterwards. He drove me over the lawn and right up to the door of my hut and invited me to come to dinner at the Dateline Hotel the following week.

All the meaningful discussion and all the warm exchanged I'd hope to have with 'Ofa happened with Victor. He was the one who put his arms around me in a very gentle way and told me I was beautiful and wrote odes to my beauty, to the fire of my hair. And I loved Victor, too. I loved Danny for being funny and brilliant and making me laugh. I loved Victor for being romantic and serious and writing poems. And I even loved 'Ofa, though why is not so clear. Maybe because he was local color. I'm a little bit embarrassed by how much I grew to care about local color. There isn't any in South Carolina. Of course, as a Peace Corps Volunteer I had an obligation to get to know the Tongan people, but not in a biblical sense. And his name was Love. even though what he offered didn't seem very deep. It seems wrong to love a man who doesn't love back, and I used to comment on that to 'Ofa. If I said, "I love you," and he didn't say it back, I'd add, "Pearls before swine" to show him that I valued me more than he did and more than I valued him. Sometimes I'd try to be flippant, "Children, love ye one another," I'd say when we were lying together in the dark on the tapa cloth and starting to love each other. "God is love, and so are you," I'd say, referring to his name. But I'd have preferred not to have had to resort to humor so often.

With Victor, there was less need to keep a comic distance. Victor is a man they call an expatriate. He lives in a beautiful house in Nuku'alofa, and we had a lot of Saturday evenings there, where we sort of established a ritual. After walking his dog, we'd go into his living room for culture shock for me. Keep in mind that I was living in a hut with no running water and no electricity, and I was eating only what grew on trees. Then once a week at Victor's I'd be sitting in a high-ceilinged house, where he'd be serving me an aperitif. Cointreau. Benedictine. Drambuie. Drinks that I'm not even sure that I can spell. He'd cook for me, and he was a good cook. I always had a sense of well-being with him, and so did the children, who became acquainted with him and his dog and were occasionally invited to join us at his home or on outings. He has a library in his home in Nuku'alofa, and I'd browse through his books. Sometimes we'd read aloud to each other.

In his home I even had some privacy. My own fale was always full of villagers, mostly children. At Victor's it was only the two of us, and sometimes he'd leave the room. He gave me the key to his house so that anytime I bicycled in to Nuku'alofa, even if he were at the hospital, I could use his house. He'd let me come even when he was in Fiji, where he often came on hospital-related business. He'd ask me to occasionally visit his dog in a part of the world where people were less inclined to play with pets than they were to eat them

It was in Fiji that he bought me perfume bearing that name but spelling it wrong, the French way: Fidji by Guy Laroche. I loved the smell and that was when I had to decide about ethics. Would it be wrong for me to wear perfume given to me by one man when I was dating another man?

No one, of course, ever asked me to see only him. Still, I wondered whether it would be fair. But I worked it out well. I did wear Fidji with 'Ofa. But I also invited Victor to attend soccer games in which 'Ofa played and brought him produce that 'Ofa started bringing me after I complained that the villagers borrowed my food to feed him. I sent Danny articles or copies of poems I discovered with Victor and with Victor I shared the issues of THE ATLANTIC MONTHLY and HARPERS that Danny sent. Everybody I loved benefitted from the existence of everybody else I loved. But it was Fidji I was wearing with each of them I loved that weekend.

It's funny that the perfume was Fidji because the capital of Fiji is Suva, and the Tonga word for sex outside of marriage is "faka Suva." Remember that faka just means pertaining to, but the Tongans use pertaining to Suva to mean pertaining to the illicit love that's practiced there, which the Fijians say it isn't. It could be that the Fijian word for illicit love is "pertaining to Tonga." I don't think the way they do things in Suva is any more risqué than the way they do things in Tonga. And I want you to understand that the way I did things in Tonga wasn't very risqué except, perhaps, for a Peace Corps Volunteer who wasn't supposed to have a social life. And I really did work hard at my real Peace Corps assignment. I cared.

I didn't really have much sex with Victor. We just kissed and necked and touched, and when we did, 'Uli'uli (his dog) would growl, apparently jealous. The funny thing is that we never made love until that weekend—an historic weekend not just for us but for all of Tonga because it was the week of their first Independence Day celebration.

But before I tell you about that week, it's occurred to me that in describing your grandfather and grandmother and uncle and possible fathers—your family—I left out me.

They left me out of the Peace Corps interview too! We had to describe everyone in our family except ourselves.

The Mother (for sure!) Who Conceived You

First of all, I want to say that I often wished that my parents had done for me what I am about to do for you: Given me up for adoption to a normal family.

And I hope it won't make you think that you have pre-marital sex in your blood, but I was born three months after their marriage. Mother said she kept trying to find someone suitable to marry, and that's why she waited till so close to the due date. Daddy said right away that he'd marry her, and she said, "I'll bet you would." She said she could see that he didn't grasp that that was not the ideal solution.

"But wasn't Daddy my father?" I asked.

"Oh, he was your daddy all right," Mother said. "How can you doubt that, with your looks? I'm the one you should suspect of not being your mama."

I have to say that I did look into that, but all the evidence seems to point to her having given me birth. But it was my dad I looked like. Height, red hair, freckles, white skin. Mother had dark eyes and hair and looked more dainty. She was the kind of person you immediately thought was pretty. She used to say that it took time to see my beauty.

"You really are beautiful, too," Mother told me when I was visiting her right before I joined the Peace Corps. She was fixing herself up for an evening at home (something that appealed to me and that I'll talk about later) and had just moved her eyes from the mirror, into which she'd been gazing lovingly at herself, to study me for a moment.

"It's just that it always hurt my narcissism that you didn't look a thing like me. How can there be two such beautiful girls in this world who look so different?"

One thing I always liked about Mother is that she never used the word pretty unless she wanted to be insulting. Beautiful is what a woman aimed to be, and no woman worth her salt settled for being anything less. "Attractive" was a word you used only for people who were really plain, and plain was reserved for offensively ugly people.

"I wish I'd married a good man the first time around," she said after I met her second husband, the one who'd left his wife for her.

"Daddy's a good man, isn't he?" I asked.

"Oh, he's good at things like saving the world. He's good when it comes to things like moral issues. But I mean a man who was good to ME. Good to US. What good is a good man if he's not good to YOU?"

And then she looked at me and kind of apologized.

"I'm sorry, honey. I know it was mean to run off the way I did."

I was amazed that she could use words like "mean," as if abandoning your little children was like an unkind remark or a thoughtless little action.

"But," she went on, "It was you or me. My life would have been over if I had stayed."

"What attracted you to Daddy in the first place? Was there a time when you cared about the world, too?"

"Oh, honey," she said, looking at me, as if she were startled that I didn't know. "It was animal magnetism. And that's why it was so wrong of me to marry him. I should have married someone else and just had an affair with your dad. That would have been the right thing to do. I knew that even then, but I'd fallen so hard for your daddy that I'd been neglecting my other boyfriends. Remember, there's safety in numbers."

But I don't want you to think that it was that philosophy that led me to the week of our conception. Mother and I are as different in the way we think as we are in the way we look.

In fact, I think I was always a little more motherly than my mother. When Mother ran away, I'm the one who took care of Peter, who was a year younger than me. ("I still hadn't learned how not to get pregnant," Mother told me years later.)

It's true that Daddy married again soon. And Helen was a brilliant woman. She graduated from Carolina Magna Cum Laude. But when I picture her, I always picture her talking on the telephone because I swear that's what she did all day long. And it wasn't great books she was discussing, either. It was gossip. She called one housewife and heard all her problems and secrets, and then she called another and got hers, and then she put them all together and made more calls. With my dad she talked about issues like what a jackass Strom Thurmond was filibustering by reading cookbooks or whether the Palestinians were like the American Indians, being put on reservations so people who needed their land could have it.

And it was when Daddy came home that Helen would read—out loud, to him—something from THE SATURDAY REVIEW OF LITERTURE or THE NEW REPUBLIC. She'd follow him around the house with articles she'd read to him while he shaved or dressed or whatever he wanted to do. And sometimes she'd make her own comments about the issues, and if Daddy thought what she said was less than brilliant, he'd yell, "What? For crying out loud! Make some sense."

It seemed so strange because Daddy would tell people that she had graduated from Carolina with honors, so he was proud of her intelligence, but I think she got on his nerves, and he seemed to have so many nerves to get on.

And so he'd call her stupid, and she'd get hurt and run to their bedroom and cry until Daddy was no longer upset and would go in to comfort her. And the door would close, and they wouldn't come out until the next day.

I often wondered what was keeping them together, and then I figured it was that "animal magnetism" that Mother had mentioned. But

Helen told me it was God. Daddy didn't want to go to church, so Helen would take the rest of us to the part of the service children could go to before they were sent to Sunday school. Being the oldest, I got to stay the longest. I liked to hear the strange, beautiful language they used at St. John's Episcopal Church—and all the magical incantations—but Helen, apparently, liked to cry, especially during the sermon when, I guess, there was time to sit and think. She'd cry and then she'd whisper to me, "If it weren't for God, I would leave your daddy. It's only God that's keeping me with him."

I still don't know whether she was praising God or cursing him. But I do know that God couldn't keep her from attempting suicide— and more than once. Then she'd be put on the J-Ward, and while she wasn't standing in the way, I'd give the whole house a good cleaning. That was the only time it got one.

When Mel and Delano were born, even though Helen breast-fed them while she smoked or talked on the telephone, I was the one who changed their diapers because she would wait so long they'd get diaper rash and the house would start to smell. To tell you the truth, the house always smelled. You could tell that there was something not quite right, just by the smell of our house. When I started dating, the boys always came to the door. That's the way they did things in the South. They came to the door to meet your parents and have ice tea with them and pass inspection. But I always tried to meet my dates outside before they got close enough to smell the house.

I used to try to clean it up. I'd go around and tuck things in and wipe off surfaces and put everything in one of the cardboard boxes we had in such abundance. Once I even tried to move the cardboard boxes out of the living room, which really made Daddy furious. He really screamed about that one. Have I told you how we had cardboard box-es—turned on their side—for our bookshelves, boxes for file cabinets? Boxes, boxes everywhere. Once a date did make it inside in spite of my efforts to get to the door before he did, and he looked around at all the cardboard boxes and asked, "Are you moving?" It always looked as if we were either in the middle of packing or in the middle of unpacking—on our way out or on our way in but never really there.

As real young kids, Peter and I liked to play in the cardboard boxes—the ones that didn't have books or papers in them. Daddy was always good about getting us more boxes. Cardboard boxes, stale bread, and canned tomatoes—those were the things we always had plenty of.

We'd each crawl into a cardboard box that fit our body just perfectly and roll over and over or rock back and forth. I guess it saved Daddy on toys. The only book of photographs he ever published that wasn't political was of Peter and me when we were little, and there we were in cardboard boxes. At first we were really excited to see ourselves in a book. To us that meant that Daddy was famous, and so were we. But as I got older—and especially when Daddy started taking pictures of Peter having his strange spasms—it didn't seem right to me. I didn't want to be famous. I just wanted some privacy. Well, let me be honest. I felt he was invading Peter's privacy—treating him like a subject instead of like a person. He'd put Peter's own words in the caption of the pictures. That just seemed, somehow, wrong. But in the case of me, I'd have been willing to be photographed if Daddy had made me look better. But he took pictures at the most unflattering time. He wasn't, he pointed out, trying to create illusion. He was trying to capture Truth. So even on an occasion when girls look really pretty —like prom night—Daddy didn't want to take pictures of me ready to go. He wanted to take pictures of me in rollers and an old bathrobe—the ritual of preparing for a prom. The same thing happened the day Kennedy was assassinated.

You know everyone's always asking, "Where were YOU the day that Kennedy was shot?" and there are hideous pictures Daddy took of the answer to that, too, and I guess it's my punishment for being so shallow.

It was the day of our annual beauty contest at Columbia High School. That was where Strom Thurmond came the year before to tell us, to a standing ovation, that the Civil Rights Bill was 'un-con-sti-TU-tional!"

so you can imagine that Kennedy wasn't grieved much. I'd been one of the few in my class who supported Kennedy in 1960 (and I loved him for starting the Peace Corps, which I'd decided to join for reasons I'll explain later), and the principal himself sponsored the Young Republicans Club. Still, Kennedy was President, and so the principal came over the public address system first to announce that President Kennedy had been shot, then to announce that he had died, and then to answer the question that had come to the minds of so many: Would the school beauty contest go on that night as planned?

"If this were a frivolous affair," the principal said, "we'd cancel it. But the beauty contest raises money for the yearbook, so the beauty contest will go on as planned."

I felt that that wasn't right. I felt that it should be postponed. So I decided I would take a stand. When I walked across the stage, I wouldn't smile.

I hope your adoptive parents have brought you up with enough sense to know that I should have refused to participate. Even my non-adoptive parents had brought me up to know. But I rationalized my going ahead and being in it with the idea that I was representing the Latin Club, which had nominated me because every club had to nominate somebody, and the Latin Club didn't have that many girls. You can just imagine how heart-broken they'd have been if I hadn't gone on stage that night. I knew the right thing to do was to mourn the President and refuse to be in the beauty contest, but it was one of those dilemmas in life: If I weren't in the contest, how could I possibly win?

And so I kept my appointment to have my hair done. It was the only time the whole year that I ever did because it was expensive—$2.50 to $3.50 twice the price of an original cast recording. But some girls had their hair washed and set every week, so I figured I could have it done once a year, for this important occasion. And of course I bribed God. If he would help me win this year, I'd say something in honor of Kennedy. ("Ask not what your school can do for you, ask...") Some Miss America contestants talk about using their scholarship money to go to medical school. I'd talk about donating my scholarship money and going into the Peace Corps.

Anyway, Daddy found out where I was getting my hair fixed and he came in with his camera. The hair-dresser had a television in his salon, and everything on TV was focused on Kennedy. So one of the pictures I have of that day is of me, in rollers once again and later getting my hair teased while I was looking into the TV screen—a reminder both of how unglamorous I was and of how shallow—getting my hair fixed for a beauty contest on the day President Kennedy was shot!

As I say, though, I deserved the punishment. And I can't even blame it on Mother, who brought us up to believe that nothing was more important than a girl's physical beauty. Daddy brought me up to have a political or social conscience. In life you pick and choose, and clearly that night I'd chosen to be shallow. It goes to show that even if you grow up in an unhappy home, you don't necessarily develop character. You might as well grow up in a happy one, and I hope you have.

But I keep getting this out of chronological order, and I don't want to confuse you.

Mother stayed at home until Peter and I were both in school, and then taking care of the house was pretty much my responsibility, though at first we had neighbors coming—and friends of Daddy's, who were sympathetic to our being left without a mother. They stopped coming after a while, though, and Daddy told me I got to be in charge from then on and he'd give me an allowance, which he did at first and might have kept doing except that I was afraid to remind him. Anyway, it wasn't like I did such a good job. The only real cleaning I ever did was when Helen was in the J-Ward. I never, ever cleaned except for washing the dishes. But I'd sweep sometimes, and I opened soup cans and took care of Peter, who being a boy seemed a lot more than just one year younger than me. We became very close and I always felt I was bringing him up pretty well. The genius part had started before Mother left and I took over, but his personality was so nice, and I figured I had a lot to do with that because I protected him from things.

Whenever Daddy and Helen would fight—and it seemed there was at least one big fight every day—I'd try to get Peter as far away from them as possible. That's when we'd go up to the attic and listen to records. Or we'd take our dog, Whitman, on a walk.

What happened to Whitman was the saddest of any incident I remember in our childhood, and all I could tell Peter about that was that Daddy meant well, but he was a madman. I knew Daddy loved animals just as much as we did, so what he did with Whitman proves he was crazy and all we had to do was keep a safe distance from Daddy and never get another dog.

Even though the house was a complete mess, there was a certain order to the basement, where Daddy developed his pictures, and we of course were not allowed to go down there. Of course we were to keep anyone else from going down there too. But one day, somehow, Whitman (named after the poet because he looked so ecstatic when he was contributing to leaves of grass) got downstairs somehow and messed up a box of Daddy's most cherished photos.

I wasn't there when Whitman did the damage, but I was there for the first part of his punishment, and I'd like to spare you the details except what I need to say. Daddy held the box of negatives to Whitman's nose and kicked him over and over again, while he held him by his collar. For about five minutes we shouted for Daddy to stop, and we didn't usually talk back to Daddy, let me tell you. But when we cried and yelled for him to stop, he just went right on kicking Whitman, and he said it was our fault because we had let Whitman get downstairs. Then Daddy kicked him out the door, and we couldn't catch up with Whitman to comfort him.

Whitman never came back.

Peter and I used to talk to each other about that a lot. We never talked about what Daddy did, just that Whitman, like Mother, ran away, and dogs were so loyal. They stayed with you no matter what, unlike mothers. We looked for him for weeks. And every night we stood at the door and called.

But Whitman never came back, and I think we believed, deep down, that Whitman had made the right decision.

It was interesting how Helen handled the situation. She was always defending Daddy to us. She'd say, even when he'd been mean to her, "Your daddy works so hard" and "Your daddy is under a lot of stress." She didn't say anything at all about Whitman for the first few days. And then one day Helen sat down with us and she said, "Children, I wanted to talk to you about Whitman." I remember tensing up.

"What your daddy did with Whitman..." And I remember thinking, "I hate her! I hate her! I hate here" because I just knew that she was going to find some way to defend what Daddy had done.

And then she said, "What your daddy did was wrong. Do you understand that?"

And we nodded. And then we cried. And I remember that was the only time I ever liked Helen or respected her. But really loved her at that moment.

And then she asked us if we'd like to get another dog, and we shook our heads no, and she nodded in agreement. And then she told us she was going to have a baby.

It was after the births of both Mel and Delana that Daddy brought another dog home. Mel and Delana seemed happier about it than Peter and I felt. And when they were petting the dog, Daddy started to cry, and he said, "I'm so sorry about Whitman." Helen put her arms around Daddy, but we just watched. Our father had good—even great—intentions, but his insanity got in the way. Who knew what he would do next?

But it turned out that he was always good to Champion, the next dog. And I'm still trying to figure out what that means. History doesn't always repeat itself? People can do better given a second chance (like I'm giving you)? Maybe you can figure out what it means. In the meantime, be kind to animals—including, I guess, parents.

Anyway, starting when we were nine and ten, Peter took care of the dog and I took care of the children and the house. I soon saw it was hopeless to try to make things neat, so the best I could do was just keep people at a distance from our house. Keep them from coming in where they could see and smell it.

I did well in school at first. I liked all the order in the classroom. It fascinated me that there was a procedure. There were rules. Everything looked neat. I remember the teacher saying, "Everything has its place" and to me that was a revelation, a creed, a wise saying to live by, the way that Christians believe and follow "Jesus Saves." To me "everything has its place" was a message from God—a message that could save the world.

And I sort of fell in love with my school supplies and my desk. At school everything DID have its place. But at home, that wasn't true. And the only place that Peter and I really liked to be at home was in the attic—with the records—or on a walk with Champion, the dog after Whitman. I have to say that, in time, Peter spent more time with Champion, and I spent more time with the records, whenever I wasn't taking care of Mel and Delana, and Peter and Champion became inseparable—especially after he started having the tics and falling under the spell of those strange spasm and people didn't like him as much anymore. However, some people were kind, and one family that was really kind was the family of the Baptist minister that lived across the street.

The Hugheses were a family that fascinated me because it seemed picture-perfect. They lived in a freshly painted white house with blue shutters (which is funny because that's the color scheme of the Mormon churches in Tonga).

They had a manicured lawn with perfectly trimmed hedges and azaleas that seemed to grow according to some divine plan. I used to think that the only thing that wasn't perfect about their home was that their front window looked out on our house across the street. Fortunately, while we had only what would grow with no help from us, there were a lot of tall pine trees hiding our run-down house with its chipped paint and crooked shutters. One good thing about living in our house was that we had a better view out than the people who were looking at our house, and I used to watch the Hugheses. I'd watch them getting in their shiny station wagon on Sunday mornings, and all the girls would be wearing hats and clutching their little black Bibles with their clean white gloves. And the son Paul would be dressed in a suit, which I thought made him look so manly because he looked like a grown up instead of a boy. My father still dressed like a boy. He didn't even own a suit and tie. He'd just quote Thoreau: "Beware of occasions requiring new clothes." But I was drawn to such occasions, and to such clothes, and so were the Hugheses.

The Hugheses were among the people who brought around casseroles when they first found out about Mother's disappearance, and then, when Peter started having problems that got the attention of people at the school we went to, they came around again—at least Pastor Hughes did.

He wanted us to know that they were praying for Peter, and I was surprised that Daddy didn't tell them not to because I never thought Daddy believed in God. Pastor Hughes invited us all to church, and once Peter and I went and they did have a special prayer for him, but when he shouted the obscenities, they thought he was possessed by the devil, and Daddy got mad and called them "primitive," "barbaric," and "stupid" right to Pastor Hughes' face, and I thought for sure after that their whole family would hate us. But anytime Peter and I saw Pastor Hughes or his wife, they were very nice to us, and they made their children be nice to us too when most children didn't have to be. They were even nice to me the year Paul Hughes and I were in the same social studies class and I entered their house, for the first time, to borrow their World Book Encyclopedia—the year that I turned twelve.

When I turned 12, it was as if my personality changed. I still loved musicals, but I wasn't "orderly" anymore. I grew too fast—mostly up—and I was skinny with just a trace of a figure. And my grades dropped. I no longer lived by "Everything has its place." Instead I lived by "Maybe it will snow the day of the test." I had the same creed when it came to social studies projects for which we were given six weeks but which I never began until the day they were due—because what was the point of getting them done on time if it was just going to snow the day we were to turn them in?

Unfortunately, it rarely snowed in South Carolina, so I'd have to say, when the teacher called on me to turn in my project, "I haven't finished it yet," which was true, since I hadn't begun it. The time I had to borrow the World Book Encyclopedia was the day we'd each had to turn in a different flag we'd sewn, and it hadn't snowed. That day I decided to go to the library to see what a flag of Portugal looked like, but there was no one to drive me because Helen was having another nervous breakdown, and Daddy was busy on a project. We didn't have any encyclopedias ourselves because Daddy said they were too "watered down" and he didn't believe in things that cost money. So I called the family next door to Paul's. I didn't want to call Paul's family because he was in my class and would know that I should have begun my project six weeks earlier, as he had. He was a straight-A student because he planned ahead, but not the way I did, planning on a snowstorm. Unfortunately, what happened was that the Morrisons, the people I called about an encyclopedia, didn't have one but said they knew that the Hugheses had one so they called the Hugheses and said they would send me over. So I had to go over there in the end. That was the first time I'd ever entered the house that looked so perfect from the outside, and it looked perfect inside too with sets of furniture of wood that shone and new, clean carpets and lamps that matched and nicely framed family pictures up on the wall and on the mantel.

That's how I picture YOUR home, and I hope that's where you are. Somewhere lovely and peaceful and shiny and safe.

Anyway, where am I? Oh, I'd just turned twelve and started not being a good student. I made C's and D's in everything except English. Somehow I managed to do well in English without trying, and then, when I saw how badly I was doing in other subjects, I started trying to do even better in English. That's when I started memorizing everything—partly to prove that I wasn't stupid, and partly because I really liked the poems. Some pieces of American and British literature had lines as great as those I'd learned from Broadway musicals.

And that's when I started having boyfriends and keeping a diary. From twelve on I was always in love with some boy or other, and I had the good fortune to be loved back. That's strange to think about because I had so much going against me. I wasn't a good student anymore—people made fun of me for never knowing the answer when I was called on in geography or math or science—I didn't have a good personality or in any way fit in. I was gawky and certainly not pretty. But there was always a boy who really liked me and treated me nicely, who would even listen to me talk or sing, who really paid attention.

To this day, I feel grateful to each one. In fact, I can tell you that I've never stopped loving any of those boys, though of course I never loved any of them the way I loved the three men who might be your father.

I fell passionately in love when I was sixteen, and that was a love that lasted all the way to the Peace Corps. We even thought of joining together.

I met Erik when I was sixteen and we started going steady almost at first sight. My father thought it was rebelliousness on my part because Erik's parents were Republicans and very well-to-do. His father was a district attorney whose appointment depended upon the Republicans getting back in. His mother was a southern belle by way of Sweden. She had been a baroness before she married Erik's dad. That was the lowest level of nobility, but it was still nobility. People used to say that they knew she was Swedish because she looked like Greta Garbo. I used to think that she probably expected her son and me to "go all the way" because that's what they did in Sweden.

But it wasn't rebelliousness that caused me to fall in love with the son of a Swedish baroness and a Republican district attorney. It was the son, Erik himself. When I turned twelve, I started realizing that I wasn't as totally different from my father as I had planned to be, and I wondered whether it was in my genes. Even though I believed what the kids at school said about it being unnatural for people of different races to mate, and I was as surprised as they were when Perry Cuomo kissed Eartha Kitt right on the mouth, like Daddy I thought it was wrong to make the colored people go to the back of the bus and to use different water fountains and stand at the back of McCrory's instead of allowing them to sit down at the lunch counters. And Erik told me I'd changed his mind about these things, too. He even promised to convert to the Democratic Party when he was old enough to register to vote.

And yet, his parents liked me. When his father first met me, he said, "Wow! Rita Hayworth." I knew who Rita Hayworth was from the movie version of PAL JOEY, but it had never occurred to me that I looked like her. She was so OLD—almost forty. Later, when I saw pictures of her younger—especially the one in the negligee—I thought Mr. Atkinson was wonderful to call me by her name. It was an image I hoped to live up to.

His mother was nice to me too. And they even seemed to re-spect my father when his book of photographs on the Civil Rights Movement came out. Other people thought he was just trying to stir up trouble, though they didn't say anything to me about it because I think they figured it wasn't my fault that my father wanted to give people this one-sided view of the Communist-inspired Civil Rights Movement. But the Atkinsons bought Daddy's book even while it was still in hardback and seemed to like it even though they had, up on their wall, antique framed documents giving them the ownership of the slaves named therein.

(One word you need to learn when you go through life is paradox.)

Anyway, Erik and I were madly in love. I hear that people have to be at least eighteen before they're allowed to see their adoption pa-pers, so maybe falling madly in love has already happened to you, and you'll understand how intense love is when you're sixteen years old. You love being together and you look forward to being together every moment that you're separated. With Erik it was just like the song in PAINT YOUR WAGON. You can hardly wait "Till the golden moment when you'll be seeing him again." It's like the song from WEST SIDE STORY, when the "minutes seem like hours, the hours go so slowly" any time you're not together. You want the moon to "glow bright and make this endless day endless night." Every love song turns out to be true.

And yet (or maybe And so), I was a virgin when I joined the Peace Corps. Even though Erik's mother was Swedish and my parents thought the Real Morality was racial equality and not virginity, I thought traditions like virginity were picturesque and I often heard that your virginity was the greatest gift you could give your husband on your wedding night, and he would always absolutely adore you if you could give him that.

I guess my mother was the wrong person to ask about this—she might have been on the defensive—but I asked what she thought and she said, "If your virginity were the greatest gift you had to offer, why would anyone want to marry you?" But I believed what other people said, that if you weren't a virgin on your wedding night, your husband would always think of you as used merchandise.

Nonetheless, while I thought this, every time I was close to Erik, I felt willing to become used merchandise, to make him a gift of my virginity ahead of time, before our wedding night, and I was grateful that he was able to hold himself back when maybe I wouldn't have been able to.

But there was something I didn't understand for months. Erik had a secret I hadn't figured out. This is a hard thing to talk about, but who knows? Maybe it will be useful to you someday, whether you're a son or a daughter.

I'd seen my brother's penis, of course, and I'd seen pictures of a penis. There was always at least one in every biology book, even if our South Carolina history book still called the Civil War "The War between the States: The South's Fight for Independence." A penis was a penis, not just The Family Jewels. But when they showed the pictures, the penis was always in a state of rest, so I didn't know that it was supposed to be engorged with blood and going up without anyone's even holding it and screwing it in. That's another thing. The words are all wrong. "Making love" of course is the most romantic way to say it. "Having sex" sounds too impersonal. But "screw" is all wrong, even if you don't care about love. The word "screw" made me think that it was difficult to get it in because it had to be twisted. If they have to use carpentry terms, they should say "nail," not "screw."

Anyway, even before I ever saw Erik naked, I could feel how big he was. I couldn't imagine it being any bigger, I thought he was just showing respect for me because we did so many intimate things, but he never tried to "go all the way." I thought he just wanted to keep me a virgin so our wedding night would have something we'd never had before and he wouldn't even have to THINK the words "used merchandise."

But then one day he told me. He was impotent. He traced his impotence back to his being molested by his baby-sitter when he was little.

I wish I could tell you that I was loving and understanding, but I showed my father's blood that night. I was furious. All along, I'd thought he was using restraint out of respect for me because he loved me and wanted to marry me and get the greatest gift I could give him on our wedding night. And all the time I'd thought it, he wasn't using restraint at all. He just couldn't. I considered this deceit, and I yelled at him. And just like Helen, he started to cry.

I felt foolish because I thought that this meant I desired him more than he desired me. I refused to see him for several days, which was the longest we'd gone since we'd met.

When I look back now, I think I betrayed him the way I reacted because when someone trusts you enough to tell you something that's hard for them to tell you, you shouldn't punish them. You should show them that they were right to confide in you. You should be understanding, and I wasn't. At least not right away.

Later we talked, and I said, "It just hurts my feelings. Even if we don't go all the way, I want you to want to."

And he said, "I do want to. I just can't."

I pretended to settle for that, but I didn't really. I wanted him to be able to and NOT.

And yet, everything else about him was so perfect. He was handsome. He was smart. He loved me. He would come inside our house and say he didn't smell a thing, and he just thought that the cardboard boxes were funny. He'd take me beautiful places like out of the house. He took me to horse races like The Carolina Cup and to the Carolina Ballet, the Palmetto Club and to Town Theater (where we saw GUYS AND DOLLS, CARNIVAL, and MY FAIR LADY) and even to summer stock in Charlotte, North Carolina (where we saw SHE LOVES ME, KISMET, THE UNSINKABLE MOLLY BROWN, THE SOUND OF MUSIC, and THE MUSIC MAN.) And he took me to Myrtle Beach, where if a girl were going to lose her virginity before marriage, she'd go to lose it. People used to say that you could hear girls screaming out in pain all along the beach. Of course, that's not what I was doing at Myrtle Beach with Erik.

If only he hadn't been molested by the babysitter. I should have been angry with her instead of with him.

But we did try to work things out. If anyone could have worked it out, it should have been me because when I first discovered sex—I guess at about the age of six—I thought it was a solo act. It seemed so natural. After all, you carry yourself around all day, and there are several hours a day when you have total privacy in bed with yourself. It seems natural that you'd start caressing yourself, and I remember thinking, "Oh! This feels good!" But somehow I knew that this was a private thing. I wasn't supposed to do it in the classroom or at the dinner table, if we ever sat down together. Later I found out there was an ugly m-word for it and that it wasn't something you were supposed to do without a partner—and it had to be a partner you were married to. (This changed with the musical HAIR, but that was a ways ahead.)

Supposed to or not, I couldn't stop doing something that felt so good, so every night I'd touch myself and then count to ten—my purification period—before saying my bedtime prayers.

So what I thought was exciting about making out with Erik was him. And now there seemed to be something wrong with him. He saw a doctor, and the doctor told him there was nothing physically wrong with him so he prescribed trying out on another girl. (This was the same doctor who told Helen, when she said that she was going to breastfeed, that breasts were for sweaters, and breastfeeding would make her breasts sag.)

The doctor thought that maybe my being a virgin was inhibiting him. But Erik said he wouldn't do it with another girl because that was what Warren Beatty does in SPLENDOR IN THE GRASS when Natalie Wood doesn't want to get "spoiled" and then she goes out of her mind from loneliness and frustration. Neither of us wanted it to end up the way it does for them, with her driving away reciting that Wordsworth poem about how looking back at splendor in the grass, glory in the flower, you'd better "grieve not but rather find strength in what remains behind." (I wish I had time to write down all the poems I think you'd love and all the lyrics to the songs to help you get through life!)

In the movie, Natalie Wood sees him one last time and meets the woman he settled for when he couldn't have her and, knowing they'll never see each other again, she drives off to marry the patient she met in the mental institution. It's like THE UMBRELLAS OF CHERBOURG, when at the end Catherine Deneuve, by chance, meets the handsome guy (Guy) she used to sing with to the music of Michael Legrand before he was drafted and sent to Algeria to fight. He never got the letters she wrote and he sent her letters she never got so she thought he'd found someone else and, to give their baby a father, she married a diamond merchant. In that last scene, she drives up to his gas station, not knowing that it's his, and he comes to the car window not knowing that it's hers, and she gets out of the car and the music that used to play for them starts to play again, only all the words are different—just in reference to the lives they're sharing with the people that they settled for. ("And the sun will rise, and the sun will set, and you learn how to settle for what you get." CABARET) Neither of them knows that the other never stopped loving them. And then she drives away knowing that they'll never meet again. FANNY is a little bit like that, but in Fanny he chooses to go to the sea. In UMBRELLAS OF CHERBOURG he's drafted. I think Tony was luckier in WEST SIDE STORY because he died so only death would part them now. Nothing's sadder than two lovers who get separated by circumstances beyond their control and have to go on living. ("But other hands and other hearts are holding me! Holding me! Only you long as I shall live!" FANNY) Nothing's sadder than that except maybe a mother and child who never even meet.

I'm not sure that Erik and I went our separate ways because of his impotence. I think there was something else that went wrong. I think as I became an adult, eighteen to twenty-one, I kept getting to be more and more like my parents. I started to be irritable like my dad and sometimes, to my horror, I found myself saying, "What?" in the same tone of voice to Erik that my dad used with Helen and anyone who got on his nerves. That's what happened. Erik started getting on my nerves, and I had to re-assess love.

I saw a movie called ELVIRA MADIGAN, and in earlier years I would have just loved the movie, which is about a tightrope walker and a married military officer who run off together and make love to Mozart's Piano Concerto Number 21, which is now the Theme to ELVIRA MADIGAN. But they have trouble getting food and other necessities, so they have one last picnic and commit suicide together. Instead of loving the movie and thinking how wonderful it was that they had died together instead of going back to reality, I was suspicious of the story. I tried to figure out what really happened—because it was supposed to be based on a true story. And I figure that the newness wore out/off after a while and he started thinking he'd really made a mistake leaving his family and his job, even though he hated it, and she started to think he was really pretty boring and wanted to go back to the circus. So he killed her when she tried to leave him, and then he felt really ashamed and like a failure because he'd left his family and deserted his regiment for a tightrope walker who stopped loving him, so then he shot himself. I kind of felt that they had died not because their love was so great but because it wasn't.

I think that was about the stage when I decided you had to think love through.

I still didn't like Mother's coldness about love, but I started to think that maybe you had to pretend to feel a distance you didn't feel in order to keep the warmth there. I started "dating" in the sense of going out with lots of different boys when I went away to Winthrop College, and I liked dabbling in relationships. I didn't make love with any of them because I still felt that Erik and I were the real couple, but I liked being asked out by lots of different people and getting to know different personalities—though I think you'd have to say they were all "southern gentlemen." I remember thinking that it was just plain wrong for a girl to open a car door or pay for anything on a date. Of course, it was also true that a girl was supposed to let the boy decide where to go, and I liked to decide myself. It really wasn't fair, I see now. I'd decide where to go, and they'd pay. The girls in the Peace Corps told me it wasn't this way where they went to school, but in the South, the only thing you were allowed to pay for, if you were a girl, was Christmas presents. And I remember that one boy I dated was really surprised to see how many gifts I had laid out in the lobby of the dormitory on the night before we had to go home for Christmas break. (Only one of them was for him.)

Anyway, I want you to know that I wasn't promiscuous and I wouldn't have to wonder who your father is if I hadn't tried to balance things. I loved Danny, but I didn't want to need him more than he needed me, so I had to find someone else to keep myself from being too needy.

There used to be a column in GLAMOUR MAGAZINE called

"Ask Daisy" that talked about teddy bear tricks—ways to keep a man interested in you. I don't know why they were called Teddy Bear tricks unless it's because people outgrow teddy bears and you don't want a man to outgrow you. Her advice was to pretend you have other interests. She said that if you really love a man, you want him to be certain of your love, and that's what kills his interest. She said you should pretend to be able to live without him, pretend to have thoughts of other things, and he'll stay interested forever.

When I first saw that, I knew she was right that men don't like a woman who's too worshipful, but then it occurred to me: Why pretend to have other interests? Why not REALLY have other interests? Why not really be able to live without him? It sounds unromantic and maybe a little bit unfeminine, but I started to think of ways to live without him, whoever he was. And with Danny, I knew that if I just pretended that there was someone else, I'd go crazy. There had to really be someone else. But the someone else I found was a Latter Day Saint whose God forbad doing what we were doing, so we could only meet secretly. So even though he wasn't impotent like Erik, he wasn't a substitute for a complete relationship where you can go out into the light. Victor was on the way to a complete relationship, but he wasn't a national, and he came after I was already involved with 'Ofa, who offered me cross-culture and continuity. I have to be faithful, even if that means adding to the man or men I'm faithful to. I don't like life to be fragmented, going from person to person. I want life to be one long novel instead of just an anthology of disconnected stories.

I wish that I could stay in touch with you.

What else can I tell you about me? I've told you that I'm not a slut and that I value continuity. I guess I'm supposed to give you facts like statistics. I'm sending you into what I feel confident will be a happy home, but you're still likely to have some of our characteristics, as I discovered by finding my parents in myself. I should have been less likely than you to take after them because I grew up around them and knew what to look out for. But you, being in another environment, will be even more vulnerable to genetic make-up because you won't see the warnings.

I'm 5 feet 8 inches and thin. In training the staff told me every single man rated me high when we had to indicate who we'd like to have in our village, and one staff member said, stifling a yawn, "'cause they all think you're so pretty and feminine." That was the American draft-dodger's view, and Victor, from New Zealand, shared it. But I was ugly by Tongan standards, so I guess you can give credit to 'Ofa for being attracted to me in spite of my lack of bulk. Tongans admire big, fat women. The fatter the more beautiful. And maybe they're on to something. Fat people are soft and cuddly. I'm getting to be like that. I've put on 50 pounds. Anyway, the word they used for the way I looked (of course I wasn't pregnant at first) was palaku—ugly—but literally it means scarface. They just meant that I was too bony. I have red hair and, while they prefer this to blond, their ideal beauty would be a fat, fair-skinned (without my freckles) brunette.

If I could give you any part of me (not counting my collection of Broadway cast recordings), I think I'd give you my memory. I don't mean the things I remember but my ability to remember what I select. It's always help out. If there's something you're not good at—like having a normal life—it helps to over-compensate, and that's what I've done. When things weren't very pretty at home, I had a head full of beautiful songs and scenes that kept on playing. And even if you have a happy normal home the way adoptees are supposed to, you might not be good at math and then you can do what I did and compensate by memorizing every poem in ADVENTURES IN LITERATURE. And when the high school did THE GLASS MENAGERIE, I knew everyone's lines before they did, and even though I was Laura, I could whisper them their lines if they forgot. So even though I wasn't a popular girl (until I joined the Peace Corps and we out-numbered the guys 3 to 1), I was voted "most talented." I hope you've inherited my ability to memorize songs and lines and moments.

There's a song in HELLO, DOLLY: "He held you for a moment,

but his arms were sure and strong. It only takes a moment to be loved your whole life long." Changing the words just a little bit (but keeping the moment), "Each held me for a moment, and their arms were sure and strong. It only takes a moment to make love to pass along."

Now I guess I'd better tell you about those moments the week of your conception.

Moments with 'Ofa

It was the week of Tonga's first Independence Day celebration, and the British—maybe to show that they were better sports than they'd been when the United States won its independence (or that there was no oil in Tonga, after all), sent a ship with Prince William of Gloucester aboard. As one of four "government girls—single," I had been invited aboard the visiting British warship to meet Prince William of Gloucester and all the crew who had embarked in Nuku'alofa for a week of receptions, parties, dinners, parades, and other celebrations.

"What do you do as a government girl—single—on a visiting British warship?" I asked the Peace Corps director, who had extended the invitation but was, himself, a government man—married. "This wasn't in our Peace Corps job description."

"Just make small talk," he said.

"Fefe hake?" I suggested. "'Alu ki fe?'?"

"Maybe in English," he said.

The captain of the ship, who looked like Oskar Werner, an actor I like, greeted me and introduced me to "the man who really ISN'T married," a very nice guy named Nigel, who showed me around, danced with me, and got me a gin and tonic, a glass of wine, a rum and coke and a Manhattan because I wanted a combination of tastes—which, as you know, was certainly what I got that week.

Nigel was a perfect gentleman if you can overlook his approval of the US's presence in Vietnam and Cambodia, his reading TIME Magazine and his patronizing comments about the Tongans.

"The Tongans have no class," he said within earshot of a Tongan waiter.

"My mother once told me that anyone using the word 'class' doesn't have any," I said. (There are times in life when you have a moral obligation to be rude.)

Nigel recovered, and he and other men plied me with compliments, which was very enjoyable and a nice contrast to village life, where I was palaku. ("When men say I'm cute and funny as around in a dance we whirl, I just lap it up like brandy. I enjoy being a girl." FLOWER DRUM SONG) But equally enjoyable was the incongruity: I was a Peace Corps teacher serving Tonga by spending an evening aboard a British warship and dismissing class. But what I really particularly enjoyed was the singing, which we all wound up doing as a result of conversations that began with poetry.

The captain, after paying me a compliment that I'm too modest to repeat here, told me that he was part of all that he had met, which is a line from Tennyson.

"'Yet all experience is an arch wherethrough gleams the untraveled world whose margin fades forever and forever when I move,'" I replied.

"You know Tennyson!" he said.

"Not as intimately as I'm sure you do," I said, but the captain asked some other men to come over and listen, and we began reciting alternate lines. The men applauded and then, instead of slipping away to have some fun, they asked for more. We recited some Shakespeare, Donne, and Milton.

"An American who knows English literature!" the captain said.

"I know American literature too," I said.

"IS there any?" he asked.

I recited evidence that there was.

Because it was supposed to be small talk, I stuck to easy-to-like poems like Poe's "The Raven" and "Annabel Lee" with an exaggerated southern accent, which they really liked. And Frost's "The Road Not Taken" plus the last stanza of "Wild Grapes" (which I'll write down for you). But I also recited "The Love Song of J. Alfred Prufrock." They thought "Oh, Captain, My Captain" had something to do with them. (It's really Walt Whitman mourning the death of Lincoln.), so I suggested Gilbert and Sullivan, which really did relate to the Queen's Navy.

I am the Monarch of the sea

The ruler of the Queen's Na-vee.

I figured if they liked that, they HAD to like Rogers and Hammerstein and Lerner and Lowe, so we moved on to Broadway, and every now and then they'd be able to sing along.

It really surprised me that, instead of people backing off and away, more gathered around as if it were a strip tease they were watching.

We sang all night, and it was "a grand night for singing." (STATE FAIR)

Nigel accompanied me back home in a taxi.

"That was the most fun we've had on the entire trip, he said. "We don't usually sing like that. You've given the fellows something to fantasize about."

"What's that?" I asked.

"Being me," he said.

I wasn't quite sure what he meant by that. Was he expecting something to happen between us? Did the label "government girl" suggest the same thing to him that it did to me? Or did he mean he would be a source of envy just because he had the privilege of escorting me home and reviewing more poetry?

He took me to the door and kissed me in a very socially acceptable way. No, I didn't kiss back. No one aboard that ship is among the men who might be your father. In fact, when you think of all the men I DIDN'T make love with, I look like a prude. (Just joking.) Drinks always arouse me, but I was reserving my arousal for 'Ofa.

"When someone with eyes that smolder says he loves every silken curl that falls on my ivory shoulder," I sang as I walked from my door to Taita's, where I hoped to find 'Ofa and did.

"I enjoy being a girl!" I sang as I entered.

I approached Taita and embraced her as a preview of coming attractions for 'Ofa. I told them about the evening and sang a medley of the musical numbers, ending with one we hadn't sung, "He touched Me" from DRAT THE CAT. It's one of the most beautiful songs I've ever heard because it describes the feeling you have when you're really attracted to a guy and the smallest contact, the slightest touch, is thrilling.

I'm not pretending, of course, that there was only the smallest contact, the slightest touch, that evening.

Anyway, I sang the song, changing the tense from past to future: "He'll touch me. He'll put his hand near mine and then he'll touch me. I'll feel a certain tingle when he'll touch me. A sparkle, a glow."

Then I sat down beside 'Ofa and whispered in his ear.

"You are a Latter Day Saint," I said, "and I am a government girl."

"Kreecht," he said, smiling

"Jesus loves you," I sang, "So do I."

'Ofa smiled and said he would see me safely to my door, and sure enough that far he saw me safely. We closed the door.

"Light the lamp. Light the lights. We've got nothing to hit but the heights!" I sang. (GYPSY)

"Shh!" he whispered, and he didn't light the lamp.

"Please touch me," I sang.

"Shh!" he said.

"If you want me to stop singing, you'll have to seal my lips," I told him, and he complied.

"So what did you do aboard the ship all night?" he asked when he took his first breath.

"I told you. We recited great poetry."

"Yes, I'm sure," he said.

"And we sang."

"I bet YOU did. And was James Bond there?"

"Victor? He was supposed to be there, but I didn't see him."

"You didn't?

"No."

"I've heard he's a ponce."

"A what?"

"A ponce."

"What's a ponce?"

"I don't know. Why don't you ask him?"

"You know what they gave me on board the ship? They gave me magic love potions guaranteed to turn me helplessly amorous towards the first handsome Tongan I gaze upon. I kept my eyes downcast until just now," I said, looking up at where I felt his breath in the pitch-black air. "I'm looking in the eyes of love," I said, staring deeper into darkness. I couldn't see 'Ofa at all, but there was strong evidence that he was there.

And that's as much as any mother should tell her child about the night that might have been the night of your conception.

But there are, I'm embarrassed to say, a couple of other possibilities.

DANNY'S LEAVE TAKING

There were so many days that I'd longed for Danny. The day he came to Tongatapu wasn't one of them.

After months spent getting off to a slow start in my job, as they had advised us to do, I was now teaching oral English classes in every grade from 8:00 to 3:00 as well as "po ako" or "night school," which was preparation for the sixth-grade exams that determined the futures of the children. It was the second night of cocktail parties, dinners, and dances during the independence celebration, and I'd arranged to have the po ako earlier in the day so as not to heighten the panic the sixth grade children and teachers felt at the approaching exams.

The teachers rewarded me by telling me I'd gotten high praise from the headmaster.

"He is pleased with me," I sang. "Our fine headmaster declares he's pleased with me. What does he mean?" (A slightly altered rendition of a song form THE KING AND I)

"He means," Tupou said, "that you are a very keen teacher."

Tupou was one of the teachers who had once told me something very reassuring. "Sela, usually if a person sing and dance in the street, people think they a foolish. But not you."

The way she looked at me made me think that maybe she had cast the dissenting minority vote, but it still made me feel good that they'd learned to regard my bursting into song as the norm, at least for me.

As Tupou, the children, and I were walking back towards my hut Tupou added to the headmaster's pleased-with-me assessment.

"You prepare your lessons and you show loving kindness to the children," she said.

"And Victor," Kili said.

"And 'Ofa," Mataiaki added.

"Every boy love to you because you beautiful girl," Kili said.

It appeared that I had both a professional and a personal reputation.

And then, in honor of Tonga's independence, I gained a reputation as a magician when I lit my kerosene stove and, in a matter of minutes, transformed flat, tiny seeds at the bottom of a pan into fluffy white blossoms that filled the whole pot and almost pushed the lid off. I left the stunned children in the next room marveling at my magic powers while I poured water into my tin to tafitafi. (The English for tafitafi is "take a sponge bath," but I'm sure you'll agree that tafitafi says it better.)

That was when Danny, who I thought was still on Ha'apai, appeared.

"Oh, Danny!" I said in a tone that could only be interpreted as "I'm so sorry to see you!"

"I called to tell you I was coming, but your line was busy," he said.

I laughed. "Are you here for Tonga's independence celebration?" I asked.

"No, I'm here for mine."

The children entertained him outside while I dressed, and then he offered me a ride to town on the back of his bike.

The children looked worried when we were setting off. Was Danny one two many? They'd already started to take sides with Victor against

'Ofa. Who, after all, came for me in his James Bond car with his beautiful black dog, 'Uli'Uli, who'd started to teach them that dogs were fun for more than target practice? Who had invited them to come along with us to the beach? Well, actually, I had suggested it, but Victor had extended a "someday" invitation to them, and Kili had asked, "What's the name of the day?" leading Victor to make a real commitment, which he'd carried out.

That was the day that I realized I had already accomplished something during my Peace Corps service, in spite of getting off to a slow start, because Kili had applied a song. There were some songs I'd never thought of teaching the children but just sang for myself, and Kili had liked one of those and asked me to teach it to her. It was "Follow Me," a song that a spirit sings to lure Merlyn away from CAMELOT.

"Other child will going or only we go?" she had asked.

"Only you," I replied.

Kili gasped. She knew that phrase! And she broke out in song:

Only you, only I.

World farewell, world goodbye!

It felt so great to know that I'd be leaving behind something besides the Mickey Mouse Club Song.

Anyway, Victor was already earning points when Mataiaki went into Nuku'alofa and investigated. He had credit at the fale kaloa (store) there. That cinched it. He was the children's favorite among my "suitors."

Even though one villager still insisted, "'Ofa is a good conduct boy, and you are a good conduct girl," Kili and Mataiaki insisted that "'Ofa not bath" and 'Ofa not enough for you."

Oh, if they only knew.

Anyway, now there was Danny, who it turned out had come to Tongatapu because he was terminating. I suggested that we meet to talk at Pesi's house after the feast in Nuku'alofa.

"Not HER house," he said. "Why, did you know she once chased a

Tongan with a frog? She's lewd and suggestive."

"Well, what do you expect?" I asked. "She's another government girl."

And so after a feast during which we kaied ke pa'u (ate till we burst) we followed Pesi home.

After telling us some Twilight Zone stories, as only she could tell them, she thoughtfully arranged to spend the night with a Tongan neighbor "so that YOU can be lewd and suggestive."

I really just felt like sleeping.

Danny felt like leaving. Tonga. Apparently he also felt like taking me with him.

("Wherever we go, whatever we do, we're gonna go through it together." GYPSY)

"Now you've been to Tonga," Danny told me. "Time to move on." ("Knowing when to leave may be the smartest thing that anyone can learn." PROMISES, PROMISES) "I'm not ready yet," I said. "I'm getting to like it." (I was "getting to like them. Getting to hope they liked me." THE KING AND I)

"Come on," he said. "Be wild. Gather up your visual aids and run away with me."

("Not too fast. Not too fast. Let it grow. Let it last." ZORBA)

"I can't," I said.

"You CAN," he said. (No, nothing from CAN CAN, but there is something from ANNIE GET YOUR GUN. "No, I ca—a—a—-n't.")

"In the big scheme of things," he said, "it won't matter. They'll forget you in six months. But I'll remember you—" He looked at me and pretended to be calculating. "For a year at least! And if you come with me, I'll never forget you because you'll never LET me forget you."

("Try to remember, and when you remember, then follow." THE FANTASTICS)

"I'll never let you forget me no matter where I am," I said, "And for another year and a half, I'll be here."

"I should never have left you alone on this island," he said.

"I wasn't alone," I said, smiling.

("When I'm not near to the boy that I love, I love the boy I'm near." FINIAN'S RAINBOW)

"That's what I was afraid of," he said.

"It's true," I said, "that things might have been different if you'd stayed on Tongatapu with me."

"Yes, you once proposed that."

"And you proposed that we get married and have some beautiful Filipino children."

("When the children are asleep, we'll sit and dream." CAROUSEL)

"Is it too late?" he asked.

I felt that it was but thought it would be impolite to say so.

"You don't feel what you felt before, do you?" he asked. "Love is so transient."

("Somebody soon will love you if no one loves you now." CARNIVAL)

"I still love you," I said. "I just don't lust after you."

"Oh, Sara. I need for you to lust."

"Maybe our relationship has transcended that," I said.

"Oh, no, you've found it somewhere else, haven't you. I've heard rumors."

"What kind of rumors?"

"I've heard that you've been faka-suvaing with some dog named James Bond."

"Oh, they meant Victor. He has a dog. They call Victor James Bond. He's a doctor from New Zealand."

"God! Not just a license to kill, but a license to practice medicine."

"He's a very nice man," I said. "But we haven't been faka-suvaing."

"(Yes, I'm always true to you, darling, in my fashion." KISS ME KATE)

Danny touched my hair and sort of lifted it.

(Grow it. Blow it. Show it. Know it." HAIR) "Your hair has grown so long. It's so wild. As a token of my esteem, let me de-lice it for you."

"I don't have lice anymore," I said. "So much has changed."

"Then let me brush your hair for you," he said. "You once told me that brushing your hair was the greatest form of seduction."

"Isn't it nice that we can joke about that now? Now that we've become pals?" I said.

("And the world discovers as my book ends, how to make of lovers true friends." PAL JOEY slightly altered)

But it was no joking matter. Brushing someone's hair IS the greatest form of seduction, and how could I refuse him? Here was a man I loved. He had been sending me his used copies of ATLANTIC MONTHLY and HARPERS for months. He once said that I was the best date he'd ever had—dinner in Hawaii, breakfast in Fiji, and lunch in Tonga. The flame of my love for him was rekindled with every stroke of the hairbrush going through my hair until a desire that I had transferred from him to 'Ofa was blazing for Danny again.

Even as I write this, I have to smile because I can just hear his higher criticism: "'The flame of my love for him was rekindled with every stroke...'? Oh, Sela, you've made it easier for me to leave you."

But Danny may not have left soon enough. He may have become a weekend father. Yours. Mahalo pe. (Perhaps)

ME AND SYMPATHY

"Tevita was helping me look for my 'Uli 'uli," Victor said when I reached his door and Tevita, his "houseboy," was leaving

"You can't find her?" I asked.

"No, she's been missing all afternoon."

The significance of this wasn't lost on me. A missing dog was more alarming than a missing child. Tongans didn't eat children. This was a feast week. Poor families—and almost all Tongan families were poor—found meat wherever they could when they felt the social pressure of contributing to a feast.

"It's a valid expression of human existence," was the phrase that played in my head because I found that hard to believe at times like this. Yes, I knew that Americans sometimes treated pets better than human beings, but as my mother said, "Animals are nicer than people."

"No, I didn't believe that. I preferred human beings. Some human beings. But I couldn't stand to see the children throw rocks at dogs, as if they were inanimate targets. I had made it a point to introduce the Tongan children to Victor's dog, both when we went to the beach and once when I borrowed the dog for a purposeful walk through the village. "This is a dog. A dog is a living thing. A dog has feelings. A dog can feel pain. A dog can love." My oral and written English sentences contained concepts that were as foreign to Tongans as was the SPCA. Eating other people's beloved pets wasn't a valid expression o f human existence for me.

And so, that day, I was already feeling a concern and tenderness towards Victor.

We took a long walk, looking for the dog, and I asked him if there were any chance that 'Uli'uli had taken off of her own volition.

"Well, she certainly wouldn't just run away," Victor said. I told him about Whitman, the dog we'd had as children, and explained (not quite fully) that he had run away.

When it was time for dinner, we didn't feel as if it were time. And so we had drinks on empty stomachs, and we talked about the celebrations of the week.

It turned out that Victor had actually been among those in a private "audience" with Prince William of Gloucester."

"I hear that you made quite a hit on board the ship," he said.

"Yes, I heard the same thing," I said. I told him about our reciting poetry and singing Gilbert and Sullivan.

"The captain kept talking about this Sara Nye," Victor said. "He said all the men were talking about you."

"I hope that doesn't give the wrong impression," I said. "I went in to get some aspirin for my headmaster, 'who is pleased with me,'" I sang, "and Dr. Atkinson told me the same thing. Then he asked me if I wanted anything besides aspirin."

Victor smiled. "What did you say?"

"No," I said.

"You're a girl who can say no, aren't you," he said, and I thought, "only to birth control pills."

He put his hands on my shoulders and then ran his fingers up my neck and to my hair, which he pushed back with his fingers. I thought of Danny. I thought of 'Ofa. (I didn't know about you yet, or I'd have thought of you too—proof that I'm not always a woman who can say no) And then I remembered what 'Ofa had said.

"What's a ponce?" I asked. Victor took his hands off of my shoulders and moved back, looking at me. After what seemed like a very long time, he said, "That's a rather rude word. For a man who's effeminate."

"Oh," I said. "I have a book locker with lots of books with English words I don't understand. Certain slang words we don't have in American English keep cropping up."

Victor looked at me, but he didn't say anything. Did I see tears coming to his eyes?

I worried that I had hurt him. I could tell he suspected that the word had been directed at him. How sad that anytime a man is intelligent and sensitive, he's accused of being a effeminate. I knew he was feminine only in ways that were good.

I put my arms around him. I loved Victor in a deeper way than I loved 'Ofa or Danny. I felt the pain that he must have felt knowing that people misunderstood and made fun of his gentle and artistic manner. I felt the horror he must have felt picturing the manner in which 'Uli 'uli may have been captured and killed.

I reached out to comfort him. We held each other, and then he began sort of nuzzling my neck. He led me to a back room where I had never been before.

That was the only time that he and I ever made love.

Almost immediately afterwards we heard the dog bark and Victor hurried to the door while I put back on the items of clothing that he had taken off me.

When I came out into the living room, he told me that a Tongan from another village had recognized the dog and saved it from the fate we'd feared. He'd brought it back home to Victor.

"He said that he knew you," Victor told me brightly. "An 'Ofa Kulalau?"

The double irony came when I later looked up ponce. It doesn't mean what Victor said it meant.

To Whom It May Concern,

I'll bet that you don't approve. Neither do I. Philosophically, I do, but not emotionally. Or maybe it's emotionally I feel okay, but not philosophically. Somehow, it doesn't sit well with me. Making love with three men on one weekend seems tacky, and who am I to tell you that it's not? As your once-upon-a-time, soon to be long-ago mother, I will advise you: Don't make love to more than one man in one weekend. (This is where you can shout back, "Oh, Mother! You're so old-fashioned! Weren't you ever young?") But why do I always assume that you're a daughter?

I think there are other things mothers are supposed to say too: "Prudence, take your pill." And I'm sure you're wondering at my ir-responsibility in not taking mine. I'm wondering too. I didn't have any pills, of course, but I certainly had access. Mother certainly would have sent them to me (along with those champagne colored, satin bikini panties she did send me). There was the Peace Corps doctor, even of-fering to give me something besides aspirin. And one of the men who might be your father was a doctor. He had access to pills as well as to abortions, privately done, without going to Japan or Sweden. I think other girls should have abortions, but not me.

Of course, I didn't want to ask for pills because of my sense of privacy. It was an announcement—at least to one person—that I was having the "social life" a PCV was not supposed to have. Sometimes I fantasized having 'Ofa's baby, but I knew it was only a fantasy and not a wise course of action. Maybe it was like a game—Russian roulette.

Will this chamber have the bullet? Will this one? Why do people play Russian roulette, anyway? Is it for money? Is is it for cheap thrills? (Maybe not so cheap)

I'm not suggesting that you were for cheap thrills. Or even that 'Ofa was. Of course, Danny and Victor weren't. I wonder if I were just giving fate a chance. If you were meant to be, you'd be. I even wonder if maybe I wanted to have a child to give up. I grew up wishing that I'd been given up for adoption so I could have parents who passed inspection and were, at least, sane. Maybe you were my way of having a child without exposing her (except in safe, clean print) to the family I grew up in and maybe even am.

But at the same time, I think I'd make a good mother. I've always liked children, thank God, since they surrounded me all day long in Tonga. And I always thought in terms of having children—and keeping them! Even now, I think of all the songs I'd like to sing to you and all the things I'd like to tell you along the way. I used to want to name my daughter after a song from a musical: Maria ("Say it loud and there's music playing. Say it soft and it's almost like praying." WEST SIDE STORY), Gigi (GIGI), Mariah (PAINT YOUR WAGON), Jenny (STAR), or Jenny Rebecca (THE YEARLING). I love "Jenny Rebecca" because the mother sings it when her daughter is only four days old. And she sings about how lucky Jenny Rebecca is, with all that she has to look forward to. "("Dolls to be caring for. Love to be giving. Dreams to be daring for, long as you're living") If you're a son, I'm so sorry there aren't any really good songs.

You would probably never have come into existence if I had been a more conventional Peace Corps Volunteer. I knew people were peeking through the bamboo poles and trying to figure out what was going on. I knew that they were spying on me every time 'Ofa and I were alone. And I kind of made a decision. I knew a love life wasn't in the Peace Corps job description. I knew there would be people who would judge me harshly if I had a man in bed with me—or even with me on the matted floor, covered with a tupenu. But I made up my mind not to pay attention to people whose values would prompt them to look between bamboo poles or to listen to reports from those who did. I really tried not to care. I was trying to go from being a southern girl to being a Great Woman, who didn't care what people thought! A Great Woman rises above the rules. By definition a Great Woman does what she wants to do instead of what other people want her to do. But I think that some of what I wanted to do WAS what other people wanted me to do—not because they said so but because we valued the same things. There's really no sense in rebelling against what you love and believe in, no matter how much you like the idea of being rebellious. I haven't rebelled against everything my father believes in. And I'll give him credit for living by several of his convictions. He just happens to be crazy. My mother seems to have so few convictions beyond her beauty, but there are pretty things about the way she lives. She dresses up, even for at home. I think maybe we should all dress up especially for home or wherever we go every day. Superficial beauty is better than no beauty at all.

For weeks before you were conceived, I kept resolving not to make love with 'Ofa, and then I would. Finally, I wrote in my journal, "I'm weak. I keep resolving not to make love with 'Ofa and then I do. If I weren't weak, I'd never make such an awful resolution." But I'm not sure that a Great Woman is a woman who gives in completely to her passion—or to her passionate comic relief. Maybe a Great Woman is a woman who cares enough to use restraint. I don't think I used very much restraint the week you were conceived.

So, what useful advice can I give you besides "Don't make love to three men in one weekend" and "Prudence, take your pill"?

Remember that your adoptive parents are your real parents. Blood may be thicker than water, but you can't drink it. Real parents are the ones who take care of you and get to know you day by day. All this history I've given you is to keep you from feeling like a continent with a missing link. And it's bound to make you more grateful for your adoptive parents!

What else can I tell you?

Remember that whoever your father is, I loved him for more than just one weekend and always will. ("Fish gotta swim. Birds gotta fly. I've gotta love three men till I die. Can't help loving those men of mine." SHOW BOAT)

Read Frost's "Wild Grapes," especially the last part.

When you're in love, never travel without the sonnets of Edna St. Vincent Millay and the verses of Dorothy Parker.

Memorize everything you love so you can carry it with you wherever you go.

Give Broadway musicals a chance.

I haven't finished the up-date of SOUH PACIFIC that I started. I was going to do a version with Peace Corps Volunteers instead of the Navy because no one ever thinks about World War II anymore (except your grandfather, who still won't buy a VW or any other product that might support the re-industrialization of Germany).

One little ditty has come to me, though:

(To the tune of "There is Nothing Like a Dame" from SOUTH PACIFIC)

There is something in my womb.
Something I can't name.
I address it as To Whom.
Is To Whom a guy or a dame?

It's funny. The very first thing a mother hears is "It's a girl!" or "It's a boy!" I wonder if they'll tell me which you are before they take you away and give you to a mother who can bring you up in a normal home.

Even if I never get to see you, I'll know you by heart, and carry you with me wherever I go.

The last lines of "Wild Grapes" by Robert Frost

I had not learned to let go with the hands,
As still I have not learned to with the heart,
And have no wish to with the heart—nor need,
That I can see. The mind—is not the heart.
I may yet live, as I know others live,
To wish in vain to let go with the mind—
Of cares, at night, to sleep; but nothing tells me
That I need learn to let go with the heart.

South Pacific as a Peace Corps Musical Reprise in 2008

"Where in Africa is that?" I wondered when I got my invitation to train for Tonga.

I had asked for any French or Spanish speaking country, and I soon learned that no French or Spanish was spoken in Tonga, and it was not in Africa. It was in the South Pacific, a musical I knew by heart!

It was the first musical I'd ever listened to. My parents had it in an album of several 78 rpm records—a record for each song—and I'd sit in the attic for hours and listen to it over and over on a little plastic turn-table. Then, whenever the house was empty—not very often because there were seven of us—I'd expand my horizons to beyond the attic and go down to the living room where there was a bigger record player, turn the volume all the way up, and go dancing around the room, doing cart wheels and tap dancing on the picnic table (the one we kept under the chandelier in the dining room because we had moved into a house much nicer than we were). I didn't know how to tap dance of course, and my cart wheels were lopsided, but what I lacked in instruction, coordination, grace, beauty, and skill I made up for in enthusiasm. That's been the story of my life.

We had large mirrors all over the dining room, and I'd greet myself with exuberance, dancing my heart out until I heard the car pull up, and then I'd stop my criminal act like a burglar in the midst of gathering the silverware, turn off the music, and jump three steps at a time back up the staircase to my room leaving "A Wonderful Guy" and all the other joyous *South Pacific* songs for another day.

For years I didn't know that there was a whole genre called Broadway Musicals, but they were my addiction even before I had the name for what I couldn't live without. I'd seen *Show Boat* performed at the Idaho State Hospital, where my dad was Head Psychologist and we kids were included in the patients' Friday night showings of movies, so often MGM musicals. I knew that I liked the kind of songs that told a story, an adult fairy tale set to music. A cock-eyed optimist found a cultured Frenchman across a crowded room, and she wondered how she'd feel living on a hill side, looking on an ocean beautiful and still.

South Pacific! I was going to serve in a Broadway Musical! There was no other region in the world where the Peace Corps went that had a Broadway Musical named after it. (Did Vista work in *Oklahoma*?) Tonga might not be Spanish or French-speaking, but it was in the South Pacific. As a Peace Corps Volunteer I could update *South Pacific* and make it a Peace Corps Musical. Keep the music. Change the words so that Nellie Forbush was a Peace Corps Volunteer in the nineteen sixties instead of a nurse in World War II. The war would be Vietnam. Men could serve in the military and go to Vietnam—that would be Cable, the lieutenant who sings "Younger than Springtime" to lovely Liat, daughter of Bloody Mary—or they could join the Peace Corps and get a deferment like the male PCVs, who outnumbered the female PCVS almost three to one. Tonga was a British protectorate, I soon learned, so Emile would be a British guy, an expatriate.

During my two years in Tonga I did, in fact, get to know and love A Wonderful Guy who was British, a hospital administrator in Tonga. He invited me into his beautiful home, cooked for me, brought me Fidji Perfume from Fiji(!), wrote and illustrated letters to me, and gave me the key to his home. That was so that when he was away and I was working at the Fasi Teachers' Retraining Center near his house, I could relax there, making myself at home. I was totally clueless back then, but now I know that the Wonderful Guy was gay (though not as trite and as gay as a daisy in May). A Wonderful Gay.

But my South Pacific musical wouldn't begin with him because I loved other wonderful guys, some of whom I'm almost certain were heterosexual, and even before I put them to stolen music, I had written about Lanai, the Hawaiian island where I was student teaching during Peace Corps training.

To the tune of "Bali Hai"

Most people live on pineapple islands.
 Lost in the Doleful Pacific seas.
Most people train for another island.
 One soon to be full of PCVs.

Tongan Isles will call you,
 As did John Kennedy.
Ask what you can do for your island.
 Find out who you can be.

I also wrote what I could in French. (It should have been en Tonga, not à.)

Dites-moi, pourquoi Je suis à Tonga.
 Dites-moi, pourquoi j'habite ici.
Dites-moi, pourquoi J'enseigne à Tonga.
 Parce que je suis un PCV.

"You've Got to Be Taught" is a song about racial prejudice. The original words are these:

You've got to be taught to be afraid/of people whose eyes are oddly made/and people whose skin is a different shade./You've got to be carefully taught.

I started a verse about fitting in with complainers after I heard they were making fun of me for being happy in Tonga.

You've got to be taught to be irate
Conform to what all your peers so hate.

Even then I was aware of not having the "right" responses to whatever was going on, but in Peace Corps training we'd been taught not to assume that our culture is the only legitimate one. However people choose to live their lives, spend their time and money, "it's a valid expression of human existence." I genuinely liked the people—Tongan teachers, other Peace Corps trainees, staff. I couldn't help it although I was more self-critical and critical of others my second year. I still loved those wonderful guys, too, and it was a valid expression of human existence to love more than one, so I could see myself singing on the beach to the tune of "A Wonderful Guy."

I suspect everyone
in the Peace Corps makes fun,
Saying I love all men who are some mother's son.
dadadadadadadadadadadada

They say faithful can be just to one, not to three.
But I'm citing my source, and according to me
dadadadadadadadadadadada

Loving more than just one, is greater fidelity.
I'm being true to each of the three.
"How can you?!" How can I not? I plea
Loving, funny, smart. They're all this to me!

I'm as faithful as Ruth to Naomi.
Whither they goest I go with each one.
    Add more than three

to this sweet melody
I have found me four wonderful guys.

Jim, my first Peace Corps love's missing in action.
I love him though he dropped out of the scene.
    I correspond
    From this island I'm on
When I'm not with another, I mean.

Jim wrote wonderful letters, and I wrote too, devotedly, and I appreciated the fact that before he left, he told Ron to take care of me.

Ron is funny and smart and so loving
It's no fun, not smart not to love him back.
    And you will see
    him in my company
Please give social life four times more slack.

There was also a priest-in-training I could sing about to the tune of "A Wonderful Guy."

Please don't think it's a sin
This sweet quandary I'm in
When I'm tempted I don't bow.
I stick out my chin.
dadadadadadadadadadadada

When you come to a feast
appetites will increase
When you hear of the love that I have for my priest
dadadadadadadadadadadada

Faithfully, I kneel here and offer my prayer for him.
Who has yet to take final vows.
Thankfully, I know that our chances are awfully slim ...
The future will hold fond memories but I won't hold him!
Chorus

I'm in love with a priest who's in training
Wholly committed to this Man of cloth.
    Deadly are sins
    But not ones we are in
We're both lively in love; there's no sloth.

My God, the verses keep coming, like manna—or locusts?—from
the sky!

Since I've loved this young priest
How my praying's increased
It's on him that my eyes, hands and arms now do feast
dadadadadadadadadadadadadadada

And they're saying right now
I should just disavow
The affection that's real
for this priest that I feel
dadadadadadadadadadadadadadada

When he's near, I feel that this island's a paradise.
Touching, I feel a warmth that's divine
Don't forget. He isn't really a priest— not yet
It's love —hear my confession—I'll never regret!

He's a Tongan, and that's local color.
I'm getting into the culture this way.

And I must say
I feel anga-lelei
When I think of this wonderful priest

He's not a priest yet; he's only in training.
I give him lessons on how couples love.
 He shouldn't miss
 What is holy—a kiss!
That I give to this wonderful priest..

I should make reference to the time he represented Polynesia and got his feet kissed by the Pope!

He deserves a vacation from pontiffs
Kissing the sole of his foot humble-y.
 I can't relate
 To a celibate state
When I think of this wonderful priest.

I know some verses right there in the Bible
"Greet one another with a holy kiss."
 Roman Sixteen
 Puts us both on the scene
"When in Rome" with my wonderful priest.

But I should work in what they taught us in cross-cultural training: "It's a valid expression of human existence." Starting with the intro to "A Wonderful Guy"

Please don't criticize me
 for what I can't resist.
It's a valid expression
 of how we exist.

dadadadadadadadadadadadadada

Hmm. How come I'm so profuse in my lyrics for my wonderful priest? They just keep coming. Is amount of doggerel a good gauge for degree of affection?

Maybe I should move on from my wonderful guys and focus on that valid expression of human existence.

To the Tune of "Younger than Springtime"

A valid expression is this
Of human existence. A kiss.
    Nobody knows
    Our friends and our foes
Are only guessing.

A valid expression are we
Of living life meaning-fully
    Please don't disdain
    What we don't explain
It's not depressing.

Okay, well. I should get Vietnam into the lyrics too since that's why there were so many more guys than dolls.

We won't go to Vietnam to the tune of "There Is Nothing Like a Dame" (intro)

We're deferred from Vietnam
But we're serving Uncle Sam
By enlisting in the Peace Corps
We are here out on the lam.

We outnumber women PCVs we've noticed, three to one.
Valid expressions are such fun!

Okay.

I never got around to finishing my re-write of South Pacific.

Stage Directions:

Write it now, July 2008, as Tina's grandmother, the one I am taking back to Tonga with me, as me, two generations later.

In case anyone is unfamiliar with the Rodgers and Hammerstein musical *South Pacific*, from 1949, it's based on James Michener's Pulitzer Prize Winning short story collection *Tales of the South Pacific* and takes place on an island.

Nellie Forbush is a young American nurse from Little Rock, Arkansas, stationed on a South Pacific island during World War II. She falls in love with Emile, a middle-aged expatriate French plantation owner before finding out that (gasp) he was once married to a Polynesian woman and fathered "colored children" with her.

Bloody Mary is the local-color character—a middle-aged woman who sells things like grass skirts to the enlisted men on the island. The servicemen regard her as funny and uncouth. (Scoop: The Bloody Mary character is Vietnamese. Tonkin is the northern-most province of what is now Vietnam.) She has a beautiful virginal daughter, Liat, stashed away on an off-limits island called Bali Hai. Lieutenant Cable, a young Princeton graduate from New Jersey, falls in love with Liat but knows that people back home would never accept her because they've all been "carefully taught" to discriminate on the basis of skin color and the perceived shape of eyes.

Unfortunately, Jim, Ron, and my priest-in-training were not expatriates. Vincent Williams would have to be Emile and instead of a French man, he'll be a Brit. That will give a different focus to the love story. It won't be Nellie's racism but her homophobia the conflict will center around—although there will be references to the life of a Peace Corps Volunteer in Tonga.

When I was in the Peace Corps, I had never heard the phrase "sexual orientation," but soon after my return to the United States (after living in Tonga, Spain, and Algeria), I started hearing about Peace Corps women who'd married Peace Corps men and never needed their birth control pills, and after developing a crush on a guy in my Masters Program at San Francisco State in 1976, I developed better gay-dar (radar for who's gay), present and past.

I've tried to find Vincent between the time I left Tonga in late 1971 and 2008, when I'm returning. If he comes forth to sue me for using his real name, then I'll finally succeed in finding him. I'd like to be a better friend now that I understand why we couldn't be lovers.

So Vincent Williams will be an expatriate whose crime was not killing a man, a bully, as it was with Emile's back story, but having sex with a man. Being gay and getting caught. Exiled. The Polynesian children Nellie could love only if they were someone else's children will be not Emile's kids by a Polynesian woman but the Tongan boy Vincent Williams loves. The boy would sing the Tongan equivalent of "Dites-moi.""

Malo e lelei is *hello* or literally *Thank you for being well*
Fefe hake is *How are you?*
'Alu ki fe? means *Where are you going?*
"Alu ai is goodbye to someone who is going
Nofo ai is goodbye to someone who is staying.

Malo e——-lelei
Mo fefe hake.
Malo e— lelei. 'Alu ki fe?
Malo e —-lelei. Mo fefe hake.
'Alu ai. Nofo ai. Go or stay.

Or maybe I can have them sing "Mo 'ofa atu" *and love to you.*
Malo e— lelei
Mo 'ofa atu.
Malo e— lelei. 'Alu ki fe?

Malo e— lelei. Mo 'ofa atu.
'Alu ai. Nofo ai. Go or stay.

Scene: At Vincent's home. Young Tongan guy pretends to work for Vincent when others are around.

I had, in a sense, met Vincent across a crowded room. First the Peace Corps doctor had invited my neighbors, Leif and Mele, to dinner to meet Vincent, but they told me that Vincent had shown much more interest in me. He told them he'd seen me walking along the road from my fale (pronounced FAH-lay and meaning hut) to school, and had wished I would get attacked by a pig so he could rescue me. Sometimes, too, he'd see me walking through what looked like a lake, which my yard turned into after a rain because it was built in a ditch. Could he rescue me from drowning?

To make such heroic feats unnecessary, Dr. Wiley had another dinner and invited me. Then Vincent invited me to dinner at the Dateline, Tonga's only hotel, built along the wharf as part of the five-year plan that was to save Tonga economically by attracting tourists. It was the brainstorm of King Tāufa'āhau Tupou IV, the now-deceased King of Tonga.

"But no one thinks the wharf is very pretty," his underlings protested.

"If they don't like it, they don't have to come," the King replied indignantly.

In the Peace Corps version, Nellie and Vincent meet in Nuku'alofa, the capital city, in 1970, on the palace grounds at Pangai Lahi. when Queen Elizabeth is visiting and eating with her fingers, faka-Tonga. (Faka means pertaining to: Tongan Style.) Then he invites her to his home nearby.

Vincent's house wasn't exactly on a hill. Our island, Tongatapu, was flat. But we could still have "Twin Soliloquies" as Emile and Nelly do on his plantation. They could be contrasting his life as an expatriate living in a house with running water and electricity and hers as a Peace Corps Volunteer in a group where there are a lot of men, some of whom are rat control inspectors and other foreigners like the Mormon missionaries. (How does a wonderful guy compete with *them*?) The lyrics will also contrast his elite British accent and her humble American one. She expresses her gratitude that he doesn't think she's ugly just because she's not fat. In the context of body size, she can use the Tongan words for bon appetit: Kai ke sino (Eat till you're fat) and kai ke pa (Eat till you pop)

ELLIE
    Wonder how I'd feel,
    Once I left the Peace Corps
    Staying here forever
    Expatriate dream.

VINCENT
    This is what I need.
    Someone who's adapted.
    Someone to share this with
    Paradise the theme.

NELLIE
    We are not alike.
    He's older and wiser.
    Has a British accent.
    I'm his culture shock.

VINCENT
    I am twice her age.
    I'm a father figure.
    With the draft the young men
    Line up on her block.

NELLIE

Wonder why I feel
I am still in training.
Can I learn Queen's English
On warm Tongan nights?

VINCENT

Shall I ask her out?
Maybe to the Dateline?
They have running water,
and electric lights.

NELLIE

He's so awfully nice.
Someone I can talk to.
Doesn't think I'm ugly
Just because I'm thin.

VINCENT

Younger men than I:
Mormons! Peace Corps!
Rat control inspectors
How do I fit in?

The music swells to the Tongan version of "Some Enchanted Evening."

VINCENT

Some enchanted morning
You may see a strange girl.
You may see a strange girl wade through a lake-like lawn.
And somehow you know.
You know even then

That you'd like to see her
Again and again.

This is the beginning of their "romance" that always stays a romance and never moves into an affair, and she thinks it's because she's a Peace Corps Volunteer and isn't even supposed to have a "social life," much less a love life. That's what they tell them in training. He, trying to appear—maybe even be—"normal," courts her but hopes that it will always stay in the courtship stage. After driving her back to her village, he returns to the house boy he really loves, and he sings to the tune of "Younger than Springtime."

Stranger than fiction are we.
A stranger addiction have we.
We don't belong.
I'll sing you a song
Of love that can't be.

I should neglect you, I know.
You should reject me and go.
But there's a force
that we can't divorce
It's love not just sex.

But it is sex too, we plead
It can perplex too, this need.
We can't complete
This love can't compete
With what's accepted.

So we'll just say we are friends
Honesty in love offends.
To lies inured

A future endured
Is ours. The end.

Etc.

I'll make "Bloody Mary" not a person but an island, Tongatapu,
the main island, and Nuku'alofa (meaning nook of love) is the capital,
so Peace Corps Volunteers can sing "Tongatapu" to the tune of "Bloody
Mary." Once again we pay homage to our rat control inspectors and
add those in Family Planning too.

Tongatapu is the— isle we love. (bong, bong, bong, bong)
It's the island we are— so fond of. (bong, bong, bong, bong)
Nuku'alofa means the —nook of love.
We're here to serve two years.

Or better yet, make that "Faka-Tonga." *Faka* means pertaining to,
in the style of...

Faka-Tonga is the way we love. (bong, bong, bong, bong)
On this island that we're so fond of. (bong, bong, bong, bong)
Nuku'alofa means the —nook of love.
We're here to serve two years.

Peace Corps Tonga is the— job we love. (bong, bong, bong, bong)
Tonga is the place we're— all fond of. (bong, bong, bong, bong)
Tonga's where the skies are— blue above.
We're here to serve two years.

Here we draw the water— from a well. (bong, bong, bong, bong)
Kerosene lamps and stoves— are just swell. (bong, bong, bong,
bong)
We'll have stories that we'll— get to tell.

Faka-Tonga's our way now.

Here's a volunteer in— rat control. (bong, bong, bong, bong)
Rats controlling thatched huts— take their toll. (bong, bong, bong, bong)
We do family planning— for the soul
We're here to serve two years.

We are going to a— Tongan feast. (bong, bong, bong, bong)
Underground oven for— every beast. (bong, bong, bong, bong)
Kai ke sino: Eat till— you've increased
Faka-Tonga's our way now.

Faka-Tonga makes the— English howl. (bong, bong, bong, bong)
Faka-Tonga—hey, folks, — watch that vowel. (bong, bong, bong, bong)
Faka isn't any— thing that's foul.
Faka means pertaining to.
Bong, bong, bong, bong

I can make reference to the International Dateline, where time begins and to the blue laws, stipulating what you are allowed to do on Sunday: Pray.

Tonga is the place where— days begin. (bong, bong, bong, bong)
We skipped Tuesday when our— plane came in. (bong, bong, bong, bong)
All that's not prayer Sunday is a sin.
Faka-Tonga's our way now.

Bong, bong, bong, bong

I can show how some Peace Corps Volunteers are trying to

assimilate, wearing the traditional Tongan clothes and eating the favorite Tongan dishes. I can introduce the ta'ovala, a mat worn around the waist, and the tupenu, a wrap-around skirt for both men and women. They can sing of lupulu, which is corned beef (from the English word *bull* but Tongans have no *b* and they never end a word with a consonant) and *lu* is the taro leaf it's wrapped in after it's been mixed with onions, coconut cream, and other condiments.

> I'd like to wear the ta'ov—ala too. (bong, bong, bong, bong)
> The tupenu . What else— can we do? (bong, bong, bong, bong)
> To show the natives, I'll eat lupulu.
> Faka-Tonga's our way now.
> Bong, bong, bong, bong

> There are piggies visit—ing my hut. (bong, bong, bong, bong)
> Goats and chickens, horses, — rats do strut. (bong, bong, bong, bong)
> I could shoo them all a—way now, but
> Faka-Tonga's my way now.

> Should we have tong, tong, tong, tong in place of bong, bong, bong, bong?
> How about fak, fak, fak, fak.

For now, let's leave bong and move on to "There Ain't Nothing Like a Dame."

In the original show *South Pacific*, the guys miss females, so longingly they sing "There Ain't Nothing Like a Dame."

"There is Nothing Like a Name" could introduce the world to Tongan names like Kili, Sione, Tevita, Tupou, Hinehina, Likua, Loiloi, Fatafehi. Or maybe "Here in Tonga's Not the Same." This could be a tribute to all that Tonga offers, including foi niu (coconuts), fales (two syllable word meaning huts), and lice!

> We've got ovens underground.
> We've got busses going to town.
> We've got coconut trees kids can climb
> To bring *foi niu* down.
> We've got fa-les with great tapa cloth and mats spread out so nice.
> What's more we've got –a head of lice!

But I hear rumors that Tonga has changed. The place with zero waste, where they used to take their baskets to town and get a cup of sugar measured out into a newspaper and folded over and put in the basket—that place has discovered plastic, and now they are contributing more than their share to the Great Pacific Gyre, that gigantic island of garbage in the middle of the ocean.

> Oh, their baskets went to town
> Where they'd put a cup of flour
> Never putting things in plastic bags
> They took sponge baths, no shower.
> They used cloth but never paper, for their lights used kerosene.
> Now things have changed. It's just obscene!

> Here in Tonga's not the same.
> Once with zero waste.
> Back when eco had no name
> Here in Tonga it's not the same.

> Now they leave baskets at home
> and get plastic bags instead
> They don't walk from place to place
> so there's a traffic jam ahead.

Etc., etc. We really must move on now.

Now, again, with no Bloody Mary, who will sing to the tune of "Bali Hai"?

Could it be the evangelist who's after only one thing: Nellie's soul? Maybe he could be the one who wrote the Tongan textbook for the Peace Corps Volunteers.

To the tune of "Bali Hai"

'Alu ai, they tell you, as you leave to move on.
'Alu ai, is what they tell you. It's the name of this song.
Nofo'ai is different. That's goodbye if you stay.
It means stay when someone's going.
Stay while I go away.

Nofo'ai, alu'ai, nofo'ai.

Okay. So much for that one.

What does the Peace Corps Volunteer, in love with A Wonderful Gay, sing instead of "I'm Gonna Wash that Man Right Outa My Hair"?

I'd like to Wash that Man Right Out of My Hair
To the tune of "I'm Gonna wash that man…"

I'd like to wash that man right out of my hair.
But I can't wash that man right out of my hair.
I cannot wash that man right out of my hair
The village well is dry.

But I can wave that man right out of my arms.

Yes, I can wave that man right out of my arms.
Yes, I can wave that man right out of my arms
'Alu ai y nofo'ai.

If a man can understand you,
Give you Fidji perfume too,
Cook a meal
Still not feel
That you've got true sex appeal.
Oh, it's oh, so insulting.
So throw him into the well.
Oh, hell! Oh, well.

But then, she admits he's a Wonderful Gay.

I expect everyone
In the Peace Corps makes fun
Of my dating a man
Who'd prefer someone's son.

Da da dut da da dut da da dut da da dut da

And they'll say I appear
To love just what is queer
While rejecting the boys who regard with a sneer.

Da da dut da da dut da da dut da da dut da

But at the time Nellie sings this song in the original World War II *South Pacific*, she doesn't yet know about Emile's shame. It isn't that he killed a man. That doesn't bother her. The shame is that he's fathered two children with a woman who was Polynesian, "colored," and not the right color to a girl from Little Rock, Arkansas.

As Nellie says in Act I scene twelve:

And—their mother…was a…was…a…

To which Emile replies, "Polynesian."

Nellie, our girl from Little Rock, is stunned and turns away, trying to collect herself while Emile says that his wife was beautiful and charming.

"But you and she…"

Then Emile says that he has no apologies. "I came here as a young man. I lived as I could."

What a nice defense of Polynesian people.

So… "A Wonderful Gay" comes later. After our Peace Corps girl has gotten over the shock. In this Peace Corps version, she'll use the word fie leti, which means wants to be a woman

Fearlessly I'll face all the homophobes serving here.
Greater by three are the guys to the gals..
They know the words like the fie leti but leer
As the man who's a Wonderful Gay appear(s).
I'm not ashamed to reveal
The earthshaking truth I can't conceal.

When she does find out about his sexual orientation, he can sing her "You've Got to Be Carefully Taught" to explain why he hadn't come out to her or even to himself for so many years.

You've got to be taught to be like them

The people who don't know what I am.
Who think fie leti's a joke that's a gem.
You've got to be carefully taught.

You've got to be taught to feel disgust
For people whose feelings cause distrust.
You've got to conform; not the boy but the bust.
You've got to be carefully taught.

You've got to be taught before it's too late.
Before you become what you are, you must date
And marry and buy with some girl real estate.
You've got to be carefully taught
To be what you really are not.

Or maybe he sings that to the boy he loves whose parents are marrying him to a Tongan girl…or maybe Nellie is courted by the gay boy Vincent loves. That would be an interesting plot twist and add to her wonderful guys..

Then Vincent, without the two people he really loves, the Peace Corps Volunteer (platonically) and the Tongan boy (carnally), sings to the tune of "This Nearly Was Mine."

If I were not gay
To the tune of "This Nearly Was Mine"
If I were not gay.
If I were like other men.
If I were like other men,
Then I could be free.

If I were not me
I could be a part of life.

Not only apart from life.
I'd be free of me.

I don't think— it's a choice
That therapy could cure.
She thinks I have a voice
That men could lose allure.

This young man I love
This woman I love but less
Loving her more for her tenderness
That nearly is gone.

This young man I can't have.
She that I'm so fond of
They leave me without a love
To escape what I know of love.
Now, now I'm alone
Me, as I was born to be
Wishing that they could see
And love that which is me.

Oh, dear. This is getting serious. More like "Sunday, Bloody Sunday," a movie that Vincent loved.

Now it's time for "Happy Talk." *Fiefia* means happy in Tongan, and *talanoa* means chat. Kole is the word for borrow, and it's a tradition, as I found out when Loiloi wanted to make pancakes and borrowed my sugar, flour, eggs, pan, and finally my stove!

Happy fiefia fiefia Tongan talk
Talk about things you'd like to do.
You'd like to take a shower.

There's no water this hour.
So talanoa and wait the hour through.

May—I borrow a cup of stuff
Flour, sugar, butter, eggs. Enough!
It's pancakes I will make
As soon as I can take
Your kerosene stove.
All's gone in a puff.

Could I borrow your spouse
To add him to my house
That's leaking now? Finding a plumber's tough.

You've got to kole too
If you don't kole too
Everything you've got's kole'ed from you

Happy fiefia fiefia Tongan talk
Talk about things you'd like to do.

I can also bring in the Gloria Tate Syllabus we used for teaching oral English, acting out every verb we taught. We'd try to get the children to laugh until we found out that when they laughed, the headmaster beat them.

Talk about the fate
Of teacher Gloria Tate
Teaching English all around the isles!
Though it seems absurd
You act out every verb
The headmaster beats every kid who smiles.

Happy fiefia fiefia Tongan talk

Talk about things you'd like to do.
It really would be nice
To get your head of lice
Back to the liceless hair that you once knew.

Now what's left? Should the PCV sing something to the tune of "Honey Bun"?

Nellie can describe how she's living as a Peace Corps Volunteer in her fale (hut, pronounced fah-lay). She can throw in some Tongan words: vai (water), anga lelei (good natured), Oku'ou potoau he lea faka Tonglish, which means I'm good at speaking Tonglish.

My hut is as cozy as a basket.
Woven mats and tapa door to door.
There's a window of wood held up with wood sticks
Having electric grid or water would be a bore…or…or…or?

A couple of years
Is all we've got
To use cross-cultured things they've taught.
Make the most of every Tongan day!

Drawing the vai from my own well
Someday South Seas tales I can tell.
Every day brings more malo e lelei.

I'm sometimes culture shocking
My way of Tongan talking
Tupenu too
What can I do
My time here I'm clocking.

I hope they'll say
Anga lelei
After my precious two-year stay
I am here and here I will stay
To say two more years
Of malo e lelei.
Oku'ou poto au
He lea faka Tonglish as I do.
I'm good at Tonglish.
Two years is nice
In Paradise.
Although I've got a head of kole'ed lice.

What more? "Cockeyed Optimist"? She can describe the sky as faka 'ofa 'ofa, which means beautiful. She can make reference to the selection process in Hawaii, when her friend 'Ana was labeled lewd and suggestive because she chased a Tongan with a frog. Nellie herself, of course, was almost de-selected for living in a dream world. Like me, she was considered a high-risk volunteer, someone who was liable to waste the tax payers' money because she wouldn't adapt or stay the course. I'll pay tribute to Sali, the Tongan teacher who told me, "Usually someone singing in the street, the people call a foolish. But when you singing in the street, nobody call a foolish. People just say "Tina."

When the sky is so faka'ofa'ofa,
It's a beauty we all appreciate.
But when I see blue skies it's fantasy
That my eyes, both rose tinted, create.

Oh, in training while 'Ana was just labeled lewd
The shrinks looked at me and identified
Me as a high-risk-don't-send-her PCV
"She lives in a dream world!" they cried.

But friend 'Ana the Lewd
Said they had misconstrued
My dream world as a negative.
"It's really your main gift
Dream worlds give you a lift
When you land on Tonga Isles to live."

I will always be grateful for the people
Who know sane's over-rated, over-praised.
For I'm now here to stay
Stay 'anga lelei
And reality been re-appraised.
I'm ama—-a—-a—-a—-a—-zed.

I'm exhausted. I've spent all afternoon writing songs to turn the South Pacific back into a musical, this time with a Peace Corps Volunteer as Nellie Forbush. But who will star when Tina takes her grandma back to Tonga? I, with my never-very-good-turned-raspy-from-misuse-and-overuse voice, am willing but too old to play the lead. But wait! Several years ago Glen Close at the age of fifty-four starred as Nellie. I wrote a letter to the Datebook Section of the San Francisco Chronicle, which chose my letter as "Letter of the Week."

Aging Actors Take Note
Tuesday, April 17, 2001

Editor — As a woman in her mid-50s, I was delighted to watch Glenn Close miscast as the 21-year-old Nellie Forbush, ready for her close-up, in "Rodgers & Hammerstein's South Pacific" (March 26) fewer than five years after playing the aging Norma Desmond in "Sunset Boulevard"! This is the direction we all hope to go in.

As I listened to Rade Sherbedgia singing "This is what I need; this is what I long for: someone young and smiling lighting up my hill," about the 54-year- old Close, I could only wonder why they hadn't got-ten Rita Moreno to play the "younger than springtime" Liat.

A friend has also suggested that we recast a few other movie musi-cals: John Travolta and Cher could be the Romeo and Juliet lovers Tony and Maria in "West Side Story"; Julie Andrews could star as Sandra D. in "Grease" opposite Alan Alda.

The possibilities are endless. And if young actors complain that all the best parts are taken by older actors, we can just tell them to wait 30 years, and they too can play characters in their teens and 20s!

TINA MARTIN
San Francisco

http://sfgate.com/cgi-bin/article.cgi?f=/c/a/2001/04/17/DD166188.DTL
This article appeared on page C - 3 of the San Francisco Chronicle
I am Tina taking her grandma back to Tonga, and my grandma is the ingénue, our Nellie.

Glossary of Tongan terms

"Alu ai = goodbye to someone who is going
'Alu ki fe? = Where are you going?
anga lelei—good natured
faka—pertaining to, about, in the style of
faka-Tonga in the Tongan style
faka'ofa'ofa=beautiful
fale (pronounced FAH-lay)=hut
Fefe hake = How are you?
fiafia=happy
fie=want to
fie-leti want to be female (slang)

foi niu=coconuts

kai ke sino—*Bon appetit, meaning eat till you're fat and literally eat for body*

kai ke pa- Bon appetit, meaning eat till you pop

kole

lu pulu—corned beef embellished with coconut cream, onions, and other condiments and wrapped in taro leaf

Malo e lelei =hello or literally *Thank you for being well*

mo—and*Nofo* ai is goodbye to someone who is staying.

Nuku'alofa=the capital of Tonga, literally the nook of love

Oku'ou potoau he lea faka Tonglish= I'm good at speaking Tonglish

'*Ofa atu*=love to you

ta'avala the mat Tongans wear around their waist

talanoa=chat

tupenu—the traditional wrap-around skirt, like a sarong

vai=water

Looking Over Tonga Clippings, 2008

Pre Coronation

PICTURE ME IN July 2008, trying to get a sense of what's transpired in Tonga since I lived there, and particularly when and why Tonga became a member of the Bush/Cheney/Rumsfeld/Blair Coalition of the Willing.

I remember something in the *San Francisco Chronicle* about Tonga—something derisive like, "So I looked into just who was in the 'Coalition' besides the U.S. and England, and I see that it's places like Tonga." I have two binders about Tonga, if you don't count the 28 journals I kept when I was a Peace Corps Volunteer there. One binder is labeled "Tonga Photos" and the other is "Tonga Articles."

For the first two decades between the years I lived in Tonga and the summer I'm going back as my own grandmother, I clipped out everything written about Tonga because finding anything was like finding a pearl in an oyster. Usually the oyster (that would be newspapers and other media) had no pearl. So in a binder I labeled "Tonga Articles," I had the *National Geographic* pearl necklace, the March, 1968 issue with two full and fully-illustrated articles. The first was "South Seas' Tonga Hails a King" about the Coronation of King Taufa'ahau Tupou Fa, which took place seven months earlier on Tuesday, July 4, 1967.

The other article on Tonga, also several pages, was "The Friendly Isles of Tonga." (The October 1967 coronation of the Shah appeared in the same issue, but it was pretty clear that the editors preferred Tonga's.)

Back in 1969 there were no online resources because—are you listening, young'n's?— there were no home computers and no Internet, an astonishing fact that has become our generation's equivalent of "And I walked to school twenty miles in the snow." So I went to Good Will and St. Vincent de Paul to get the back copy, and I found several. But even though my binder begins with the fulsome 1968 *National Geographic* spread, it has nothing else until the 1990s although I do believe I had a tiny clipping about a Peace Corps Volunteer who was stabbed to death by another Peace Corps Volunteer on Tongatapu in 1976, when the murder occurred. It was only a couple of paragraphs until Philip Weiss wrote a book in 2004 about every detail of the murder..

So, if you take a look at my binder, you'll take a leap from 1968 to 1992, when Paul Theroux's "In the Court of the King of Tonga" was published in the *New York Times Magazine* as an excerpt from *The Happy Isles of Oceania*," published by G.P. Putnam's Sons. Bill Shoaf, a friend and colleague at City College of San Francisco, provided me with that.

Next is an article from the July/August 1996 issue of *Motorland*, the former name of the magazine Triple A (California State Auto Association) puts out. It's called "When you're a palangi…in Tonga they love ya." Palangi literally means "sky jumper," because that's how the Tongans saw the Europeans when their ship appeared over the horizon. It's now used to mean a foreigner, particularly a white one.

Then comes a black and white clipping from the *San Francisco Chronicle*, Sunday, June 29, 1997, "The Tonga Connection," by Zachary Coile, of the *San Francisco Examiner* staff back in the days when the *Examiner* and the *Chronicle* brought out the Sunday paper together. That this article was in the section COMPUTERS & TECHNOLOGY came as a surprise because when I lived in Tonga, electricity was scarce, and there was no technology, no technological connection. But lo and behold, two men pictured on a boat in still water, Eric Lyons and Eric Gullichsen, were selling domain names on behalf of Tonga. There's an inset photo of the Crown Prince Tupouto'a, described as "an Oxford graduate and self-described computer geek." These enterprising website designers named the domain "tonic" as in Tongan Network Information Center.

Then from a year and a half later, on December 28, 1998, there is a clipping under World Report "Cyclone Whips through Islands In South Pacific," from the *Chronicle* News Services by way of Wellington, New Zealand.

"Not a single banana tree was left standing" after being hit by Cyclone Cora with winds up to 100 mph." What surprised me when I first read the article was the news that the Tongans "were without electricity or phone lines," implying that they usually had them.

This is followed by a March 11, 1999 article about the Hillsborough home of King Taufa'ahua Tupou IV, for which he'd received a permit to add four bedrooms to the 6,000-square-foot house. Apparently neighbors had protested, but it was explained by the Tongan Consul-General Emeline Uheina Tuita: The Tongan government "doesn't have anything in New York. We don't have anything in Washington. We chose San Francisco because it is more central for the U.S. Tongan community… I have a large family. We can't all fit in the house right now."

That's followed pretty closely by Ellen Goodman's "Going Thin In Fiji" column of May 27, 1999. The article doesn't mention Tonga at all, but it's all about Tonga. Just replace every mention of Fiji with Tonga:

First of all, imagine a place women greet one another at the market with open arms, loving smiles, and a cheerful exchange of ritual compliments:

"You look wonderful! You've put on weight!"

Does that sound like dialogue from Fat Fantasyland? Or a skit from

fat-is-a-feminist-issue satire? Well, this Western fantasy was a South Pacific fact of life. In Fiji, before 1995, big was beautiful and bigger was more beautiful — and people really did flatter one another with exclamations about weight gain. In this island paradise, food was not only love, it was a cultural imperative. Eating and ...

Goodman goes on to lament the "western Mirror that the Fijians (and Tongans) got in 1995, when television came to the islands. The girls in "Melrose Place" and "Beverly Hills 90101" became the ideal, and within 38 months the risk of teenagers at risk for eating disorders more than doubled to 29 percent. She mentions the "recent" Columbine High massacre.

Then in July 1999, John Carman, TV reviewer for the *SF Chronicle* wrote, "Clear Sailing for Geraldo in Millennium." Geraldo is shown by water with a caption saying he plans to meet the millennium at the International Date Line.

"The King of Tonga apparently is a big Geraldo fan." Geraldo describes the king as "a real fun guy."

And then comes what many chose to call the new millennium: 2000. And less than halfway into the year (May 28, 2000) there's an article in the *SF Chronicle*, "Living on Tonga Time/Don't work too hard or undress to swim in these South Pacific islands." Susan Spano/*Los Angeles Times* I remember Tongans going into the water fully dressed both out of modesty and because they didn't have a swimming suit.

Next comes "Looting the Tongan Gene Pool" from *Funny Times*, March 2001. This article claims that an Australian biotech corporation calling itself Autogen Limited has purchased the exclusive global rights to the entire gene pool of the people of Tonga. Apparently Autogen wants to be the only company allowed to perform genetic studies on the Polynesian race, whose gene pool is valuable because of their having been genetically isolated from other populations of the world and being, for that reason, "pure." The Tongan government will get royalties from any drugs developed from the Tongans' DNA.

Hmm. A kingdom getting royalties. Sounds right. The article

reports the question that has been raised: Is this bio-piracy? I rush from my hard copy of old news and Google to find out whether this really happened. I find The Indigenous People's Council on Biocolonialism.

On the other side of the hard copy is "A royal endorsement/Tonga's king praises Stanford conference on islander health." (Bill Workman, *Chronicle* Staff Writer.) Under a picture of the king, there's the caption, "King Tauf'ahau, put his people on a diet to deal with their love of huge fatty meals. At his heaviest he weighed 462 pounds but lost 200 pounds by following a fitness routine that included "power walking behind the royal palace accompanied by a military escort carrying his throne." He also bicycled 15 laps a day, five days a week, perhaps without his throne.

The next sheet protector has a Dave Barry column "Tonga court jester not such a wise guy," from November 18, 2001. I remember this one. This story, about the court jester stealing $26 million dollars from Tonga, is a news story that was covered fairly widely for a Tonga news story. According to Dave Barry, Tonga had raised the money by selling Tongan citizenships to people who needed a new country and had among its clients Ferdinand and Imelda Marcos. The King was afraid that if the money were left in Tonga, the government would just spend it on roads, so he deposited it in a Bank of America checking account, where a man named Jesse Bogdonoff noticed it. He became a financial adviser for Tonga, and I guess he was for that kingdom what Madoff was to be for ours. Bodgonoff persuaded the king to make him the official court jester. Then, as the official court jester, Bogdonoff got the king to put the money into a new company in Nevada called Millennium Asset Management, which soon ceased to exist. This led to resignations. But there were also rumors that some of the missing money was lost in the dot-com company written about on a previous page of my binder, and sure enough His Royal Highness Crown Prince Tupouto'a helped set that up. A report not written by Dave Barry also appeared in the *SF Examiner* on September 27, 2001, by way of the *London Independent*. "Tonga account short $20 million."

Where, I wonder, did Tonga get $20 million? Its annual budget is $28 million. Apparently the money was made in the 1980s after the king approved a scheme to sell Tongan passports for up to $10,000 each to Hong Kong Chinese anxious about the colony's being given to mainland China. (The Marshall Islands and Kiribati did the same thing.) The king didn't want the money wasted on "public works projects." George Chen, the HK businessman behind the passport scheme, put it in a B of A checking account. Between 1983 and 1991, more than 5000 Tongan passports were sold, raising $20.7 million. The disgraced former head of the Hong Kong Stock Exchange, Ronald Li Fook-shiu, Chen Din-hwa, a HK textile millionaire, and Michael Nyland, the GM Co. vice president were among the takers. Then Bogdonoff, who worked at the bank, noticed that millions of dollars was "inexplicably invested in a checking account." Bogdonoff got royal permission to invest the money and made it grow by $12 million. He asked and got the king's permission to take the money when he left the B of A.

This article says that Bogdonoff, as a member of the Buddhist Soka Gakkai International, got the organization to give the king a humanitarian award and an honorary doctorate after the king had proclaimed Bogdonoff, born on April Fool's Day, "Court Jester." It's hard for me to resist going online for more, but I have to move on through this binder of clippings. I haven't even gotten to the Peace Corps murder yet—more than a mention, I mean.

The next page goes back to December 31, 1999, which puzzles me until I see that it was sent to me in early January 2002 from a Lost Friend with whom I used to have pre-dawn e-mail communion before she sent me a poison pen letter. But I digress. This article contains no jesting! Tonga, just hours before it became one of the first places on Earth to begin the New Year, was hit by a massive tropical storm. This time it was Cyclone Waka, which whipped Niuafo'ou island, 350 miles north of Nuku'alofa. My Lost Friend had sent it to me on January 2002. Hm. What took her so long? Oh! She was telling me that journalist Mark Morford referred to the December 31, 2001 piece in his column. Communication was lost! For my Lost Friend and me. For Tonga. Oh, I guess this was the second time we celebrated the millennium.

The next thing in my collection is from April 8, 2002, the *SF Chronicle's* list of New Movies Opening Friday. I was focused on "The Other Side of Heaven," which I took my unsuspecting mother and brother to see on one of our outings that didn't involve lunch at the Sizzler. (Back then it was The Sizzler. It's Applebee's in 2008.) Meanwhile Jodie Foster's "Panic Room" won at the box office over "High Crimes" (not "…and Misdemeanors"). It also won, no doubt, over the "Other side of Heaven," about a young Mormon missionary who learns to speak fluent Tongan by going out by himself and reading the *Bible* translated into Tongan. Just for nostalgia purposes, I note that following at the box office were "ET" and "A Beautiful Mind." "Amélie," "Monster's Ball," "Y Tu Mama También," "Gosford Park," and "Iris," back when it was Iris Murdock's great mind that was bringing in diminishing returns.

Then the Tongan Court Jester is back in June, 2002, in an article by Suzanne Herel in the *SF Chronicle*. The only new thing I learn here is that $20 million were invested in life insurance policies of terminally ill patients who failed to die. Another $4 million bought stock in Trinity Flywheel Power, developing electricity-producing devices. Another half million was invested in FailmAsix.com, which planned to develop electronic distribution of films but went bankrupt instead. Electricity, which I had lived without in Tonga. Electronics! And our villages hadn't even been on the electric grid back in the early 1970s.

The suit against Jesse Bogdonoff, Tonga's court jester, was filed on June 3, 2002. I see that my son sent it to me in an e-mail message on August 8, 2002 with the heading, "Have you heard about this?" I guess I'd failed to tell him just what it was I was clipping out and saving.

I now come to the first thing in the binder printed from the Internet: Villa Mamana, on Telekivava'u Island in the Kingdom of Tonga. Do they mean the whole villa—3 houses, 3 boats, fully furnished and equipped (with electricity?)— is selling for $525,000? 2700 square feet? Shall I buy it while I'm there? TV CVD, Stereo, fans, satellite dish & tower, fridge, a/c power, hot and cold water!!! How futuristic that sounds from my era of no running water.

Now I turn the page to a letter dated July 2, 2004, from Mike Monti, a New Zealander I met and kissed (just once or twice) in Tonga back in 1970. He had gone from New Zealand with three inches of snow on the hills to a beach in Tonga, where the temperature was 82 degrees F "Passed Veitongo, Vaini, Ha'ateiho draped in black, Pea. Stayed at Nerima Lodge operated by a Japanese woman, the widow of one of Posima Afeaki's sons."

The VSAs, New Zealand's volunteers, were leaving that year, 2004, because the locals weren't taking over; they were just getting cheap labor from NZ.

Tupouto'a=Crown Prince—nephew of the Siaosi V.
Pilolevu—king's only daughter married Tuita, the noble

Mike says she's reputedly worth $5 million. Is that where some of the $28 million went? No, they say she earned it through ownership of an Internet provider. Mike says there's rumor that, since the Crown Prince has not produced an heir and doesn't seem inclined to, Pilolevu might take the throne. (But it's Siaosi, the oldest son of the late king, who is scheduled to be crowned in 2008.)

My New Zealand friend visited ZCO, where he had worked in 1970, and found that they were still using the piece of classical music he chose for funeral notices on the radio. He spoke of a local TV channel along with FM and AM radio. Some priceless tapes—like the king's first visit in 42 years to Tin Can island (Nuiafo'ou)— was gathering dust and stretching with age. Some tapes were mis-filed or put into wrong boxes or lost some other way. I had asked about a recording of the *Messiah*, which the Tongans sang beautifully in Tongan a cappella. I'd attended a performance of it in Nuku'alofa with the handsome Australian archeologist who wanted to save my soul. I've always wanted to have a recording of the Hallelujah Chorus sung in Tongan.

Mike was witness to the Tonga Rugby team's first overseas tour, the one they took in 1969 to New Zealand. Mike had helped cover the landing on the moon that year.

I see a mention of VOA and have to look it up. It's what they took when Apollo 13 re-entered the atmosphere over Tonga early 1970. It turns out to mean Voice of America.

I also see mention of the visit by the British Queen and the King's visit to Nuiafo'ou for the Agricultural shows in 1970. Mike had also helped introduce soccer to Tonga. Langi Kavaliku and Father Line were two who were involved. They took two teams north on the agricultural tour to play demonstration games.

Then there's a Jon Carroll Column on Jan 8, 2004. He's talking about the US-VISIT program, "designed to discourage people from visiting the US" after September 11, 2001. But, Jon Carroll asks, why are they being particularly unwelcoming to countries like Samoa, Tonga, Costa Rica, Bhutan and Mongolia?" He also mentions that Americans are geography-challenged, unable to find China on a world map. He quips, "And you're coming from Tonga? Is that like Togo? OK, we'll say 'Asia' Again."

That's what I had thought, back in the summer of 1969, when I had gotten an invitation from the Peace Corps to train for Tonga—that Tonga was in Africa.

Next there's "Emotional Baggage" from *Travel*.

After that the binder holds some of the many print-outs on the Peace Corps Killing that started appearing in late October 2004, 25 years after the murder, when the sensational book came out.

The title has always intrigued me: *American Taboo: A Murder in the Peace Corps*. So now we know what's taboo in America. Murder's okay, but not murder in the Peace Corps!

I Have an e-mail from Jim (see "Dates I Know by Heart"),

referring to Deb Gardner, the PCV who was murdered, and writing, "Fortunately you escaped death in the tropics, as well as death in the desert and death in the hot-blooded Iberian sun," referring to my years between 1970 and 1976 in Tonga, Algeria, and Spain.

Also in 2004, I have a 20-page print out from the blog of Tom (Tomasi) Riddle, writing about Tavi.

This was the year I was back from a trip south of the Border, where I spent ten days with MyMeque (mejor que un esposo, better than a husband) but never with any of his friends or family, who were having a reunion without me.

This was also a year before I was interviewed by both Swiss writer Alex Capus, who was writing a chapter about Tavi in a book, and by a Dane named Leif Moeller, who was making a documentary about Tavi. They'd both heard from Tavi's sister that I was the only woman Tavi had ever sought to marry, but I had responded that he was too much like Jesus Christ, and I was too little like Mary Magdalene.

I have a print out of Emile Hon's Coconut Wireless, a 2005 review of what was happening with those who'd served in Tonga.

Emile is the reason I'm going back to Tonga. I don't remember how he and I made contact, but I think it was through Tom Riddle, who wrote so extensively about the Tavi he knew. Tom told me that Emile was "the friendliest person in the world." He's also the one on the cover of the book *American Taboo: A Murder in the Peace Corps,* but not as the killer. He was friends with both the Peace Corps Volunteer who was killed and the Peace Corps Volunteer who killed her.

After we met, Emile kindly scanned photos I had of my days in Tonga. He now sometimes goes back to Tonga with the San Mateo police, who are trying to understand the Tongan Community in San Mateo by visiting the land that the Tongans come from. Emile is their advisor.

I hadn't planned to go back to Tonga. I wanted to remember it as it was. But Emile convinced me to join him and a small group of friends going there for the King's coronation.

I want to read on, but there are other things I need to do before I pack. I want to imagine what it would be like to go back into that motel room in San Jose for a 15-minute sanity test. How would I describe my family now? And who exactly is my family now?

2008 Conceit—
Back to that Motel Room

It's 2008, and before returning to Tonga, I'm picturing myself back in the motel room with the Peace Corps psychologist who's going to sum me up on the basis of a fifteen-minute interview about my family.

It was in 1969 that I first met this man— whom I found relatively attractive because I liked dark, hairy men, and he was probably even Jewish—before they sent me to Peace Corps training in Hawaii.

I realize I am now my own grandmother, going back to Tonga, and I want to reflect on changes in me and in my family.

Now in my imagination I'm back there in that stark room with only a couple of armchairs, a desk with a Gideon Bible, and a shrink ready to sum me up. But this time, I'm coming armed, with essays I've written about my family, but just who is family at this time?

The two men I married and divorced (sequentially)? The man in my life right now? My son?

And what about me? Don't I count?

Since the day I walked into the motel room in October 1969, I've lived two years in Tonga, one year in Spain, and two in Algeria. I've gotten my MA, married, had a baby, divorced, and taught at both City College of San Francisco and Golden Gate University.

"I see your father is no longer living," the psychologists says.

Oh, yes, he is! I think. He may be dead, but he's still very much a living force.

DADDY, OXYGEN, AND OTHER LIFE FORCES

Of all Daddy's expressed insights, the one I keep thinking about is this: We experience everything at least three times: In anticipation, in the moment, and in memory. I had already been aware of how in remembering we re-experience (not to mention distort and re-write), but I'd never stopped to think that anticipation was an experience too. That helps comfort me when I look at his last postcard, referring to an upcoming reunion we were planning for the Christmas of 1999. He had been in San Francisco with my son, my sister, my brother and me the previous June and planned a more inclusive reunion at Christmas time. His last postcard, sent two days before he died, began, "I love the idea of a Reunion." He even capitalized reunion.

I know how important it is to have something to anticipate, and I think that Daddy was starting to worry that all he had to look forward to was Assisted Living. For several years, he'd made plans to leave us, writing a Living Will and setting up a trust for us adult children as well as for his grandchildren. This was from a father who had been pathologically frugal as we were growing up, watering our milk, making us believe that instead of buying a new two-dollar pair of shoes, we should just use a rubber band to re-attach the sole that was falling out of our old pair. (Let's be fair though. He did get us tickets to *Man of La Mancha* and *Cabaret* in August 1969, and he did treat my son and me to Cuba with Global Exchange in 1998.)

Anyway, I refused to believe that he would soon leave us, and, I regret to say, I rationed my sympathy to last till he turned one hundred and one.

I was less blasé though when, a year before his death, I got a call from a nurse saying that Daddy was in the hospital.

"Hospital!" I exclaimed.

"He's on oxygen," she went on.

"Oxygen??!!"

Oh, my God, I thought, and my thoughts paced the room in a panic that lasted until the nurse put Daddy on the phone.

"Tina," he began, not sounding at all weak. "I've been thinking that we should transfer some money from the Martin Trust to give it to the people of Nicaragua."

This was at the time of Hurricane Mitch, so I said, "Yes, you're right, Daddy. Hurricane Mitch has killed ten thousand people!"

Then my dad's response boomed back. "That's nothing compared to the devastation United States policy has caused."

Daddy sounded just like Daddy. There was no oxygen shortage that I could perceive.

I felt increasingly relieved when I found out that young Hollywood stars went on oxygen just to look more beautiful.

I shared this tidbit with Daddy, who said, "I sure hate to be in *their* company."

"And in Japan, there are oxygen bars," I said. "They say it's life enhancing."

"Well, if I weren't using oxygen, there wouldn't be any life to enhance," he said.

Still, I couldn't imagine Daddy's taking his last gasp.

Then I got a call from my sister, Dana, whom I'd been trying to contact for months without success. Every time I called her, I got a message saying to leave a message for Tina, whose identity she sometimes borrowed the way sisters borrow a blouse or a pair of earrings—without always asking. She told me that Daddy was dying and we'd better get down to Columbia to see him right away. "They say he may not be able to go home. He may have to go to assisted living."

But after we'd booked a flight, Daddy was home again, and when I talked to him on the phone, he said he was on his way to a party at the Unitarian Church and was trying to figure out which oxygen tank to take. After our reunion, he was the one who drove us to the airport.

Maybe that's when I stopped worrying enough. I knew Daddy was very tired and probably more than just a little bit afraid. He was worried that he was sleeping too much, and I wrote him on Sunday afternoon while my son, his college-age grandson, was sleeping in the adjoining room. "It doesn't matter what percentage of the day you're sleeping," I told him, "as long as, when you're awake, you're as glad as I am that you're alive."

A day after Daddy's death, I got the postcard from him saying that he was looking forward to the Reunion. Some people might joke about the longer distance I'd have to travel for a reunion with him now, but I don't feel the distance. I feel the emotional closeness that was enhanced when Daddy chose to move into a retirement home instead of living with my son and me. As much as I loved my dad, I acknowledged that he was as difficult to live with as I was. I'd think, "I'd rather die than turn my back on my dad, so if he wants to come live with us, I'll kill myself." Once the physical distance had been established, our relationship flourished. We dared to share more personal feelings and experiences. As a child, I'd been afraid of my father because he seemed so different from other fathers, and I thought he was crazy. As an adult, I was able to write verses celebrating his uniqueness.

To the tune of "Carolina in the Mornin'"

If we had a normal dad how bored we'd all be.
We celebrate the fact that he's he."

I also came to know his kinder, gentler side and became better acquainted with his humor. A lifetime activist, he quipped, "The only reason the FBI doesn't come after me is that I'm so ineffectual."

But that self-effacing comment was belied by one of the tributes paid to my father at his memorial service in 1991. A black psychologist credited my dad with having unofficially integrated the University of South Carolina in 1960, when Daddy, Chief Psychologist at the

South Carolina State Hospital, recruited and hired black psychologists from the under-funded, under-supported black State Park Hospital in Columbia. For their training seminars, Daddy brought them together with his graduate students from the all-white University of South Carolina.

Shared memories. Another way of experiencing life.

On Father's Day I think of my dad, who was unlike most dads in his radical political beliefs, which led him, in retirement, to give half of his income to Central American causes "to counter-act meddling by the United States."

After his death, when as executor of his estate I got all his mail, I made a gigantic poster of the word DADDY formed by the return addresses of the causes he believed in and supported. I called it "Daddy's Soul," but even that couldn't quite capture it.

There's a saying, "With a death, a life ends, but a relationship continues." I believe that a relationship continues, and I continue to think of my not-quite-normal dad in the anticipation, moment, and memory of each day.

MOM

"And your mother is eighty-six years old?"

"Yes." She had been forty-nine and beginning a new life—one without my father—my first time to Tonga.

Now she was coming to the end.

I'd written an essay in her honor for my students, who preferred downloading to reflecting and telling the truth about their parents and themselves. I thought that if I wrote something really personal, my students might dare to reveal—or at least reflect upon—some truths, some things that mattered. I wrote it as if the readers were outside the class.

This I Believe—in My Mom

My mother has been away on a two-week cruise around Hawaii with her partner of twenty-eight years—a period of time even longer than the quarter of a century that she was married to my father—so we postponed her October birthday until this weekend, the same weekend I'm creating an assignment for my ESL students at City College of San Francisco. My students studied a unit in their *NorthStar* textbook called "The Landscape of Faith," which begins with a peer interview "Religion in Your Life," with the apparent assumption that religion was and is and always will be in the lives of the students. But it turned out that many said they were atheists who believed in themselves, not in "imaginary things." This led to a discussion of the Twelve-Step Program, which requires that the person ask help from a "higher power." Is that necessary? If so, can the higher power be within the person? How about within the person's mother? This I believe—in my mom!

I asked the students to choose a proverb that they believed in—something that represented their philosophy of life or some guiding principle, a source of inspirations when they needed encouragement. I know which one I would choose. From Viktor Frankl's *Man's Search for Meaning*: "Everything can be taken from a man but one thing: the last of the human freedoms—to choose one's attitude in any given set of circumstances, to choose one's own way." I think my mother has done that. Whatever has happened to her, she's found a way to respond that's kept her from becoming discouraged, cynical, or self-pitying. Probably for her the chosen "proverb" would be a quote from Camus: "In the midst of winter, I finally learned that there was in me an invincible summer." I once gave that quote in a frame to my mother because it represented her. As I was growing up, I saw her face an unhappy marriage and children with special needs. But she kept an optimism and a zest for life while dealing with major problems. She cried a lot, and she slammed doors, but she never wasted her energy fretting about things over which she had no control. After she divorced my father, which she did when most of us five children were adults, her life improved, and she made the most of new opportunities like finishing college, which she had left to marry my father, type his PhD dissertation and have five children. She started to live with and travel with the woman who has become her life partner. She was roller-blading and taking tap dance lessons until she was eighty. Then some things began to change, and she had to face the problems of age. Her eyesight is still better than mine, but about ten years ago she was diagnosed with myasthenia gravis and macular degeneration, and the medicine she takes for these problems has side effects, which makes it harder for her to be as active as she used to be. In addition, she has started to forget things and sometimes feels confused. She doesn't pretend that these problems are easy for her. Once on a trip we were taking mostly for my brother, who has serious neurological problems that require around-the-clock care, she was spending more time than usual in the restroom, and I asked behind the locked door, "Is there anything I can do to help you?" She responded, "Not unless you can get me a new body." But this was a lament, not a whine. She was acknowledging that she was in distress over something new: signs of growing old. But the attitude she chose when faced with this problem was one of being honest about her distress. She could have stayed home and kept us from knowing about her problem. Once on the road, she could have chosen to whine, to complain, to make her problem the focus of the trip. Instead she dealt with the problem the best she could and we had a fairly nice trip. She continues to travel. When she was visiting my older sister in Chicago, my sister's ex-husband told my mother, "You're my hero." Mother was surprised and touched by this comment, but I know what my ex-brother-in-law means. I don't really admire people who have an easy life. I'm not even sure I envy them. I think people who have an easy life have kind of boring lives and are kind of boring themselves, and what kind of example do they set for the rest of us, anyway? A model for having a boring, easy life? The people I admire are people who have obstacles in their path but keep on going, keeping an interest in life, not giving up. Instead of having people's sympathy, my mother has people's admiration because she is bravely getting on with life in spite of the challenges she is facing. She's still good company. She remembers more than she forgets, and her mind is kept sharp by the crossword puzzles she does every morning and by the books she reads. She also has a way with words and other talents. When we were children, she made all our clothes. Now she's knitting hats for homeless people. Until my son moved to New York, he and my mom gave us concerts twice a year—he on the clarinet, she on the piano, and we're all impressed by how well she still plays the piano in spite of the arthritis in her fingers. We're also impressed by how she stays active and informed, doing work for the Diablo Valley Peace Center, protesting against the war on Iraq, supporting Obama.

By chance as I was planning the assignment on proverbs, I came across the book This I Believe: The Personal Philosophies of Remarkable Men and Women. The blurb on the back describes the "personal credos" in the book as "inspiring and invigorating." That's my mom! I believe in Viktor Frankl's creed, which she so well illustrates. So, as we celebrate her eighty-seventh birthday, I can say

This I believe—in my mom!

Two weeks before my departure for Tonga, I'd spent a weekend with my mother while her house-mate and companion Kathy was away. She was still often very lucid and always *interesting*, that Chinese curse. Reading aloud a column a friend and former professor, Manfred Wolf, had written, we talked about the themes, truth-telling, times when we should demand the truth and times when we shouldn't, times when we should tell it and times when we shouldn't, privacy versus full disclosure in friendships and romantic relationships, etc. We also watered the plants, trees, and bushes in her very big yard, and I was amazed that an eighty-six-year-old woman who was quite a bit overweight (sino faka 'ofa'ofa—beautiful body—by Tongan standards) was managing to keep up her yard while the sixty-two-year-old daughter, who was less overweight, was pretty much depending upon nature, a gardener, and an automatic drip system in her own back yard. I confessed this to my mother and said, "I feel like a criminal."

My mother, who retired from counseling/probation work when she was seventy-two, said, "Tina, don't say that. As an ex- probation officer, I have the duty to report you. Oh, but you're not in my county. Thank God!"

She was joking then, but she wasn't joking when I returned to her house after doing some errands and she asked, "So what are *you* doing here?"

I told her I was staying with her, and she said, "How nice. Can you come in for a few minutes? You can't spend the night because Tina's—Kathy's—here."

I knew she was confused because Kathy had left on Sunday and wouldn't be back until the following Saturday.

Did she think that I was Kathy, returning too soon?

I asked, "Are you sure Kathy's back?" and my mom said, "Yes, because we've already had a fight."

"Then where's her car?" I asked.

"I guess she left to do some errands. I thought you were her when you pulled in."

Mother looked confused and uncertain, as if she were doing an acrobatic groping stunt.

I suspected that she had thought I was Kathy even when she had first seen me, and Tina, not Kathy, was the person who was there, whose place I couldn't take if I were Kathy, not Tina.

Yeah, that made it all clear.

"But why did she come back so soon?" I asked.

"I don't know."

I thought that maybe for some reason Kathy *had* come back, so we went into the house to find Kathy, whose car wasn't there, and there was no sign of her in the house, either.

"But I was just talking to her," Mother said.

"Maybe on the phone?" I suggested.

"No, she was right here." Then Mom looked really worried. "I've been calling her all over the house. She'd better be here or I'm losing my mind."

Oh, yes. That.

Of all the things I've lost, I miss my mind the most. Who said that?

When I had first heard that Mother had been showing signs of dementia, I said, "So have I, since I was eight years old."

My sister, relating "evidence," said tearfully, "She's mixing up her all words when says she something," which made me wonder whether it was my sister who was having problems, not my mother.

But then my son, getting together regularly with Mom to practice their music for the JoNani Duo (she on the piano; he on the clarinet) reported incidences too. They'd watched a Giants game together, cheering at the upset, the surprise win by the Giants. Then ten minutes later she'd asked, "I wonder whether the Giants game is over."

For the past five years or so, she'd called me regularly to ask about my sister, Dana, who never returned her calls.

"Have you heard from Dana? I want to knit her something," she'd say, "but I don't know what color. I've left messages, but she never returns my calls."

Mother didn't mention that Dana's message machine had my name on it. She had been using me as an alias for several years.

"You know, Mom, Dana never picks up the phone or returns calls unless the spirit moves her, and the spirit doesn't move her very often."

"I guess you're right," she'd say, and then she'd tell me she had to go. But soon she'd call again, maybe later that day, maybe the next day.

"Have you heard from Dana? I want to knit her something," she'd say, "but I don't know what color. I've left messages, but she never returns my calls."

And I'd say, "You know, Mom, she never picks up the phone or returns calls unless the spirit moves her, and the spirit doesn't move her very often."

"I guess you're right."

Then, a short time later, she'd call back.

"Have you heard from Dana? I want to knit her something, but I don't know what color."

Perhaps the sixth time, I changed our dialogue.

"Red," I said. "Knit her something red."

"Does she like red?" Mother asked, surprised.

"No, but I do," I said.

Now it was just a couple of weeks before my departure for Tonga, and Mom was confused about just who was in the house.

We called LA, the home of Kathy's ninety-one year old aunt, and Kathy was there, not here.

"Oh, Kathy," Mom said to Kathy on the phone. "I feel like I'm losing my mind."

I tried to reassure Mother.

"Maybe right before I got back, you'd had a dream, and I woke you up, so that disoriented you."

This idea, a reasonable explanation, or an explanation of reason, comforted Mom a bit.

"Maybe so," she said. "But that was kind of weird."

"Well," I said, sharing perhaps too much, "someday we may all wake up and realize this life was the dream, and we'll say, 'Yeah, I thought that was kind of weird.'"

The rest of the time my mom was fully in touch with reality except for my last night with her, when she was knitting (not something red) as I was reading Vendela Vida's *And Now You Can Go* novel aloud to her.

At one point, she stopped knitting and said, "Tina, can I ask you something? Is this really my house?"

I said yes, and she said, "Then where's my mother?"

I said, "This isn't the house you lived in with your mother. This is the house you live in with Kathy."

Then she asked, "Then why did my mother call? My mother *didn't* call. *Kathy* called. But why did she think I was here? Because I *was* here."

She got out of some of that confusion all by herself.

I always tell my students that self-correction is a sign of great progress.

And she still did the *New York Times* crossword puzzle every day, first thing. With a cheat sheet.

I told her about an Amnesty International Lead a Delegation to Congress about Guantanamo Bay event a friend had volunteered to head. We'd be having an eight-thirty breakfast at my house before leaving for Jackie Speier's office for an 11:00 AM appointment.

She could grasp that.

I told her about the messages I'd gotten from Emile Hons, the Returned Peace Corps Volunteer who'd lived next door to the beautiful Peace Corps Volunteer who'd been stabbed to death (twenty-two times) by another Peace Corps Volunteer, and I reminded her that she was the one who'd first found a tiny article about that murder and had sent it to me when I was living in Algeria. (I was wrong. I returned to the United States in August 1976, and the murder took place in October, when as a graduate student I was living in the dorms. If she had sent it to me, she had sent it to the dorms.)

"Anyway," I told her, "Emile is the one who's organized the group to go back to Tonga for the king's coronation. We're all getting together on Monday night. But MyMeque is joining us tomorrow. To see you."

"Oh, good! He's such a nice man."

MyMeque wanted to take us out to dinner, but Mom was having digestive problems.

"I'm so sorry," she told MyMeque. "I hope you understand."

"We'll bring you back dinner," MyMeque said.

She said she just wanted to sleep.

"But I don't want to dream," she said. "I don't want to dream."

Mom was apologetic when Kathy first asked me to stay with her (Mom) for a week while Kathy was caring for her aunt in Pasadena, but I was looking forward to seeing her. It's rare that I ever see her, one-on-one. Since my brother was admitted to Napa State Hospital in 1968 and since he was transferred to Garfield in 1998, she and I have been a team, regularly taking my brother to lunch. We also get together on birthdays and holidays. Still, it's rare that we get together just the two of us.

But she thought she was imposing.

"I just think it's asking too much for you to stay with me a whole week," she said.

"But, Mom, you sometimes stay with Dana a week. Even longer than a week," I told her.

She said, "You think I'm as interesting as Dana?"

I said yes, though nobody is as interesting as Dana.

DANA BEFORE TONGA

Dana is a performance artist, and the world is her stage.

Dana disappears for most of the year. Maybe she disappears into Tina. She uses my name. I've seen her business card although she doesn't have a business other than being beautiful and getting men to serve her and going clothes shopping eight hours a day and trying on clothes after the stores close.

For a while she was running a dating agency, and I thought maybe she was using my name because it was really an "escort service" designed for call girls and the boys who wanted to love them. Dana would be a great madam. Anyway, her business card has a picture of her looking like a sweeter Cleopatra and says, "Tina Martin Attachments 20,000+

Singles." Then it gives her hometown and zip code and her e-mail address, which repeats the tinamartin. When I asked, "You're borrowing my name without even asking?" she pointed out that her e-mail address says tinamaratin2. I get to be tinamartin1, the original.

But Dana is the original original.

So when she disappears, I'm not sure where she goes. I don't get any response to e-messages or even presents that I send. Then she'll show up in San Francisco for a meeting of the American Psychological Association. She's not a psychologist, but she's divorced from a psychiatrist, and they still attend conferences together.

Now when she shows up, it's to see her son, who lives in San Francisco—if he slips and lets me know she's coming when she has not let me know.

The last time she was here, at the end of her visit she said, "The most interesting part of my visit was not meeting your meque." {As mentioned earlier, my meque is my _me_jor _que_ _un_ _e_sposo _or better than a husband,_ with whom I established a very private club, which to protect his privacy, I'll call the Club Dos Meques.}

She pretends to think that I'm ashamed of her. But I'm really just worried about her dazzle. Already a bit frumpy myself—my God, that's the first time I've ever used that word; until this very moment, I was using drab—I don't need any comparisons. I don't think I'm jealous of her, though I know I'm threatened by the thought of comparisons. But maybe more than that I'm afraid of the thought of disappearing. When I'm with her, I don't exist. Now, of course, as I get older, to many people I don't exist even when I'm not with her.

People are taught not to look away from the physically disabled because looking away implies that they don't want to be noticed, don't want to be seen in their "defective" state, that they would rather we pretend they don't exist. People are taught not to look away when they meet someone in a wheelchair. But people aren't taught not to look away from people who are no longer young, no longer beautiful.

That's probably why Dana refuses to give up being young

and beautiful. While I was, in my youth, "pretty for a Peace Corps Volunteer," Dana was always stunning. Dana always dazzled. I saw and understood this. I even accepted it. I wasn't jealous until someone would say, "Wow your sister's gorgeous. I'll bet you're jealous."

People who are taught good manners know another way of saying this: "Wow, your sister's gorgeous *too*." But I have, on several occasions during my life, met people who were not taught good manners.

It's obvious that my meque has been taught good manners or at least has picked them up somewhere (borrowed them, perhaps, from all those people left saying, "I'll bet you're jealous"). He's so polite that he won't even mention one woman to another, which allows him to live parallel lives, living with one person for fifteen years without any of their colleagues knowing that they're living together. Taking walks with another woman for three years before you find out. "Yesterday? I took my car in to have the oil changed." That's how he spends every other Thursday because he would never even mention one woman to another, much less make insensitive comparisons.

For the first four years of our Club T-M, I was "la mujer mas linda que hay," and now I'm "la mujer mas preciosa del mundo." I was moved to frame a card he got me because it has a woman wearing a *Beach Blanket Babylon/My Fair Lady* hat layered with praise: "¡Oye, dulzura! ¡Oye, preciosura! ¡Oye, diosa de perfección sin igual, princesa de increíble belleza, ejemplar de juventud perpetua!"

Spanish is full of enough cognates that you can probably translate this for yourself. Notice the "Paragon of eternal youth."

My meque brings me flowers each time he comes and hides the surprise on his face that today I'm looking "tired" instead of the paragon of eternal youth.

And yet…

When he first saw a picture of Dana and me together and asked, "Who is this?" with much greater interest than he usually takes in my pictures, he forgot his good manners.

Dana has given me permission to let people know just how she has maintained the beauty she was born with. So I said, "She's my older sister, but she looks younger because she's had cosmetic surgery."

"It worked!" My Meque replied.

I work against their meeting not because I think My Meque will make a cruel comparison to me but, maybe, because I'm afraid he'll make a sad comparison in his own mind—maybe feel a little bit sorry for me. And maybe fantasize.

And maybe this is a good time to talk about fantasies. I have a lot of fantasies, including sexual ones, but I am faithful in my fantasies. All my life the man in my fantasies has been the man with whom I'm in a relationship. Now my fantasies are always with my meque, never with another man. I've heard that other woman fantasized Richard Gere or George Clooney or Brad Pitt. I don't. And I don't like the idea that a man I love and am being faithful to even in my fantasizes is fantasizing being with another woman. It's not what a man does that threatens me as much as what he wants to do. I feel pain at being what a man "settles" for. I cannot stand that thought. I'd rather settle for No Man At All than settle for a man who's settled for me.

Dana was able to put this into words long before I was, and I was impressed. Before I left for Peace Corps training for Tonga in 1969, I stayed with her and her husband for a few days. They had a kind of cocktail hour from about six o'clock to midnight, when we finally had dinner, so there was plenty of time and liquor for candid—even careless—revelations. One of her husband's was about a really gorgeous woman he knew back in college.

"But I lost her because I was too timid, too unsure of myself," he said. "I feel bad about that."

"That's not what I want to hear," Dana told him. "I want to hear, 'Thank God I didn't have the nerve to pursue that girl back in college because what if I'd wound up with her instead of this much more gorgeous, beautiful, wonderful wife I have now!'"

Before my second trip to Tonga, Dana writes to warn me that, because her computer is acting up, she might be forced to call, so

"DON'T ANSWER."

"dearest tina 1:
im havving bad time comput—mite b forzd 2 call u
DONT ANSWER
DANA

I can't understand everything in that message, but I know she has said some very sweet things about my being the closest to her of anyone and wanting to have a funeral for me, beautiful, in good taste. "Put the FUN back in FUNeral," She doesn't want to do Mother's funeral.

Her visits are few but dramatic.

The moment she walks in the house she says, "We've got to see each other more often so we won't be so shocked by how much we've changed."

She hasn't changed. I am the shocking one.

That's why I don't want my meque to meet my sister. I don't want him to be so dazzled that I am a bit of a shock.

My Meque is very Latino in the sense that he knows all the standard phrases men are supposed to say to women. Everything has to be hyperbole. But he does get one of the phrases wrong. He always says, "I want to be the man who's loved you more than any other man ever loved you." I say, "I want you to be the man who's loved me more than you've ever loved any other woman."

(So that I'm not letting my own dazzling self-absorption dim his light, let it be known, that he is the man who best combines the romantic and erotic. Who'd ever know? He looks like everyone's favorite granddad.)

I want him to be the man who's loved me more than he's loved any other woman…even in his fantasies, but we can't control the fantasies of the man we love. All we can do is keep him away from Dana.

Should I send Dana a postcard from Tonga? She is so uninterested in travel. It might actually annoy her to get a postcard. She might have to make a derisive comment like, "Oh, doesn't she have anything better to do with her time than leave the comfort of home? What a waste she's made of her life."

What would the psychologist say?

DAVID

"And you have a brother, David, age 60, in Oakland."

In that motel room in San Jose, for reasons I explained earlier, I'd broken down into sobs when the psychiatrist came to the name of my brother.

I didn't burst into tears when I was writing to my sister and son about my brother a couple of months before I returned to Tonga in 2008.

In 1968, he'd voluntarily been admitted to Napa State Hospital, where a short time later he was elected President of his ward. ("That's what I'm here for!" he told us, when we praised the way he was looking out for the interests of the other patients.) But his condition only deteriorated. In the 1990's because of budget cuts, Napa was closed to everyone but hardened criminals. Former patients less lucky than my brother wound up on our streets. My brother was admitted to a neuro-behavioral center in Oakland. That's where he was in 2008, when I wrote this letter.

Thursday, June 12, 2008

Dear Suzy and Jonathan,

David was pretty alert and pleasant today. He was very courteous, as he was the last time we took him out and when I visited him after the Garfield quarterly. For example, when Mom got seated in the front seat, he handed her the seat belt from the back seat. He told the waiter in Applebee's, "My sister doesn't have any eating utensils." On our way from Garfield to Applebee's, he said he was for Obama, "But are you… not upset, about…about the lady?"

"About Hillary Clinton?"

"Yes! That she didn't get her dream to achieve her destiny."

We said we were sorry, but I pointed out that she had voted to authorize military force against Iraq and therefore was a war criminal.

"I didn't know that!" he said.

Later in the restaurant, I said, "Maybe the word you were looking for was sympathetic. Were we sympathetic to Hillary Clinton not achieving her destiny?"

David said, "No! Because she's a war criminal like the Nazis."

See what I mean about courteous? He was paying attention to what I said and taking it to heart. Who else does anything like that?

Also, when Mom and I were talking about something else, David asked, "Could I change the subject?"

"To what?"

"Politics!"

Right before we took him back, I asked him about his new (1/2 year?) roommate, and he said, "He's groovy." I asked what showed his grooviness and David said, "He cares about people."

The only negative was when I asked him about NIAD. {National Institute of **Art and Disabilities**}

"It's all right."

"What are you making or working on now?"

"A picture."

"Of what?"

"A person. I don't want to talk about NIAD. Today's my day off."

When he'd eaten his shrimp and steak down to the last bite, and we commented on his healthy appetite, he said, "Well, it's not every day that you take me out."

Mother commented on the second meaning of "take you out" as in contract killing, but David seemed unfazed.

He asked, "When's my next home visit?"

Mother said, "Well, while Kathy's away and Tina's staying with me…" Then she thought again. "Maybe when the weather is cooler."

Kathy's planning the farewell for you, Jonathan, on June 29 after you go to Stern Grove, so I volunteered to organize something around July 4. I also told Kathy I could have the farewell party, and she could do July 4, but she said it was just too hot in Pleasant Hill for the Fourth of July.

Mother was really good company too—funny and alert. She insisted on giving me $5.00 for picking her up and taking her back—to pay for the gas.

David was tired. We started to go to Walden Books, but both he and Mom opted out in favor of the ice cream parlor, which was closer than the bookstore and cooler than the walk. Once inside, he put his head down on the table. When I asked, "Do you want to go back to Garfield instead of going shopping?" he said yes, but it turned out that he did want to stop by Walgreen's to get some chew just in case they were out of it at Garfield, so we got some.

I checked with the woman who (finally) came to the door. They had plenty, so I kept the stash we got for David for another occasion.

Love,
TinaMom

THOSE NOT GOTTEN TO IN 1969

MISSY AND SUZY

I MENTIONED RELIEF that the psychologist never got to Missy, the sister who was living 3000 miles away from the father of the child she was carrying in 1969. I regretted that he hadn't gotten to Suzy, the sister who seemed sane and well-adjusted compared to the rest of us.

Before that day of staging in San Jose, my mother had gifted my sister Suzy and me with a trip East so we could see Missy and our father in Harrisburg and Southern friends and relatives in Atlanta, Columbia, and Virginia. I was seeing my First Great Love in Columbia and a guy I'd had a crush on all through high school, whom I'll call Craig. Craig and I had become closer through the letters we exchanged through our four years of college in different states. We were meeting for the first time since we graduated from high school and I moved away. I was not at all disappointed in our reunion although Suzy was far too attentive as a chaperone. But Craig and I did have some time together after I'd begged Suzy to let us have some time alone, and Suzy didn't tell me until later that she could hear every word we said through the vent downstairs where she was sleeping.

But that's another story.

The part that pertains to Missy is our arrival at our father's Town House in Harrisburg. Craig drove us there from Virginia. Our father asked me to let him know when we were almost there so he could come down and meet us. Missy was far enough in her pregnancy that she was not to be seen. But after we arrived and while we were talking in the parking lot of the town house, Craig noticed that someone was waving from the window. It was Missy. Had I even told Craig that she was living with my father? I don't remember. But I'm sure I hadn't told him why.

In 2008 it would be different. An unwed mother-to-be could be seen. The shame would be in not inviting Craig to lunch after he'd driven two hundred and twenty miles!

But in 1969 the most important consideration was keeping secret her unwed pregnancy. After all, this wasn't France, and Missy was not Catherine Deneuve.

In 1969 Missy gave her newborn baby boy up for adoption, and in the following years she married a man who lived in Harrisburg, and together they had three daughters as well as in-laws she adored, who lived right down the street.

But by 2008, Missy had moved farther than 3000 miles away.

In 1994 when she was 44 years old, our father was living with her and her three daughters after she had a nervous breakdown and her husband's response was "I can't take this anymore." He had left her and filed for divorce after taking a second mortgage on their home, which made it difficult if not impossible for Missy to pay the mortgage. Our father paid it off by selling some Merrill Lynch stock. Missy's in-laws, who had been an integral part of her daily life, no longer welcomed her in their house, partly because Missy's ex-husband wanted primary custody of the daughters, and Missy went to court to keep them.

Daddy was always there with her and her three daughters except for one week when he went to Texas for a hip operation. He'd chosen Texas because he had a sister there who wasn't working and could take care of him after his operation. That was the weekend I got a call in San Francisco from my uncle, who told me to sit down because he had some very bad news.

"It isn't your dad," he told me. "He's doing okay. It's your sister Missy."

He told me that two of her children, coming back from a weekend with their dad, had found her dead in the kitchen.

This was while I was making a video for Missy, who I had heard wasn't eating right. Her children, too, were eating too much junk food. So I, a terrible cook, decided to make a video cookbook which I called "The If I Can Make It, You Can Make It Too Cookbook." I never actually appeared in the video because I was behind the camcorder, one of those enormous things we used to mount on a shoulder—with the video cassette measuring $7\frac{1}{3} \times 4 \times 1$ inch inside. But I followed myself around the kitchen and videotaped what I was making. That was before I'd become a vegetarian, so I was showing her how to make a Chinese chicken salad, one of the dishes I actually got to turn out okay.

Missy was a great letter writer. I went back to the last one she'd written me, and it sounded too much like a sad farewell. She wrote about her "beautiful girls in this ugly world." Her death came a month before her ex-husband was to marry again.

Our sister Dana said Missy had died of a broken heart. Did she think the children needed to be with their father in a more stable home than she could provide for them?

I called my mother and Kathy, who were away on vacation that September of 1994.

Then my sister Suzy and I made a video with photos of Missy and talked about the photos and what we loved most about her.

Suzy wrote a beautiful poem describing a photo of them together, "Moments in Sisterhood/Snapshots from an Album, From my Mind."

Easter, 1960?
Matching dresses, mother-made
Yours with yellow ducks
Mine, lavender bunnies
Two brown-haired girls smiling
My hand in yours.

Summer four years later
Squatting in the dirt
Our backyard baseball diamond
Snowball posing too, fluffy white
We smile at the camera
Your pixie, my crooked braids

You'd pedal a blue bike
Me on the seat
Up Forrest Drive
To the donut shop
Knowing the clerk would whisper
"Y'all like a lemon-filled today?"
Your talkative friendliness, the welcome currency
Then back towards home
Down Forrest Drive to Stratford Road
Me perched on handlebars
You pedaling strong

Saturday night, the Stones
You me David
Entire jars of Spanish olives!
Hotdogs—on buns!
Spaghetti—from a can!
And a peacock spreading a tail of living color

Bedtime
Our white and turquoise room upstairs
Double bed beside the window
Watching pines against the sky

Moments in our childhood
Like squares of an afghan

Sewn together for a lifetime of warmth
You and me
Sisters.

I wrote something prosaic, but no less heart-felt.

Missy, Everybody's Little Sister for Quite a Few Years!

One of my warmest memories of Missy is of the year that we were at Schneider Elementary School in Columbia, South Carolina. She was in the first grade, and I was in the sixth grade, and after her class let out, she'd come upstairs to talk to the big kids in sixth grade.

I don't remember exactly how this started, but I think she thought that if her sister were in the building, of course she should come in and say hello. She always assumed that because she was so welcoming, she would be welcomed, and she was.

We had a teacher that year who seemed to understand that part of education is feeling connected to other people, and the teacher liked Missy as much as the kids did. So she'd let Missy come in and show us her drawings and give us the scoop on what was happening in first grade.

Missy became everybody's little sister that year, and we always looked forward to her visits. Years later my friends from that sixth-grade class attended a different high school, so I'd see them only occasionally. But when we met, they'd always ask me how I was doing, and then they'd ask, "And how's Missy?"

After all, she was their sister, too!

This memory of Missy represents some of the qualities that I loved so much in her. She was very friendly and very warm. She loved her family, and she was always welcoming more people into her family. None of us will ever forget the special brightness she brought into our lives.

To put in the new VCR for Missy, of course I had to take out the one I'd been making earlier, the "If I Can Make It, You Can Make It Too."

She hadn't quite made it.

By 2008, Missy had been gone for fourteen years. On that Peace Corps form for the 15-minute mental health clearance, I'm not sure whether they had a space for family no longer living.

Suzy, though, would be listed.

SUZY

If we had gotten to Suzy in 1969, what would I have said?

Just two months earlier, she and I had traveled together back to the South. I adored her even though I'd been a bit miffed that she'd been too attentive as a chaperone.

When Suzy was a little girl—I was ten when she was born—I really wanted to be her mother.

I taught her to love musicals and show tunes until she got old enough to know that I was a bad influence and she started to listen to people like Tracy Chapman.

I still have notes she wrote when she was just beginning to learn to write.

I can still remember the cute-Suzy stories I collected and retold when she was a child: I used to write down things that she would say.

"How do babies get into the mother in the first place?" She asked me.

"Well, it's like there's a seed inside the mother. And it grows into a beautiful flower," I said.

"Who waters it?" She asked.

I don't know how old she was when she stopped going to Sunday school, but I remember a conversation that may have been around that time.

"What would you do," she asked me, "if you believed in Jesus, but a lot of your friends didn't?"

I can't remember my answer, but I remember her next question.

"What would you do if a lot of your friends didn't believe in Jesus and you didn't either?"

Her teachers were impressed by her apparent intelligence and had her tested almost every year to be in the gifted class. I remember her coming home and saying, "I had another test, and I found out I'm not GIFTED! They asked me how many feet in a yard. Whose yard? Whose feet?" She knew it was all relative. How could there be just one correct answer?

She asked such good questions on the subject of religion.

"Tina, is Jesus the son of God or the son of Joseph and Mary?" I told her "both." Then she asked, "Do you believe more in God or in Jesus?" She told me "I believe more in Jesus 'cause I've seen more pictures of him."

I didn't know it then, but this was the beginning of a very thorough analysis of religion on my sister's part. A few weeks later she said, "Did you know that the devil was once an angel but then he was bad so God sent him down to be a devil?"

"Well, Suzy," I said, "You certainly do know a great deal about religion."

"Yes," she said proudly. "On Christmas Jesus was born, on Easter he came up from the dead, and…I don't know what he did on Halloween."

One day as Mother was getting ready to leave the house, Suzy began a very casual but intense discussion.

"Mother, what would you do if some of your friends didn't believe in Jesus, but you did?"

"Well," Mother replied, "if it became confusing to me, maybe I'd talk it over with my parents."

Suzy paused for a moment.

"What would you do if you had some friends who didn't believe in Jesus and you didn't either."

"Well, I think I'd tell my parents."

"So I'm telling you," Suzy said.

Mother had to leave at that moment, so she handed Suzy over to me. Suzy wanted to know if all Jews would be punished for not believing in Jesus. I gave her an unorthodox "no." She then wanted to know whether if there were no Jesus Christ, people who believed in Jesus would be punished.

'Oh, I don't think so," I replied.

Suzy took a very "adult" attitude towards attending church. It wasn't really necessary. "If you love God, he knows, so you don't have to go to church to tell him about it."

And Suzy didn't go to church without being coaxed.

When my other little sister Missy was attending a predominantly Catholic school, she became confused about terms.

"The Catholics believe in everything," Missy informed me. She listed them for me. "God, the Lord, Christ, Jesus, Mary, Joseph…"

She asked me what the Virgin Birth was. I explained it as well as I could, and she asked me whether I believed in it.

"I don't know," I said. Do you?"

"Well," she said, pausing. "It's unusual."

Suzy listened as we talked and then said, "I believe that Jesus was just a good man. And I don't believe that God is what the Catholics or Episcopals (SIC) say he is. I think he's the sky and that everything in the sky is what God has made."

That left a lot of land and even more of ocean, where I'd be going in 2008.

SUZY in 2008

"And your sister Suzy, I see, lives in Oakland?" I imagine my Psychologist asking.

"Yes, she lives in a little cottage there."

Would I think of mentioning that she and I had lived together in

Madrid, Spain, her junior year of high school and my first year out of the Peace Corps?

"So how would you describe her?"

"She's very smart and kind of sassy. Much surer of herself than I am. Very good at sports. My sister Dana and I were always the last to be chosen for the team because the captains knew what they were doing, but Suzy was the captain of her basketball team."

"So are you close?"

I know he doesn't mean geographically.

"I used to feel very close to her. I even think she felt close to me. But that isn't true anymore, and it hasn't been true for years. We communicate about our brother David, and she's wonderful to him. Patient. Warm. Enthusiastic. Attentive. Interested."

"And she's not that way with you?"

"I was shocked to find out that she goes to a regular appointment within walking distance of my house and never mentioned it or suggested that we have lunch together. I care about her. Not too long ago, I got her an iPod because I thought it would transform her life the way it has mine. We both listen to a lot of books on tape. My iPod has made it so much easier. But how would I get it to her? That's when I found out that she regularly has an appointment just a couple of blocks from where I live, so she could pick it up on her way there."

"So what does she do?"

"She avoids me."

"No, I mean as a job," the psychologist says.

I never learn. I responded that way when he asked about my father too. Why do I never think of professions when I describe family?

"She's a marriage and family therapist," I say.

Would the Peace Corps psychologist like that?

And were we getting any closer to my old home in Tonga?

Ah, but I also put down my son on the Family List for my imaginary return to the Motel Room Interview. In 2008 he's family.

JONATHAN

Imaginary Return to the Motel Room for 50-minute Sanity Test
Jonathan, Son, NYC

"I see you have a son, twenty-nine, who lives in New York City."

"Yes, he just moved there this year. After his father, my first husband, died. He knew his father was ill, so he stayed in the area. Then his father died in April, and Jonathan gave notice on his job."

"His job as…?"

"As Project Manager for UC Berkeley's University Health Services. This year they've gone online with scheduling at UC Berkeley, and the same month that he gave notice that he was leaving, they went live. He also gave notice on his apartment in Berkeley. And he sold everything except for personal items. Right now he's living with friends in New York City. A lot of people he knew at Berkeley—and even in middle school—moved to NYC before he did. It's what his generation is doing instead of joining the Peace Corps. Now some of his life is stored I boxes in my basement—mostly the souvenirs from his first love, someone who suffered from depression. We had a New York New York concert in honor of his new home."

"Are you suffering from the empty nest syndrome?"

"No. I love him. I guess he's the most important person in the world to me. But he moved to Berkeley back in 1997, and even then I felt close enough to him emotionally not to suffer. Of course, we could get together a little more often when he was living in Berkeley. We formed a mother-son book club last year. The JoMama Book Club. We were getting together to discuss books. Well, now we won't be doing that in person every month. But after he finds a place to live, we will get back to it, maybe online. So much has happened this year. His father's death. His father's sister and her husband sold their house—one Jonathan's dad lived in at one time—and moved to the Sequoias in San Francisco."

Is he letting me ramble like this? Why doesn't he stop me? Oh, because he doesn't exist. Not now.

"It's now possible to get videos made into DVDs, so I did that at Ritz's on Market near Church, and that took me back to Jonathan's fifteenth birthday. That's when Jonathan and my mother started the JoNani Duo. He plays the clarinet and she plays the piano. They give us concerts twice a year—on his birthday in March and on her birthday in October."

"That sounds nice."

"Yes, it does sound nice. Jonathan has a real talent. In those high school competitions when a judge comes to rate the playing, in five of those, he got five Command Performances. That's the highest anyone can get. Besides being musical, he's really clever! Maybe three or four years ago he started sending me topical praise on Mother's Day and on my birthday. Things like 'The World's Best Mother, Under 80 Division.' Because my mother is also a mother, and she's the World's Best Mother in the 80 and Over category. Anyway, he'd do it like The Question Man. 'Tina Martin has been called The World's Best Mother under eighty. What do you think?' And then he'd have pictures of those people being interviewed in The Onion—their names and professions. 'You bet she is. Those twelve million other moms with the Best Mother tote bags and mugs are living a lie.'"

"Oh, I see you've memorized it."

"It's like poetry—and even better than Ogden Nash verse. Last year when Jonathan's gift to me was to be helping me get a new computer and setting it up, I got a letter from Alberto Gonzales, the Attorney General, saying that the computer help that Jonathan had promised me would be carried out by him and the others in the Bush administration because they already had so many of my files. Something like that."

"Very clever."

"Yes! And when I was taking a creative writing online course through UC Berkeley, he had such clever comments when I showed him the transcripts of my talk with the writing instructor. That should be framed. A lot of things are. We've traveled together a little bit too. To Cuba after he graduated from high school and to Chile after he finished college. Jonathan was going with me to see David for a while too. It's usually been my mother who goes with me to visit him, but my mother—who was always so outgoing—developed a shade of agoraphobia. What I was mentioning earlier. Jonathan went with me to a NIAD presentation that David was involved in. a couple of months ago."

"He sounds like a good son."

"Yes, this year he helped me buy a dining room table and set of chairs, and I'll never forget the desk he put together for me three years ago. It came unassembled with a 48-page instruction manual. I know I'd have given up after step three. But he just kept going—just long enough to glance at the directions. He never even had to ponder. It took a long time because there were so many pieces, so many steps, but there was no hesitation. It was amazing. He's helped me make decisions about the apartment I rent out in our basement. Whether to raise the rent and how much. Whether to refund the cleaning deposit. At one time he helped me screen applicants. He's a good son and a good person. But I try not to make too many demands. We do things that are enjoyable as well as things that have to be done. This summer we went together to hear a friend play in a jazz band at Socha's, a place in the Mission District in San Francisco, before he moved to New York. I don't want to be the mother he has to look after. I don't want him to associate me with tasks. I want us to have an emotionally close relationship, where we can talk about things. Like…"

"Like…?"

"This year, after his father's death, he asked me about my split with his dad. He'd never asked me before. He told me his dad had said, close to his death, that he should talk to him about the split. I don't think he ever did. But I did."

"I'm afraid we're running out of time."

Shouldn't there be limitless time in my imagination? My imagination should have made time and place for MyMeque,

My mother eventually got around to asking about him.

My Meque, My Better Than A Husband

"So who is this man you love?" My mother asked me about a year after I'd first mentioned him.

"I wish I knew," I answered. "I think he's either a CIA agent or a drug dealer."

"Well," said my mother, "I hope he's a drug dealer because I don't think CIA agents are very nice people."

I pointed out that not everybody thought drug dealers were all that nice, and my mother responded, "It depends on the drug."

That was in 2003, five years before my trip back to Tonga and more than a year after I'd first met this man I love, for whom I created a new word, meque, an acronymn for "MEjor Que Un Esposo," Spanish for better than a spouse. To respect this privacy, I'll refer to hm from here on as MyMeque, as if that were his name. Together MyMeque and I had formed the Club Dos Meques. (I thought of myself as better than a spouse, too.) He was the President, which meant he paid for meals out, and I was the secretary, which meant that I wrote up the minutes to our meeting in Spanish to be read and corrected by him. Ours was an exclusive club, with only us as members.

My mother, Nani, who was never intrusive or inclined to live through me, met MyMeque two years later in March 2005, when she and my son Jonathan were giving a small family concert of the Jo-Nani Duo, and MyMeque and I arrived carrying picket signs fresh from a peace march, just one of the many activities of our club.

While I held the peace signs, My Meque presented my mother with a bouquet of flowers. Then he excused himself to use the bathroom or whatever CIA agents or drug dealers do when we're not looking.

"He's so nice!" My mother said.

"Yes, I know," I said. "And I love him. But I know he lies."

"That could work," my mother said, and when I laughed, she elaborated. "I mean, as long as you know he's lying."

What did that mean? Deception was okay as long as there was no *self*-deception?

I did ask to meet both his housemate and his ex-wife to be sure there wasn't a wife or wife equivalent that he was betraying.

It appears that the only one I have to betray is me. My second marriage ended almost twenty-five years ago. Since my son left home almost twenty years ago, I've liked living alone, but I also like exclusive relationships, sharing a life if not a home. I love MyMeque, and I love continuity.

But I no longer demand full disclosure. MyMeque compartmentalizes his life. We see each other only on weekends, and even though we exchange about 1400 e-mail messages a year, he doesn't really tell me what he's doing during the week.

Our club has forced me to practice being in the moment. But I still think of other moments, past moments, which turned out to be stolen moments.

Before I met MyMeque, I dated another charming man, whose business card I lost twice in an hour—as if I had some unconscious approach-avoid conflict, and I'm sure that I did. We met at the beginning of spring break, when I was teaching at City College, so he gave me his number and suggested we get together before I had to go back to campus. I thought because of my carelessness (and my approach-avoid conflict), all was lost, but when I returned to my office after spring break, there was a message from him. He'd gotten my office number from the college's switchboard.

He told me he was divorced, but I always had the feeling that he was living a double life. He would disappear from time to time on "business trips."

"If he has to make a business trip on his birthday or on major holidays," I thought, "I'll know he's not monogamous."

Sure enough, he had to.

I told my first love, Steve, someone I'm still in contact with after fifty-two years, that I was going to London with this Double Lifer, and Steve called on New Year's Eve, when the Double Lifer was watching me unwrap the Christmas presents he'd gotten for me—a delayed activity because, he said, he was on a trip with his sons at Christmas. I let the message machine do its job and heard Steve say, "I just want to wish you a happy new year and a good trip with the Double Lifer you're going to London with."

It was after the trip to London that I got a phone call from someone named Jackie, letting me know that I was the Other Woman.

I didn't want to be The Other Woman. But neither did I want to be a wife again—or even a live-in girlfriend. I wanted a passionate, loving, exclusive relationship with a man whom I'd be there for and who would be there for me—but preferably only on weekends.

I missed having a man in my life, but there were too few hours in a day. I wanted to brush up on my Spanish, and I wanted to date, and I knew that the only way I could do both was to date a Spanish-speaking man.

On campus in the duplicating room I was reflecting on this when a man of retirement age walked into the room and greeted me politely. I noticed that he had an accent.

We talked, and I found out that he was from a Spanish-speaking country! He found out that I was going to Oaxaca in a couple of months and that I really wanted to work on my Spanish.

As we talked, he started to look younger and younger and more and more interesting.

We eventually set a date and when he picked me up and complimented me on my nice house, I asked him where he lived. "I can't really say," he said.

Oh! I thought. A married man. He said that he had three houses, one of which he'd bought outside the city with another person, an old lady, because neither of them could afford to buy a house on their own.

"What address do you have on your driver's license?" I asked him. It was the one with the old lady.

It could be true, what he was telling me. That day we went out of the city, where we walked, had lunch on the water, and switched to Spanish midway through the day.

This is perfect! I thought. He was charming, warm, a lot of fun to be with—and all in Spanish! So when he said, "Would you like to get together again," I prefaced my "Yes! Oh, yes!" with a statement a friend had made around that time.

"You know, a friend of mine was saying, 'I'd like to do less more slowly.'"

He said, "Well, we could get together once a month."

I wanted to take back what I'd just said about less more slowly. I wanted more, faster. But I just said, "Once a month, like a book club/"

"Why not?" he said.

I liked his "Why not?" spirit, and after he dropped me off, I wrote up the minutes for our first club meeting. I wrote them in Spanish and left them in his faculty mail box for correction. The next month, when we went out again, we spoke exclusively in Spanish and I offered to pay for lunch because he'd paid the first time, but he said, "No, it's my job to pay because you write up the minutes of our meetings."

"Then if I'm secretary," I said, "you can be president. By acclamation."

He accepted my unanimous vote and took on the position, even suggesting that we have an objective for our club. *Para promover la paz, la tranquilidad, la alegria, y el cariño entre socios*, which translates to promote peace, tranquility, joy and affection between members.

That's when I knew I would love him forever.

I created a letter head for our club stationary, which I used for all the minutes.

To the question "Are there any additions or corrections to the minutes as read?" there were always corrections, and while my Spanish may not have become better by leaps and bounds, I occasionally learned from my mistakes.

In our third month, during a particularly warm embrace, I informed MyMeque, who often gave me compliments but had never said he loved me, that I would never make love with a man who didn't love me.

"Te quiero!" (I love you!) he said, without missing a beat.

Soon he was signing all e-mail messages, "Te adoro," and I was signing mine "Te quiero," and our club was meeting weekly and sometimes in faraway places like Costa Rica, South America, and China.

He and I both love rituals. The flowers that he brings me are always brought into the bedroom before we make love, and we always make love in the morning. He gives massages at other times too, and he is gifted, so I am blessed. We both love reading the newspaper and sipping tea and planning ahead, but planning less. We both want to do less more slowly.

The Club Dos Meques celebrated five years last fall, and MyMeque still brings me flowers every time he arrives at my front door. He wrote it into the bylaws of our club.

I still sometimes wonder, "Who is this man I love, this other member of our club? A CIA agent or a drug dealer?" Then I remember what my mother said, "That could work." I think our special relationship has worked, and my family consider us a couple. Of course, he never includes me in his own family gatherings, but I've gotten over needing that.

Maybe that's why it never occurred to me to suggest that he go back to Tonga with me. I wanted to go back to my village, where I had lived as a single woman, and I wanted to go singly.

The We in Tongan

"**Emile has organized** a group of us to go back to Tonga for the King's coronation this summer," I told MyMeque (my *mejor que un esposo* or better than a husband), in March 2008, "and we'll be leaving July 27th!"

"Wonderful!" MyMeque replied, with an interest and excitement that he didn't usually show in my activities when they didn't include him.

It hadn't occurred to me that he would think the *we* was inclusive. English makes no distinction between the *we* including the person spoken to and the we excluding the person spoken to, but the Tongan language does, making it more merciful because it can prevent misunderstandings and hurt feelings later.

In the sequel to this volume, *Letters of Apology for My First Memoir*, I describe how I once thought I was included in an outing at my new workplace because of interpreting the *we* as inclusive when the manager of the office, expecting me to stay behind and take care of clients, said, referring to the higher-ups, "We're going to Sausalito for lunch." "Great!" I said. "When are we leaving?"

I loved MyMeque and often traveled with him, but I wanted to go back to my village in Tonga the way I'd lived there—as a single woman, now Tina's grandmother. I wasn't staying in Nuku'alofa with Emile and the others in our group. I'd arranged to stay in my village, Ha'ateiho—through the kindness of 'Ana Taufe'ulungaki, who pretended to remember me fondly when I was contacting Tongans before the trip. She and I had birthdays just six months apart and had started teaching in the same village of 'Atele in 1970—she at the boys college there, 'Atele Lahi. (I was diagonally across the street at 'Atele Si'i.) I was also aware of the huge difference between traveling alone and traveling with someone else. Both can be wonderful, but traveling alone is more intense and immediate, usually offering more interactions with the native population than a couple traveling together can have.

I wasn't even aware that MyMeque would have welcomed being included until several days after I made the announcement.

I don't remember at what point he stated, "You didn't invite me to go with you," but I was stunned and felt really bad. I had done him wrong—not by going solo but by not explaining to him why I felt I needed to go alone. I wanted him and me to be *we* but not in Tonga.

Coming of Old Age in Tonga

Two Weeks for Two Years: My Return to Tonga 2008. As Tina's Grandmother

Sunday, July 27, 2008

See? I did learn something I should have and could have learned in Tonga. I learned to write the day, date and YEAR!

Last night, Saturday, July 26, 2008, MyMeque accompanied me to Walgreens and Radio Shack to get the suggested Ziploc bags, Excedrin PM, insect repellent, Dramamine, eye mask and 5 green bags. He treated me to Fresca, the Peruvian restaurant on West Portal. Today he took me to the airport, where we met up with Emile, Linda, Pat, Cathy and Jim, friends of Emile who were not in the Peace Corps but liked the idea of a coronation. We also had a Food Court dinner with Linda, Emile, and Pat, which didn't preclude MyMeque's also getting us tea and a cupcake. We (he and I) had our separate, quiet farewell before the rest of us went through security, where they didn't check carryon items beyond the x-ray and didn't ask about the thermos for water.

My baggage is light on clothes—my red-orange dress for the coronation, my green sleeveless top and black capris, and my white-and-brown sleeveless top with skorts plus what I'll wear under my three outfits—pretty and new in case I have to hang them on the clothesline.

But my luggage contains gifts including the collages I've put together. One is of the children's drawings—such colorful works of art on newsprint with felt-tip pencils—which I kept all these years and then had laminated this week so they look like placemats. Others are photos of my fale in Ha'ateiho and the people I hope to see again—children as adults, adults still living and around?

Of course I have a to-do list:

Give 'Ana and other Tongans green bags and other gifts—Elizabeth Schultz, ocean poet.

Attend king's coronation.

Revisit my fale.

Revisit my school.

Go into Nuku'alofa.

Go to Fahefa for Andrea and take pictures of her old fale and school.

Send postcards to MyMeque, David, etc.

Find Kili, Kalala, Loiloi, Fatafehi, Hinehina, Line, Fuiva and Langi, Tika.

Find out where Likua's family is living. (Alaska?)

I like a to-do list that includes "Attend King's coronation."

Why is it only now that it occurs to me that *my fale* is pronounced a little bit like *my folly*? Granted, it's more like Fah-Lay, but *folly* goes so well after *my*.

Tuesday, July 29, 2008

I know I was awake for Sunday, July 27, after MyMeque left and I got on the plane with Emile and friends, and I assume that Monday disappeared behind the International Dateline, but I wasn't conscious. When I woke up to the announcement that we were about to land, the woman next to me was looking at me with wonder. She told me I'd missed dinner and breakfast, "but I wish I could do what you did and sleep all the way there."

We were at the airport in Auckland, New Zealand, and we had a six-hour layover. I loved being with Emile and the others, who dared to leave the airport. I probably would have stayed and read had it been just me.

It was raining, and Emile's very kind girlfriend Linda lent me one of her raincoats. As usual I looked for a newspaper so I could see the headlines from a local perspective: "National's lead over Labour gets even bigger." We checked our carry-on luggage and took an Air Bus into town, where we ate at a place called Mecca along the water and had a waitress originally from Chile. I tried Vegemite for the first and possibly the last time. We saw the Needle/Sky Tower and walked in the rain. Of course I thought about Andrea and my January 1971 trip in this incredible country I love, but this was a totally different part of it, and I was traveling with a group. Lesson Learned: Traveling alone is totally different from traveling with one other person, and traveling with one other person is totally different from traveling with a group.

When we returned to the airport and had gotten our luggage, I wrote postcards. The first was to MyMeque, the part of the *we* not included on this trip. The second was to David. He does most of his traveling through us, I think. Then Carol/Caroline/Koralina and her daughter Tara arrived and joined us for the flight to Tonga.

Everyone in the group will be staying in Nuku'alofa except for me. Will I recognize Ha'ateiho? Will Ha'ateiho recognize Tina's grandmother?

9:30 PM We've landed—just an hour later than scheduled. All the luggage is here except Kathy and Jim's.

Wednesday, July 30, 2008

After I last wrote, we were met by two Tongans, Alan and Feauna, who took me to Ha'ateiho, not within view of my former fale. Arriving at night made everything seem more dream-like. I was greeted by 'Ana's son Palei and his wife Vika, who had been watching "Lawrence of Arabia" on TV! This house has electricity and running water—even hot—even if it doesn't have mats on all the walls, ceiling, and floors!

Vika showed me to the bedroom, where the linen is much finer than anything I've ever had, and I got the essentials: A towel, a washcloth, and a brand-new red Digicel phone! I've never had a cell phone before.

I woke up around 3:30 this morning and wrote while waiting for the Tongan sun to come up.

After sunrise, I peeked out the window of my bedroom and saw a big van parked on the side of the house, covered in a canopy. Finau, one of 'Ana's sisters or cousins, brought in breakfast. 'Ana came around 8:00 am, and we talked. She emphasized that Tonga has changed a lot. 'Ana has changed a lot too. The very quiet, gentle Tongan woman I remember now seems strong and frank but still very kind. After all, she's welcomed me and put me up here. She seems bemused, with a wry sense of humor. I think of that Dorothy Parker poem, "Three be the things I shall have till I die./Laughter and hope and a sock in the eye." She seems like someone who's had all three—like me. (So basic to my existence that I had it done in calligraphy and framed for my living room wall.) I distributed the green bags, and I gave her a book of poems I'd brought along because they were written by someone my poet-friend Leslie Simon knows, Elizabeth Schultz, and they pertain to the ocean.

Finau drove me to town for what they call the Fai Kava in the Pangai Si'i, across from the Pangai Lahi and palace. That's a traditionally Tongan way of celebrating the coronation. The *Fie Palangi* way comes later. (Lesson: *Fie* means want and *palangi* means white man/foreigner, so fie palangi means putting on the airs of a foreigner instead of doing things the Tongan way.) Feauna called herself on my cell phone to get my number. I thought, "What high tech!" But I looked around, and it seems that everyone has a cell phone. It used to be that they'd take a basket to the market. Now they take their cell phones.

Nuku'alofa didn't look terribly familiar, and maybe that's good. It was never the world's most beautiful capital. Sort of like a town in a black-and-white Western—a town just getting started or one about to become a ghost town. Now most of it is pretty and pretty unrecognizable. But I recognized the area where Loiloi and I used to watch Line and the rest of the Ha'ateiho team play soccer back in the days when we made their sandwiches and the king would be driven from his palace just yards away to the field to watch the soccer game. Our team would always win because, the other team complained, with the priest playing, we had God on our side.

What's new in Tonga? For one thing, a flyer featuring Barak Obama is on the front door of the post office. "Would Obama be Good for Tonga?" it asks. Someone named Michael G. Horowitz is addressing this question the evening after I leave on Monday, August 11. Too bad I won't be able to attend. I've never heard of Lolo Masi Hall, where the lecture will take place. But Nukualofa has improved—and not just because Obama's adorning the post office door. They even have some nice restaurants. I met Emile and the rest of the group. We ate at a restaurant that wasn't here before, Friends, and then took a walk through the market. I'm sorry to say that they're selling the tortoise-shell bracelets and earrings that I, clueless, wanted so badly back in 1971. The woman selling the tortoise shell was wearing a tee-shirt saying "Global Warming is so hot right now." We went to the Dateline Hotel for drinks, and even though that's where Sione took me for my birthday in 1971 and I went there on other occasions with Vincent and was even in a fashion show there, I hardly recognized it or the spot that it was in.

From there we walked to Emile's village, and he showed us where the murdered Peace Corps Volunteer had lived. Emile is actually on the cover of the book *American Taboo: A Murder in the Peace Corps*, but not as the killer. I read the book soon after it came out in 2004 and gave to Andrea to read on our 2005 cruise of Turkey. I remember commenting, "Now we know what's taboo in America. Not *murder*, but a *Peace Corps* murder!" Emile is on the cover posing back in 1975 or so with the beautiful Peace Corps Volunteer Debora Gardner, who was murdered, and the Peace Corps Volunteer Dennis Priven, who stabbed her 22 times because she didn't show the interest in him that he felt for her. Jim told me soon after he read the book, "Tina, that could have been you" and I said, "You make me feel that I didn't have the full Peace Corps experience," but I know I should be ashamed for making quips like that.

We went to the Deep Blue, where everyone but me is staying. Ben, a taxi driver, offered his services, so we took his taxi to the Blue Banana, a beautiful resort owned by Shane and Chris in the western part of island (Konikokoli). There was an incredible sunset. Took more pizza to Ben and sat with him. Asked about getting back to Ha'ateiho. Talked on the phone to Feauna, who was mad at Emile for taking us away from Nuku'alofa, but the whole time I was talking to her, I thought I was talking to 'Ana. When we finally got back, 'Ana showed me what to prepare for breakfast because Vika will be eating separately. They have an electric water kettle, something I'd like to have back in SF. I showered and collapsed immediately on the very fine linen.

Thursday, July 31.2008.

Something else I should have and could have learned in Tonga and actually did: If you write about a dream, indicate when a dream begins and when it ends: Dream: Last night I dreamed of scaling a building to get to my house. End of dream.

This was a great morning. I had papaya and coconut for breakfast before I rode into Nuku'alofa with 'Ana and Finau, who dropped me off to explore as I wished. I hoped to see Line and thought he would be at St. Mary's, so I walked until I was almost there. I wondered whether he would recognize me now that I was Tina's grandmother—not a young woman in her twenties but a woman in her sixties. I stopped short of St. Mary's—4 blocks. Away. Then I went into a book store and bought *The Tongan Past* by Patricia Ledyard and *Tales of the Tikongs* by Epeli Hau 'Ofa & 7 coronation pens to give as gifts. I went to the Café Escape to write postcards. My first one was to MyMeque. My second was to David. I ate lunch with Tara, Linda and Emile. Finau picked me up around 3:00 to go to the market, and I was finally allowed to help out by paying for several of the items for the feast. 'Ana and her family have been so generous with me. Those who plan the coronation get $20.00 from each person (household?) in the village, so in the end the money I gave Finau is for her and her family to pocket. I want to be sure they understand that I'm not in Ha'ateiho because I can't afford Nuku'alofa. I'm here because it's my village. I'm not trying to save money. I'm just trying to reconnect with the past, my granddaughter Tina's past.

I interrupt this diary for a major news report:

"You can't go home again" when your home has burned down, and that's what happened to mine. This is an interesting coincidence because while I was still living in Tonga, I was fictionalizing my life here, and one of my pieces began, "It's not true that I went mad and burned down my village."

Apparently the person who did this, the son of one of the women I knew back when, was not mad but just intoxicated when he put a pot on the stove and forgot it until the whole hut was on fire, and he woke up just in time to escape.

Think of all the kindling—all the beautiful mats and pieces of tapa cloth on the ceiling, floor, walls! It was really the most beautiful Tongan fale I'd ever seen, a fale woven into a dream. That must have been quite a fire. Where was the rest of the village while he was in his drunken stupor? Oh, but water is scarce! Even if they had seen it, would they have had time to draw water from the well? And what if the well was dry?

The cement floor of my fale is still there, so I asked, "Are you sure this isn't just the top of the tomb, and my fale is buried underneath?" But they didn't do an excavation to satisfy my curiosity.

"Well," I said. "I guess I can't move back in."

I've already taken walks through the village, and I've seen *fie palangi* houses where none had been before. One stands out as more of a mansion than a house, but I don't ask "Who lives there?" because my interest might be misconstrued as admiration.

I saw Lolo in the market, and she remembered me. After all, her older son was the one who burned down my fale. Her younger son is in Iraq. I remember Lolo, who was a beauty, and her little girl Pesi. In fact, I'm holding Pesi in one of my collages, and there's a little boy beside us. Could he be the one who grew up and burned down my fale? I guess I should acknowledge that it really wasn't *my* fale. 'Ana cooked tuna for me and we talked a bit. She asked me whether I had ever married or had children. I guess my coming here alone makes it look as if I'm unattached, and my having the surname Martin doesn't show that I'm a mother or that I was married twice or that I left behind someone who makes my first person singular plural!

Friday, August 1, 2008 The King's Coronation Day Fie Palangi Style

I wore my long red-orange dress with the slit up the side and a short-sleeved jacket for the King's Coronation at 10:00 am in Kolomoto and met Nolini, Sila, and Maui—daughters of 'Ana and Finau—and went in to Tonga High School with them. A pen I was writing with broke and bled blue ink all over my hand and on the front of my dress around my left breast. Fortunately, the jacket covered the "marked woman" me, but it was very hot outdoors, and I wanted to take off the jacket. I may have had the chance to enter the church. The ink stain showed me as a blue blood, and it certainly looked as if the guards were welcoming me. But since I didn't have an official invitation—apparently, they were intended but never sent out—I kept walking, finally setting up with others at an observation point on the road, covered with tapa cloth. I was carrying my huge black handbag and the PBS bag a group of us at City College had been given for the material we helped write for the local educational TV station, and when I put it over my left shoulder, it covered a lot of the ink splotch.

When I was here in 1970-71, I had an Instamatic camera. Now I have upgraded to a Canon Elf! I took pictures of the church, tapa cloth, girls from Queen Salote High School. I met a couple of current Peace Corps Volunteers, Brian and Stacy, who commented that it was unfortunate that the invitations had never gone out, but I felt fine outside the church. My only regret was not being able to sit down.

We saw the king-to-be ride by. He was declared king after his father's death in September 2006, but there were delays in his official coronation. First, there was a six-month mourning period for his father. Then there were riots in November 2006, when the Parliament had a recess without having made progress in democratization. After most of the government buildings and stores were destroyed by fire, the king wanted to focus on rebuilding the capital before being crowned.

Afterwards I walked through the palace grounds and found Nolini on the other side, marching with Tonga High School. My camera battery died. Later I went to Café Escape to write postcards to MyMeque and David as well as to others. I wanted them to be dated the day of the king's coronation.

I ran into Jim and Kathy Prescott, who'd been pulled in to the coronation ceremonies when all those whose invitations had never been sent out failed to show up.

I walked to the bus stop at 2:00.pm and waited for bus for one hour. Finally I got a ride with the police, so I can say I was deported from Nuku'alofa and returned to my village! I had assumed that the police would know where I wanted to go, but of course I had no address, just 'Ana's name and the general area. They drove around the house a couple of times, and 'Ana told me later that they had seen the police coming around and assumed they were looking for a criminal. That would be me, with my huge carbon footprint. I then watched the Coronation on TV . Found out 'Ana had abusive immigration experiences in the USA. She was pulled aside and questioned, as if she were a threat to US security. She also told me that there used not to be a problem with juvenile delinquency, but now when Tongans go to the United States, New Zealand, and Australia and get into trouble, they are sent back to Tonga.

'Ana made a delicious fish pie. 'Ana knew in advance that I don't eat meat, but I'd considered eating it here because my main objection to eating meat is that the animals in factory farms are never given the chance to live before they're slaughtered. But in Tonga, they do have freedom of movement and can follow their instincts, so I don't feel as sorry for them. But there's been plenty to eat with resorting to animals—except for sea animals—and 'Ana seems to understand the concept of not eating animals.

In the evening I went to the Tutupakanava with Nolini, Sila, and Maui. This is a traditional torch lighting following a coronation. I treated them to a log, one of the 30,000 used as torches to honor the new king. Very pretty.

Saturday, August 2, 2008

I talked with Vika , 'Ani's lovely daughter-in-law, at breakfast. She's a doctor in the hospital that Vincent helped plan and open in 1971. I gave her a green bag and a Wrap n Mat, which she seemed to appreciate. When I spoke of the I eco-wise Tongan traditions I remembered from the early 1970's, she said, "That's right. I remember my mother would say, 'Go get the basket.'" Now plastic bags are popular, and she says they burn them, which of course isn't good for the air.

I took a walk to 'Ateli Si'i to see my old school, and it looked very much the way it had in 1971, when I'd last seen it. I noticed that it had been built just after World War II. It really doesn't seem to have changed much since that time, either. After I took a look—no classes in session—I walked in the opposite direction to the Farewell Cemetery.

Nolini and I went into Nuku'alofa at 12:15 and peeked in at the palace ground and lunches. We ordered takeout from Two Sisters Restaurant and watched the dances—two sets. Ma 'ulu 'ulu is the seated dance. Laka laka is the other. Wrote postcards. Read *Tales of the Tikongs* by Epeli Hau 'ofa. Saw Japan's Crown prince's limousine collect him. Got coconuts. Drove through Ha'ateiho and 'Atele. Nolini came with fish cakes.

<u>Sunday, August 3, 2008</u>

Dream: Grandmother Robison was starving upstairs. End of dream.

Saw a little rat or big cockroach. A good rain right before 5:00. Read *Epili Hau'ofa*. Washed my hair and let it air dry. Watched preparation of the 'Umu at 'Ana's house 8:30-10:00. Pulato, Sione Vea's adopted son, Liku'a's nephew, and Finau's husband prepared it. Nolini did all the food to go into the 'Umu. Went to New Weslyan Church (designed by Tavi but extended) and saw Malia Lau Si'i, who remembered me—maybe with a little help from Nolini— and invited us to a barbecue on Thursday. Called Feauna. Ate delicious umued dishes. 'ufi, palu sami, 'ika. Read Hau 'Ofa and Patricia Ledyard's *The Tongan Past*. Went in to Nuku'alofa to say goodbye to Kathy and Jim, who are leaving tonight, and checked on Carol and Tara, who was sick.

<u>Monday, August 4, 2008</u>

This was the day we Peace Corps Volunteers got together officially at the home of the country director Jeffrey Cornish. We were all interviewed for the newspaper, and I was interviewed for Tongan TV.

But before that I read some of *The Tongan Past* and went into Nuku'alofa, where I'd planned to go by bus. But I got a message from Nolini that because it was raining, Finau would come for me at 9:00 so I wouldn't have to wait in the rain. In Nuku'alofa I bought 30 postcards and went to the Blue Banana, where they're selling green bags similar to the ones I brought from the USA. They say 'OUA 'E TALI TANGATI MILEMILA, which means don't use plastic. Started writing post cards. Went to the PO, where Obama was still posted, and asked for stamps for the postcards, but no one seemed sure how much postage was needed for the USA. I went to the market for tomatoes and butter. Waited for the bus at noon and got back home around 1:00. Then Feauna got me over to the country director's house, which is so close to the ocean that it seemed we were on a houseboat. I was the first to arrive. Other RPCVs and new PCVs arrived. A cute young Tongan guy named Poli interviewed us for the newspaper, and as I mentioned, I was interviewed for Tonga TV.

<u>Tuesday, August 5, 2008</u>

Today I went to her office with 'Ana and talked with Malakai, a Mormon born in the US of Tongan parents. I showed him the collages, and he asked what I was doing now back in the US. When I told him that I was teaching at City College of San Francisco, he asked, "What else?" I told him, "I'm reckoning with my past and bringing it up to date in Tonga."

I checked my e-mail and found MyMeque had just sent me a message. I responded, and it turned out that we were online at the same time, so for a few minutes, emailing back and forth, we were together in Tonga.

'Ana called Kalala's office and asked her to come over. I wonder whether she'd have recognized me now that I'm Tina's grandmother if she hadn't known that's who she'd be seeing. I guess I'm not the only one self-conscious about changes. Kalala thinks she's gained too much weight. I reminded her of how almost 40 years ago she told me, after I got stung by a bee and my face swelled up, that she wished a bee would sting her all over her body to make her fat.

I was thrilled to see her again! I treated her to lunch at Two Sisters Restaurant, where we had a very intense conversation. I learned something that I really hadn't known before. She was always such a charming, animated little girl that I had the impression that things just fell into place for her, but she told me that she often felt out of place and alone and scared. It hadn't been easy for her to be at the Side School, where she was away from the other village children, even though she did well there in terms of learning English and getting good grades.

After lunch we went to get her children, who are at the Side School—at least I think that's where we were when she picked them up. She seems like a very warm and adoring mother, maybe giving her children the kind of attention she wishes she had been given instead of being designated as the one who would bring distinction and prosperity to the family—in the generation after her uncle Line, who played that role in his generation. I don't think we talked about her Uncle Line, although I might have said in passing that I'd like to see him.

We didn't sing together, Kalala and I, but then that's something I did with the kids at my school. She was just my sometimes little girl. But she remembered the books I read to her, especially "Green Eggs and Ham."

I later returned to Ha'ateiho, had dinner, and got the news that Loiloi was back in Ha'ateiho!

I couldn't wait to see her. It turns out that she's the one who lives in the house that looks more like a mansion! (Back in the 1970's their house looked as if it were made of cardboard, but people told me it was Masonite.) I managed to compliment her on her house without adding, "Fie palangi," and she was very friendly and warm—a bit teary-eyed. The rest of her family wasn't there. When I later asked to use the bathroom in her deluxe abode, she told me that there wasn't any water.

When I got back to Palei and Vika's, I found out that I had appeared on TV. It was the interview from yesterday, Monday, August 4, 2008, at the country director's house.

Tomorrow I'd like to find out where Likua's son and daughter-in-law are living so I can get in touch with them when I get back.

Wednesday, August 6, 2008

Went into Nuku'alofa again and took pictures—even one of me under a matapa (the archway). A Tongan obliged. A bookstore clerk told me she'd seen me on Tonga TV 3, and when I asked, her, "What did I say," she said, "Don't use plastic." I met a very nice clerk at Digicel when I was looking for Masao Soakai, the father of Likua's song Mongohea. She made the call for me, but I never connected to Masao Soakai. The clerk let me sit down in the air-conditioned office and look up names.

When I returned to Vika and Palei's place, they weren't home and the house was locked, so I went to Loiloi's, and Fatafehi and Amilia were there with their children. I was so happy to see them after all these years and with kids older than they were when I last saw them. We looked at the collages I made, and Amilia told me her children had never before seen photos of her as a baby. Apparently, Hinehina and the baby that was born in 1971 won't be returning to Tonga while I'm here. We all went to see Fuiva, who lives just a block from them. I don't think that's where she and Langi were living in 1971, when Fuiva pierced my ears and later had me over for a farewell dinner. In any case, she wasn't there. Then we went back to Loiloi's and had lunch together—haka, which means boiling vegetables in a big pot that looks like a cauldron.—kumala and 'ufi—sweet potatoes and yam. We went back to the remains of my fale to take pictures. I heard about the Miss Galaxy Contest and invited Loiloi, who accepted, but there was something of a delay waiting for the person who would drive us.

The Miss Galaxy Pageant is a contest to crown the most beautiful "fakaleiti". That's new since I lived here.

Leiti is Tongan for *lady*, and *faka* means pertaining to, so fakaleiti is "like a lady," which may be slightly different from "lady-like." I think most of the contestants are transgender rather than men dressing up as women just for the night. They are really gorgeous and they radiate the joy of being female! It makes me happy that these people, maybe the most glamorous Tongans I've ever seen, can be applauded and maybe even crowned! I feel like being their coach and leading them into a couple of stanzas of "I Enjoy Being a Girl," which I think is an even more exuberant celebration of female trappings than "I Feel Pretty." But I pale beside them, and not just because I'm now Tina's grandmother.

I'm usually the one who falls asleep at events, but Loiloi fell asleep tonight. I love her for that—and for other reasons like her seeming happy to see me. But it did make me aware that sometimes an invitation can be an imposition. Maybe she'd have preferred being in bed to being out in the galaxy.

Tomorrow I'm meeting Feauna and 'Ana for lunch at Friends Restaurant. Later Nolini and I are going to Malia and Pepe's for dinner.

August 7, 2021

This morning 'Ana told me that the other Peace Corps Volunteers and I were in the newspaper *Talaki*, so I went around town trying to find a copy and finally did. They'd translated what I said in English into Tongan, so I needed help in understanding what I'd said! A very nice Tongan at the Café Escape helped me. But of course I feel ashamed. If it had been in French or Spanish, I'd have understood. But my Tongan was always rudimentary. My excuse, of course, is that they wanted me to speak English to the children so they'd do better on the exams they took in sixth grade. But I think my not learning more Tongan had more to do with my fatigue and my mistaken notion that I'd never have the chance to speak it again after I left Tonga. Of course, I do see that through my very last diary, November 1971, I was still jotting down new Tongan phrases—and words to songs

Lesson: Use the language, wherever you live, not the good excuses for not using it.

Feauna, 'Ana and I had planned to have lunch at Luna Rosa but found out it's not open for lunch. We talked about the upcoming election in the US, and 'Ana said someone was commenting that Americans can overcome their prejudice against Blacks but not against women. I think she and Feauna were rooting for Hillary. I found out that special English schools will be outside the Ministry of Education. I guess that would include the Side School? I managed to pay the tab when they weren't looking, something they described as "naughty."

'Ana left around 2:00, and Feauna and I talked,. We called Cindy Soakai, the half-sister of Likua's son Mongahea Soakai, but it didn't lead to any more info on how to contact Mongahea. I gave Feauna my copy of Konai's poems (Konai Helu Thaman) and got another. Konai is a Tongan poet, no longer living in Tonga, the same age as 'Ana and me.

I took the bus back, and then Nolini and I left for Malia's before

6:00. They have a white picket fence right around their porch. They prepared a meal quite different from the ones we shared almost 40 years ago. Malia remembered that I'd given her my kerosene stove before I left.

"Where is it?" I asked. But they just laughed.

We ate with her, Venna and Tui and Malia's brother or nephew, who had po ako while we were there. I should have audited! An opportunity lost. But I did notice that they had electric lights.

Friday, August 8, 2008

Got up after some dreams woke me up around 4:00 but didn't record them Went back to 'Ateli Si'i (east of Ha'ateiho) when classes were in session. Met Ika and Veiongo and other teachers. Sat in Radio Hour with teachers. Saw the actual write-up of the radio broadcast for Class 6, Term 1, under Tongan Government and "The Day of Rest."

"It is written in the Tongan Constitution that 'The Sabbath Day shall be kept sacred in Tonga forever/A Sunday in Tonga is a day of rest.' Tongan people are to go to their own churches and Sunday schools… Trading is not allowed on Sunday so the shops are closed. No one goes to the garden to plant or dig crops. No films are shown except religious films by church groups. There are no dances. Travelling by plane, bus or taxi is not allowed. If church groups want to go to another village, they must apply to the Minister of Police 4 or 5 days beforehand for a special permit to use a bus."

Took pictures where 1970 ones were taken. It turns out that one of the teachers, Fanga, is the daughter of Tonga (a proper name as well as the name of the kingdom), a teacher I taught with in 1970. She posed with me in the same spot her mother was standing the day she told me there was a kutu (louse) on my forehead. Veionga invited me to come back to see his English class later, and Fanga cut class to take me to see Tonga, who was sick in bed.

I then visited Loiloi before going back to Veionga's room for English class. They're no longer using the Tate Oral Syllabus. Another change from 1970: A cell phone rang during story time!

I went back to Loiloi's, and Loloma (their designated driver?) took Fehi, Sione and me to the Ha'ateiho Beach. It was beautiful! The two years I lived in Ha'ateiho, I never saw a beach except when I went into Nuku'alofa—unless that's where Vincent took the children and me, and I just didn't know it. There used to be bush hiding the water.

Then we went to the 'uta, the inland. which they used to call "the plantation," the farmlands where they grow 'ufi (yam) near the king's villa. I liked seeing the 'ufi in the foreground and the coconuts in the background. Loiloi prepared a tomato salad with kapa ika.(canned fish). Then I went back once again to my old school to watch the 'Atele Si'i kids hiku the veve, pick up rubbish, which they do in troop-like lines, marching forward. Children and cars exited between 3:00 and 4:00 pm.

A teacher told me I was a "wonderful person," and the teacher standing beside her nodded. I have no idea what prompted that. Just my being interested? I certainly wasn't doing anything to help, and they weren't asking me to sponsor them back in the USA. I should have asked them why I was wonderful, but I didn't want to put them on the spot.

I forgot to mention that the day we met in the rain at the market, Kalala said she'd come by for me on Friday evening for dinner, but she never came. Nolini and I looked for bread and ice cream (Chateau.) Picked up Finau and took her for ice cream too, and saw a concert to raise funds. Donated!

Saturday, August 9, 2008

Went to 'Ana's at 7:30. We went together to the flea market at Tofua. She surprised me by commenting that vegetables that aren't so beautiful might be better because they're grown more naturally. I went to the bookstore for coasters and got one saying "BACK TO MY ROOT TONGA." 'Ana and friend looked for refrigerators and stoves. I thought that buying them a stove or refrigerator would be a good way to thank them for putting me up, but 'Ana said no.

We took a picture at the matapa (archway) at the Royal Palace. Then I went back to Loiloi's at 11:50 am or so. Loloma took Fatafehi, and me to the Stalactite Cave Scenic Reserve on the Anahulu Beach in the east of Tongatapu. Loiloi told me that Ha'amonga 'a Maui, Niutoua, is where her family is from. It was Captain Cook's Landing place, and that's where they have the stone trilithon they sometimes call "The Stonehenge of the Pacific." Back at Loiloi's, she called Line's cell phone to arrange a meeting. In the meantime I got a new card for Digicel and couldn't get into Vika and Palei's place, so I stopped by 'Ana's and found her and her family sitting in the dark. 'Ana said, "We're watching a stupid movie." I said, "Good!" But I turned down their invitation to watch "Men in Black" in favor of wandering. Palei returned with the key, so I got into my "quarters." Nolini and Sila came for me at 6:20 to drive me to the Deep Blue to pick up Emile and Linda for dinner at the Luna Rosa, which was closed. We wound up at Little Italy, where the food was like something I would make—not good! What about the 'Ofa atu? Was that it by a different name? What about the Beach House? We took a taxi back.

Sunday, August 10, 2008

Dream: I was in a pizza-heating business enterprise. End of dream.

This is my last full day in Tonga, and I'm going to keep a blow-by-blow account.

Looking again at my to do list from July 28th, I see missions accomplished and missions missed.

I've given 'Ana and other Tongans green bags and other gifts—Elizabeth Schultz. Beyond that, I've even appeared on TV talking a green streak.

I attended the king's coronation, standing room only outside.

I revisited what remained of my fale.

I revisited my school.

I went into Nuku'alofa.

I've sent postcards to MyMeque, David, and others almost every day. When I travel, I always intend to send postcards to people I especially like, and then I realize how many people I especially like. (Tavi once told me that the only thing he ever needed money for was stamps.)

Of the lost and found, I've found Kalala, Loiloi, Fatafehi.

Tika is nowhere around although 'Ana has worked on a translation of the New Testament into contemporary Tongan with him.

But no Kili. Only very indirect contact with Line. Is he avoiding me because he's not interested in me or because he wants, as I did for so long, to keep the illusion that memory creates? Fuiva and Langi haven't been home.

I still don't know where Likua's son and family are living, and I need to get to Fahefa, on the west of Tongatapu, for Andrea..

In the meantime I'm reading the verses of Konai Helu Thaman and plan to write a few verses of my own.

Nolini and I are going to church, and there's almost always a feast after the church. Loiloi lives just a stone's throw from the church, so maybe I can be thrown there.

Well, I took a photo of Fatafehi and her son after the church service, but there was no room at the inn—or at the last supper. It takes a village, but the village isn't taking me—not to lunch. Am not sure what Nolini and Fatafehi were saying in their native Tongan, but this is what I imagine.

N: You're inviting her to your Sunday feast, aren't you?
F: No. There's no room.
N: It takes a village!
F: We've already taken her to see all the sights. We've done our part.

But Andrea's Tongan was better than mine, and she thought my offering a reward for the return of my basket was my thanks to the Tongans for their loving kindness. All I really understood of the heated exchange between Fatafehi and Nolini was that I was the charge.

It does take a village, and Nolini and the rest of 'Ana's family have been a whole village onto themselves.

Nolini and I are now at the Vaiola Hospital, the hospital Vincent helped plan and open in 1971. She's getting a child's prescription filled.

Nolini says she'll take me to Fahefa!

For Andrea, Fahefa, where she was 'Ana

What a quiet village. It's in the far west "corner" of Tongatapu. I never really had a sense of where any of us were. I took a lot of pictures, but we didn't see a soul. Andrea came back here with Roger in spring 1986 shortly after she married him in 1985, and they brought four-year-old Jenny along. But their return was fewer than 15 years after their departure. My visit to her village comes a whole generation after theirs.

Kolovai!

I never thought of Tonga as having tourist attractions, but they've made the Houma Blow Holes at Kolovai very attractive. Somewhere along the route, though, I lost my camera case and little notebook. I thought about the diary I lost in 1971, shortly before I left Tonga. I still have my bigger diary.

Lupe, Daughter of Havea

Am now at Loiloi's in her bathroom with no water. They'd finished their big meal, and Loiloi asked me why I hadn't come to eat with them.

I hazarded a guess. "Because I wasn't invited?"

"Look who!" Loiloi told me, and I saw Lupe, the daughter of our village chief Havea. The Lupe who had lived with me the first months of my stay in Tonga. We talked a little bit, and she told me some things about people close to her who've been in prison because of drug dealing, "the poor things." I don't really have to come into the bathroom to write. There's always a lot of back-and-forth planning I stay out of, so it's the way it used to be. I have time to write. Loiloi says we're going over to see Fuiva and Langi now.

Well, guess who was at Fuiva and Langi's home! Line, a bit heavier and white-haired but still Line to Tina's grandmother. Fuiva and Loiloi sat on the floor while I, wearing my red-orange dress with the blue ink splotched concealed under the jacket, posed with them, with Line on my right, Langi on my left, both of them sitting in chairs. I tried to join Fuiva and Loiloi on the floor, but they wouldn't let me.

Line said he had had sent Amilia by for me last night—just after I'd left to have dinner with Emile and the rest of the group. ("You summoned me?") I showed them my collages. Soon there will be another one—with them, with us.

Just heard that Kili is back from New Zealand! Nolini, granter of wishes, drove me over to her place right away, but someone in her family told us she's at the Catholic Hall in Ha'ateiho near the village clinic. We're on our way!

Most important mission accomplished! When she saw me, Kili cried out, "Tina Peace Corps!" I told her how much I'd wanted to see her, how well I remembered her. Then I got a bonus. Katalina, another of Line's nieces and Kalala's sister, was there with her family too. She'd grown from an adorable child of five to a mother of almost five adorable kids. (I counted four.) She took off her lei and put it around my neck. Why did they have leis? Had they all just flown in? Kili was about to sing with a group, but I had two other calls—one from Lilieta Soakai and another from Line, so we've promised each other that sometime between now and my departure tomorrow, we'll get together to talk.

Nolini says that Line wants to see me at Loiloi's, another summons. I'm there almost as regularly as I'm at Vika and Palei's home. I go by to see Loiloi as if I feared that she would disappear if I didn't keep watch.

Loiloi, Line, and I talked on her porch as we sat beside her husband Fonomanu, who has memory loss. No wonder Loiloi fell asleep at the Miss Galaxy Pageant. She's returned from Australia with goods to sell in front of the house Fatafehi owns—a mansion with no running water—and she's taking care of a husband who isn't all there anymore. She stills smokes, something she picked up from Line, who has given it up. Loiloi doesn't think that's fair.

I told them how wonderful 'Ana and her family have been and that without them I'd never have been able to stay in Ha'ateiho. I mentioned a place for tourists that I'd looked into, but it seemed too far removed from the real village. Line knows Vivienne Puloka, the woman who runs the bed and breakfast, and offered to take me to see the place I thought was too touristy. Did we invite Loiloi to come along? We should have—just in case her imagination was greater than Line and I were. I told Line how much I loved Loiloi, and Line said something like "She's one in a million" or "She's the greatest." Something superlative.

Our conversation was friendly and polite—as if he were a priest and I a parishioner—but not like the ones in *The Thorn Birds*. Neither was there any of the sparring that we just naturally did back in the early 1970's, when I think we were the poor person's Benedick and Beatrice. Now, as our own grandparents, we were being so careful, so correct, and I thought about Jim Canning when I saw him again in 2003, the first time we'd been alone together in twenty-eight years, and we'd seemed like distant cousins whose parents wanted us to meet. But in the case of Jim, we were our parents meeting again. Line and I are the age to be our own grandparents.

The only thing I said that was at all flirtatious was "I like you with white hair. It makes you look very distinguished. Sort of like a priest." He laughed. "You were a mere boy when your hair was black like that limousine that drove the King of Tonga those few yards from his palace to watch you play soccer." He told me his game was now golf and that, while we'd never ridden in a limousine together, he reminded me that we'd once been brought back to our villages by a mini-moke, one of the taxis with the driver on a motor cycle and us passengers in an open cart in front of the driver. He asked me something like "So how's life?' and I said "Good" and gave a few examples including MyMeque. He reminded me that he'd visited me in San Francisco when I was married and the mother of a two-year-old. I'd forgotten that, but I know I have some pictures from that day, the only pictures I have of Line and me together.

He asked whether I wanted to go back with him to Loiloi's or be dropped off at Vika and Palei's, and because I really wanted to see Kili, I chose Vika and Palei's, where Kili knows I'm staying.

Before I got out of the van he was driving, I gave him an affectionate kiss on one cheek but refrained from asking him to turn the other. He smiled and said, "Ciao, Bella." I should have taken one last look at the foot that was once kissed by the Pope when Line was in training in Italy, representing Polynesia, but he put it on the accelerator and departed.

So here I am, back at Vika and Palei's, with the hope of seeing Kili later.

***(See "Finding Kili.")

The day of my departure, 'Ana and her family gathered in front of the house and wished me a warm farewell. They couldn't see me off,

'Ana said, because they had to go to work, and two girls were going to school—Tonga High. Three members of her family were taking me to the airport to see me off. They must have been relieved to see me go. We all know the proverb about fish and guests and three days before the stench, and I'd been there two full (very full) weeks. But the same kindness that had compelled 'Ana to host me in the first place prevailed.

I visited Kili outside her fale, and we took pictures. But I had no further contact with Loiloi and her family until I was walking to board the plane and saw in front of me Amilia, the child I used to hold to my hip while I slaved over my kerosene stove. Loiloi and others were waving goodbye to Amilia and her kids, going back to Australia, and while they were at it, they called out to me. Later at the airport in New Zealand, Amilia and I talked some more and I walked them to their gate for their flight back to Sidney.

From the Auckland airport I was able to access WiFi and sent a letter to MyMeque, who greeted me at the San Francisco Airport with a sign saying "Club Dos Meques."

I am back from Tonga, back with the man I love, and back to using the inclusive we.

I hear that now Peace Corps Volunteers are told to prepare a reply of one or two sentences to answer the much-too-broad question, "So, how was it?" That's how long they have before eyes glaze over. I'm teaching my students at City College relative clauses. How long of a sentence can I get away with?

Who's Who in Tonga— Exercising Relative Clauses to Sum Up my Return to Tonga, 2008

KING SIAOSI TUPOU V is the king whose coronation I went to with a group led by Emile Hons, whom I'd met through another RPC, Tom Riddle, who told me that Emile was the friendliest person he'd ever met, which seemed to be the case when I met him earlier because of Tavi, who was the subject of both a book and a documentary for which I'd been interviewed, and found out that he was also the one who lived right next door to the Peace Corps Volunteer Deborah Gardner, who was murdered by another Peace Corps Volunteer, who stabbed her twenty-two times, which was written up twenty-five years later in a book called *American Taboo: A Murder in the Peace Corps*, which indicates just what is taboo in our culture, from which I first flew in 1970, when I held hands all the way from Hawaii to Tonga, by way of Fiji, with a Peace Corps Volunteer named Jim, who after telling me I was the best date he'd ever had (dinner in Hawaii, breakfast in Fiji, and lunch in Tonga), sailed off to Nomuka, an outer island, and in six months dropped out of the Peace Corps and returned to the states, where he got a singing part in the original cast of *Grease*, which startles people when they find out that he's the one who's singing in a recording of "Ave Maria" that I've put online and the Tongan classic "Angi Mai," which he sent me at my request before I took my second trip to Tonga, which was without him and even without my meque (which is an acronym I created for mejor que un esposo, which means "Better than a husband," in Spanish, which is my meque's native tongue), in 2008, when I went, which is what I was saying earlier, with Emile Hons and a group that he'd gotten together, which consisted of his girlfriend, Linda, a fire dancer, Pat, who was wearing the International Peace Belt, which was made of coins from all around the world, and Kathy and Jim, who were a married couple and who were later let in to the New Wesleyan Church for coronation ceremony, which took place the Friday after we arrived in Tonga and which was preceded by the Kava Ceremony, which in the Tongan tradition makes a man a king, for which King Siaosi Tupou V was presented with between seventy and a hundred pigs which had been 'umued, which means cooked in an underground oven, which is something I also got to watch the following Sunday, when we rested, which is the only activity allowed on the Sabbath, according to the Tongan Constitution, of which Article 6 declares "The Sabbath Day shall be kept holy in Tonga and no person shall practise his trade or profession or conduct any commercial undertaking," which the preparation of the 'umu, though labor-intensive, is not, so I witnessed the building of the 'umu, which followed our flight, which was on New Zealand Air and the most comfortable one I'd had in ages, which meant that I slept all the way from San Francisco to New Zealand, where we toured Auckland for six hours while waiting for our connecting flight, which would include Carol Graham, another RPCV and her daughter, Tara, who was a photographer and who, along with Emile, had a press pass and a camera much fancier than mine, which was a Canon Elf digital, not the instamatic which I'd taken to Tonga thirty-eight years earlier, when I'd been in my twenties and lived in a hut which had no running water or electricity, which was in great contrast to the home into which I was welcomed by the family of 'Ana, the lovely woman (and later Minister of Education), who had started teaching the same year I had back in 1970 and was hosting me in a house that had hot running water, a microwave, and some appliances I was living without in the USA before I arrived in Tonga, where I spent two weeks first at coronation-related events in Nuku'alofa like the Tutupakanava, which is the traditional torch spectacle on the water around Nuku'alofa, which I went to the night after the coronation, which was also the day that the Tongan police transported me from Nuku'alofa to my village, and where I spent a second week re-discovering the Tongans I'd known long ago, such as Losa, whose son burned down my hut (which is kind of funny since my first attempt at fictionalizing Tonga was a story that began, "It's not true that I went mad and burned down the village"), which I visited with Losa herself and which was right next to the home of Malia, who greeted me in church with "Tina Pisi Ko!" and invited me to dinner the following Thursday, when I found out her daughter Mele, whom I'd know when she was a little girl, was now living a few miles from San Francisco and who later became my Guest of Honor, after I'd returned to SF with Tongan body oil and newspapers that her mom had sent through me and when I gave a party to extend our vacations on a Sunday, which I instructed my guests was a time they HAD to stop work and play instead, which, to avoid getting ahead of myself, was what I was doing in Tonga, where I visited my old school, which hadn't changed much except for the fact that water shortage made it impossible for the children to brush their teeth in the school yard, which they'd done back in the early 1970s, when the teachers had no cell phones in their hands and there were no SUVS, which have become so prevalent in Tonga that people don't walk anymore, even around the corner, where they say they have to drive because of all the dogs, which never bothered me when I went on my many walks, including the one which took me to 'Atele Si'i, where I met the teachers, who still wore the ta'avalas and used the chalkboard instead of computers or duplicated materials or overhead projectors, which required equipment and facilities they didn't have, and where I discovered that one of the teachers was the daughter of a teacher with whom I had taught back in the 1970s and with whom I appeared in a collage I'd put together for the teachers, which led the daughter and me to posing together in the same spot and then taking her son's red car to go back to the village to see her mom, who lived right across the street from the home of 'Ana's son and daughter in law, Palei and Vika. who were sharing their home with me while I stayed an extra week, which brought me reunions with some of the people I'd loved most, who...

To be continued in spite of shouts of "Stop! Stop! Stop!"

I wanted to write more about Tonga, so the voice I heard was saying, "Start! Start! Start!"

FINDING KILI

KILI WAS A Tongan child I remembered as having, maybe being, the spirit we all seek—in others and in ourselves. She stood out among the children, already out-standing, who walked me home after school and lined my hut. When Vincent, the British hospital administrator I'd met through the Peace Corps doctor, drove up to my hut to ask me out (there were no phones in the village), Kili was among the children who asked him where he went in that shiny white car of his. (There were no *cars* in the village, either.) Vincent politely said that someday he would drive us all to the beach in that white car, and Kili jumped for joy, applauding in the air. Then, feet hitting the ground, she asked, "What's the name of the day?"

I adopted Kili's phrase on the spot and still use it to get a commitment out of vague suggestion.

"What's the name of the day?"

Vincent named the day, and when it came, Vincent took us all to the beach, thanks to Kili.

Kili was the first to learn the songs I taught the children at school—the songs Welsh governesses and Austrian nuns teach kids—and she even picked up the songs I just sang around the hut.

There was one from *Camelot* with the words "Only you, only I. World farewell, world goodbye."

When Kili asked, "Who is going to the beach besides Salika, Paula and me?" and I said, "Only you," Kili sang out, "Only you, only I. World farewell, world goodbye!"

Just what I'd always dreamed of: Someone who knew that life should be a musical with people dancing down the street and bursting into song when given the proper cues.

When I went back to Tonga in 2008, Kili was one of the people I wanted most to see.

But upon my return to Ha'ateiho, the villagers told me that Kili wasn't in Tonga because her brother had died, and she'd gone to his funeral in New Zealand.

So I'd settled for the coronation of Kingi Siaosi Tupou as well as the eco-message I wanted to take back to Tonga (the place I'd learned it), and a stay in Ha'ateiho with the son and daughter-in-law of 'Ana Taufe'ulungaki, a remarkable Tongan woman who'd begun teaching English the same year I had and in the same village, 'Atele, adjacent to Ha'ateiho. Thanks to 'Ana and her family—and of course Emile Hons, who was largely responsible for my going back—my two weeks in Tonga had the kind of reunions I'd dreamed of. Still, something was missing. Kili.

Then the last day I was in Tonga, the Sunday night before the Monday I was to return to San Francisco, I heard that Kili was back from New Zealand. Nolini, one of 'Ana's nieces, drove me to her house, which was close to where I was staying and just a few yards from the spot where my *fale* (hut) had once stood.

But her son said Kili was at the Catholic Social Hall, so Nolini drove me there.

When Kili saw me, she said "Ouiaoue! Tina Peace Corps!" And after we'd hugged, she introduced me to her whole beautiful family.

Later that evening, she walked over to see me at home. I feared that Tongans never walked anymore; they all seemed to have humongous vans. So I was impressed that she was walking. I was also impressed by her total recall. She said she remembered all the songs I taught them—including old melodies with new words—and was so mad when the radio got them wrong. I asked her about "The Twelve Days of Christmas" because I'd forgotten what Tongan items I'd substituted for the English ones, and she remembered every single day of Christmas!

On the twelfth day of Christmas my true love gave to me

Twelve girls who could hiko
Eleven who lakalaka
Ten men drinking Kava
Nine boys drawing water
Eight women beating tapa
Seven ducks a swimming
Six goats a grazing
　　Five turtle rings!　　　　　　　　(I'm sorry. I didn't know in those
　　　　　　　　　　　　　　　　　　days that we should let turtles
live!)
Four ukeleles
Three 'umued pigs
Two matted slippers
And a flying fox in a toa tree.

Kili could even get the song to scan.

When I commented on her amazing memory, she told me she'd only gone through Form 2 or Form 3 in school because she had to go back to Niua, her island, where there was "Nothing flour, nothing sugar, nothing eggs, nothing anything!"

There were no boats to get her to school, but if she'd been able to go on to Form 4 and 5 and 6, she could really have done well. As it was, she worked hard and had gone to New Zealand to plant tomatoes in the freezing cold so she could earn money…to buy a van.

We talked and sang and recited special memories, and she apologized because, she said, "I don't speak English properly."

I thought her English was just beautiful, and so was she—
still the spirit of Ha'ateiho, found again!

Finding Kili

Eco-Bore Takes the Good Old Days Back to Tonga

I THOUGHT OF my village in Tonga as my Walden Pond though David Thoreau might not have recognized it. It was in the South Pacific instead of in New England, and while Thoreau went to the woods to live deliberately, my woods had coconut trees. The pond was the Pacific Ocean — or maybe my lawn every time it rained, since my hut had been built in what appeared to be a ditch. Still, it was deliberately that I went to live in a hut with no electricity or running water. For two years I used a kerosene lamp and kerosene stove, drew water from the well, and bathed by soaping myself and pouring a quart or two of water over my body for the first and final rinsing. Everywhere I went, I took my hand-woven basket, and when I wanted a pound of sugar, it was poured onto a piece of recycled newspaper, which was wrapped into a package and placed in my basket.

For almost forty years I told people about Tonga, where nothing was wasted. Tonga, where I had come of Eco-Age.

Then, about the time that San Francisco banned plastic checkout bags at supermarkets and the mayor banned plastic-bottled water at City Hall, I heard that plastic had attacked, invaded, and occupied Tonga, and I flew off to rescue the island that I loved.

Granted, there were other reasons for going. There was a coronation coming up, a Peace Corps reunion, and some Tongans I really wanted to see again, but I had a mission: Taking the good old days back to Tonga.

Four decades earlier, one of my jobs in Tonga was at a teachers re-training center, where I taught methods of teaching oral English to children. Now I would be re-training them to do what they'd taught me: Reduce, Reuse, Recycle.

Now, before I go any further, I should mention that I'm cursed by a passion for all sorts of things that produce gaping yawns in others. My office mate, Bob, whose imagination soars so high that he was hoping the coronation was mine, gives his students writing assignments allowing them to be Koko the gorilla and explain how frustrating it is that Dr. Penny and her Stanford-educated staff can't learn one word of gorilla. Meanwhile I'm asking my drowsy students to write about the evils of bottled water. I was going back to Tonga as Eco-Bore — bearing a message, boring the people. But there was no stopping me now.

I packed green shopping bags and Wrap-n-Mats, (squares of cloth with plastic centers to wrap around sandwiches to keep them fresh and then, once opened, to serve as mats for the sandwiches) something that appears to be modeled after the food packages Tongans put in the 'umu, their underground ovens. Tongans used banana leaves and taro leaves instead of cloth and plastic for the food packages they put in 'umus, and they tied them up with the rib of coconut leaves instead of Velcro's, but the principle was the same. I would give these bags and Wrap-in-Mats as gifts. I packed other things, of course. Knick-knacks from Walgreen's San Francisco Souvenirs aisle and pictures of Tongans and me, 1970–1971, which I'd made into collages and laminated like placemats. I also threw in something to wear to the coronation and something to wear every other day. Like the Tee-shirt, I would say, "I Recycle. I wore this shirt yesterday." And the day before. And the day before that.

Once over the International Dateline, where we dropped Tuesday and got right on to Wednesday, I was taken to a house in my former village of Ha'ateiho, where I found electricity and running water — even hot — as well as a microwave, and, gulp (or not) bottled water! Lots of bottled water with the Tonga label. The son and daughter-in-law of 'Ana, who was hosting me, were watching "Lawrence of Arabia" on television, an invention that had never been seen by most villagers back in the 1970s, when we could see English-language movies in coconut sheds that had electricity and translators with good imaginations or in Nuku'alofa, where we paid 10 sentini (about ten cents) and once saw "Romeo and Juliet" with the reels reversed, so that the lovers killed themselves for love of each other before they met. Now there were DVDs and TV. I was given a towel, a washcloth, and a cell phone, which doubled as my clock. I peeked out the window and saw a van under a canopy of net and soon noticed that in a village where people went by foot or by horse and cart back in my time, there was now a car on almost every lawn, and most of the cars were big. Well, Tongans were king size, and so were their families, but considering the price of gas, I suspected that Tongans were earning more than my 1970 living allowance of thirty-two dollars a month. I soon learned the word "Remittances." They are now the main source of income in Tonga, it turned out, where relatives living in other countries send money back for SUVS and the other fine things in life. People also hire entire shipping containers to send home things like furniture and clothes. Some of the people living abroad had been deported back (recycled?), and Tongans were concerned about this. In the US, they'd learned "bad habits" like crime, and now they were back to teach those still at home what they had learned. (Re-used?)

I quoted the headline from the *SF Chronicle*: "Gas prices turn drivers from gas guzzlers to gas sippers," but I benefitted from the big bad vans. By my third day I had contributed quite a bit to global warming, making round-trips into Nuku'alofa to see the Kava ceremony where the King was presented with about a hundred *'umued* pigs, another to go shopping at every market on Tongatapu to get food for the coronation feast, another to see the coronation itself, which turned out not to be mine (Sorry, Bob), and still one more for the Tutupakanava, the traditional torch-lighting spectacle around the wharf in honor of the newly-crowned king. I went shopping with the driver, Finau, and we must have driven to every market and store on Tongatapu to get the food that would be prepared for our village's contribution of ten tables. Everyone in the village was contributing twenty pa'anga. I "treated" at the counter whenever they'd let me. And I put what I could into the green bags.

On the day that I decided to support the bus system, after an hour of waiting I decided it wouldn't support me, and when a van full of policemen drove by, I hitched a ride back to Ha'ateiho, only I wasn't quite sure just where in Ha'ateiho the house was once we got off the main road. Didn't the police know? After leaving our carbon footprint all over the neighborhood, I called 'Ana on my cell phone, and she walked outside to where we were making the call about three yards from her door.

'Ana, who had already told me about the bad effect of deportees sent back to Tonga, told me, "We kept seeing the police drive by, and we thought they were looking for someone who'd committed a crime."

"That was me," I said, thinking of my carbon footprint. "They found me and deported me from Nuku'alofa." I gave her another green bag.

It turned out that a shop in town, near the Café Escape and just yards from empty blocks where buildings had stood before the 2006 riots, sold green bags that said "'OUA 'E TALI TANGAI MILEMILA." Don't use plastic bags. But everywhere I looked people were using them.

When I gave a green bag and a Wrap 'n' Mat to Vika, 'Ana's daughter-in-law and a doctor at the Vaiola Hospital on Tongatapu, she told me, "I remember the days when my mom would take us shopping and she's always say, 'Go get the basket.'" Were those days over?

My thoughts soon turned to water — the subject of water, that is. I found out that 'Ana and her family had had to go to their other house to get water because their tank no longer had any. I didn't understand this business of tanks. When I was in Tonga in 1970–1971, I drew water from the well and poured it a bucketful at a time into a Gerry can, and when I needed water, I scooped it out a cup at a time. But how did tanks work, and why did the house I was in still have enough? I wondered, too, if I was depleting the water supply. I visited the school where I had taught in 1970, and it seemed unchanged except for the cell phones in the teachers' hands and the vans that picked up the children who in past ages had walked to and from school; and, while there was a water tank, there wasn't enough water for the children, who were asked to bring water from home. Back in the 1970s, the children had lined up to brush their teeth. They didn't do that anymore. Water was too scarce.

I stared at the bottled water with the label Tonga on the kitchen sink — the bottles 'Ana had provided for me. I could see through them to the grassy lawn and the coconut tree. But where did they come from? Who were the bottlers? Did they deplete the water supply? What was this about ground water? Rainwater? Tanks?

I went to a beautiful new home owned by a family who had lived in a hut forty years earlier. It was a mansion. But there was no water for the toilet.

Then my Eco-Bore persona felt an assignment coming on: a research paper for any students unfortunate enough to sign up for my class instead of Bob's, where they could be writing from the point of view of Koko the Gorilla or advising George Bush on the difficulties of learning their native language if he thought English was too hard. But, hey, my students were finding web sites like tapping.com, giving not just three reasons not to consume bottled water but twenty, including that it would give you smoker's lips: those unsightly fine lines and wrinkles from constantly wrapping around an object.

THEN CAME SUNDAY, when the Tongan Constitution makes it unlawful to work. Article 6: "The Sabbath Day shall be kept holy in Tonga and no person shall practise his trade or profession or conduct any commercial undertaking. But it also stipulates that "Before the morning service, each family prepares the special meal for lunch. Different kinds of food are baked in the earth oven ('umu).

Before church I got to watch every step of the ritual of the *'umu*, the underground oven, at 'Ana's home. I'd never seen such a labor-intensive task, but since I wasn't among the laborers but did get to eat what came of it, I can say it was worth all the effort and art, and it was one hundred percent natural (if you don't count the cans of corned beef) and nothing was wasted.

Here's the recipe for an 'Umu Casserole

Preparation Time:
All morning before church on Sunday.

Serves: 50 *palangis* (non-Tongans) or 15 Tongans. (I should add that I'm a Tongan in this case.)

Ingredients:
   Banana leaves
   Taro leaves
   Hardwood
   Volcanic rocks
   Mackerel (or corned beef, beef, chicken or nothing)
   Chopped onion
   Coconut cream
   Salt
   Taro
   Breadfruit
Yams

Prepare the 'Umu: Dig a two-foot hole. Put firewood in the bottom of the pit (smaller pieces in the bottom and larger pieces on top. Wood used must be hardwood, otherwise the stones will not heat properly.) Once fire is well lit, put volcanic rocks on top. (Too many and the food will burn to a cinder and too few will mean uncooked food.)

Make 'Umu dishes (for food packages): Clean and de-rib banana leaves. Soften banana leaves by warming them over the fire.

Assemble food packages: Place taro leaves on each banana leaf. Add about 1 1/2 cup of canned mackerel or other filling (corned beef, fresh fish, beef, chicken, etc).

Add chopped onion and coconut cream.
Sprinkle with salt.
Wrap up taro and banana leaves.
Secure with a rib of banana leaf.
Identify with aluminum or other marker.
Once firewood burns down and stones are white hot, remove remaining big pieces of wood from the pit, and spread stones evenly on the bottom and sides of the pit.
Put taro, breadfruit, and yams on top of stones.
Put thin pieces of wood on top of food to ensure air circulation.
Put in food packages on top of these pieces of wood.
Cover with banana leaves.
Cover banana leaves with a flour sack or blanket.
Cover with dirt. Let bake 1/2 hour.
Serve after church.

The next day we had a the Peace Corps Reunion to celebrate the fortieth year of Peace Corps Tonga. It took place at the country director's home so close to the ocean that I had the impression of being in a houseboat under a floating palm tree. There six of us were interviewed by a reporter from the Tongan newspaper *Talaki*, and I, as the oldest Return Peace Corps Volunteer, was also interviewed for Tonga TV. I made a point to thank 'Ana Taufe'ulungaki for hosting me and even spelled her name — down to the glottal stops. I gave my Eco-bore spiel.

Two days later when I went into the Vanuatu ABC Book Store in

Nuku'alofa, the salesclerk said, "I saw you on television last night!"

"Oh, really?" I asked. "What did I say?"

"You said that we should go back to taking our baskets to market and not use plastic."

I had gotten my message across!

Next I went to the Post Office, where I passed through a door with an ad for the commemorative stamps of the coronation of Kingi Siaosi Tupou V on one side and a flyer with Barack Obama on the other, saying "U.S. President Obama? — Good for Tonga?" Following it was "Commentary by Michael G. Horowitz, Ph.D., University Dean." But it was scheduled for Monday evening August 11, the day I was leaving Tonga.

When I approached the window to buy stamps, the postal worker, not disgruntled, said, "I saw you on television last night!"

"What did I say?"

Her report was much the same, but she added, "You said you were glad we still had the 'umu."

My message had been heard! I gave back to Tonga what Tonga had given me.

When the *Talaki* came out, there were the six of us with our pictures Question Man style, responding to a question about the *"hilifaki kalauni,"* which is the coronation. (Kalauni is crown, not clown, in a language that has no r, no consonant clusters, and where every word ends in a vowel sound.) Under my picture was "Tina Martin, 62." On another page, there was a report on our impressions of Tonga, translated so that it looked as if we were speaking fluent Tonga the way we should have been.

"Oku ou faka'amu ke foki pe 'a e kakai Tonga ki he 1970 'o ngaue 'aki 'a e kato 'oku lalanga mei he louniu ke fa'o me'akai ai kae tuku atu 'a e milemila."

In other words, "Don't use plastic bags!"

Eco-Bore strikes again.

LEARNING TO READ IN TONGA

March 2019

My mornings begin at 3:00 am. A friend points out that I'm not an early riser; I'm a middle-of-the-nighter, what I became when I was in Tonga and would mistake the moonlight for the light of day and rise with what I thought was the rising sun but wasn't. Then I learned about segmented sleep from a Tongan legend named Tavi, who placed first in his engineering class of 1946 in Denmark by practicing segmented sleep and recommended it as a way to live life fully.

Here at my home in San Francisco, instead of lighting my kerosene lamp, I light the two huge candles in my fireplace—what I call vertical logs—and put my teakettle on an electric burner instead of on a kerosene stove. No need to draw water from the well or even from the Gerry can.

Then with my tea tray by my side, I start what I call my breakfast buffet of books, an assortment of reading matter that includes periodicals as well as books and, these days, my diaries from Tonga, 1970-71 and, because my son is turning 40 soon, I'm also looking at a Mother's Memory Journal I kept when I was forty and he was seven. My breakfast buffet of books usually also includes the month's selection for the JoMama Book Club, which my son Jonathan (Jo) and I (Mama) founded in 2007 so we'd have a guaranteed book discussion every month. This month, his birthday month, we're reading *The Brain that Changes Itself: Stories of Personal Triumph from the Frontiers of*

Brain Science by Norman Doidge, something recommended by Jenny Goodman, the incredible daughter of My Best Friend in Peace Corps Tonga, Andrea.

But my real reading began in Tonga, when I got the book locker we Peace Corps Volunteers were given—black cardboard shelves filled with about 250 paperback books. Going back to the 28 diaries I kept in Tonga, I see that some of those books were *Cat's Cradle, Naked Lunch, The Tin Drum. Age of Innocence, We have Always Lived in the Castle. Life with Picasso, and The Painted Bird.* Tonga was one Peace Corps country where volunteers couldn't improve their language by reading books in the target language because there were no books in Tongan except the Bible and a history book I'd never seen. English it was, and in 1970 I read seventy books. The second year I also read The Book of Mormon (because every village on my island, Tongatapu, had a white and blue Mormon church with a basket ball court) and the Bible—in English, memorizing most of The Song of Solomon.

When did I have time to read all the books I read in Tonga? "Get off to a slow start," they'd advised us in cross-cultural training, in terms of our job, not in terms of our reading. We were also advised to be people-centered, not job-oriented, if we wanted to be happy and accepted. I was dedicated to my job of teaching oral English and devoted to the children I taught, who came back with me at the end of the school day and filled my fale (FAH lay, meaning hut). I'd sometimes read aloud to them—"The Animal Book," "The Berenstein Bear Bike Lesson," "Green Eggs and Ham"—but I soon learned that they could be there contentedly talking to one another while I read silently. This was true of the whole village, always concerned that I not be lonely. They would come, and I would serve them tea or hot chocolate, and after I'd said all I knew how to say in Tongan, we'd switch to English "for the good of the children," whose academic future was determined by a test taken in English in the sixth grade. In my fale I'd teach them songs in English, then they and other visitors would start speaking in Tongan to one another, proving the adage that you can be alone in a crowd. Surrounded by Tongans, I would read, and sometimes my Tongan visitors would too, as I can see by this diary entry:

"Melaia's reading *Human Sexuality* at the moment and just asked me what *human* means."

Why had it taken Tonga and the book locker to get me reading? I'd been an English major. I came from a home where parents read. My father read mostly non-fiction—lots of politics and history—with his red pencil in hand to underline salient points even in the newspaper. My mother as a child of ten was reading books with words in small print—books like *Les Miserable* (the one written by Victor Hugo not the one produced by Cameron Mackintosh), whereas I at the age of ten—in spite of having her and my father as models— was reading, under the tutelage of my big sister Dana, *Photoplay, Modern Screen, Motion Pictures* and *True Love Comic Books*, with dialogue that was in all caps and always ending in exclamation marks. (OH! I COULD LOVE HIM MADLY!) I got through high school by asking a friend during lunch period to tell me about the book we'd been assigned and would be writing about on an essay test the next hour. In my essay, I'd show unbounded enthusiasm for the classic, and no teacher wanted to discourage an enthusiastic reader by giving less than an enthusiastic grade.

My real enthusiasm was for listening all night to long-playing records of musicals like *West Side Story, My Fair Lady, Camelot, Kismet,* and *Gypsy.* (I was giving a rest to *South Pacific* and *Oklahoma* after listening to them on 78 rpm records for several of my formative years.)

My parents' vocabulary revealed readers. Mine revealed someone who'd memorized every lyric from every Broadway show. I knew the word *convivial* only because Julie Andrews as Queen Guinevere sang about the "harmless convivial joys" of maidenhood. I knew *vacillating* only because Henry Higgins used it in "Why can't a woman be more like a man?" *Diffident* was from *Hello Dolly*, (though I incorrectly guessed it meant arrogant rather than timid). This vocabulary enrichment had begun after I saw the movie *Kismet*, which led me to *prosaic, panacea, iota, iambic, trochaic, onomatopoeia, multifarious, Burnoose, Mosque, kiosk, minaret, parapet, pertinence, miscellaneous, extraneous, caravan, Afghanistan, dromedary, Rahat Lokum, kumquat rind,* and *Mesopotamia*—and that was just one song. There was also *varicate, cogitate, genuflect.* Every word I knew I'd learned from musicals, and it was songs from musicals I taught the children in Tonga. There was no electricity, so a turntable was not a possibility. We sang a cappella—all the songs nuns and governesses teach kids in Broadway shows.

It was, in fact, probably a Broadway show that led to the name of the Jo-Mama Book Club. My son told me that he always called me Mom, not Mama, but when I quoted him, I'd say, "And Jonathan told me, 'Okay, Mama, I'll try your new dish.' And then he took a bite and put his fork down and said, 'It's delicious, Mama, but I don't think I'm quite the person to like it.'"

"I call you Mom, not Mama," he told me.

When he drew this to my attention, I figured that I'd gotten that vocabulary word from *Gypsy.* "If Mama Got Married" has nineteen Mamas. That's followed by "Rose's Turn," which has another nineteen.

My son Jonathan was willing to incorporate my misquote of him into the name of our book club because that way it would have three syllables and sound more Italian like the Jonani Duo, which my son and my mother had formed about fifteen years earlier, Jonathan on the clarinet and his Nani on the piano. Ours would be the JoMama Book Club and maybe it would help my son and me feel a little bit less the loss of the Jonani Duo, which was performing fewer concerts for the family because even though my mother could still play the piano, Alzheimer's was filling her with anxiety over their performances..

Jonathan and I began our discussions in San Francisco with *Cheating at Canasta,* a book of short stories by William Trevor. Then when Jonathan moved to New York City, we continued to meet monthly online, having "chats" that lasted three hours and printed out into 15 to 25 pages each.

We've kept the tradition of monthly "meetings" from 9 to 12 PST, and now I have eleven binders of our discussions, representing the eleven years of our club. These "transcripts" are often like a personal diary because when we start our chat, we talk about both what we've been doing and how what we've read connects to our lives—or doesn't.

When I'm in New York or Jonathan is in San Francisco, our discussions are usually in his apartment or in my house, but we occasionally have our discussions in restaurants or parks, so I have a record of where and what we ate while discussing Peter Cameron's *Someday This Pain Will Be Useful to You*, Karuki Murakami's *A Wild Sheep Chase*, Eileen Chang's *Lust, Caution*, and Ian McEwan's *Saturday*, among other books.

But going back to my 28 Tonga journals, I see how my "social life" affected my reading as much as the Peace Corps book locker did. We were told that there'd be no social life, but I definitely had one, made up of some of the smartest, funniest, most loving men I've ever known—men who enhanced my reading in a lot of ways. Here are some of the diary entries:

Jim sent me *All You Ever Wanted to Know about Sex and Were Afraid to Ask, Zelda,* and *Papillion*.

"Vincent lent me *The First Circle* but took it back when I was going on a non-reading holiday."

"Went to Vincent's house with the key he gave me—Returned *Mount Olive* and got *Clea.*"

"I'm going through a *Time Magazine* (Skinner, Sept. 20, 1971) Tavi lent me Sunday."

"Sione's house for supper. He read Antony's speech to me a couple of times and then did Brutus. I declined to read Portia's speeches. I remembered his saying that he'd read *The Sensuous Woman* and thought it was supposed to be satirical but had been assured that it

was supposed to be taken seriously."

"While Ron cooked, I read *Living Poor* aloud to him." and, on another evening, "Ron cooked while I read the cover story on Gloria Steinem in *Newsweek Magazine*.(August 16, 1971)"

Here's an illustration of what makes men like Ron so wonderful: When I said apologetically, "I just sit here and read. Shouldn't I be helping you make dinner?" Ron replied in his sardonic way, "Tina, cooking is a man's job." This was particularly nice because the cover story I was reading aloud to him was "The New Woman.")

Jim sent me a Romantic Story comic book dated December 1969 (when we were together on Hawaii) and featuring a Peace Corps Volunteer in New Guinea who says things like, "TEACHING SCHOOL ISN'T EASY...THESE CHILDREN HAVEN'T ONLY TO LEARN HOW TO READ AND WRITE BUT THEY'VE GOT TO CATCH UP ON 5,000 YEARS OF CIVILZATION IN A FEW SHORT MONTHS."

(Didn't she learn that their civilization is a valid expression of human existence? And why is an American PCV saying "haven't only to learn"?)

As I discuss books with Jonathan, it occurs to me that he's another smart, funny, loving man. When we are at odds—and we're both very gentle in our disagreement, though perhaps he's more diplomatic than I am—I think of the December before he was born, when his father and I gave each other books for Christmas and then went to a cozy cabin at Moore's Redwood in Yosemite, where I read the ones I'd given him, and he read the ones he'd given me—a reversal of "The Gift of the Magi."

I've heard laments about book clubs—that people don't read the books, that people hardly discuss them at all, that people drop out.

But our discussions are always stimulating, and our book club of two is still going strong. We always go back to particular passages that made an impression, sometimes going through the books chapter-by-chapter and sometimes by theme.

We occasionally read a classic, as we did recently with John Steinbeck's *Of Mice and men*. We more often read contemporary fiction like the novels *Go, Went, Gone by* Jenny Erpenbeck, *Transit* by Rachel Cusk, and *Less* by Andrew Sean Greer and short stories like "Krakatau" by Jim Shepard and those in Alice Munro's *Dear Life*. The plays we've read include those by Shakespeare, Moliere, T.S. Elliot, and Anouilh— *Much Ado about Nothing*, *The Misanthrope*, *Tartuffe* , *Murder in the Cathedral*, and *Becket* . But we've also read more contemporary plays like Annie Baker's *The Flick* and Stephen Karam's *The Humans*.

Just as frequently we read non-fiction, including Ann Fadiman's *Ex Libris* and Ann Patchet's *This Is the Story of a Happy Marriage*, *Lit Up* by David Denby, and *Books for Living* by Will Schwalbe. The choices we make are sometimes seasonal. We read *Joy Luck Club* for Mother's Day in 2010 and *This Is for You, Mom, Finally* by Ruth Reichl in 2018. In December 2013 *A Literary Christmas: Great Contemporary Christmas Stories* (published in 1994) and in 2017 *A Christmas Carol* because my son had never read anything by Charles Dickens.

Our book choices can also be political. After the 2016 election, we read and discussed *What We Do Now: Standing Up for Your Values in Trump's America*.

Jonathan managed to get us tickets for *Hamilton* in NYC in September 2015, so we had a special discussion of Jeremy McCarter and Lin Manuel Miranda's *Hamilton The Revolution*, reading the text together as we listened again to the songs here in San Francisco.

We also read books by authors we know, notably Manfred Wolf, Daniel Handler, David Hathwell, and Alex Capus. Alex Capus is a Swiss writer I met when he was writing *Sailing by Starlight,* which included a chapter on Tavi. who also got the attention of Leif Moller, who made a documentary on Tavi. I met Leif Moller and his crew in

San Francisco, but my German pen pal from 1963 Jutta Brockhaus and I made a pilgrimage to see Alex Capus in 2014—all the way to Olten, Switzerland. Jutta was reading his most recent novel in German (a language I don't know at all) when she and I got together in Paris in 2016. My son and I read two of his earlier books, the non-fiction *Skiddo: A Journey through the American West* and the novel *Leon and Louise*.

Our book choices sometimes relate to a trip we've taken; we read Graham Greene's *A Quiet American* after visiting Vietnam. Sometimes they're related to a present concern or in honor of someone. After my mother's death, we chose *A Tree Grows in Brooklyn* because she had loved that book so much. Earlier, when she had been diagnosed with Alzheimer's, we read *Still Alice*, Alzheimer's from the perspective of the one afflicted, and Martin Suter's *Small World*, a novel about a man whose Alzheimer's replaces his short-term memory with long-term so that he recalls a sinister past wrong that he can now set right. But guess which book most resonated in terms of my mother? The book of the Broadway musical *Next to Normal*, which I kept recommending to friends going to New York City.

"If you want a really good musical about mental illness—" I'd say.

"If you're looking for a musical about a bipolar mother—" I'd begin.

So few did. So few were. But Jonathan and I made that our book club selection in June 2010, when I visited him in New York City and we saw the play *Next to Normal*. By that time *Next to Normal* had won the Grammy for Best Score and the Pulitzer Prize for Drama.

For Mother's Day 2015 my son answered my question, "Of the 80+ books we've read together, which were your favorites?" (I sent him the complete list.) His answer came in a pdf and then a Word file "onT heWorld'sBestMotherBookClub," only temporarily altering the name of the JoMama Book Club. His favorites were *Being Wrong, Brooklyn, Dear Life, Freedom, How to Live, or a Life of Montaigne in One Question and Twenty Attempts at an Answer, Olive Kitteridge, Saturday, Survival in Paradise, Then We Came to the End* , and *What Is the What* by (respectively) Kathryn Schultz, Colm Toibin, Alice Munro, Jonathan Frazen, Sarah Bakewell, Elizabeth Strout, Ian McEwan, Manfred Wolf, Joshua Ferris, and Dave Eggers. It's time for us to update this to include the latest three and a half years—and my list. *Less! Less! Less*!

For my 70th birthday in 2015 we read something I wrote—(Kinko-bound)—that appears in this volume: To *Whom It May Concern: I Am Your Mother*, a short novel in the form of a letter a Peace Corps Volunteer in Tonga writes in 1970 to the baby she is giving up for adoption, telling about the three men who may be his or her father. She doesn't know the gender, so she includes in her Peace Corps adaptation of *South Pacific*, to the tune of "There Is Nothing Like a Dame" this verse: There is something in my womb./Something I can't name./I address it as "To Whom"/Is To Whom a guy or a dame?") The letter also recommends musicals, poems, and even books for To Whom to read.

When I took a creative writing course in All about My Family and Other Difficult Subjects, my classmates criticized my essay about the JoMama Book Club for not having enough conflict, so I'm trying to find some. Certainly Jonathan and I go at different speeds when we type our responses. We Martins rush in. We're quick and careless. My son is very thoughtful and cautious. As a baby, he would crawl to the threshold of a room and look inside until he really knew the territory and all the inhabitants. I marveled at this and still do.

On an online chat, I write faster than he does—whatever comes into my head comes out into the chat box. If I'm impatient seeing those three little dots that mean he's writing as I wait for him to enter that thought, I can go to the kitchen and make a snack.

I'd been impatient with him when he was a toddler too. His little friend Jessica was already identifying types of dinosaurs, Stegosaurus, Tyrannosaurus, Diplodocus, Coelophysis. Jonathan hadn't yet said "Cat." When, at the age of two, he started talking, he spoke in well-crafted paragraphs (he'd had two years for his mental rough drafts), but it was a year later that his kindergarten teacher came running out of the school to tell me, "Jonathan talked today!" Why had he held out at nursery school for an extra year? I felt there was some catching up to do, so when I read him his bedtime story, I'd occasionally point to a word to see whether he could decode it.

"Mom, just read," he told me.

From then on I did, and if you are a nervous parent or know of any, please note that a kid who says "Cat!" when he sees a raccoon and "eyebrows" when he sees a cat's ears can still grow up to get into Berkeley and graduate at the top ten percent of his class. He can even mature enough not to let anyone know about the Phi Beta Kappa key he was offered but declined—something his mother would have worn proudly had she learned to read in time to graduate Phi Beta Kappa.

Jonathan expresses disagreement with me from time to time, but he does it kindly. (Do you think my ideas will be ridiculed by a son who says, "It's delicious, Mom. I just don't think I'm quite the person to like it"?) I have more of an edge to my personality, but I usually find his comments enlightening rather than off-track, so it's easy for me to show respect for his opinions and his take on what we read.

I do have one regret: This book club that brings us together every month also appears to be an excuse for his waiting to respond to my messages. I notice that when he's visiting here, he's in touch with his girlfriend more than once a day. He doesn't respond to my messages on a daily basis. He usually waits, and if our monthly meeting of the JoMama Book Club is coming up, he waits for that.

When I first heard a mother say that she spoke to her daughter on the phone every day at least once, I thought that must be a foreign custom because my own mother didn't do that, and I wasn't doing that with Jonathan. Then I heard another and then another American-born mother speak of these daily calls, so I mentioned this to Jonathan, who showed shock and fear and assured me, "Mom, you're doing just fine!"

The morning after our online discussion, I read over what we've said and often send him a follow-up message, which he doesn't answer for a few days. He's quicker in responding to my calls for help—concerns about my brother, computer problems, and things like that. When I asked him, eight years after his move to New York City, whether he thought he'd ever move back to the Bay Area, he said, "Oh, yeah. For sure!" When I asked, "When?" he paused for just a moment and said, somberly, "When you need me."

Most women worry about appearing "needy" to the men in their lives when these men are not their sons! I don't want my son to communicate with me out of duty or sympathy. I want to be a mother whose son enjoys her and comes to her in time of his need. Reading over "A Mother's Journal" which I started keeping when he was seven, I see an entry about thanking him for being observant and noticing things I might fail to notice. "You really help me a lot sometimes," I said, and he replied, "Well, you help me a lot sometimes too."

I'd thought that was my job, to help him, all the time.

Now that we're both full-fledged adults, I see that helping each other applies to our book discussions. We help each other see things the other might have missed, and I think for the most part, the JoMama Book Club is something we both enjoy.

So I marvel at this: Though *Everything I Should Have Learned I Could Have Learned in Tonga* implies that I failed to learn what I should have and could have, I can call this chapter "Something I Managed to Learn among Many Things I Could Have Learned in Tonga." The joy of reading— then with the Peace Corps book locker and those wonderful men and now with the JoMama Book Club and a wonderful forty-year-old son.

I focus more on wonderful women later.

A Letter to the Sanity Shrink Following the Death of My Brother

Is a dreamworld a valid expression of human existence?

June 28, 2019

Dear Dr. Reshon,

This letter is, in a way, inspired by a 90+-year-old friend I have who, back in the 1960's, wrote a 158-page letter to her son's therapist. She let me read it last month, right before I left San Francisco to go to a 55th high school reunion. But I don't think my letter will be that long because you're not my son's therapist, I can't type that fast, and I'm going to my brother's visitation in 12 hours. Also, I'm not as brilliant as my

90+-year-old friend. I don't think I could hold your attention for one hundred and fifty-eight pages. But fifty years ago I held your attention for fifty minutes.

I'm attaching a portrait my brother David did of me. even though it's not a perfect likeness, to help you remember me after fifty years. I know what you're thinking: "As if I needed any help!" (That's joke. When I visited you in 1969, you didn't know a joke when I made one.) I visited you again in 2008, but only in my imagination, before I went back to Tonga for the first time since my Peace Corps "service" there in 1970 and 1971. (I put "service" in quotation marks because I'm not sure exactly how I served although I loved teaching songs from Broadway musicals to the children there. ESL English as a Singing Language. My brother David could sing the alphabet but not say it. He and I had things in common.)

But back in 1969, I really did meet you—in a hotel room in San Jose, where we Peace Corps recruits were getting our mental health evaluated to make sure we weren't too risky to send to Molokai for training. I was thinking that our sanity tests were only fifteen minutes, but now that I've found the diary I kept in training, I realize each recruit had 50 minutes. That gave you a little bit more time to make me cry and then comfort me. (I'm writing this facetiously. No one *makes* me do anything. I'm almost 74 years old, and I realize that I am the captain of my soul and the master of my fate. Wasn't I that back in my early twenties?)

Maybe you remember that in staging, we each had an appointment with you or another psychologist, waiting for us in various motel rooms there. I thought it was funny, and I thought it was an ice breaker when I said, "Well, it's not every day I'm asked to see a man alone in his motel room." But you didn't laugh. You thought I was trying to seduce you.

I won't go into all the details of our 1969 sanity session. If you're curious you can read my memoir, *Everything I Should Have Learned I Could*

Have Learned in Tonga, which I hope to get out this year, the 50th anniversary of that sanity test I somehow passed in spite of describing the members of my family. And in spite of breaking down when we came to my brother, David. I'm in the process of writing my memoir, but now I just want to get it off even though I know it's not ready. I don't want to work on it any more. I want to work on my brother's life and make his dreams come true now that it's too late. You've heard of paper sons, deceit and counterfeit making possible a brighter future. I'm trying for a better past for my brother. When I talked to you in 1969, he wasn't yet twenty and had been a patient at Napa for only a year. He died this past Saturday at the age of seventy, locked up somewhere else.

Back in 1969 you had me describe all members of my family. But in a way, David is a portrait of our family. He's sort of like the picture of Dorian Gray—not Dorian Gray, who stayed young and handsome, but the portrait itself, taking on not David's character defects but ours. Mine.

I'm writing to you on this day of the visitation, when I'll see my brother for the last time.

I'm writing because among all the things I should have and could have learned in Tonga is something I did learn, from you, even before I was out of staging: the best way to find out about a person is to have them describe the people in their family. I'm going to begin—and maybe even end (my friend Beth is picking me up in 12 hours) by describing my brother, and maybe the best way to describe him is in terms of his dreams.

DAVID

My social studies teacher in junior high school, Barbara Langford (later Hayes) told us that we should never give the date a person died at the beginning of a report on that person. George Washington was born on February 22, 1732nd died on December 14, 1799. We should keep the date of death until the end. I don't think she meant that it would be a plot spoiler. She probably had a good reason, but I'm going to begin with David's death, which was last Saturday, June 22, 2019.

We were mourning his loss long before then because he'd had a really hard last couple of years. Not that the rest of his life was easy. After all, it was when we came to his name on the list in 1969 that I burst into tears. Back then he'd been a patient at Napa for just one year, and he was not yet twenty-one years old. Now he's no longer living, dead at seventy.

My son Jonathan and I are planning two memorial services for David— one at his care facility with his care-givers and one at home with our friends who really didn't know him but care about him—and us. We'll keep it upbeat at the urging of my son Jonathan, who doesn't want to mourn David's life the way some mourn a death.

We'll focus on what gave him pleasure, what seemed to make him happy. Favorite TV shows. Until he couldn't seem to see them. Eating. Until he couldn't hold his fork. Chew until he lost his short-term memory and forgot he was addicted. The Beatles. Until he no longer knew who they were. Our visits, even after he no longer knew who we were or who he was. And we'll focus on the caregivers who made his life as good as it could be these last few years. They're my heroes.

I don't know how to write an obituary about this brother I loved, who spent most of his life in mental institutions, who had well-defined dreams that didn't come true. But in the past few days, the dining room table has become a huge altar. I always have flowers there. I can see them from my study and then look out over them to the front window and the beautiful park across the street. Isn't that good feng shui?

But I've added framed photos of him and the cards people have started sending.

The books and stories we connected with David are piled up now.

Flowers for Algernon and *The Light in the Piazza*. In one the protagonist gets an operation to make him smarter. In the other, a mother finds a way to get her brain-damaged daughter a "normal" life married to a privileged Italian. I used to wish that we could "find a girl" for David to marry, as he would ask our father—the way the mother in *The Light in the Piazza* does (at first unintentionally) for her daughter with the mental age of ten.

Of Mice and Men makes me wish that David had had what the intellectually slow Lennie has— a buddy with whom he forms a working team because Lenny is strong, and as his friend George says "He's dumb as hell, but he ain't crazy." David wasn't, in the beginning, "dumb" at all, but he was brain damaged. He wasn't crazy either, in the beginning, although his medicine made him dopey, and he often had a faraway look in his eyes.

He was better-functioning than Benji, so I haven't included *The Sound and the Fury*. He didn't have historic good fortune, so I haven't included *Forrest Gump*.

Maybe most representative is The *Idiot* not just because, like Dostoevsky, Prince Myshkin had severe epileptic seizures, but because he was in Dostoevsky words "a positively good and beautiful man." One day after we'd given David a little bit of pocket money for his "money in my pocket" wish, we happened to pass a "Save this child" donation jar, prompting David to empty his pocket into the jar. Then looking doubtful, he asked, "Was that a stupid thing to do?" We were touched that he wasn't smug about being generous but rather self-critical about his impulse to give— like an idiot. David had, like Myshkin, an open-hearted simplicity and guilelessness.

My son Jonathan and I read *The Light in the Piazza* with David in mind. I used to think that maybe David could "pass" for normal, but as soon as my friends met him for the first time, they'd pick up on his "uniqueness" and look at me sympathetically. That happened in

Mexico, where I was living with a Mexican family while doing volunteer work in Zamora, Michoacán back in 1967, and my father drove down (more than 2000 miles!) with David. I'd told my Mexican sister that I had a brother who was her age, and she was interested. But as soon as she saw David, she looked alarmed and gave me a "Why didn't you tell me?" look. Another time Mother brought David by to see me in the home where I was renting a room after returning from Mexico for the fall semester of school. David giggled a lot, and after he and my mother left, my landlady said, "He's a jolly one, isn't it." I nodded in agreement, happy to see that she'd interpreted his laughter as good humor, but then she added, "He's not quite right, is he, dear."

It just occurred to me that I should have a book that David himself read, a skill we'd been told he'd never develop because of his brain damage. But a reading specialist visited David one summer and taught him to read, a skill that brought him a lot of pleasure, whether it was the want ads he'd read around Thanksgiving, when we let him circle what he'd like for his December birthday and Christmas, or a simple Word Find book. He seemed to need to read—unless I'm projecting. *I* need to read, the way I need to write. I've kept notebooks for decades, and I simply have to write. I know you're not a neurologist, but have you read the book *Midnight Disease: The Drive to Write?* (Here I am, driven to write to a psychologist I met in a motel room fifty years ago.)

David also liked to read the magazines we'd get him like an anniversary issue of World War II or a magazine about the Beatles, the musicians he enjoyed the most.

But when I think back on our childhood, I know there were two stories our parents associated with him. My father told my sister Dana and me, when we were both under the age of ten, that the poem "Little Boy Blue," made him think of David, and I wondered why. At that time David had been having seizures for a couple of years, and he often had a faraway look in his eyes. But in the poem, I understood that the little boy had died after tucking his toys in bed.

"And while he was dreaming an angel song awakened our little boy blue."

David wasn't dead then. Did that "angel song" mean that his mind was being carried away from his body? Or did our father think that David would die from too many seizures, those brutal attacks on his brain?

Our mother said the short story "Silent Snow, Secret Snow" made her think of David. In that story, a boy simply chooses to leave reality and live in his own world, a world of snow, beautiful white snow, like a blizzard in his brain that finally settles down and buries him. I'd like to think that David was entranced, enchanted, bewitched, not disturbed and haunted by what went on in his mind.

Maybe he was entranced, enchanted, bewitched. Maybe he found something beautiful and comforting in his life away from us and our reality.

I just thought of something I should add to the altar—Anne Frank, a person he admired and maybe identified with to some extent. Had he had to go into hiding?

But to get back to how my dining room table has become an altar. Beside the pile of books are a lot of binders. The binder I kept of all the documents needed to renew his conservatorship each year. The binder of the quarterly reviews. The binder of letters he and our father exchanged over the years. (My father kept all of David's letters as well as carbons of what he wrote to David.) Binders of David's art work, most of it done at NIAD, the National Institute of Art and Disabilities, but also a self-portrait he did when he was a younger man at Napa and still had hope of a future.

I've already shown you the picture he painted of me. He also made me a teapot. The most beautifully obscene and masculine teapot I've ever seen.

I've spent the hours since his death making collages of him— as a child, as an adolescent, with his caretakers, his art.

I've made an album of pictures of him from birth until shortly before his death, and I just want to turn the pages and talk about him.

I feel this intense "Hurry up! Please! It's time!" urgency. As if my death were encroaching and I'd better get finished with my brother's death before I go gentle into this good night myself, which I plan to do in spite of Dylan Thomas' order not to. I want a good death, a gentle and accepting death. And I want my brother to have after his death what he didn't have when he was living.

I want the world to know him. I want him to be my saddest confession. I'll put him online, narrating a slide show as a tribute to his care-givers and to David's courage and character. His character in loving us in spite of our failure to rescue him and his courage in continuing to live after his dreams had died—unless they didn't die. Unless he found a way to live somewhere else in his mind. "The mind is a terrible thing to waste." So let's use it to the highest heights of our imagination.

That's what's at the center of the altar. His dreams, as he expressed them in a composition written for his special ed class.

My son Jonathan, who will be coming here from NYC for the memorial, doesn't think we should mention or show what David wrote when he had those dreams in front of him because it's just too sad, too much like a mourning for our "upbeat" memorial service. But I'll share this with you.

Our father saved this, written in what looks like the handwriting of a third-grader. David wrote it in 1968, when he was nineteen years old—just months from when he self-admitted to Napa State Hospital, where my mother and I helped him "check in." He probably thought that they would cure him of his psychomotor epilepsy and then discharge him so he could get on with his life. I don't remember what we thought—just that he would be safe there—maybe until we could find a better "solution." We'd already tried a board and care home, which had given him more freedom—the freedom to take a walk along the freeway, where the police had found him, looking disoriented and battered—maybe from foul play, maybe from a seizure.

Anyway, getting back to David's dreams, I found them clearly stated in a composition he wrote for a special ed class his last year of high school—about why he was in school and what he wanted out of life.

Dear Mrs. French,

I am in school because I want to learn. I want to learn how to get along with people. I want to be a good citizen. I want people to like me. I want to learn math and history. I want to be a good father to my kids. I want to get a good job when I get out of school. I want to get a nice home. I am working on math. I am in school to learn so when I get out I will be ready for a job. I want to be smart. I want to learn and at the same time have fun. I want a good job. One that pays good. And I want to have money in my pocket.

David Elmore Martin

Now I want to grant those wishes in some soul-saving imaginary way if only on paper to be cremated with his battered and bruised body. If I could sew (you should see the pocket I made!), I'd make a patchwork quilt out of his dreams. But instead, I've made a collage of images in paper.

Money in my pocket

"Money in my pocket." That has always been the easiest of his wishes to make come true. We always gave him spending money even when he wasn't getting out and had no place to spend it. He could fold the bills and let the loose change jingle in his pocket—until he could no longer use his hands and had to be put in a hospital gown. He died in a hospital gown that had no pockets, so I've made him one. I'm determined that he will leave this world with money in his pocket—and with some of his dreams tucked in there too—along with a pocket watch and Jane Seymour, wishes that came later.

It was after he'd been a patient at Napa for a few years that he wrote this to our father after Daddy's insistence that he "Write out a plan."

1. **Get out of the hospital.**
2. **Get a good job. You and I were talking about me a postman.**
3. **Or maybe I could be a board and care home owner.**
4. **When I get the job as a postman or a board and care home owner, I will get married. I do not want to run blindly into this.**
5. **I would like very much to go on a trip and find a girl. I ain't crazy. I know what I want in life!**

Once when David was hospitalized on the brink of death (changed medicine, pneumonia, status epilepticus), he told the doctor, "I'd like you to cure my epilepsy while I'm here. I can't get married if I have seizures."

The doctor replied, "Well, there are a lot of people with epilepsy who have good marriages."

"And there are a lot of people without epilepsy who don't," I, twice divorced, intoned.

"There are two things I'd like to do," David told the doctor. "Stop the seizures and grow some hair." By that time he was balding and looking for hair growth products at Walgreen's. He was also looking for Jane Seymour.

Somewhere in Time

At least a decade after he'd been a patient at Napa (with "intermissions" when we tried and failed to find alternatives like board-and-care homes) David's favorite movie was "Somewhere in Time," a time-travel story, and I believe he imagined himself in the role that Christopher Reeves played, the handsome man who wanted to go back in time to meet the Jane Seymour beauty from 1912.

I see that in a letter to our father on April 16, 1990 he was fantasizing this. This was a letter he dictated. It was very hard for him to form words in writing. Even signing his name was laborious. Anyway, he said in a dictated letter he signed, "I know what I want for my birthday: to go to the Grand Hotel up at the opposite end of where Dana lives. It's on an island."

Dana is our older sister, who lives outside of Chicago, also on Lake Michigan like the beautiful Grand Hotel on Mackinac Island.

That's where "Somewhere in Time" was filmed. It came out in 1980. Had he been fantasizing about it for a decade?

No one took him to the Grand Hotel, but my mother, Jonathan, and I did take him to a hotel in Reno, closer by, around 2001, when he told us that his birthday wish was to go to a hotel, something I'd never heard him request before. (At that time I hadn't seen his letter to our father.) He also wanted a pocket watch, like the one the Christopher Reeves character had been given by a mysterious old woman calling him back to her youth.

When we got to the hotel in Reno and were retiring for the night, David clutched his pocket watch, closed his eyes and counted, but he never left the year that we were in. The only traveling back he did was to his care facility, the neurobehavioral center where he lived— unless the dementia that came later took him somewhere else. It didn't look to us like somewhere better.

I printed out a picture of David at his most handsome about forty years ago—wearing a three-piece suit as he always did when he came home— and one of him smoking a pipe and looking professorial, and I've put him in a scene from "Somewhere in Time," standing beside a close-up of Jane Seymour's beautiful face, where Christopher Reeve once stood, and sitting with her by the water.

I WANT TO LEARN

David did learn. He learned to read after we'd been told that he was too brain damaged to learn but a reading specialist wanted to give it a try. I don't know where she came from, and I'm not sure how old he was when she worked that miracle. I picture her sitting in the back yard with David and a book that he did learn to read. For years after that reading brought him a lot of pleasure. I'm sure he never learned to read with much speed. When he was given a battery of tests at Napa, the notes said that it took him two hours to complete 47 items, so they started reading the questions aloud to him. I'm surprised that he was able to do 47 items in two hours.

But he could decipher words and read captions until he got totally out of practice. When his vision failed, they couldn't keep a pair of glasses on him, and even though we always brought a pair of reading glasses when we visited him, they quickly disappeared, and reading matter must have become a blur.

But our sister Dana says that at one time when she and her husband visited him—we can't figure out the year but she didn't see him often— they took him to Walgreen's, where she was astounded to hear him reading aloud what was written on medicine bottles. I haven't learned to do that. Have you?

I WANT TO GET A NICE HOME

I'm not sure where David was living at the time he wrote this composition, January 1968. I thought he was at home, our mother's home, after our parents separated and our father moved to the East Coast. Maybe by then he was in the board and care facility our mother found for him after she got her full-time job and couldn't look after him all day when he wasn't being supervised in his special ed classes.

But just six months after he wrote this composition his "nice home" was a ward at Napa State Hospital and then, when Napa was closed to all but hardened criminals, a neurobehavioral center.

When he was at Napa, David commented more than once that he had "the life of Riley." Is that a phrase he heard from someone who had a job on the ward taking care of David and other patients? Did David really believe that, or was he being sardonic? He had a sense of irony. I looked up the expression and found that it means "living the easy life, an existence marked by luxury and a carefree attitude." Once our older sister Dana commented that David's goal in life was "to make the least effort possible." I used to stare at a pot shot by Ashleigh Brilliant, my favorite epigrammist (Oscar Wilde comes second) that said, "It's good to know that, if I behave strangely enough, society will take care of me."

David was "taken care of." But something tells me it wasn't the life of Riley.

I guess the nicest home David ever had was our mother's, where he'd come back for holidays and his birthday. Our father at one time talked about their building a cabin together, out in the woods, where David could have a dog. I never saw our father put a hammer to a nail. His way of putting up a picture was to scotch tape it on a wall. But he talked about building that cabin in the woods with David. A place where David would have freedom of movement, in the great outdoors. That was going to be after our father's retirement.

I don't think David's fantasy was a cabin in the woods with our father but maybe with Jane Seymour, Dr. Quinn, Medicine Woman, a later version of the beautiful actress at the Grand Hotel on Mackinac Island. That cabin in the woods grew to mythic proportions. By the time Daddy retired, it was too late. So I Googled "cabin in the woods" to add that to the money in his pocket, and it turns out that there's a horror picture by that name. I Googled again and used a different picture. Then I pasted "Somewhere in Time" next to the cabin.

I WANT TO LEARN TO GET ALONG WITH PEOPLE…
I WANT PEOPLE TO LIKE ME

When he was in school, kids made fun of him. When he was in his early teens, three years younger than me, and we lived in South Carolina, he said, "The kids would be a lot nicer to me if they knew I had a famous sister." He meant me. He didn't know that kids in junior high and high school had made fun of me too—often for being too eager, too friendly, too "open" even before that became a term. I'd gotten through the mocking and bullying and started appearing in amateur productions in Columbia's Town Theater and winning offices and awards by the time I was a junior in high school, so he'd see me in *The Columbia Record*, our small-town newspaper, where the Kennedys and other famous people appeared (though not in the school section), so he thought I was famous like them. He said, in reference to a TV commercial at that time (early 1960's) "If I were Tina, I'd be sailing down the highway on Firestone tires!"

You can see why I loved him. He thought I was so much more than I was, and he made TV commercials his own. He had a good imagination. I hope it served him well.

Around the time he wrote that composition on what he wanted from life, he was a senior in high school in Pleasant Hill, California, where we'd moved in 1966, and he was about to graduate from special ed classes. When the prom was approaching, two girls called him on the telephone and said they wanted him to take them to the prom. David was elated. They told him where to get them corsages and what time to show up. You might say that it was like something out of "Carrie" except that the cruelty was bloodless, and David didn't have telekinetic powers to get revenge. He was too guileless even to want to. Our mother stopped the prank while the girls were still on the phone, ending the dream before it could become a nightmare.

But years before that our mother said he could be duped out of anything in his effort to get people to like him. She said she was afraid to send his Dilantin to school with him for fear he'd give up his mid-day dosage in his attempt to make a friend. Once at a quarterly review, his case worker from the regional center asked, "And David, do you have any friends here?" David looked startled and just said, 'Friends?' As if he'd heard that word before but couldn't quite remember what it meant.

But he did have a friend once, a psychologist friend of our father who befriended David. He used to take David out to get something to eat and just talk. Later, David would tell me what they talked about. David was fifteen then, and he was wondering why parts of his body were behaving in new ways. "Jim told me a boner is the Good Lord's way of telling you what girl to marry," David told me.

Jim, that psychologist-friend of our father who befriended David, had an unusual last name—Rybeck. I see that in a letter to our father David mentioned wanting to take a trip and visit Jim Rybeck. So I Googled Jim Rybeck, and I found a couple of addresses for him. This letter to you is taking a long time, but I plan to write a letter to him and send it to both addresses—after I finish this letter to you and after the visitation. I want this man to know how much his friendship meant to David.

I wanted to be David's friend, too, and I wish I could have been closer to him physically and just held him. But whenever I gave him a hug, he'd give me his lecherous grin and laugh. It frightened me because an incestuous closeness wasn't what I had in mind with my artist-brother, who made me a teapot with an erection.

David worried about my getting raped. He advised me to carry pepper spray with me wherever I went because, he said, "You're getting to be a very pretty girl, and one of these days some guys are going to want to rape you."

Anyway, he did have one moment of triumph in that wish to learn to get along with people. Early on at Napa, I guess when he was about twenty years old, he was elected president of his ward. He was advocating for the patients who elected him, and when I praised him for doing so much to help them, he said, "That's what I'm here for." (Later, when our mother was in a facility for people with dementia, she thought the people around her were her clients. Let's hear it for defense mechanisms, even if they're insane.)

The psychologist who wrote up the testing results had this to say: "Mr. Martin related well to the examiner. He was friendly and cooperative." That's getting along with people.

I think he knew that we liked him as well as loving him. We "got along with" him and I hope it wasn't just because, after he left home at nineteen, we weren't charged with being his real caregivers. I have a lot of photos of his caregivers smiling at him and him grinning back. Is that getting along with them? Is that being liked?

I WANT TO BE A GOOD CITIZEN.

He wanted to be a good citizen, and he was. In my imaginary return to the Motel Room Sanity Test Site in 2008, I reported on how he was following the upcoming election and liked Obama, who'd just won enough caucuses to be the presumed presidential nominee from the

Democratic Party. But he was concerned about the dashed hopes of "the lady whose destiny was to be president." He was paying attention and he cared. I wonder whether he ever had the chance to vote. I'm pretty sure he didn't vote in 2016. By then he was probably not "qualified" because of his rapid cognitive decline. (If only more people with cognitive decline had been disqualified.)

One of my favorite memories was when we got him a weekend pass from Napa one summer in 1973 and took him to Stinson Beach one weekend, and he told me that his ward hadn't been able to see the movie they wanted to see because they didn't have enough psychiatric technicians to take them. (It was *Brigadoon* of all things! Sort of like *Somewhere in Time*! Love transcending time!) He told me that he wished that I could get a job there as a psychiatric technician "because you're kind, you get along with people, and you're every bit as pretty as Susan Dey on *The Partridge Family*." (That was a popular TV program in those days. I hope he had some beautiful life experiences through TV, with TV families.) Anyway, that's when he said, "But that bastard Ronald Reagan has cut our funds, so we don't have enough technicians." I commiserated, saying, "Yes, Governor Reagan is really one sick politician!" and he said, very calmly and thoughtfully, "Yes, he may be sick. But if he were a patient and you were a technician, you'd have to treat him decently, just like anybody else."

Now if that's not a good citizen, I don't know what is. So I've folded that story into the pocket I made for him, along with the collage of him and Jane Seymour beside the cabin in the woods where he can have a dog.

I WANT TO LEARN MATH AND HISTORY.

He could add and subtract for a while. I don't think he ever got to multiplication and division. But history he did learn—at least through the Second World War. He was always fighting the Nazis. He used to have dreams that I was a nurse, and the Nazis were trying to rape me. But he paid attention to documentaries and looked over intently (reading?) the magazines we got for him that featured special battles and treaties—something like *Life Magazine's 100 People Who Changed the World*. The last real book I saw him reading was one about Anne Frank, another brave and innocent person in a locked facility. He learned.

I WANT TO BE A GOOD FATHER TO MY KIDS.

Of course, he never had a family except ours (if we don't count the ones on TV). We praised him for being a good uncle to his nieces and nephews, but the truth is that he rarely saw them except in photos with the exception of my son Jonathan. I have a picture of him holding Jonathan both when Jonathan was an infant and when Jonathan was about three years old. After that Jonathan was really nice to him but more as a caregiver than as someone David could take care of, be a substitute father to. Jonathan was directly involved in helping David through a nasty experience that must have been humiliating to him. He struck out at Jonathan, who was trying to help him. When our mother and her partner Kathy could no longer have David spend the night in our "ancestral home" (bought 1966), we celebrated Christmas at my house, and David spent the night but didn't make it to the bathroom for a bowel movement Jonathan was trying to help him clean up. The next morning when his social worker Kazuko asked, "So how was Christmas?" David said, "Awful." When she asked him why, he said, "I don't want to talk about it." So David, who wanted to be a "good father to my kids," was instead the "charge" of his nephew Jonathan. Another nephew, Karl, was also good with David, but he came into the picture after David was in his fifties, and as with Jonathan, the roles were reversed, and it wasn't David who was the good father.

I'm not sure that David ever even had sex other than the kind people have all alone. (I hope no one told him that it would cause hair to grow on the palm of his hands or was the cause of his being on a mental ward, in the first place, at Napa, where he couldn't have sex with anyone else.). What chance did he have? In more than one letter to our father, he asked that they go on a trip "So I can meet a girl and get married." But as far as I know, he never met a girl. I think early in the time he served at Napa State Hospital, they told us of a girl on the ward and how they were doing their best to keep David and this girl apart. How sad for David and the girl to be so well-protected!

But I really don't think he ever had contact with women in a sexual sense except those on the pages of *Playboy Magazine*, which he'd get with that money in his pocket, usually at Walgreen's or Walden Books, where we'd take him after lunch on the days we took him out. At his neurobehavioral center, he taped pictures of these nude women on the wall over his bed. When a staff member asked during a quarterly review, "David, do you really think you should have up those pornographic pictures on your walls?" David replied, "I think they're groovy."

He'd kept that word groovy from the Summer of Love, the year before he was admitted to Napa State Hospital.

Later, there were no *Playboy Magazines* around, but he found pictures of women in magazines and held them close to his mouth, whispering suggestively, more than "sweet nothings," until he could no longer whisper or even hold the magazines. I wonder where his mind went then.

I WANT TO GET A GOOD JOB—ONE THAT PAYS GOOD.

His death certificate will say under *usual employment* "never worked."

He mentions a job three times. "A good job—one that pays good."

At first, he wanted to be a brain surgeon, as in "physician, heal thyself." Then he wanted to be a highway patrolman, like the police officers who picked him up when he was wandering along the freeway before we restricted his freedom to wander along freeways. He had had a brutal reality check that he related to me. He'd asked someone at the hospital if by some miracle he someday no longer had seizures, whether he could become a highway patrolman and wear a gun.

David reported, "He told me 'Nope.' Just 'Nope' and nothing to go with it."

He then said he might be a board-and-care owner, like the one who'd housed him until he made his escape. There was some talk of his working at a post office or carrying mail. But he never had a job beyond educating us and finding something to live for in a 24/7 locked facility.

I WANT TO BE SMART.

It was a good insight on David's part that when we share our hopes and are told "nope," we need something to go with it, something to soften the blow! David wanted to be smart, and sometimes he was, and I loved him for his insights and the sometimes poetic way he expressed them before he lost the use of language in his last two years.

I WANT TO BE SMART.

That battery of tests they gave him in 1992 must have been killing, soul-destroying. I have their write-up. He went in for testing for nine days in May and June, just a few months before they started letting us know that Napa was going to close. Were they trying to "ascertain" whether he could live independently?

It was really a battery, as in assault and battery.

ASSESSMENTS UTILIZED:
    Diagnostic Interview/Chart Review
    Neurobehavioral Mental Status Examination (NMSE)
    Wescsler Adult Intelligence Scale-Revived (WAIS-R)

Minnesota Multiphasic Personality Inventory (MMPI)

Rorschach Ink Blots Test (Rorschach)

Trail Making Parts A& B (Trails A & B)

Reitan-Indiana Aphasia Screening Test (Aphasia Screen)

Reitan-Kover Sensory-Perceptual Exam (Tactile, Auditory, Visual,
Tactile finger recognition, and Finger Trip number writing)

Lateral Dominance Examination

Advanced Progressive Matrices Set I ((Raven)

California Verbal Learning Test (CVLT)

They wrote that he could add and subtract simple numbers, but he couldn't multiply or divide.

As a toddler, when he was barely able to speak, he started counting in a way that the psychologists who worked with our father thought was precocious. He could manipulate numbers. But that was before all the brain damage from the seizures and the side effects of the medicine that didn't always control them. {Our father, who studied journalism before becoming a psychologist, kept copies of the letters he wrote to psychologists, psychiatrists, neurologists starting in the 1950's trying to help them get the every-changing balance of medicine right.}

They didn't have his "relevant history" quite right, either. They had records showing that he had been "receiving services" at Napa since October 5, 1977. What about the nine years before that? Had something happened to their records?

David was diagnosed with "Organic Personality Syndrome, Explosive Type, and Personality Disorder, Not Otherwise Specified." What does that mean?

They also noted that he was stubborn because he insisted that his birthday was December 10, 1948, and the records they had clearly showed his birthday was December 8. The records were wrong. David was smarter than the records.

Not to digress too much into the testing—I'll enclose those pages separately; they might mean more to you than they do to me or did to David. But I saw that their records hadn't been updated. They give as the cause of David's seizure disorder encephalitis that he had at age four. They didn't know that in the 1980's I did a search into the biological past of our mother, an adoptee, and found out that we had an uncle whom David resembles and who also had epilepsy. Our mother's birth mother had died during a lobotomy.

But back to the business of his wish to be smart. I wonder what it was like for him to sit there and go through all these tests that he knew he was "failing." He had, after all, according to the EEG tests "diffuse cerebral dysfunction focused in the right frontal and right temporal areas." The doctor, Michael David, who tested David in 1983, had acknowledged "moderate to severe, diffuse, organic dysfunction." He described David as being "*very slow* during testing, requiring three to four times as much time to evaluate as even the most impaired patients I see." He also reported that he believed that "some of Mr. Martin's slowness was deliberate."

I don't think it was deliberate. He wanted to be smart. I think he was paralyzed by the thought of not being. I had an experience once, after I'd written a really good paper that the professor used as an example of how to analyze a poem and enhance the pleasure instead of destroying it. But he didn't know who I was because I'd always been so quiet in class, feeling that everyone else was so much brighter and more articulate than I was. So when he asked me a question as a follow-up, instead of feeling more confident because my paper had been praised, I could think only of being judged, and my mind went completely blank. I couldn't say a word. I can still feel that moment of silence. I had stage fright right there in the junior seminar class, and that was after my paper had been praised. David probably had stage fright too. Or maybe he managed to escape the assault and battery of tests by taking his dysfunctional brain somewhere else, some island closer to Jane Seymour, where he could be handsome and smart.

Here's a paragraph of what the testers saw:

Mr. Martin attended the testing sessions promptly and was dressed casually with good hygiene. He is a tall, Caucasian male of average build, who wore a bicycle helmet throughout the testing. Mr. Martin has numerous scars on his face and head resulting from injuries obtained during falls and seizures. He exhibited dystaxia which seemed to worsen after sitting for long periods of time, and during one longer walk that he took with this examiner when he needed to rest his hand on my shoulder for support.

Support! As for his wanting to be smart, take a look at what the testers noted:

Mr. Martin occasionally used words inappropriately, for example, during a Rorschach response he said "descreption" when he seemed to mean "discrepancy." Mr. Martin's use of such words seemed to be his way of trying to impress the examiner. He did generally seem to be searching for words when expressing himself, which may relate to limited formal schooling.

(Me again: Who could he talk to on the ward? He could watch TV, but who was there to hear him, to listen when he spoke? What practice did he have in speaking?)

Mr. Martin appeared motivated to perform optimally throughout the testing. This was evidenced by his wanting feedback about his performance, and by some embarrassment when he assumed he would not do well. (For example, on the math section of the NMSE, he said, "I can try it but I'd only look foolish.")

How well I can understand that!

Nine days of testing, of wanting to be smart and knowing that he looked foolish.

They noted that he was on anticonvulsive medications (Tegretol and Phenobarbital) "which may have interfered slightly with his speed of responding." Yes, and what about his brain damage?

They also thought he saw himself as "broken" because of his answers on the Rorschach test.

ASSESSMENT RESULTS (Psychological/Personality): …

The most prominent characteristics from the testing results related to Mr. Martin having a very negative self-image. He seems to see himself as broken or damaged in some way, and likely realized the need for assistance. This self-perception seems to conflict with the positive way in which Mr. Martin would like others to perceive him. He is probably reluctant to openly ask for help and chance weakening his positive façade, but in doing so he sacrifices working on and strengthening his limitations. Mr. Martin's negative self-image seemed very apparent on the Rorschach where several of his responses had morbid content, (e.g., a rabbit with feet "blasted away by a hunter," a bat with a wing "knocked off" and an infant with "a cut-off leg."

Have you read the story "Flowers for Algernon"? It's about a mentally-disabled man (they used mentally retarded when it was written) who wants to be smart and is given an operation that triples his IQ, bringing him the love and respect—and choices—that had been lacking in his life. But it doesn't last. He sees what's coming because Algernon, the mouse they tested the procedure on, dies. They made a movie out of it, *Charly*, with Cliff Robertson playing that part, in 1968, the year David checked into Napa.

Those psychologists in 1992 thought he slowed down deliberately when told that the testing was coming to an end. What did his slowing down mean? Did he think that these tests might determine his freedom, his discharge out into the real world? Did he think his time was running out to prove that he was smart?

They noted that "the longer Mr. Martin took to respond to a problem, the more he seemed to become frustrated and confused. He seemed to attempt to solve most problems with a strategy in mind, yet when the initial strategy failed to provide the necessary result, he would abandon the strategy entirely and respond in a random manner and/or express resentment."

I hate to think of his enduring all this!

He was unable to complete Trails B—whatever that means!— because of his lack of ability to recite the alphabet. (He could sing it but could not say it. Shouldn't he have gotten extra credit for singing it?)

His IQ was evaluated as borderline, but from the report you'd think considerably south of the border. They say he'd tested consistently in the mid-70's range since 1961. That's when we were living in Columbia, South Carolina, and he was attending special ed classes. Did they test him in school, or was that when he was taken out of school because he was having so many seizures? I don't know.

But I can't help thinking that he'd have done a lot better if they'd given him the test you administered to me and other Peace Corps recruits and asked him to describe his family. We could have been the ink blots on his Rorschach tests, too.

He did show his smarts when our sister Dana visited him after years of being at a distance. He asked her, "Dana, do you still hold that grudge?" and she said, "What grudge is that? I hold a lot of grudges." David replied, "If you don't remember, I'm not going to talk about it." Wasn't that smart?

I WANT TO LEARN AND AT THE SAME TIME HAVE FUN.

I think David did have fun when he wasn't being tested. Looking back to when David lived at home, I know he watched TV shows, and our father sometimes took him and our two younger sisters Missy and Suzy to Five-Points, a section of town where they could get ice cream at Zesto and see musicals at Five-Points Theater—even old Jeannette McDonald-Nelson Eddy ones. David liked those. Later he liked the Beatles. His favorite "fun" game was Twenty Questions. I was looking over a kind of log I've kept on my computer for about 15 years. I call it Just the Facts because I simply list facts about what happened in a given day, so it's not personal like the diaries I used to keep. I found something from Thanksgiving Day 2010. It turned out to be our last Thanksgiving Day with our mother in the home she shared with Kathy. I looked under Twenty Questions and found this.

Thursday, November 25, 2010 Thanksgiving Day. Mom about David: "He's going to wonder why I look so old. White hair, no teeth." Kind of messy but pleasant Thanksgiving. We benefit from Kathy's organization, and she wasn't there. (She was in LA with her brother and 100-year-old aunt.) Things look prettier. Played 20 Questions. David was Hitler. "Hell, no. You don't live if you shoot yourself in the head" response to the question "Are you living?" Suzy was Peter Pan, and David guessed it. Me to MyMeque: "You have to play whether you want to or not. You're our guest." David had one seizure if we don't count his telling MyMeque, "Fuck you!" and making a motion that he was going to hit him when MyMeque took David's arm to help him to the car. David apologized later.

Does that represent fun?

I wish I could play Twenty Questions and let him win after death.

Were you a male? Yes!

Did people like you? Yes! (No fair to add info, but just for the reference, look back.)

Did you get along with people? Yes! (See note above.)

Were you a good citizen? Yes!

Did you have fun? Yes!

Were you a good uncle to your nieces and nephews? Yes!

Did you have a job? Yes! (Educating us. Being brave. Finding something to live for in a 24/7 locked facility.)

Were you smart? Yes! (He had insights that were worth hearing, and his score would have been much higher on that battery of tests if they'd asked him to describe his family. Even if our scores would have been lower.)

Did you have a nice home? Yes. (Besides the one that locked him in, where he was "living the easy life, an existence marked by luxury and a carefree attitude," he went home—to our mother's home with Kathy, to my home, to our sister Suzy's home, to his nephew Jonathan's home on special occasions—if not to that cabin in the woods. Until his mental and physical disabilities made leaving his facility too much of a chore for him.)

He knew what he wanted, and he must have known that he never got it—unless, in some recess of his brain, he did recreate this world and him in it. David didn't mention a dog in that letter he wrote in 1968 stating what he wanted from an education (special) and life. But he loved all the dogs we had over the years when he was living at home, where it was possible to have a dog to love and be loved by, a living being to be allowed to hold. So I've put in a picture of him with a dog he loved who loved him back. I think he named the dog Napoleon. (Learn history. Check.) But maybe it was Chipper.

He should always have had a dog. I used to fantasize winning the lottery and being able to buy him a place in the country where he could learn to love nature as much as he loved Jane Seymour and he could have a dog as well as a caregiver to keep him from walking along freeways. But they didn't permit dogs in his locked facility, and what good was my fantasy of winning the lottery when I never even bought a lottery ticket?

I know a couple who have a son with Asperger's, and they founded a whole school for him when he was a little boy, and after he became an adult out on his own, they worked with the police to create a video so that the police would know what to look for and not shoot.

Our family wasn't heroic that way. I guess we did our best. Unfortunately, our best just wasn't all that good. Still, we were better than Charlie Gordon's mother in *Flowers for Algernon*, who threatened to kill Charlie if her husband couldn't find another place for him to live, and we didn't keep him locked up in the attic the way Edward Rochester did Bertha Mason.

Why do I feel that isn't exemplary?

Anyway, what I failed to do in life, I want to do in death. His life. His death. David's dreams I've described here are now safely tucked into the pocket I made so that he can leave this world with wishes granted. But maybe David, who so much of his life had a faraway look in his eyes, managed to be where he wasn't and have what he didn't. It often seemed like a nightmare, but maybe he had a dreamworld too.

Lewis Carroll said (Have you read his complete works?) that we should always stamp and address an envelope before writing a letter because what good is a letter if it can't be mailed?

I have an envelope and a stamp. Please send me your address. But how can you if you don't get my letter requesting it? Instead of

dropping this letter in a mailbox or slipping it Through the Looking Glass, maybe I'll add it to that pouch granting my brother's wish for "money in my pocket."

Then I'm going to submit *Everything I Should Have Learned I Could Have Learned in Tonga*—a memoir of my inadequacies that I couldn't have written if you hadn't given me a pass on my 1969 sanity test, validating my expresion of human existence. Here's to yours.

Tina

CPSIA information can be obtained
at www.ICGtesting.com
Printed in the USA
BVHW071154260921
617288BV00010B/58